Americanization and Anti-Americanism

AMERICANIZATION AND ANTI-AMERICANISM
The German Encounter with American Culture after 1945

Edited by
Alexander Stephan

Berghahn Books
New York • Oxford

Published in 2005 by
Berghahn Books

© 2005, 2007 Alexander Stephan
First paperback edition published in 2007

All rights reserved. No part of this publication may be reproduced in any form by any means without the written permission of Berghahn Books.

Library of Congress Cataloging-in-Publication Data

Americanization and anti-Americanism : the German encounter with American culture after 1945 / edited by Alexander Stephan.
  p. cm.
  Includes bibliographical references.
  ISBN 978-1-84545-487-6 (alk. paper)
  1. United States--Relations--Germany. 2. Germany--Relations--United States. 3. Anti-Americanism--Germany. 4. Americanization. 5. United States--Foreign public opinion, German. 6. Public opinion--Germany. 7. Popular culture--Germany. 8. Politics and culture--Germany. 9. Germany--Civilization--American influences. 10. Germany--Foreign relations--1945-   I. Stephan, Alexander, 1946-

E183.8.G3A626 2004
303.48'243073'09045--dc22

2004045084

British Library Cataloguing in Publication Data

A catalogue record for this book is available from the British Library.

Printed in the United States on acid-free paper.

CONTENTS

Acknowledgements   viii

Alexander Stephan
Introduction   1

PART 1: POLITICS OF CULTURE

Russell A. Berman
Anti-Americanism and Americanization   11

Michael Ermarth
Counter-Americanism and Critical Currents in West German
Reconstruction 1945-1960: The German Lesson Confronts
the American Way of Life   25

Bernd Greiner
Saigon, Nuremberg, and the West: German Images of
America in the Late 1960s   51

PART 2: POPULAR CULTURE

Jost Hermand
Resisting Boogie-Woogie Culture, Abstract Expressionism,
and Pop Art: German Highbrow Objections to the Import
of "American" Forms of Culture, 1945-1965   67

Kaspar Maase
From Nightmare to Model? Why German Broadcasting
Became Americanized   78

Heide Fehrenbach
Learning from America: Reconstructing "Race" in
Postwar Germany   107

Part 3: Film

David Bathrick
Cinematic Americanization of the Holocaust in Germany:
Whose Memory Is It?   129

Sabine Hake
Anti-Americanism and the Cold War: On the DEFA
Berlin Films   148

Thomas Elsaesser
German Cinema Face to Face with Hollywood: Looking into
a Two-Way Mirror   166

Part 4: European and Global Perspectives

Richard Pells
Double Crossings: The Reciprocal Relationship between
American and European Culture in the Twentieth Century   189

Rob Kroes
Anti-Americanism and Anti-Modernism in Europe: Old
and Recent Versions   202

Winfried Fluck
California Blue: Americanization as Self-Americanization   221

Volker R. Berghahn
Awkward Relations: American Perceptions of Europe,
European Perceptions of America   238

Part 5: Outlook

Karsten D. Voigt
Crisis or Cooperation? The Transatlantic Relationship
at a Watershed   253

Bowman H. Miller
Germans and Americans: Understanding and Managing
Change   257

Bibliography   263

Contributors   276

Index   283

Acknowledgements

This book received generous support from the following institutions and organizations:

The Mershon Center, Ohio State University
Deutsches Programm für transatlantische Begegnung, Bundesministerium für Wirtschaft und Arbeit, Germany
German Academic Exchange Service, New York
Deutsche Forschungsgemeinschaft, Germany
Department of Germanic Languages and Literatures, Ohio State University

INTRODUCTION

Alexander Stephan

When it comes to cultural issues, the United States and Europe have had a difficult relationship during the last one hundred years, a period that has been labeled the "American century." But what was for the most part a slow-burning subterranean disagreement blazed into a widespread fury over America's second war against Iraq. Suddenly, a clash of cultures looms, exposing deep-seated differences over the deployment of military force, concepts such as "just war" and "preemptive strike," the role of multinational organizations including the UN and NATO, the rule of international law, and fundamental human values and principles by which we all live. Many commentators signal the start of a new world order. The Cold War division into two power blocs, which for over a half century kept the world in precarious balance, is dissolving into complex and short-lived constellations described as "axes of evil" or "coalitions of the willing." Europe, whether the smaller "old Europe" or the expanded "new Europe," no longer automatically allies itself with the United States. In short, Europeans and Americans are receiving the message that, from now on, they should get used to living in different worlds.

Anti-American invective on one side of the Atlantic and Euro-bashing on the other set the tone of the times. In Europe, George W. Bush is depicted as a trigger-happy cowboy, or Rambo, who serves as the front man for a zealous group of right-wing ideologues and greedy corporations unconcerned about the public good. Terms such as US imperialism, unilateralism, and hegemony appear frequently in newspapers throughout Europe. Europeans worry that the United States, as the only remaining superpower, may see no further reason to abide by international treaties and the rules of bodies such as the UN and the International Court of Justice, which many Americans have disliked all along because of a perception that they infringe upon US sovereignty.

According to this view, politicians in Washington, driven by a widespread religious fundamentalism, have appointed themselves "globocops" bent on imposing their own brand of democracy and free market economy on all corners of the world, regardless of how people in other nations view the American model of economic growth and its corresponding consumer mentality, which by no means functions flawlessly even in "God's own country."

Americans in turn accuse the Germans and other Europeans of being too soft and accommodating to defend themselves against global terrorism, whose ugliest manifestation so far was seen in the attacks on New York and Washington on 11 September 2001. Since 1990, Europe has clung naively to the notion of a peace dividend, Americans claim, and envy is the real motive behind anti-Americanism. Terms such as "Eurotrash" and "Europe's postmodern paradise" are circulating throughout the US press. One frustrated American senator has argued, consistently enough, that the physical remains of US soldiers who died in Europe in the first and second world wars should be retrieved from the ungrateful continent and repatriated. Other politicians suggest inflicting economic damage on the obstinate Germans by closing American military installations in Germany or transferring them elsewhere, to Eastern Europe. Meanwhile, a debate rages in the US Capitol about whether to change the name of French fries to freedom fries, and French toast to freedom toast, in the congressional cafeteria.

The essays in *Americanization and Anti-Americanism: The German Encounter with American Culture after 1945* were completed in early 2003, when relations between America and Europe reached their nadir during the debates about the war in Iraq. It is no wonder, then, that many contributions represent direct responses to the frictions that arose between Germany and the United States during this period. They include an article by Karsten D. Voigt, coordinator for German-American Cooperation at Germany's Foreign Ministry, who opens his chapter with the hesitant statement: "Transatlantic relations remain as important now to Germany—indeed, even more so to Europe—as they have ever been in the past. If Europe and the United States were to oppose each other's policies and positions, their shared attempts to address global issues would be jeopardized in terms of military and economic matters, and also those related to democratic culture and environmental protection." Diplomatic phrasing employing subjunctive verb forms and subsequent protestations to the contrary cannot disguise Voigt's worry that, at the start of the twenty-first century, the pillars of transatlantic relations are in danger of collapsing. The unrestricted partnership between the United States and Germany that had been solid for more than fifty years, he implies in the title of his essay, "Crisis or Cooperation?", may be consigned to the museum hall of history.

Voigt's concerned reaction to the signs of the times is echoed in the contribution by Bowman Miller, director of the Office of Analysis for Europe in the US Department of State. The task of reflecting on German-American relations is now more "timely" than he had thought until recently. The notion of "sustained national sovereignty" and even a "'go it alone' foreign policy" (which represents, as Miller points out, an "icon or article of faith" in the United States) alarms Germans, who have learnt to distrust nationalism and think that problems are better solved through international institutions. Moreover, since the opening of the Iron Curtain, Germany "no longer represents a special, primary concentration or concern among US leaders."

Russell Berman sharpens the statements of politicians in Berlin and Washington by advising German intellectuals critical of America, such as Martin Walser and Peter Sloterdijk, that anti-Americanism amounts to a "denunciation of the historical American defense of democracy against Soviet expansion," is tinged with anti-Semitism, and represents "fundamentally an expression of hostility to … the historical development toward democratic capitalism," a "social model" that "retains enormous attraction for populations around the world." Other contributors try to defuse the culture clash between Europe and the United States, interpreting the German attitude as "anti-Bushism", as Volker R. Berghahn argues, rather than anti-Americanism. Still others prefer to view "American entertainment" as "more cosmopolitan than 'imperialistic,'" as Richard Pells writes in his chapter, or talk less of Americanization or "cultural imperialism" than of global forms of a modern or postmodern culture powered by new technology (themes addressed in contributions by Kaspar Maase, Thomas Elsaesser, Rob Kroes, and Winfried Fluck).

Americanization and Anti-Americanism: The German Encounter with American Culture after 1945 aims to explore the recent background and the most significant views in this increasingly strident conflict between the United States and Germany (indeed, between the United States and most of Europe) that is manifested not only in politics but in culture and cultural diplomacy. At the heart of this conflict lie the controversial concepts of "Americanization" and "anti-Americanism." Case studies and retrospectives on the transfer of American culture to Germany since 1945 give some necessary context to the current debates, which at times have been highly emotional.

This book is divided into five sections. "The Politics of Culture" opens the volume with two broadly designed essays looking at the genesis and the current state of the German debate about anti-Americanism and counter-Americanism, while a third contribution zooms in on Germany and the German image of the United States during the time of the Vietnam War. The next section, "Popular Culture," contains studies about the lost battle staged by German elitist art against American pop art; about the commercialization, democratization, and modernization of broadcasting; and about a new German debate about race with regard to black occupation children. The three contributions in the section "Film," which is arguably one of the best researched areas in German-American cultural relations, focus on the Americanization and globalization of the Holocaust, on anti-Americanism in East German movies, and on the double transfer of ideas and people in the film industry across the Atlantic. The following section on "European and Global Perspectives" looks at the experiences of other European countries and asks to what extent German-American cultural relations are rooted in a worldwide trend in which multinational techniques for the production and distribution of cultural products (for example, in the film industry), the runaway digital revolution with its postmodern intertextuality, and new, somatic forms of reception are rendering obsolete the traditional discourse on cultural transfer and cultural imperialism. It concludes by suggesting that a new age is dawning in German-American relations and the intellectual apparatus for analyzing and describing the transfer of cultural products needs to be rethought. Contributions by two key players in the political arena, Karsten D. Voigt and Bowman H. Miller, close the volume by providing inside perspectives on the current tensions between Washington and Berlin and by carefully hinting at what might be the beginning of a Second American Century.

In discussing the wars against Afghanistan and Iraq, American government spokespeople and journalists have repeatedly cited the case of Germany, as well as that of Japan, as a model for freeing a country from a totalitarian regime and turning it into a democracy that provides open access not only to basic human rights but also to largely US-manufactured cultural products such as television programs, popular music, and Hollywood films. Such forecasts of unproblematic nation building may seem exaggerated—as likewise may the concern of many German intellectuals that Washington has fallen prey to delusions of its own omnipotence and that Germany is turning into a cultural province of the United States. On the other hand, the perception that the Federal Republic is, if not a model, at least a special case, or *Sonderfall*, of cultural Americanization is not altogether false.

The essays in this volume focus on four main features of the theme of Germany as a *Sonderfall* of cultural Americanization. First, the delayed unification of Germany in the nineteenth century and the brief and unhappy experience with democracy during the Weimar Republic meant that elitist social structures and traditional concepts of *Kultur* and *Geist* prevailed in Germany deep into the first "American century." Many Germans thus resisted the consumer culture and lowest-common-denominator mentality said to exist in the United States (as well as America's unbridled faith in technology and progress) longer and more intensively than other Europeans (a theme explored in this volume by Michael Ermarth and Jost Hermand).

Second, Germany, like Japan, lost much of its political sovereignty and all of its military autonomy with its defeat in World War II and had its moral certitude and national identity shattered in ways that are still visible today. As a result, after 1945 the country was wide open to a radical cultural reorganization from the outside (a topic taken up by David Bathrick), which neither the generosity of the American government in its "soft reeducation" policies nor the largely positive relations between the civilian population and the US occupation forces could disguise (see chapter by Heide Fehrenbach). In Germany, the United States worked hard to win the hearts and minds of future leaders by arranging official visits and semiofficial exchanges under the auspices of philanthropic organizations. No other country in Europe was blanketed after 1945 with such a network of American cultural institutions (*Amerikahäuser*); nowhere else were there comparable programs for the translation and dissemination of American books and films.

Third, Germany represents a special case within Europe because from 1945 to 1990 it was divided into the Federal Republic and the German Democratic Republic, which faced each other on the front lines of the Cold War. Sabine Hake addresses this issue in her essay on anti-Americanism in movies about Berlin produced by the East German film company DEFA. On the other side of the Iron Curtain, American cultural policy in West Germany largely reflected the global propaganda war between the United States and its communist adversaries, for instance, in the work of organizations such as the Congress for Cultural Freedom, which was run by the CIA and financed in part through European counterpart funds to the Marshall Plan. Fourth, unlike Britain and France on the one hand or Poland and Russia on the other, a unified Germany after 1990 had to redefine its position regarding the United States and the real or presumed American claims to (cultural) hegemony at the end of the Cold War.

The significance of Germany's history as a European *Sonderfall* of cultural Americanization should not be underrated. But an equally dominant line of thought arises out of international concepts such as modernization and globalization that asserts that many or most developments in German postwar culture resulted not from a deliberate policy of Americanization but from trends evolving throughout all Western industrialized countries and, to an increasing degree, in other parts of the world. In other words, West Germany might well have Americanized itself eventually even without any direct American influence.

Numerous data supporting this theory can be found in the essays assembled in this volume. Maase, for example, cites the so-called German economic miracle of the 1950s to show that new forms of consumer behavior and an increase in leisure time were stimulated less by American models than by the rapid growth of financial opportunities and reduced working hours. Young Germans' discovery of new ways to listen, view, and behave went hand-in-hand with the development of novel, inexpensive, and increasingly mobile and thus more accessible and user-friendly technological innovations such as record players, portable radios, audio and video cassette recorders, CD players, and internet swap shops such as Napster and Kazaa—innovations that in turn influenced the content of radio and television programming. The auteurs of New German Cinema (such as Wim Wenders, who coined the contradictory mottos "rock saved my life" and "the Yanks have colonized our subconscious") have been replaced by transnational filmmakers such as Wolfgang Petersen and Roland Emmerich and producers such as Bernd Eichinger, who operate on both sides of the Atlantic and use "post-Fordist methods" and a style of "European internationalism" that no longer differ much from the techniques of the American film industry (all topics addressed by Elsaesser). And intellectuals who warn that the digital revolution threatens the creativity of individual artists by creating a Borgesian "virtual library" of texts and images characterized by "patchwork," "fragmentation," and "interchangeability" are no longer anti-American Europeans in the old sense but see themselves as critics of a certain type of modernism (a theme explored by Kroes). Moreover, whereas in the past American pop culture was said to manipulate national markets, current discussion of the mass media is governed by supranational concepts such as "self-cultivation," "access," and "unmediated," "body-centered" emotional reception (ideas explored in Fluck's chapter).

Finally, the essays in *Americanization and Anti-Americanism* tentatively broach another topic: the possibility that, in the not-too-distant future, a united Europe with a common cultural identity could play a central role in the worldwide confrontations with the United States. Europe, with its regional differences merged into this new identity, would then constitute a third way, not specifically German or French, but a model operating as a supraregional political, economic, and cultural center of power offering a form of "soft globalization" as an alternative to the American empire. Within this pan-European zone, a modern, open mass culture, powered by technology and democracy and available to the maximum numbers of people, could enter into a fruitful, give-and-take relationship with older forms of high culture. The distribution of cultural products on market principles of supply and demand would be supplemented by targeted state subsidies. The new Europe would remember its experiences with multicultural coexistence reaching back into the Middle Ages. By drawing on the positive aspects of a common past, and on the structures for multinational cooperation that exist today within its borders, a united Europe might avoid the leveling of cultural diversity that accompanied what once had been interpreted as the American melting pot. At the same time, such a united Europe could dodge the overly optimistic claim of the United States to represent, as Pells puts it, "a replica of the world." The chaos of postmodernism in which everything is possible would be disciplined by the traditions of European modernism, allowing us to resume debate on the utopian themes of the Enlightenment of how to live together more humanely.

This kind of dialogue between partners of equal status could put an end to European anti-Americanism in its traditional aristocratic, elitist form as well as its communist and postdemocratic shapes. Equally, it could soften the recent flare-up of Europe-bashing in the United States that has gone on, in a low-key fashion, for a long time. Cultural imperialism of the kind Europeans practiced for centuries toward other nations, and especially toward the Americas, would then become as obsolete as the US attitude of exceptionalism that marked the first "American century" and now seems to be extending itself with a vengeance into a second one. Claims by any single country or region of the world to define culture must give way to broad international exchanges. A new, genuine transatlantic partnership could replace the "Athenian complex" of the Europeans and the American quest for imperial domination.

* * *

The volume *Americanization and Anti-Americanism: The German Encounter with American Culture after 1945* differs in four respects from other publications on recent German-American relations. First, unlike such books as *The American Impact on Postwar Germany* (edited by Reiner Pommerin, 1995) and *Die USA und Deutschland im Zeitalter des Kalten Krieges* (edited by Detlef Junker, 2001, English translation, 2004), the present volume focuses exclusively on the cultural relations between America and Germany, even though most contributors root these relations in general historical and political debates. Second, in contrast to the specialized studies of Klaus J. Milich (*Die frühe Postmoderne. Geschichte eines europäisch-amerikanischen Kulturkonflikts*, 1996), Gerd Gemünden (*Framed Visions: Popular Culture, Americanization, and the Contemporary German and Austrian Imagination*, 1998), or Uta G. Poiger (*Jazz, Rock, and Rebels. Cold War Politics and American Culture in a Divided Germany*, 2000), this book offers a broad spectrum of themes ranging from the history of the concept of "counter-Americanism" to German reactions to the Vietnam War (Bernd Greiner) and to discussions of film, radio, and a new race politics after 1945. Third, more so than in earlier studies, many of the contributions look beyond the German *Sonderfall* to the context of Europe as a whole. And, finally, this volume presents preliminary reactions to the cultural clash between the United States and Europe, which sharply intensified with the international debates on the wars against Afghanistan and Iraq and with the publication by the Bush administration of *The National Security Strategy of the United States of America* in September 2002—a clash that no doubt will continue to feature in the transatlantic dialogue for many years to come.

– *Part 1* –

POLITICS OF CULTURE

Anti-Americanism and Americanization

Russell A. Berman

For a brief moment after the fall of the Berlin Wall, it might have appeared that anti-Americanism had disappeared, or nearly so: in Germany to be sure, where decades of American foreign policy—the airlift, John F. Kennedy's appearance in Berlin, Ronald Reagan's call to tear down the wall—culminated in a clear victory. Yet that triumph cast a glow far beyond Germany. The Soviet Union, the overriding opponent in one of the defining conflicts of the century, had been defeated. America and the values of liberal democracy and neoliberal capitalism were the undisputed winners. The European left, the traditional locus of most anti-Americanism, stood in disarray. The only remaining opponents were on the right, the isolated ideologues of anti-American anticapitalism, such as Hans-Jürgen Syberberg in Germany and Alain de Benoist in France.

Yet the moment was indeed brief, ending quickly with the onset of the Persian Gulf War in 1991, which elicited a widespread peace movement, notably in Germany, in which the American-led international coalition against Iraq was characterized as an expression of imperialist design rather than a response to the Iraqi occupation of Kuwait.[1] Although a new historical epoch had indeed begun—the Cold War had ended, and with it the Soviet inspiration for anti-American propaganda—an anti-American political culture flourished. In fact, that hostility grew throughout the course of the decade, providing the defining framework for debates around an ever-shifting set of topical concerns: the Israeli-Palestinian conflict; the emerging anxiety regarding globalization; international economic relations, particularly around the General Agreement on Tariffs and Trade; and the efforts to develop an international agenda for ecological concerns that came to be associated with the

---

Notes for this section begin on page 23.

negotiations in Kyoto, Japan. No matter how the specific topic migrated, a discursive framework remained constant in which America was cast as the fundamental source of discord. This analytic predisposition was nowhere more common than in Germany. While the terrorist attacks of 11 September 2001 produced a momentary solidarity effect with the United States, they did not significantly mitigate the anti-Americanism that became increasingly widespread in the German public. Grotesquely, the anti-American predisposition could even blame the events of 9/11 on the United States in mutually exclusive ways. While some critics suggested that terrorists carried out 9/11 because of an allegedly provocative American foreign policy, others could insinuate that it was the Americans themselves who had engaged in a secret plot in order to gain political advantage by acting as agents provocateurs. The latter, conspiracy-theoretical proposition is of course outrageous but ultimately cannot be disproven to those who dwell on such flawed thinking and are always willing to believe the worst and most macabre claims about the US government. The former position, interpreting the attacks as a plausible response to American foreign policy, is equally obnoxious, to the extent that it is intended as an implicit justification. As I will argue later, there may well indeed be a relationship between the attacks—standing now as the supreme expression of anti-Americanism—and aspects of US policy, but in a very different sense than a justification. For now, however, suffice it to say that anti-Americanism has become an important factor in contemporary political life in Germany and elsewhere—despite the end of Communism and despite the terrorist threat. Hence the urgency of posing the question: where does anti-Americanism come from?

To pose this question in the context of claims regarding a process of Americanization pushes the inquiry in a particular direction and depends on certain assumptions. The set of ideas, images, values, and tropes associated with anti-Americanism—Jean-François Revel calls it an "obsession"—are presumed to stand in some to-be-defined relation to a social process describable as Americanization.[2] It follows, then, that we are engaging in an inquiry about the relationship of a set of ideas to society, of ideology to social process, or rhetoric to "the Real," and so on. Each of those several formulations implies different sorts of methodologies and understandings regarding the relationship of thought to experience. In general, one can say that the problem of anti-Americanism and Americanization is, at least initially, a particular case of the general problem of the relationship between political ideology and lived experience.

In addition, positing some relationship between anti-American rhetoric and a notional "Americanization" implies that that latter term itself is a useful descriptor and not only a displacement of some other animus: antimodernization or antiglobalization. Is it in fact a matter of some uniquely and particularly American material inserted into other national contexts that elicits opposition? If that were the case, then one could indeed claim that "Americanization" provokes "anti-Americanism." Or is the putative "Americanism" only the packaging or the outer shell of processes that are ultimately not the expression of a specific national identity nor of a national interest? In that case, the conflict around American signs would in fact have little to do directly with America but with some other, presumably more significant social transformation.

Furthermore, to pose the question as one of "Americanization and anti-Americanism" could be taken to suggest a causality, no matter how complex: something that might be called "Americanization" is presumed to take place, and "anti-Americanism" is imagined to be the response to it. For this scenario to make sense, plausible or not, one would have to agree to define Americanization as the transfer of various institutional structures, social practices, and cultural values from the United States to the foreign setting, in our case, Germany, and one would then propose accounting for anti-Americanism as a negative response, perhaps even a resistance to those transfers. In addition, this model surely presumes that the transfer takes place in the context of unequal power and that inequality is the precondition for the transfer.

Let me dwell on a couple of examples that may help illustrate what is at stake and may lead us to an evaluation of the causality claim. During the mid-1960s, British popular music had a considerable impact on the emerging youth culture of the United States. One can regard this so-called British invasion as a significant cultural transfer. However, it did not elicit any pertinent anti-British sentiment, nor could one plausibly posit anything like a power differential marked by British dominance over the United States. As much as British music dominated, British military power did not. At least since 1945, in contrast, American popular music spread in Germany, and while it found a very large public reception, there was also a noticeable, frequently cultural conservative resistance to it, more often than not tinged with racism. One scenario might describe that cultural transfer as "Americanization," and the hostility to jazz or rhythm and blues as "anti-Americanism," in effect an effort to resist the power to impose the cultural taste of the victors on the defeated nation. What speaks against this scenario, however, are the reports of an underground attraction to jazz in Germany even before 1945, that is, before the assertion of American power. Thus one might propose an alternative hypothesis that does not depend on the same cause-and-effect: whatever the vicissitudes of power, musical taste may be significantly autonomous from it. One may be for or against jazz in Germany or in the United States; therefore the dissemination of American music may be a pretext for hostility to the United States, but it is not clearly the cause. (One could push this argument further by asking about the reception of American music in venues where

American military presence was largely absent, for example, in Central and Eastern Europe.)

Parallel to popular music, American models of higher education—a second example of cultural transfer—gained some currency in West Germany, but on a much more limited scale. For example, the Free University of Berlin, founded at a key moment in the Cold War, was historically associated with certain American features—at the very least, the suburban campus setting as well as some considerable American funding—that distinguished it from traditional German universities. It would nonetheless be difficult to suspect every critic of the Free University of anti-Americanism. Similarly, American educational models figure prominently in current debates about the reform of German universities today. Leaving aside the question as to whether the image of American higher education circulating in Germany has much to do with American reality, one has to concede that positions for and against the various reforms, for example, the transformation of the degree system, can hardly be mapped onto the question of anti-Americanism. In other words, this prominent example of cultural and institutional Americanization, the presumed transfer of American forms into Germany, cannot be linked obviously or intuitively to phenomena of anti-Americanism.

There are two correlated assertions that follow from this preliminary discussion. First, specific or *sachlich* opposition to a circumscribed American material does not alone indicate anti-Americanism. One can oppose jazz or the BA without being anti-American. *Mutatis mutandis*: serious criticism of American foreign policy regarding Iraq should be taken seriously and not dismissed with a denunciatory epithet: as long as it is serious. Second, however, opposition to jazz, or the BA, or to Iraq policy surely does not preclude anti-Americanism; indeed, while any of those matters may be legitimately debated on their own terms, they may, in some instances, also be mobilized as pretexts to express a sentiment reasonably labeled "anti-American." Anti-Americanism is indicated when reasoned argument gives way to sweeping generalizations and hostile innuendo, and the thought-structures of prejudice and stereotype prevail. Criticism of jazz is a possible aesthetic judgment; denouncing "Negro music" (*Negermusik*) is obnoxious. Opposing George Bush on Iraq is similarly possible; conjuring up nonspecific American conditions (*amerikanische Verhältnisse*) is unreasonable. Prejudice, as an obsession, typically magnifies the power and presence of its presumed opponent, turning it into a ubiquitous generalization. McCarthyites saw Communists under every bed; anti-Semites imagined Jewish power everywhere; and anti-Americans imagine Washington's hand controlling every conflict. Given that fictional omnipresence, causation might be confused with a plausible explanation, at least by the true believer: American power is everywhere, ergo universal opposition. Yet this only means that the causation hypothesis is a function of the obsession rather than a useful explanation. The character of prejudice is that it ultimately has very little to do with its object. In this sense, one can claim that the discourse of anti-Americanism has little to do with American reality, although it may be quite revealing of the character of the anti-American.

This leads to my central claim: Anti-Americanism is not a response to Americanization. It may of course, indeed typically, point to an allegedly ubiquitous American presence in order to legitimate itself as a response, but this insinuated causality is ultimately not plausible. Anti-Americanism has a secret life of its own and cannot be correlated to specific instances that might be credibly understood as an American presence: American music, education, and so forth. Hence the proposition that anti-Americanism is independent of American presence (or "Americanization") and not explicable in a transparently cause-and-effect manner.

This decoupling can be proven in various ways. While anti-Americanism is surely only a minority position in most national populations, one can find evidence of some anti-Americanism in many different settings: in countries with histories of a considerable American presence (like Germany) as well as in countries with very different histories of involvement with the United States (like France). Yet if a comparable (if not fully identical) anti-Americanism colors political culture in those two countries, then clearly the specific history of occupation and Americanization in Germany is not a pertinent variable. Western European anti-Americanism evidently takes place in countries with very different degrees of Americanization. One could make the same argument even more strongly with reference to distant parts of the globe where an American presence has been minimal (and much less than in France), but where expressions of local anti-Americanism may well be found. Anti-Americanism may appear whether or not there has been a significant American presence: in Japan, with the history of the occupation, and in Australia with no similar history.

If we focus on Germany, three further observations bolster the claim that anti-Americanism is not explicable as an effect of Americanization. First, while it appears that currently, at least, German anti-Americanism tends to make reference to American foreign policy, it seems that the element of American foreign policy most relevant to Germany—support for unification—has dropped out of the discussion.[3] Perhaps one can assume that an underlying resentment of unification, at least in PDS circles, fuels anti-Americanism today, in which case the problem could still be explained in Cold War terms. Yet this does not seem convincing as a comprehensive account: German anti-Americanism appears to extend far beyond the post-Communist camp. The fact that it is American foreign policy that is under attack, while American foreign policy vis-à-vis Germany is excluded from the discussion, suggests that some other dynamic, some displacement, is at stake: in any case, it is evidently not American actions that elicit hostile sentiment.

Second, at least anecdotally, anti-Americanism in Germany has increased precisely as the American presence in Germany has decreased, in the wake of unification. The willingness of leading German public figures to engage in hostile characterizations of the United States is greater, even though there are fewer Americans around, and presumably less American influence. Yet one need not make the strong case: greater anti-Americanism in the context of a reduced American presence. It suffices to point out that the reduction of an American presence has simply not led to any corollary reduction in anti-Americanism. It is evidently not the American presence that drives the hostile sentiment. For example, during the peace movement of the 1980s involving the NATO double-track decision, much was made of presumed restrictions on West German sovereignty due to the postwar power relations and the dependence on the United States; a certain hostility to America followed, or was imagined to follow, from that situation. At the very least, one can note that, with unification, that restriction on German sovereignty has disappeared, but the same hostility nonetheless continues to be directed at the United States. Thus the claim during the 1980s that anti-Americanism was due to the perceived restriction of German sovereignty by American power has clearly been disproven: German anti-Americanism has nothing to do with that aspect of German-American relations. Indeed it may be independent of the real character of those relations altogether.

Yet a third observation clinches the argument, demonstrating the independence of anti-Americanism from Americanization: not only is anti-Americanism found in contexts where no significant Americanization (or occupation) has taken place, not only does anti-Americanism evidently postdate significant American presence in Germany: in fact, anti-Americanism long predates the post-World War II occupation and anything that might properly be described as Americanization, including the experience of the Weimar Republic or the responses to the Versailles Treaty. In fact, ever since the so-called first contacts of European travelers with the "New World," Europeans have given expression to anxieties regarding brute nature, the presumed absence of history, and a nondifferentiated homogeneity projected onto the western hemisphere.[4] These are precisely the standard tropes of anti-Americanism, with a long history. A German discourse of anti-Americanism became prominent, at the latest, in the early nineteenth century, as romantic authors such as Nikolaus Lenau increasingly described the United States in pejorative terms, associated with their negative judgments both on its capitalism and its democracy. In contrast, Goethe's opposition to that romantic reaction indicates the initial phase of a positive German attraction to America and the values the country represented.[5] In other words, German anti-

Americanism cannot be explained as a response to the putative imposition of American political and economic forms on Germany: while one might entertain that claim regarding cultural imposition after 1918 or 1945, it can surely not be made in the years around 1800. Yet it is precisely in the romantic early nineteenth century that the terms of the discourse are set out. Thus, it is not anything that the United States does to Germany, no recognizable "Americanization," that elicits anti-Americanism. It is rather the mere fact of the presence, on the globe, of a society defined in terms of capitalism and democracy that scandalizes sectors of German and European society. It is not an intrusive imposition of democratic capitalism that provokes the protests, but the mere temptation that it represents.

This formulation, however, sheds a new light on the causation problem. To say that anti-Americanism is not caused by Americanization means two things: it is not a result of specific American actions, cultural transfers, etc., and it is not primarily a response to the projection of a specifically American identity, national interest, etc. However, if anti-Americanism is decoupled from what one might have expected to cause it, that is, Americanization, it does not follow that we should fall back on a postmodern account, treating it as a free-floating set of texts, independent of experience. On the contrary, anti-Americanism does indeed represent a response to genuine forces of historical change; what is at stake, however, is not the remaking of the world in the image of America—a possible working definition of "Americanization"— but rather the historical development toward democratic capitalism, which during the twentieth century has transpired disproportionately through America. Anti-Americanism is, fundamentally, the rhetoric of opposition to this historical process of political and economic emancipation.

It is in the nature of such political rhetorics that little value is placed on consistency. Like other obsessive ideologies, anti-Americanism is internally heterogeneous, and it draws on multiple cultural-historical currents. One can, however, distinguish heuristically among different registers of anti-Americanism, in particular the three enumerated below.

- Predemocratic anti-Americanism, which gives expression to an aristocratic (or imitatively aristocratic) disdain for the life of democracy, deemed to be too ordinary and lacking in quality; given the vicissitudes of aristocratism in modernity, this stance has migrated largely into the arts, generating for example the notion of America as lacking in culture or appealing to an aestheticization of politics.
- Communist anti-Americanism, which was generated by the apparatus of the Communist world during the nearly seventy-five years between the Bolshevik seizure of power and the collapse of the Soviet Union. The global struggle between Russian interests, masked as Communist,

and the democratic agenda under US leadership structured much political and intellectual life for most of the past century. In the battle with twentieth-century totalitarianism, the United States sometimes entered into unholy alliances with nondemocratic regimes; such is the complexity of politics. Moreover, it should surprise no one that foreign policies, like any government-generated practice, might be internally inconsistent. These inconsistencies became targets for Communist propaganda. With the collapse of the Soviet empire, American foreign policy is gradually returning to its core values and the predisposition to support governments that are democratic or moving toward democratization.[6] (It is interesting to note that Marx largely admired the dynamism of American capitalism and did not participate in the anti-Americanism that became the hallmark of Communist thought in the twentieth century.)[7]

- Postdemocratic anti-Americanism, by which I refer to current complaints that the United States remains reluctant to surrender elements of its sovereignty, understood as a democratic expression of popular will, in order to transfer them to international bodies. Whatever the standing of these bodies, they are, in any case, not elected institutions. At best one might say that they are institutions set up by several states; yet many of those states are barely democratic, if at all, and the very presumption that a state might subordinate itself to the will of others in institutions with no external control runs counter to democratic expectations. In addition, the prominence of nongovernmental organizations (NGOs) in contemporary international debate highlights a sensitive distinction between democratic sovereignty and private advocacy.

As noted, the three ideal types may overlap and certainly coexist with reference to the same material. Thus one finds all three variants evidenced in the German responses to September 11. Predemocratic anti-Americanism is characterized by a typically strained effort to maintain composure, to foreground a cool, even cold, attitude, in order to suggest that the terrorist attacks were ultimately not very important. Representatives of this position attempt to demonstrate how one is oneself simply too important to be concerned with the suffering of the day, the significance of which is denigrated. The goal is to demonstrate successfully a lack of concern. Thus the award-winning author Martin Walser on his experience of September 11:

> I had to give a reading in Bamberg [on Sept. 11]. I asked myself whether it would really be appropriate to read from a novel called *The Life of Love,* but the organizer said we should proceed in any case. And then I gave into a whim and said [to the audi-

ence]: "The Americans are getting in my way again." The audience was irritated, so I explained that the premiere of my play *Larger than Life Mr. Krott* was scheduled for November 21 1963, but it was cancelled due to the Kennedy assassination. Then I gave my reading, and afterwards two listeners said to me: "You helped us forget today's events." That was a wonderful experience for me as an author.[8]

Walser's point is to demonstrate a studied lack of sympathy by hiding behind aestheticism as an aristocratic posture. It is the work of art that counts, and not the count of the victims. Hence a similar willingness on the part of popular philosopher Peter Sloterdijk to dismiss the scope of the tragedy; with an en passant reference to the "catastrophe landscape" of the twentieth century, he diminishes September 11 to a "small, hardly noticeable incident," although of course in magnitude the sheer number of dead dwarfed postwar terror attacks in Europe.[9] Indeed, even when one thought the body count was considerably higher, the editorialists of the *taz* eagerly trivialized the event: "as regrettable as the death of 7,000 people in New York may be, compared to what else is going on in the world, it is in comparison just a bagatelle."[10] In all these examples, the scope of the American dead is denied through the appeal to something always greater. Aside from the revealing lack of human sympathy, one is struck by the political misery of this aristocratism: desperate to diminish the importance of the events, it even blinds itself to the political consequences, especially with regard to the likely transformed relationship of the United States to the world: hardly a "bagatelle." The real triviality is the likely standing of Germany in future foreign policy arrangements. Yet this reduction is a result of a consistently wrong arithmetic in parts of the German public sphere: fifty dead in Jenin is a "massacre," while thousands of dead in the United States is a "bagatelle."

Communist anti-Americanism, the second variant, recycles motifs from Cold War propaganda and redirects them, once again, toward the United States. For example, a PDS leaflet distributed in Hamburg commented on the attacks with the slogan "What goes around comes around" ("*So was kommt von so was*").[11] In other words, the terrorists were justified in repaying like with like, and the Americans got what they deserved, presumably due to their abrasive foreign policy. More notoriously, another aspect of Communist vocabulary has reappeared: the pathos of the anti-Hitler rhetoric, turned against the United States, in particular against Bush. What the German minister of justice said in her equation of Bush and Hitler was not exceptional; one hears similar remarks frequently in Germany. A noteworthy instance involved a large banner displayed during the May 2002 demonstrations against Bush in Berlin, showing pictures of Hitler pointing to the burning Reichstag and Bush in front of the crumbling World Trade Center. To make the identification complete, they share the same cartoon bubble of speech:

This attack means that our nation must set out on a long march to war and forget the debilitating trust in civil liberties! But do not fear, my people, for this just fight will only add to our glory!! And although this attack seems to be made to order to make you forget my disputed seizure of power and to pave the way for blind obedience to my orders, I want to have you believe that my security forces had nothing to do with it. Thank you very much. See you later in Poland or Iraq, and then around the world!![12]

The poster tells us little about Bush and Hitler, but a good deal about the political culture that could tolerate this sort of distorted representation. For starters, of course, in a classic Communist manner, the anti-Semitic character of Hitler's rhetoric and National Socialism is simply expunged. In addition, the conspiracy-theoretical innuendo that American security forces carried out the attack on the World Trade Center is clear. More generally, the equation of the legal systems in Nazi Germany and contemporary America is striking: either it means that the contemporary post-Communist Germans imagine that Nazi Germany was basically like the United States, and therefore not all that bad; or it implies a grossly distorted view of the United States and the standing of civil liberties. Yet we know that the justice minister herself described the American legal system as lousy. Thus Communist imagery structures anti-Americanism in two ways: in its denunciation of the historical American defense of democracy against Soviet expansion, and in its characterization of capitalism, and especially the most developed capitalist society, as fascist through the association with Hitler.

While the predemocratic and Communist variants of anti-Americanism represent residues of obsolete political formations—no matter how these ideologies retain a contemporary afterlife—postdemocratic anti-Americanism, the third model, reflects an emerging divide: on the one hand the widespread predisposition, perhaps more so in Germany than elsewhere, to shift decision making to supranational and therefore nondemocratic units—the European Union, the United Nations, an international court—and on the other the American insistence on the priority of national sovereignty as an expression of the popular will. The process of sovereignty transfer may correspond to larger pressures toward globalization or, alternatively, a logic of bureaucratization: one more way to allow for the deferral and dispersion of decision making. To the extent that Germany, in particular, buys into this process, however, may reflect its own ambivalent relationship to its national past and its impaired self-esteem (although there is plenty of willingness to engage in symbolic self-assertion as long as the opponent is the United States).[13]

In the responses to September 11, this postdemocratic perspective emerged in expressions of concern that US policy inappropriately responds to domestic constituencies. In other words, there is an underlying assumption that policy, and in particular foreign policy, ought to be decoupled from democratic political discussion and decision making, that is, a diminishment of the domestic public sphere. Apparently American politicians should listen less to voters and more to NGOs. Thus, as Klaus Theweleit said,

> It is frequently overlooked that Bush could only win the elections with votes from the Bible Belt, the votes of fundamentalist Americans, religious fanatics. ... And then Bush does not understand when armed religious fanatics come back from other parts of the world.[14]

Leaving aside the bizarre analogy of cultural conservative Christians with armed terrorists, one notes the implicit objection that this particular group, perhaps any particular group, should be able to participate in the electoral process. Does Theweleit mean that Christian voters should be disenfranchised? Yet if one assumes that fundamentalist Christians do indeed have the right to vote—a right that Theweleit seems to dispute—then one cannot object to the possible consequence that they might have political influence. The same objection recurs even more frequently with regard to the Jewish vote, evident in the tedious German paranoia regarding a "Jewish lobby" somehow steering American foreign policy.[15] This anti-Semitic content regularly lurks behind the standard complaint that US policy in the Middle East is a function of domestic political concerns. Yet again, just as I bracketed the anti-Christian substance of Theweleit's comment on fundamentalism, one can see beyond this anti-Semitism in order to focus on the much more obvious and revealing complaint: the notion that domestic politics ought to be excluded from foreign policy can mean nothing else than decoupling foreign policy formation from the democratic process. The logical conclusion would entail separating foreign policy from democratic government and relocating it in an independent foundation or an NGO of objective experts: absurd options, to be sure. In any case, given this European suspicion of the US system as excessively democratic due to its propensity to respond to domestic politics, it is only consistent that much European public opinion does not proceed from a basic solidarity with democratic states, particularly in the Middle East. In contrast, one of the important successes of current US policy has been the ability to focus international attention on the urgency of democratization throughout the region.[16]

These three types of anti-Americanism may overlap and intermingle. Moreover, they take on specific colorations in different national contexts. French anti-Americanism is more commonly marked by a cultural denigration of America; hence, for example, Jean Baudrillard's celebration of the 9/11 terrorists as noble savages, living authentically, in contrast to what he chose to refer to as the "banality" of American life.[17] Meanwhile the geopolitical element in the French discourse is typically more oriented toward inventing space for France to imagine remaining among the key global players, in contrast to German provincialism, eager to defer to Europe or the UN.[18] In Germany, too, one can find the cultural criticism, for example, the televised remark by the celebrated theater director Claus Peymann (with his own history of support for terrorists) that chewing gum is the only American contribution to world culture.[19] Communist-inspired accounts of twentieth-century history are more common in Germany than in France. More frequently, however, German anti-Americanism is haunted by the anxieties of German national history: the desperate need to relativize the Nazi era past by imagining that the United States, or Israel, or both are equally criminal. Hence the long history of denouncing America's *alltäglicher Faschismus* (everyday fascism) and, in the 9/11 discussions, the constant parallels suggested between the allied bombings in World War II and the air war in Afghanistan: both, so the analogic argument goes, are wrong. In other words, lingering resentment about the US role in World War II contaminates the German judgment on current foreign policy. Evidence of current American wrongdoing seems to provide Germans an absolution for their past.

What then is the source of anti-Americanism? My first thesis was negative: anti-Americanism is not a result of specific processes of cultural or institutional transfer that could be construed as entailing "Americanization." Yet this does not mean that anti-Americanism is nothing more than a free-floating discourse, with no relationship to real historical processes. On the contrary—and this is the second and concluding claim—anti-Americanism is fundamentally an expression of hostility to societies of democratic capitalism. This dynamic sort of social formation involves a set of institutions that developed particularly through the history of Western culture and its values, and it has flourished particularly in the United States, which has defended this model in the hot and cold wars of the twentieth century. Yet democratic capitalism and its associated values are not narrowly American or even exclusively Western. On the contrary, as a social model, it retains enormous attraction for populations around the world, one result of which is immigration, as well as the remarkable capacity of immigrant groups to integrate into the US polity very quickly. Against cultural relativists, it is important to assert that democracy is not a parochial artifact of American culture but rather an objective potential for all humanity, even if it is the United States that has become its sometimes reluctant vehicle.

Anti-Americanism is therefore not a response to the Americanization associated with the spread of jazz or youth culture; it is not fundamentally about the bombing of Dresden, or the proliferation of McDonald's in Paris, or even the sanctions on Iraq (although each of these might be taken as a pretext and each, one can add, might well be debated on its own terms). Instead, Anti-Americanism involves a global judgment, an enormous stereotype, driven by fears regarding democracy and capitalism. The fact that the American model exercises such a magnetic attraction globally exacerbates the anxieties among those who do not emigrate and especially among national cultural elites, who resent their compatriots' opting for an American life-course. But this process, again, is not about the narrow assertion of American national interest or the particular contents of American culture (e.g., jazz). Nor is the key issue immigration, although the universal attraction of America—to peoples from very different cultural backgrounds—is quite telling and proof of the universalizable character of the specific set of values. The point is that the principles objectified in the American Revolution, to be sure, products of particular cultural traditions, have proven to assert universal appeal because they speak to basic aspects of the human condition everywhere. "Here or nowhere is America" ("*Hier oder nirgend ist Amerika,*") spoke Goethe's Lothario: the political and social revolution of democracy ought to be pursued in Germany and not, primarily, through emigration to the United States.[20] Lothario can only have meant that the structure of emancipation modeled in the United States was worthy of emulation elsewhere. It is that potential of progress in human history that anti-Americanism resists.

Notes

Parts of this essay appeared in revised form in my *Anti-Americanism in Europe: A Cultural Problem* (Stanford: Hoover Press, 2004).

1. See "The Gulf War and Cultural Theory in the United States and Germany: Nationhood, Popularity and Yellow Ribbons," in my *Cultural Studies of Modern Germany: History, Representation, and Nationhood* (Madison and London, 1993), 175-200.
2. Cf. Jean-François Revel, *L'obsession anti-américaine: Son fonctionnement, ses causes, ses inconséquences* (Paris, 2002).
3. Philip Zelkiow and Condoleezza Rice, *Germany Unified and Europe Transformed: A Study in Statecraft* (Cambridge, Mass., 1995).
4. See Suzanne Zantop, *Colonial Fantasies: Conquest, Family, and Nation in Precolonial Germany, 1770-1870* (Durham, 1997), 18-42.
5. Dan Diner, *America in the Eyes of the Germans: An Essay on Anti-Americanism* (Princeton, 1996), 37.
6. *The National Security Strategy of the United States*, September 2002 (Washington D.C., 2002), preface, n.p. (p. iii).
7. Diner, *America in the Eyes of the Germans*, 46.
8. Cited in Henryk M. Broder, *Kein Krieg, Nirgends: Die Deutschen und der Terror* (Berlin, 2002), 93. Note that the Kennedy assassination took place on November 22, 1963, not November 21 as Walser states.

9. Ibid., 10
10. Ibid., 123
11. Ibid., 200
12. *The Times of London*, 23 May 2002.
13. Cf. Tom W. Smith and Lars Jarkko, "National Pride in Cross-National Perspective," paper of the National Opinion Research Center, University of Chicago, April 2001. Available at <www.issp.org/paper.htm>.
14. Broder, *Kein Krieg, Nirgends*, 186.
15. William Safire, "The German Problem," *New York Times*, 19 September 2002.
16. On the urgency of democratic reform in the Arab world, cf. Claire Nullis, "Report: Arab Economies Need Reform," *Washington Times*, 8 September 2002, re "Arab World Competitiveness Report" of the World Economic Forum.
17. Jean Baudrillard; "The Spirit of Terrorism," in *Telos* 121 (fall 2001): 138; cf. Alain Minc, "Terrorism of the Spirit," *Telos* 121 (fall 2001): 143-45; and more generally, Philippe Roger, *L'ennemi américain: Généalogie de l'antiaméricanisme français* (Paris, 2002).
18. Regarding provincialism, cf. Karl Heinz Bohrer, "Provinzialismus (II): ein Psychogramm," in *Merkur* 45, no. 3 (March 1991): 255-61. Thus Bohrer: "[...] *daß auch das vereinigte Deutschland als Folge des nationalsozialistischen Traumas im Ernstfall nicht als westliche Macht mit entsprechender politischer Mentalität, sondern als mitteleuropäisches Grauzonenland ohne demokratische Tradition politisch spontaner Öffentlichkeit einzuordnen ist.*" (256).
19. Statement addressed to Hans Ulrich Gumbrecht in the German television broadcast *Philosophisches Quartett*, ZDF, March 2002.
20. Johann Wolfgang Goethe, *Goethes Werke*, ed. Erich Trunz (Hamburg, 1962), VII, 431.

COUNTER-AMERICANISM AND CRITICAL CURRENTS IN WEST GERMAN RECONSTRUCTION 1945-1960
The German Lesson Confronts the American Way of Life

◆ ◆ ◆

Michael Ermarth

> The modernization of the world is in truth its Americanization.
> —Rupert Murdoch (1994)[1]

> Germany can certainly not be converted to "Americanism" nor will she become a satellite of the United States. She will probably have to walk a long road, with detours and blind alleys, before she becomes the society of free citizens we call democracy. Many differences between America and Germany do not stem from German faults or shortcomings; but neither do they bar a common perception of values, interests, and purposes.
> —Norbert Muhlen (1953)[2]

The German-American Imbroglio of 2002/2003 in Historical Perspective

Whether real or imagined, German anti-Americanism is back in the headlines with the special force that blows with the winds of war. Prominent and ordinary Germans are disputing US insistence that the world after the terrorist attacks of 9/11 is facing the sort of absolute either/or "decisionist" moment that earlier Germans in the vein of Carl Schmitt brooded over and acted

---

Notes for this section begin on page 48.

upon, only to be met with the catastrophic consequences of two total world wars, systematic genocide, and enduring infamy. Such extreme moments of existential decision are said by their proponents to compel the absolute separation into oppositional camps and exclusive categories, such as "friend" or "foe," "us" or "them," "hammer" or "anvil," "subject" or "object"—to cite but a few of the master dichotomies in the former German vocabulary of absolute polarization used to define world politics in the period when Germany aimed to be a world power in its own right.

Needless to say, the Germans have been burned several times over by their previous rigid categorical framing of world conflicts. They have a painfully acquired, systemic autoimmune allergy to Schmittian absolute decisionism and its lethal momentum of categorical, all-or-nothing positions. By way of mitigation, such an unconditional either/or formulation could be reframed in the terms of another notorious German Carl—that is, the Prussian military theorist Carl von Clausewitz—who observed that war conducted in the modern post-Napoleonic age of national states and international alliances should seek to restrain its inherent dynamic toward "absolute war" (as a kind of ghostly "thing in itself") and rather should strive to remain flexible, modifiable, as war is in essence "nothing but a continuation of political intercourse, with a mixture of other means."[3]

The contrast between the two German Carls finds its latter-day parallel in the contrast between the two American presidential Georges—the more liberal, multilateralist, consensus-building father, and the more tough-talking, unilateralist son. Germans have registered vastly more favor and confidence in the flexible Clausewitzian stance of the elder Bush, who promoted German unification and led the first war against Iraq, than in the peremptory, hard Schmittian posture of the junior Bush. History seems to be teaching different lessons on different sides of the "widening" Atlantic. As shown in the embarrassing episode in which the former German justice minister compared the younger President Bush to Hitler in the use of foreign war as a deflection from domestic political predicaments, the German lesson regarding hubristic tendencies in their the own history is swelling suspicions about kindred forces at work in American policies—the latter being driven more by the profligate American life-style rather than race-based mythomania and expansionist biopolitics.

Of course, the putative lessons of history and the practice of politics itself—including the tangled dialectics of justifiable wars and democratic politics in the present, media-saturated age—remain susceptible to very divergent interpretations and applications. Times change, and so do the dominant interpretive lessons of past events, transformed by new exigencies the present. There can be no doubt, however, that Germans continue to feel a special burden in trying to bring their own harrowing experience to the task of construing historical lessons. Here a lasting German specialness persists, despite talk of ongoing "normalization," as nested in the widening concentric circles of Europeanization, Westernization, globalization, and modernization. Whether and how the concept of Americanization fits in with this orbital ordering of encompassing processes remains a loaded issue, as will be treated below. If America represents the world's sole remaining superpower, it is just as true that the ready label of Americanization remains the favorite superconcept for epitomizing the unsettling changes sweeping over much of the world. As once enunciated by Joschka Fischer before he became Chancellor Gerhard Schröder's effective and popular foreign minister, the view that the vaguer, amorphous term "globalization" is really in essence an oblique or euphemistic label for the more abrasive "Americanization" remains commonplace in Europe and the world at large.

The German-American friction of most recent times concerns the real, underlying rationale for a war against Iraq at a time of astonishingly close electoral campaigns and razor-thin outcomes, continuing economic slump and severe budget crises, an inflamed Middle East situation, and gnawing uncertainty about the real direction and impact of globalization—all agitated by acute public fear at the potential global reach of high-tech and low-tech terrorism. The once happy, hybrid notions of "glocalism" and "thinking globally and acting locally"—the felicitous fusion of global awareness and immediate grass-roots participatory activism—have taken on a much more sinister meaning. Under conditions of democratic politics and global (yet also obdurately national) public opinion, the domain of hard geostrategic policy shades over into the vaguer hinter-realms of culture and civilization, principles and values, ideologies, and ways of life. As often remarked by editorialists and political commentators, hard strategic power remains inextricably linked to soft "cultural" power, in the form of tacit values, public opinion, and the osmotic sway of popular culture—including the "memory culture" that keeps alive the lessons of the past. Contrasting and even excruciatingly antithetical lessons of history surge to the forefront in the current German-American altercation, even as concerns core values of close partnership in support of peace, democracy, and human rights. Such bedrock values may at once guide and transcend particular historical exigencies, but they do not escape from the problematizing pull of what different nations and peoples consider the main historical lessons of the past.

In the impasse of early 2003, the German lesson as invoked by many outspoken and ordinary Germans was presented as being utterly at odds with the American imperative of joining in a preemptive, full-scale war and radical regime change in Iraq. The Bush administration insisted that such actions were necessary for protecting and promoting basic human values, security, democracy, and decent ways of life in Iraq, the wider Middle East, and the world at large. There are complementary concentric patterns at work here, too: these democratic values and ways of life are claimed to be at once American, European, Western, Middle Eastern, and universal. Both sides of the argument for and against the second Iraq war have struggled to occupy the moral high ground by marshalling momentous analogies from the past. The American side has invoked Hitler, the illusory Munich agreements of 1938, persisting genocidal potentialities, as well as the positive reconstruction for post-Saddam Iraq along lines similar to Germany or Japan after World War II. The German side, on the other hand, has tended to evoke Vietnam, Hiroshima, Iran, Beirut, and the ongoing problem of pacifying and democratizing Afghanistan. The Americans have depicted war for regime change as having worked utterly successfully in Germany and Japan, whereas the German regime itself has not been so convinced or flattered by the parallel, however loosely intended. Indeed, during the fall election of 2002, Chancellor Schröder invoked the old, fraught term of "the German way" at the very time President Bush argued for pressing ahead with the special way of "American internationalism," reserving the right to preempt or override the United Nations Security Council. As it turned out, no such UN resolution was secured to provide international sanction for the American-led invasion of Iraq.

German-American differences continue to remain serious, if not truly acute. Despite the designation of October 6 as official, annual German-American Friendship Day, commentators on both sides of the Atlantic continue to wring their hands at the increasing erosion, "rupturing," and even "poisoning" of the previous pattern of close partnership. Indeed, veteran commentator Josef Joffe has referred to Chancellor Schröder's calculated gamble of "making hay with careful anti-Americanism."[4] In the terms of this essay and in the light of recent history, it can be argued that "counter-Americanism" rather than "careful anti-Americanism" is the proper (and far more pertinent) term for Schröder's general stance. But whatever the precise nomenclature, German and American positions have never seemed so far apart as in the contentious situation of 2003, which some believe shows signs of much deeper, continuing fracture or irreparable seismic shift. Tracing some of the incipient fault lines back to the distant period of postwar West German reconstruction can serve to cast light upon the sharper edges and deeper contours of this discord.

The rifts so evident in German-American relations both before and after the spring 2003 Iraq war can be viewed as reflecting divergent readings of the German lesson and of the American way of life, as these have respectively developed in the first and second halves of the twentieth century. Robustly unilateral American internationalism as a kind of generalized exceptionalism has run into a latter day, semi-normalized version of the German-European way, which is far from enthralled with what it perceives as the rampant excesses of the American way of life. Whether the imbroglio of 2002-2003 turns into a long-lasting fracture will depend upon many contingencies, as well as the real underlying depth of mutual reservations and doubts. But clearly German (and European) misgivings about the direction of American policy under the second Bush presidency also concern the worrisome larger "cultural" tendencies of the fabled American way of life, especially as it has been represented to Europe and the rest of the world in America's own media. To many non-Americans exposed to the wares of mass media moguls such as Rupert Murdoch, the American way of life appears to be a complacently consumerist, narcissistically self-indulgent, celebrity-obsessed lifestyle, which remains woefully indifferent or inimical to almost anything different from itself and its hard-sell, self-promoting interests.

Murdoch's glib summation of the ultimate "essential" trajectory of modernization and globalization—as everybody's eventual way of life in a global world—hardly elicits the sort of enthusiastic 24/7 cheerleading that his networks and media outlets routinely provide for this phenomenon. Moreover, the frenzied hyperbole surrounding the wondrous "New Economy" as a global capitalist *Wirtschaftswunder in excelsis* emanating primarily from America has turned out to lack the happy ending—or even broadly benign interim tendency—to cushion the "creative destruction" of this worldwide transformation. Globalization is seen as a euphemism for an engulfing Americanization, which much of the world detests or disdains.[5]

The December 2002 report by the Pew Research Center, entitled "What the World Thinks in 2002," concludes under the headline "Americanization Rejected" that "[i]n general, people around the world object to the wide diffusion of American ideas and customs. Even those who are attracted to many aspects of American society, including its democratic ideas and free market traditions, object to the export of American ideas and customs. Yet this broad-brush rejection of 'Americanism' obscures the admiration many people have for American culture and particularly U.S. science and technology." On the question of the spread of American ideas and customs, 67 percent of German respondents characterized this spread as "bad," and 28 percent said that it was "good." German views toward "Americanization" were only slightly more favorable than those offered by French respondents (of whom 71 percent characterized Americanization as bad and 25 percent stated that it was good).[6] Outside the community of "Atlantic values," the percentages were considerably more lopsided toward the negative side: Turkey showed a ratio of 78 to 11; Egypt 84 to 6; Pakistan 81 to 2; Argentina 73 to 16; and Indonesia 73 to 20.

The expansive, protean epithet "Americanization" has a long history of being inverted against its own positive and benign native meanings, so that instead of signifying the promise of democractic dignity, individual freedom, and societal flourishing for the vast majority of humankind, it turns into a self-serving presumption of opportunity and plenty for the gluttonous few but abjection and want for the many, who remain misled by its dazzling cosmetic allure. It is an old suspicion that stretches back well before the mid-twentieth century (as the inception of the high water period of the now elapsed "American century") and even well before the twentieth century itself. The critique of Americanization has been richly elaborated by German intellectuals and commentators, who often pointedly made use of cognate critiques from indigenous American sources in order to bolster their foreign "outsider" viewpoints with immanent "insider" testimonies. If once these German critics labored in the exalted cause of a distinctly German way (or sometimes a conjoint German-European way), they now argue from global rather than national or continental premises. The well-being of global humanity, the conservation of its different cultural embodiments, the survival of the natural environment, and of the very planet itself are all marshaled against the continuing sweep of global Americanization.

The shift of "orbital" premises from narrower national ones to more expansive global ones, however, has not altered the basic thrust of the inveterate German-cum-European critique of Americanization. As an unprecedented combination of will-to-power in two kinds—both soft and hard power—Americanization continues to be presented as a rampant, even demonically uncontrolled, hybristic force tending toward inhumane excess rather than the common human good. Or, stated differently, German critics of Americanism and Americanization have a penchant for regarding the American way of life as altogether too much of a good thing—whether through the consumption of calories, gallons of oil, or hours of television viewing. Whether this view is based on appearance or reality may be becoming irrelevant in the eye of the beholder in this Murdochian world of 24/7 hyper-reality: Americanization tends to become whatever the viewer wants to make of it. And many of the things Americans tend to regard as good in the process—good for themselves and, by extension, for others—others regard as very bad. Under different global conditions, the wonted American way of life becomes the wanton way of life.

Americanization as "Concept of the Century" and Counter-Americanism as Its Alternative "Other"

Americanization has recently been deemed "the concept of the century" by the discerning German historian Phillipp Gassert, who has charted its course in Germany through several crucial decades of the twentieth century. Even if thousand-year epochs and empires may no longer seem possible or even conceivable to our shortened, media-saturated attention spans, the "concept of the century" might well turn out to be the mantra of the millennium.[7] The key question is whether it deserves this momentous status by prevailing in actual force of fact or rather in name only, as once the venerable and indispensable occult element "phlogiston." Americanization flourishes as phantom as well as phenomenon, bearing out the adage that the most important matters are often the most difficult to formulate clearly. The modes of "real existing" and "rhetorically persisting" Americanization may never really be satisfactorily sorted out but rather ritually passed along as the brand name stock-in-trade of modern self-understanding, groping for some easily identifiable, iconic self-image. Already in the late nineteenth century—that is, well before the semantic explosion of the term "Americanization" in Europe following World War I—German commentators presciently observed that something very much akin to then-current ideas of Americanism and Americanization would be transpiring in the modern world even *without* the United States to give the specifying proper (or improper) name and strikingly oversized iconic image to the multiple processes lumped under the term.

After a full century of intense scrutiny and invective-ridden debate, Americanization remains no easier to fixate or to model than the other master ideas and *Sinnstiftungen* of modern history—such as rationalization, secularization, democratization, "technification," globalization, or modernity itself. Whether it serves as a popular self-cliché for modernity or as a convenient common orthography for multiple, proliferating vernacular modernities, the notion of Americanization seems routinely to elude stable conceptualization. Its very dynamism lends it both its fascination and confounding evasiveness. With their holistic or *gestalt*-like, half-Hegelian habits of mind, German interpreters have been the most ambitious interpreters of the shifting dynamics of Americanization—and not only of their own successive forms and phases of it but of others' experiences as well. Although the Americanization of Germany has often been described as especially thorough (as during much of the Weimar Republic and the duration of West German Federal Republic), German commentators have tried, in the manner of Robert Müller's counter-Americanism, to project progressive pathways of alternative development that would overcome the alleged failings of Americanization. The German urge to such "trump" patterns of alternative advancement contested the view that the American way of life somehow constituted the "end of history" or everybody's common future, as in Rupert Murdoch's scenario. Both nature and culture were brought to the fore in the cause of counter-Americanism.

Whatever its ultimate scope, dynamics, and direction, Americanization remains almost an interpretive article of faith among German and American historians for encapsulating or "modeling" what happened in West Germany in the postwar reconstruction period. Arnulf Baring has recently insisted that Americanization was "the real revolution" that transformed West Germany after 1945.[8] Similarly, Anselm Doering-Manteuffel has called the two decades from 1945 to 1965 "the core epoch [*Kernzeit*] of Americanization in the whole modernization process of the 20th century."[9] Such testimonials to the seismic shift of Americanization in West Germany during this period could be cited literally by the hundreds. For my part I am more inclined to agree with Lothar Kettenacker who argues that "the so-called Americanization of West Germany is a very superficial description, which does not stand up to scrutiny."[10] Of course, it comes down to what one means by Americanization, which turns out to be hardly anymore univocal and clear-cut than "the whole modernization process of the 20th century"; one becomes embroiled in a logical chicken-egg conundrum of the first order.

The concept of Americanization becomes more and more kaleidoscopically complicated, as it has shifted among different registers and valences. For West Germany, these variants have included: (1) the pursuit of official policy by the United States; (2) the establishment of constitutional and institutional structures and codified practices; (3) the embedding of self-conscious patterns of belief and collective ideology; and finally, (4) the diffusely tacit osmosis of unreflective suppositions, behavioral choices, and lifestyles into everyday life and climates of opinion. Because of its constantly proliferating yet directional or telic qualities, Americanization will probably continue its double-existence as both a tendentious *Kampfbegriff* as well as a neutral analytical, academic term of analysis. Despite major efforts at careful refinement (including the company of commentators gathered in this volume), the idea of Americanization continues to stalk the world as an "in-your-face" bumper sticker notion, driven by a sort of Schmittian friend-or-foe polarization, even when it is adduced from a detached or ulterior perspective. At present, the widespread view that globalization is really an ulterior Americanization under another name does not serve to foster greater forbearance for its ill effects.

With concern mounting at the souring and even poisoning of the German-American partnership, it seems an appropriate time for rethinking—and rephrasing—the prevailing view of Germany's Americanization—especially as it pertains to West Germany in the crucial foundational years of 1945-1960. It seems long overdue to address a groundbreaking but also longstanding designation for an alternative way of confronting an Americanizing mode of modernity on its own terms—individualistic, liberal democratic, free-market capitalistic, mass industrial, and advanced technological—without entirely surrendering Germans' own special terms, including a more pronounced sense of social solidarity, of personal reflectiveness, and of less commercially oriented forms of personal, public, and cultural life. In my view, the strikingly new but century-old term "counter-Americanism" can serve as a much needed missing link or dimension in the weighty German "discourse on modernity." It also provides a more illuminating focus to the proverbial but overworked motif of congenital German ambivalence about modern civilization, whether in the form of Hamletesque indecision, schizoid *Zweiseelentum*, "reactionary modernism," "defensive modernization," and the like.[11] The German idea of counter-Americanism carries its own historical cogency and rich contextuality; furthermore, it offers a valuable way to move beyond the tired Schmittian either/or categories of pro- or anti-Americanism. The latter alternative remains more political than historical—and it is time for history to prevail over present day politics, at least where history itself is concerned.

The term "counter-Americanism," or *Konträr-Amerikanismus*, came into limited public circulation in the late Wilhelmine era with interesting but idiosyncratic credentials. Robert Müller, the obscure avant-garde Expressionist Austro-German writer and journalist, insisted in a series of works written after 1910 that counter-Americanism should be pursued as the cooperative German-European pathway to a common flourishing future.[12] The Germanic vocation was to forge a progressive new "United States of Europe" that would thrive culturally and economically in the emerging global "world-world" of burgeoning competition among vast continent-sized states, international industrial conglomerates, and huge overseas empires.[13] This joint task necessitated a whole new constellation of positive, activist beliefs and ideas. Rather than calling it neo-Germanism or pan-Europeanism, Müller dubbed this forward-looking, progress-affirming, technology-friendly, socially conscious worldview as counter-Americanism. As an ardent admirer of the American triumvirate of Ralph Waldo Emerson, Walt Whitman, and Thomas Edison, Müller was adamant in distinguishing his constructive but still incipient notion of counter-Americanism from obscurantist anti-Americanism, whether of the socialist left or traditionalist right. Müller's progressive conception does not fit within the parameters of what Fritz Stern, George Mosse, and others have explicated as the illiberal civilizational pessimism of the "Germanic ideology."[14] Nor does it coincide with what Jeffrey Herf has identified as the technology-affirming but reactionary strand of German reactionary modernism. This current of counter-Americanism was socially liberal, progressive, and pan-European, remaining especially intent upon preserving European cultural diversity and distinctiveness.

Viewed from the trump vantage point of Müller's Germanic-European counter-Americanism of 1910, indigenous US-Americanism at this time represented a threatening excess and lack of self-control. Its self-stoking, obsessive economism and frantic success ethos, its heedless exploitation of nature, its threat to inner-directed depth and cultural variety, its interest-driven, plutocratic politics, its inhumane labor and workplace practices, and its emaciated social conscience—all these recent traits of Americanism forfeited the true promise of an earlier, original America. Hence Müller regarded current big-business, power-seeking Americanism as the fading wave of a soon-to-be superceded way of life rather than as the wave of the future. Thus, for Müller, the obsolescent form of recent US-Americanism represented what ironically would later be laid upon Germany precisely as "reactionary modernism," whereas his vision of counter-Americanism was believed to sublimate and supercede current Americanism for something more progressive and humane. With the collateral impulse toward a confederal United States of Europe, Müller touted his conception of counter-Americanism as the sole salutary and efficacious future course for both Germany and Europe as a whole. It should be stressed that, in a phrasing quite similar to Müller's, later German and European interpreters would likewise invoke a remedial, corrective form of modernity beyond current ideas of Americanism in the guise of what they called "serum modernism," "second-order modernity," "reflective modernity" and even "transmodernity."[15]

The persistence of something akin to Müller's conception should hardly cause surprise among historians, although its layered complexity may rattle those insisting that modern development proceeds with the Schmittian categorical clarity of either pro- or anti-Americanism. Americanization as the "concept of the century" did not go without its own shadowy, dialectical counter-conception, even if the latter became obscured or renamed along the way. German thought on modernity has been notorious for its radical, decisionist, either/or oppositions, but it has also elaborated some intriguing counter-diagonals, dialectical syntheses, and trump-transcendental third ways. Something akin to Müller's counter-Americanism served to reinforce the more liberal, European-oriented versions of the German *Sonderbewusstsein* and *Sonderweg* conceptions, whose historical significance for the first half of the century must be assessed alongside the cardinal concept of Americanization itself.

If often indicated more by subtle inflection than by forthright designation, counter-Americanism continued as a discernible current of reform democratic socialist and social liberal thinking through the period of postwar West German occupation and reconstruction. Moreover, these critical currents were recognized and to some extent supported by American officials at different levels in the Office of Military Government (OMGUS) and the US High Commission for Germany (HICOG), raising interesting questions about mutual accommodation and convergence. (The idea of counter-Americanism may also apply to Japanese occupation and reconstruction, undoubtedly with special sociocultural accents there, too. A comparative study of counter-Americanisms—as distinct from outright anti-Americanisms—would be an invaluable cross-cultural undertaking.) Counter-Americanism thus recommends itself as a fresh historiographical concept for what was a longstanding German or European disposition—one that is unlikely to recede in influence in the "Europeanizing" and globalizing future, regardless of its formal designation. Calling such a stance "anti-Americanism" or even "careful anti-Americanism" is a clumsy misnomer. The honest acknowledgment of such a third way might serve to detoxify the present atmosphere somewhat by shifting the historical thresholds of perceived threat and misrepresentation.

Several different strands of German counter-Americanism have emerged in the twentieth century, and some certainly qualify as outright anti-Americanism. This article addresses only the reformist social liberal and social democratic currents that appeared to run in tandem during the first decade and a half of the reconstruction period. In ways that seem surprising today, some major voices during this time argued that the softer "American lesson" concerning the latently inhumane or incrementally harmful perils of American-style civilizational progress corroborated rather than refuted the hard "German lesson" of the murderous calamity of Nazi totalitarianism. If perhaps "overlearned" and overinterpreted in the wake of German collapse and disorientation, these two tandem lessons prompted an abiding suspicion of the general susceptibility of modern civilization to mental conformity, collective manipulation, and the erosion of both culture and nature. These profound lessons still resonate in Germany and Europe, even though the original postwar alignment of "isms" has been largely dismantled and swept away.

I should emphasize that I am dealing here not with the avowed antipathy toward Americanism and Americanization issuing from the radical socialist/communist left and traditionalist or nationalist right (and hybrid crossovers of both). Rather, I am concerned with the middle-of-the-road social liberal, moderate Social Democratic, and Christian Democratic sectors of the political landscape, which were in many ways eager to stay on the good side of American power and policy while also holding to a refurbished German-European path forward. Specifically, I refer here not to the likes of Bertolt Brecht, Friedrich Sieburg, Wolfgang Koeppen, Hans Zehrer, Günther Anders, Erich Kuby, Hans Abosch, Bruno Brehm, holdover *Tatkreis* figures, the Naumann Gruppe, or the Frankfurt School. Rather I am referring to moderate liberals, with proven democratic credentials, such as Wilhelm Röpke, Walter Eucken, Alfred Weber, Alexander Rüstow, and even at times Konrad Adenauer himself, especially in his later years as chancellor. These figures were firmly avowed believers in parliamentary democracy, the constitutional and federal *Rechtsstaat*, and individual and civil rights, so their strand of counter-Americanism can hardly be said to translate into anti-Westernism or antimodernism. Indeed, their moderate Western "modernism of measure" reinforced their deeper worries about the excessive tendencies of an immoderate, Americanized way of life—both at home and abroad.

Postwar Social Liberal and Reformist Social Democratic Doctrines of the Third Way as Progressive Counter-Americanism

The general course of Germany after 1945 has been summarized in retrospect by Kurt Sontheimer in words that suggest an inexorable, single path to the future via a reprise and restoration of Western liberal values: "Germany's special way through modern history had ended [in 1945] in a dark dead-end. Now there was no other choice. The way forward was in a certain sense a way back, to the origins of the idea of freedom and justice in Western thought, to the Enlightened, natural-rights, and liberal tradition which the German spirit had successively abjured to the point where, as 'German spirit' under National Socialism, it went completely to the dogs."[16]

But after the maniacal, rabid "dog years" of Nazi Germany, this unswerving affirmation of Western liberal humanist values did not necessarily mean the embrace or promotion of Americanism or Americanization—not for many distinguished German voices who declared themselves Western humanist liberals and not even for some American military government officials who sympathized with their concerns. Ideas of American-style progress and the German "way forward" were not necessarily convergent or compatible. There was a complex divergence or cross-tension in this crucial area of sociocultural reconstruction and "reeducation," which played out at different levels of opinion and official policy. In striving to accommodate some key German values and attitudes, American policy and practice proved flexible enough to include its own internal kind of homegrown "counter-Americanism."

The early postwar and Cold War years after 1946 saw the strong, broadbased reassertion of the older conception of an alternative third way forged between Anglo-American-style free-market, liberal capitalism and fascist or Soviet-style, statist-collectivist planning. At this time, third-way advocates were bolstered by the close linkage of Nazism and Stalinism, joined under the general rubric of totalitarianism. As an all-enveloping collectivism relying upon the most advanced means of coercion and manipulation, modern totalitarianism was regarded as the ominous outcome of the boundless and twisted cravings of "mass-man" and "mass civilization." The notions of mass-man and mass-civilization had long informed the European view of Americanism and Americanization, the latter of which was often presented as a soft or conformist totalitarianism of mental manipulation, herd mentality, and thoughtless conformity. The delayed but remarkable success of the 1930 work by Spanish philosopher José Ortega y Gasset, *The Revolt of the Masses*, which became a faddish bestseller in West Germany in the 1950s (much as Oswald Spengler's *Decline of the West* dud in the 1920s after World War I), did much to meld sharp ideological differences at the surface level into a deeper similitude of looming mass civilization.

Under the umbrella of totalitarianism, the postwar reconstruction period witnessed a tortured intellectual triangulation among the ideologies of Fascism/Nazism, Soviet Communism, and Americanism, with the tendencies of each "ism" being attributed, oddly enough, to its other two historic adversaries. As surprising as it might seem today, extensive commonalities between Sovietism and Americanism seemed obvious to some German social liberals, Social Democrats, Christian Democrats, moderate national neutralists, trade union leaders, and educators, who continued to be as worried about the erosion of spiritual-cultural, communitarian, and environmental values as they were terrified at the prospect of a US-Soviet superpower confrontation turning into nuclear annihilation. This "convergence doctrine" regarding Sovietism and Americanism was hardly the sole property of former Nazis such as Martin Heidegger, Otto Dietrich, and Giselher Wirsing. It attracted adherents among moderates and liberal centrists, who had little affinity for the eschatological radicalism of either the left or right but who nevertheless aspired to chart a viable, humane third way between the untenable systems of Americanism and Sovietism. This idea of the third way presupposed an odd *coincidentia oppositorum* in which Americanism would come to resemble its opposite.

In 1949, the cultural sociologist Alfred Weber, younger brother of the more famous Max Weber, expounded in *Der Monat* upon the sociocultural symmetry of what he called the two behemoth, secular "social religions" of Sovietism and Americanism, which were battling and proselytizing over a prostrate Europe trapped between them, not yet able to articulate or advocate "its own characteristic, third social religion, the democratic-socialist way."[17] Dismissing the likelihood of any broad revival of traditional religious absolutes, Weber tried quixotically to articulate what he called a new "immediate immanent transcendence" that would "ground" Europeans in their difficult encounter with the two opposing, giant, social religions.[18] Weber went on to delineate three great ideological blocs of activistic/practical belief operative in the modern world: democratic capitalism (or "Americanism"), democratic socialism (or "Europeanism"), and Soviet Communism ("Sovietism").

Weber insisted that any future all-European democratic socialism would have to remain "antibureaucratic" and "antistatist," staying close to ordinary people and their everyday concerns while fulfilling the mission of conserving nature on both local and planetary scales. A pronounced sense of the limits to human power (both state power and consumer power) and limits to growth were seen as imperative for a viable future for humanity at large. Weber emphasized the cardinal importance of environmental concerns in his call for a European third way under the heading "Man and Earth," in which he discussed the impact of a world population of 3 billion by 2000 (a staggering *under*estimation by half).[19] He predicted that this scenario would result in the steady degradation of water, soil, and forest. Recasting the noxious Nazi notion of *Lebensraum*, Weber asserted that the idea of a "truly livable *Lebensraum*," previously exploited by brutal dictators in a collectivist, nationalist, or racialist vein, would become an increasingly dire global problem. Writing in 1950, Weber prophesized that "the true apocalyptic of history" did not lie so much in the awesomely dramatic power of the atomic bomb as in man's everyday quotidian relation to nature and to his fellow man.[20] In its overreaching Faustian grasp for power and influence, Americanism, like Sovietism, was not conducive to a truly livable and humane world. In contrast, the more modest *homo europaeus* would strive to conserve a greater balance of humaneness and respect for nature between the mutually escalating, power-crazed ambitions of the dominant "types," *homo sovieticus* and *homo americanus*.[21]

Weber's position was echoed and reinforced by others in the West German centrist sector of opinion. Arguing in 1949 for a "conservative social democracy" based upon a "true and honest socialism," the liberal, former head of the Weimar DDP, Willy Hellpach, ridiculed any trace of "vulgar-cultural conceit of European superiority," but went on to warn against the engrained American tendency toward unthinking excess on a vast collective scale: "The most dangerous inner enemy of all predominant power (*Vormacht*) is excessiveness (*Unmass*)."[22] Hellpach was referring not only to tendencies in American military-strategic power (recently hard-pressed by the Soviet announcement of its own A-bomb) but also to its inherent civilizational dynamic, which showed a surfeit of escalating individual desire and collective self-aggrandizement in the clutch of self-righteousness. It is worth noting that these social democratic and social liberal German (cum-European) misgivings about American mass conformity, homogeneity, and consumerism found a concurrent American echo in George Kennan's dark prognoses about the absentminded, largely inadvertent steamrollering of the diversity of European cultural distinctiveness by uncontrolled Americanism.[23] Unequivocally taking the side of America in the Cold War did not necessarily mean embracing Americanism and Americanization, as the latter had come to be perceived over decades of development.

Americanization as the mass dynamic of *Unmass*—as the mass-minded tendency to hubristic excess in terms of worldly desire—was too much of a good thing, at the incalculable cost of culture, nature, and a humane social order. Historian Thomas Reuther has recently summarized the ironic ambivalence of West German grass roots counter-Americanism in the postwar reconstruction years. Referring to the American media's homegrown hopes for democratization among broad elements in the Western zones, he concludes pointedly that "it was precisely the social forces and elements that the American media considered to be especially suited for a democratic reconstruction of West Germany and that had played a special role in plans to advance the cause of grass roots democracy—these same forces and elements resisted especially the Americanization of West German society (*widersetzen sich in besonderm Masse*). To these forces belonged Social Democracy, the churches, and the unions."[24]

It seems highly arguable, however, that US policy makers were really intent upon imposing "Americanism" or a characteristically American model of democracy or free market economy on the West Germans. As early as December 1945, General Lucius Clay had observed emphatically: "There is no easy road to democracy. The Germans must find this road themselves and the pilot cars on the road must be driven by Germans themselves."[25] Despite all the perversions of Germanness under the Nazis, West German democracy would have to be identifiably German as well as democratic, even though the combination entailed a certain element of resistance to what was deemed Americanism. The sheer numbers and influence of German émigrés and experts among the "pilot" planners and advisers for the reconstruction would argue against any template or fax theory of one-way, top-down modeling or piloting. The sort of reconstruction favored in America's Germany, it would seem, entailed a decontaminated, denazified form of re-Germanization.

After an initial period of unilateral proconsul military government, the United States tried to accomplish what has aptly been called a "Munchhausen feat" of prompting the Germans to pull themselves out of the swamp by their own mangled and charred topknots. This "grass roots as hair roots" approach had the virtue of demonstrating confidence and faith in ordinary Germans and their potential for sustaining a participatory democracy and exercising independent critical judgment, even if the roots seemed quite shallow and fragile. Trust in ordinary Germans and in the appeal of democracy, civic freedoms, and broader economic prosperity—beyond specific American stipulations as to form—became the modus operandi. In his report (and later published article)"America's Intentions in Germany," US Department of State specialist John Hilldring insisted that the United States deliberately eschewed hard-sell propagandistic methods, tempting as it was for quick results, because that was precisely what the Germans had been rendered immune against—and such a stance would surely backfire.[26] Rather curiously, veteran observer Richard Merritt has summarized the overall US posture during the OMGUS and HICOG periods as "modified colonization"; but at the same time Merritt himself cites a considerable array of American sources who remained outspokenly opposed to the imposition of "our own particular way of life on the Germans." These voices recognized the potential for short-term backlash and long-term resentment.[27] At the same time, a degree of counter-Americanism was recognized as a potential force for positive reconstruction and fit in with giving Germans a sense of having a stake in their own immediate initiatives and long-term future.

Historians' adherence to the notion of model systems may satisfy the taste for clear and distinctive labeling, but it obscures the element of shrewd, sometimes cooptative, accommodation that American officials consciously built into policy-positions and practices. These officials sanctioned a measure of indigenous critical, counter-American conviction precisely in order to allay charges of "colonialism," obligatory orthodoxy, imposed conformity, and coercive *Demokratur*. Americans too could live with a certain degree of critical counter-Americanism. (The same journal *Der Monat* that published Weber and others' pleas for an alternative third way was later revealed to be secretly subsidized by the OSS/CIA.) In sum, it seems fair to say that West German reconstruction was more a matter of German-American *Mitbestimmung* or mutual codetermination than full-fledged "hegemonic" Americanism or Americanization—with the qualifying proviso that the latter, in a genuinely liberal and pluralist sense, included emphatic support for self-determination. The assertion that the United States achieved a long-term "hegemony by invitation" in the face of the stark Soviet strategic threat of takeover in the west remains plausible for the high plane of grand politics; but at the same time this judgment obscures deeper sociocultural currents of opinion that harbored more complex attitudes, including what deserves to be called "careful" counter-Americanism.

If one refers to actual institutional structures and socioeconomic frameworks in practice, it is probably more apt to speak of the "Scandinavization" rather than the "Americanization" of West Germany.[28] The emergent West German social market economy of "freedom with responsibility" or "Rhenish capitalism" was a complex theoretical conception and evolving practical institution. While an exploration of this system's development is beyond the scope of this chapter, it is sufficient to say that this model drew more heavily in conception and execution upon Catholic social doctrine, reformist Social Democratic ideas, the putative lessons of Weimar and Nazi Germany—as well as Scandinavian precedents—than on any American model.[29] The famous social-market slogan of "as much freedom as possible, as much planning as necessary" was meant to steer a middle course, including avoidance of the "jungle capitalism" and "elbow society," which persisted as cautionary epithets for the ill-effects of unfettered American-style capitalism.

Following the postwar years of extreme deprivation and intensifying through the so-called miracle years of the mid-1950s, substantial elements in the churches, unions, and political parties came to assert strong and sometimes orchestrated objections to the excessive new West German focus upon material success and mass consumption, mental conformism, and possessive individualism at the expense of inward reflection and genuine individualism, spiritual enrichment, and communitarian social values. Americanism played in the background of these discussions. The lament that early postwar Allied policy, especially the Americans, focused too heavily on economic aims at the expense of spiritual-cultural regeneration remained a refrain of the Swiss "green" humanist writer-scholar Hans Zbinden, whose views were echoed in Germany by publisher Lambert Schneider and by liberal humanist thinkers such as Wilhelm Röpke and Karl Jaspers.[30] As several of these thinkers had spent years of residence or exile in Switzerland, they may have been inclined to favor Swiss rather than American models of democracy and public culture. In the endless chicken-and-egg question about the relationship between prosperity and democracy, these critics worried that too much emphasis upon assuring ever-increasing levels of prosperity would not only undercut spiritual and cultural pursuits but also basic democratic civic values.

Whether labeled properly or not, Americanism and Americanization routinely figured as the salient framing terms for debates about core sociocultural values and deeper identity. Without the black despondency of a Theodor Adorno or Max Horkheimer about the direction of Western rationalist-capitalist civilization and its engulfing "culture industry," the social reformist elements urged more critical awareness (and sometimes public regulation) to counter the effects of subtle new means of mental manipulation. The calculated management of opinions, tastes, and daily habits was not confined to odious, power-crazed totalitarian regimes but tended to gain sway in otherwise open, liberal societies that were predominantly profit- and consumption-oriented. The liberal culture critic Oskar Nell-Breuning was scathing toward what he saw as the immense pervasive power of the "hidden persuaders" of American-style advertising, which exploited "the most refined methods of depth-psychology." Propaganda and advertising, he argued, subliminally "influence man without his own knowledge by way of the unconscious: an incomparably greater attack on human dignity than outer physical mistreatment and the theft of freedom." The appalling "depth-psychology" cynically practiced by mass advertising required a countervailing kind of reflective "depth" to offset its manipulative, dehumanizing effects.[31]

The intellectual "founding fathers" of the West German social market economy, Röpke, Eucken, and Rüstow, were careful but insistent in rallying the true traditions of European culture and Western humanism against the dominant tendencies of modern civilization toward excessive "economism," possessive "sham individualism," and indifference to social solidarity and community. Their abstinence from explicit use of "Americanism" *expressis verbis* in their formulations did not diminish the thrust of their argument but rather broadened it to the larger, moving target of Western mass-oriented "dehumanization." Röpke was particularly vehement in his warnings against the growing impersonalism, the fixation on material success, and the erosion of civic *Gemeinschaft* and cultural-spiritual *Geist*—two venerable German ideas that the Nazis had totally "driven to the dogs" with rabidly racialist-nationalist meaning. Röpke did not shrink from invoking these two revered Germanic compass points, despite their recent murderous perversion by the Nazis: "The center of gravity of our society is being pushed upward away from the genuine, readily comprehensible communities of human warmth toward an impersonal state administration and other mass organizations lacking in spirit."[32] While pillorying romantic anticapitalism as a dangerously absurd phantasm, Röpke also offered stern words of warning against capitalistic *metastasis* and commercialistic excess: "The capitalist impregnation of all sectors of life in our society is a curse which we must banish, and the free expansion of the economy must not lead to the perversion of genuine human values."[33] Röpke denounced the arrant will-to-power of totalitarian collectivism both left and right; but he also strongly deplored the ever-escalating excesses of individual desires under modern free-market capitalism, which he felt undermined human solidarity, despoiled nature, and eroded the civic core of true democracy.

Rüstow's increasingly acerbic depiction of West German society as driven by a frenetic, depersonalizing ethos of "managerialism" was evident in his citation of a bitingly clever anonymous ditty entitled "Song of the Managers" circulating in the FRG the mid-1950s. The song elaborated the lethal effects, bodily and spiritually, of the fast-paced "manager-sickness" of a failing heart, which gives out literally only after it has gradually become bereft of humane feeling for self and others:

> As behind our windblown hats
> So we chase toward deadlines
> From sheer haste and work mania
> Our inner life lies wasted
>
> We carry stop watches in our vests
> And gargle evenings with pep-up coffee
> We rush frantically from business to pleasure
> And think incessantly in exposé-mode
>
> We continue calculating in the work break
> And smoke twenty packs per deadline
> We come home most of the time
> Only to pull on a fresh outfit to start again
>
> Day in, day out, we are in the harness-traces
> And hardly sit still for a real meal
> We notice that we have a heart
> Only when the pump gives up the ghost[34]

About this same time in the mid-1950s, the young radical Jürgen Habermas, bridging social liberal and Marxist critiques of market society, highlighted the growing "misrelation" between culture and consumption in modern Western societies. In 1955 he assailed the subtle, insidious "pleonexia" of modern consumption as the self-stoking expansion of desire for goods and conveniences, which becomes all the more obsessively "lascivious" as the quantity and quality of goods increases exponentially.[35]

The "Ordo" social liberalism of the Freiburg school was an adaptive offshoot of the erstwhile "liberal socialism" of Weimar theorist Franz Oppenheimer and the hybrid, semi-market "open corporatism" of Wilhelm Vershofen, both of whom were influential mentors to Ludwig Erhard, the postwar economics minister and later chancellor who was the practical executor of the "economic miracle." Erhard's somewhat facetious claim of being an "American invention" who remained stalwartly "more American than the Americans" carried a subtle, parrying thrust, whose multifaceted counter-Americanizing meaning should not be overlooked. The traditional American emphasis upon massive scale, hard-sell advertising, mass production at lowest cost, and short-term profit margins would best be countered by a reinvigorated German emphasis upon high quality and precision, broad distribution, and faithful follow-up service. At the same time, the German notion of the social market economy would also foster high regard for the dignity of the individual worker and the humaneness of the social order.

In a 1947 review of Röpke's works, the influential commentator Rudolf Pechel labeled these promising, broad new conceptions as "economic humanism" (*Wirtschaftshumanismus*). He also designated this stance as a fundamentally recast "new liberalism" and "third way between capitalism and socialism."[36] It seems quite plausible that the Freiburg social liberals and reform Social Democrats cultivated a judicious counter-Americanism not only in order to compete for European and overseas markets in the new Bretton Woods world trading order but also to ward off a more radical wholesale anti-Americanism. Volker Berghahn has shown that the powerful and percipient Hamburg industrialist Otto Friedrich advocated a selective or "steered" Americanization of West German industry precisely in order to resist *"Vollamerikanisierung"* and its concomitant "despiritualization." Friedrich may be regarded as a herald of adaptive semi-Americanization precisely in order to hold on to a revamped German (or German-European) alternative.[37]

As the elastic notion of Americanization was stretched from the work-crazed managerial ethos of the West German business class all the way over to the rebellious youth counterculture of the *Halbstarken*, liberal-minded humanist critics found scant difficulty in reconciling this seeming contradiction by adducing the cunning dialectics of modern mass civilization. The dominant business establishment and the boisterous youth culture were tending in the same direction of mass, mental homogeneity. Like Hegel's dialectic of development, Americanization was encompassing enough to enfold its own self-contradictions into itself. The liberal writer Jean Amery found an Americanized conformity even in the demonstrative urge for difference among West German youth, who sought differentiation from their parents' generation by seeming to be "more American than the Americans." Punning on the name of teenager star Connie Froebess, Amery pilloried "Connyformism" in 1960: "In fact we have the feeling that Connyformism corresponds to the conformism of a great part of German youth." He observed that the teenager as free-spending, sybarite consumer played an integral part in the contemporary West German economy. He further remarked upon "the complete Americanization of German youth, which looks with more intense fascination to the golden west across the Atlantic than the youth of any other nation in Europe or perhaps the entire world." Writing with a certain mock earnestness about the "German Elvis" Peter Kraus, Amery insisted that, in doing so, he was not carping in the vein of the curmudgeonly old conservatives but rather merely reporting the objective (*sachlich*) truth about an unprecedented new condition: "But the fact remains: the total Americanization [*Vollamerikanisierung*] of German youth has been accomplished, and Peter Kraus is the most palpable expression of this fact." Amery noted Kraus's "lanky limbs, which look like baseball training [sic], his protruding lips and high cheek-bones. Can anatomy Americanize itself? Obviously so."[38] Regardless of his jabs and jibes, the urbane and temperate Amery could hardly be charged with serious anti-Americanism, but his tone of cautionary counter-Americanism seems as palpable as anatomy itself.

Even Konrad Adenauer's unwavering commitment to the cause of *Westbindung*—what has aptly been called his "high wire act in the Western direction"—did not preclude serious reservations about the long-term trends of this direction, which, despite all the effusive homage to the "Western Occident," also tended to become negatively typed as Americanization.[39] In October 1951, Adenauer spoke to a CDU gathering, sounding very much like the proverbial German cultural Jeremiah: "We are all in agreement that we live in a time in which everything is in question—all ties, all goals, all knowledge." The "curse" of the age, he declared, was "restlessness, haste, distraction, and superficiality." The stamp of the times was "the lust for pleasure, the exaggerated, the hyperbolic, and the overestimation of the material factors." He spoke of the "nervousness" of the contemporary age and its "inclination to materialism that passes over into nihilism." Adenauer did not invoke the customary, coded A-word of "Americanism" but directed his wrath at creeping "materialism" and generic "massification." At the climax of the Strassen-Schiene Konflikt of 1954 concerning pedestrian versus motorist rights-of-way in reconstructed city centers, Adenauer remarked only half-facetiously that, if he were not already head of the largest party in West Germany, he would found "a party against *Automobilismus* that would be even stronger."[40]

Americanism and *Automobilismus* had long been related terms in German thinking, notwithstanding obvious German prowess (and pride) in producing VWs, BMWs, and Opels.

Adenauer was not given to indulging the engrained German-European civilizational "fallacy of misplaced concreteness" in laying these generic modern ills directly at the capacious, oversized doorstep of Americanism. Nevertheless, he continued to insist that modern life was marked by steady "nervous degradation" *(Nervenverschleiss)* and that one in twelve Americans was "mentally deranged" owing to the inhumanly hectic tempo of work. In an address of 11 July 1953 in San Francisco, he carried old German cultural coals to a New World Newcastle of corporate capitalism in warning of the slippery slope imperiling Western values. The excessive way of life of the west threatened to undercut its own core values in a tragic manner that Germany had already traversed to its disastrous outcome: "The danger of depersonalization is very much wrapped up with the development of modern technology. Depersonalization and massification open the way to the total state."[41] Totalitarianism continued to be assigned many beguiling guises and cunning directions in the modern world, even in the modern Western places where it was most vociferously condemned.

Counter-Americanism as the German "Young Shatterhand"— Trumping *Homo Americanus* on the New West Frontier

The visceral debate about the Americanization of West Germany focused broad public attention on sensitive and sometimes raw issues of culture, character, and identity. It also testified to the salutary, vigorous, free give-and-take within an emerging civic *Streitkultur* arguing about the most basic direction of modern civilization, society, and culture. Americanism in its better sense (including its own internal critique by Americans themselves) could be said to have "worked for the better" in fostering a serious civic debate about many of its own questionable or objectionable aspects. The alleged excessiveness of too much of a good thing could be countered by a critical discussion of where and how to draw lines and standards.

Of course, much as the term "Americanism" could encompass a multitude of traits under one catchall rubric, so could counter-Americanism crossover into outright anti-Americanism. Robert Müller's idea could turn more destructive than positive and edifying. In his dyspeptic essay of 1958, "The Transition from Today to Tomorrow," the renegade writer Rudolf Pannwitz raised the clarion call of resistance to Americanism as sheer "cultural colonialism" to be countered only on a broadly European rather than a narrowly German foundation. In his forward-looking summons to a truly European bloc against Americanism, Pannwitz used some very deeply Germanic terms that could hardly fail to reverberate uncomfortably on several sides:

> We must resist and preserve ourselves from American cultural colonization and its overweening domination. That requires that we must become much more than a merely economic Europe—but rather a genuine, strong, and concerted European *Reich*, as a community of peoples and a federation of states. Our thousand year old religion of humanity and humanism allows us to eschew all ideology, but never to forfeit the primacy of man over his world and never to give up on the type *homo europaeus*. This type should be as diversely manifold as its peoples and nations and only in the highest sense.

Chastising West Germany as "a land saturated with Americanism," Pannwitz insisted in a vein redolent of nationalist conservatism that "the transformation of the mass into a people is in our time the first and last task of the politician. [...] It is the principle of boundless and uncontrolled material progress that leads—and must lead—to chaos." Pannwitz concluded summarily: "The American world policy is not the right one for Europe, just as the American world culture is not the right one for Europe."[42]

German misgivings about Americanization and its supposedly fateful trajectory involved a strong (and sometimes frankly acknowledged) element of searching self-reflection and agonized self-criticism rather than some easy, self-congratulatory postulation of qualitative cultural difference from America. In dealing with such tangled cross-cultural matters, any thoughtful judgment about the recognition of "otherness" tended to struggle in the coils of projection, interpolation, and introjection. The discussion of Americanization was enmeshed with West German qualms about the fundamental directions and tendencies of the Federal Republic, of Western Europe, of Western civilization, and of the world as a whole—each orbit of which harbored its own "inner America" in both good and bad senses. German liberal humanist critics worried that the practical American spirit of can-do striving tended to overshoot the mark and become boundless *Unmass* or "immeasure." As it once afflicted and clouded the German spirit, the "Faustian" drive of Americanism too easily inclined toward excess rather than measure.

For purposes of illustration, German counter-Americanism could be personified into a venerable counter-cowboy figure once familiar to generations of Germans before their vaunted *Vollamerikanisierung*, which, if this essay is pertinent, stands in need of serious modification. I am referring to the updated, more youthful reincarnation of what historian Joachim Radkau has called the recurring "Old Shatterhand mythos" in German thought and practice. Drawing loosely upon the immensely popular novels of Karl May set in frontier America, this Shatterhand mythos centers on the deeply decent but cunningly adept German doer-of-deeds, clad in suitable frontier garb, who "goes native" (i.e., Native-American Indian), stays close to nature, and flummoxes the greedy, hard-driving "Yankee" Americans with many of their own devious means and methods. But the Shatterhand figure always strives by clever means toward higher ends, including greater humanity, respect for nature, and esteem for indigenous native peoples and customs. In short, the heedlessly exploitative ethos of predatory "Yankee" or "cowboy" wild west Americanism has elicited an adroit response of counter-Americanism rather than outright anti-Westernism.[43] If Gerhard Schöder were ever invited to the western White House in Crawford, Texas and put on a supersized cowboy hat with the younger President Bush as a sign of renewed transatlantic German-American amity on the immense soil of "the world's only remaining superpower," the German chancellor would almost certainly not call attention to German power as unvarnished "*deutsche Macht*" (as he did in a nationally televised speech at Magdeburg in October 2003 marking the thirteenth anniversary of German reunification)."[44] But there would most probably still be an unmistakable dash of German counter-Americanism in whatever photo-op garb he might choose to put on.

In their urge to find meaningful patterns in historical development, the Germans have long tended to historicize and problematize not only the elapsed past but also the immediate present and the impending expected future. They often did this in order to point beyond or to transcend temporal phases that seemed to oppress or threaten their often fragile sense of identity and cultural grounding. "Americanization" continues to persist as an engrained and expansive holistic term for a vast array of unsettling transformations. It has called forth many oppositional, countervailing, and trumping responses, and a liberal-democratic West German counter-Americanism of the third way clearly belongs in this range of responses.

Almost by dint of its own sheer immanent dynamics, Americanization seems to invite notions of its progressive supersession. More than seventy years ago, the liberal neo-Kantian philosopher-psychologist Richard Müller-Freienfels projected the following vision of a liberal-progressive "trans-Americanization":

> The Americanization of the soul need not be a stationary condition; on the contrary, it may and will be, like all historical epochs, a phase of transition to new forms of development, which will build themselves upon it as on a new direction. ... Whether we must of necessity undergo the process of Americanization is no longer in question, and it is foolish to rebel against it and lament the past; the question is rather how we are to pass through it and transcend it. The Americanization of the soul will not be overcome from without, but only from within; it will be overcome only if it is "uplifted," sublimated in the Hegelian sense; only if the good in it is retained, that new forms of life may be created from it.[45]

Notes

1. Rupert Murdoch quoted in *Der Spiegel* 32/94, 124.
2. Norbert Muhlen, *The Return of Germany: A Tale of Two Countries* (Chicago, 1953), 300.
3. Carl von Clausewitz, *On War,* ed. Anatol Rapoport (New York, 1968), 402.
4. Josef Joffe, *The New York Times*, 23 September 2003. For the American side of the discord, see for example, Jackson Diehl, "The Poison Lingers," *The Washington Post*, 14 October 2002.
5. See for example Ziauddin Sardar and Merryl Wyn Davies, *Why Do People Hate America?* (Cambridge, UK, 2002), where it is asserted that "American-led globalization, by imposing a single set of American standards, is increasingly transforming cities of developing countries into monuments to the American will to power." 128, and passim.
6. "What the World Thinks in 2002," The Pew Research Center for the People and the Press (Washington D.C., 2002), 63. Available at <www.people-press.org>.
7. Phillipp Gassert, "Was meint Amerikanisierung? Über den Begriff des Jahrhunderts," *Merkur*, no. 9/10 (Sept./Oct. 2000): 785.
8. Arnulf Baring, "West Germany as We Know It—An Episode," in *Legacies and Ambiguities: Postwar Fiction and Culture in West Germany and Japan*, ed. Ernestine Schlant and Thomas Rimer (Baltimore, 1991), 43.
9. Anselm Doering-Manteuffel, "Dimensionen von Amerikanisierung in der deutschen Gesellschaft," *Archiv für Sozialgeschichte* 35 (1995): 11.
10. Lothar Kettenacker, *Germany since 1945* (Oxford, 1997), 172.
11. See Jeffrey Herf, *Reactionary Modernism: Technology, Culture and Politics in Weimar Germany and the Third Reich* (Cambridge, 1984); Hans Ulrich Wehler, *Das deutsche Kaiserreich 1871-1918* (Goettingen, 1973); and Thomas Rohkrämer, *Eine andere Moderne: Zivilisationskritik, Natur und Technik in Deutschland 1880-1933* (Paderborn, 1999). On the question of an alternative modernity that might be considered "counter-American" in the sense of this essay, see Björn Wittrock, "Modernity: One, None or Many? European Origins and Modernity as a Global Condition," in *Daedalus* (winter 2000): 31-60; and Goran Therborn, *European Modernity and Beyond: The Trajectory of European Societies, 1945-2000* (London and Thousand Oaks, Calif., 1995).
12. Robert Müller, "Kritik des Amerikanismus," *Schaubühne* 20/10 (May 14 1914): 542. Reprinted in G. Helmes, ed., *Robert Müller: Kritische Schriften* I (Paderborn, 1993), 170-74. Müller (1887-1924) was in his time praised by Robert Musil, Alfred Döblin, and Hermann Hesse. His futuristic novel *Camera Obscura* (1921) was set in the "Americanized" capital "Oaxa" of the "United States of Europe" in the year 2000. See Robert Müller, "Europaische Wege. Im Kampf um den Typus," in *Gesammelte Essays* (Paderborn, 1995), 266-67. His "positive" equivalent of defiant "Konträramerikanismus" was a robustly autonomous, activist "Germantik," equidistant from both flighty Romantik and worldly Materialistik. Ibid., 192. Müller was also a fervent admirer of the "great emancipator" Abraham Lincoln. On Müller's sententious "Expressionist" neologisms, one should heed Erasmus' acute observation: "Every word was once a neologism."
13. Müller's counter-Americanism was a concerted neo-German "trump" to the ideas articulated in British journalist W.T. Stead's *The Americanisation of the World, Or The Trend of the Twentieth Century* (London and New York, 1901). The redundant, pithily planetary pun "Weltwelt" was touted by Maximilian Harden, editor of the progressive journal *Die Zukunft*, to suggest a whole new (if less than wholesome) global world; see *Die Zukunft* 75 (1911): 217-18. Harden was called the "alter-emperor of public opinion"; see Harry Young, *Maximilian Harden: Censor Germaniae* (Muenster, 1971).

14. Fritz Stern, *The Politics of Cultural Despair: A Study in the Rise of Germanic Ideology* (Berkeley, 1974); George Mosse, *The Crisis of German Ideology: Intellectual Origins of the Third Reich* (New York, 1964).
15. On the related themes of "second modernity," "reflective modernity," and "alternative modernity," see Ulrich Beck, *Reflexive Modernisierung* (Frankfurt, 1995) and *Risikogesellschaft: Auf dem Weg in eine andere Moderne* (Frankfurt, 1996), Ulrich Beck, Anthony Giddens, and Scott Lash, *Reflexive Modernization: Politics, Tradition and Aesthetics in the Modern Social Order* (Stanford, 1994).
16. Kurt Sontheimer, "Der "Deutsche Geist": eine Tradition ohne Zukunft," *Merkur* 36 (1982): 238.
17. Alfred Weber, "Geschichte und Gegenwart," *Der Monat* 2, no. 14 (1949): 145. The equation of Americanism and Sovietism was by no means restricted to fearful German culture critics pleading for equidistance in order to conserve cultural diversity. In 1951 British radical-liberal philosopher and *Monat* contributor Bertrand Russell observed: "The country which has a philosophy most similar to that of the United States is Soviet Russia. There, also, there is optimism and energy, there is almost boundless belief in human power, there is determination to regard Nature as providing opportunities rather than obstacles." "The Political and Cultural Influence," in *The Impact of America on European Culture* (Boston, 1951), 10. Russell also found "an excessive preoccupation with utility," 13.
18. Weber, "Geschichte und Gegenwart," 148.
19. Alfred Weber, *Kulturgeschichte als Kultursoziologie* (Munich, 1950), 480.
20. Weber, *Kulturgeschichte*, 455, 487, and 494ff. In 1956 the former *Tat* writer and Nazi intellectual Giselher Wirsing painted a much more catastrophic scenario for the twentieth century in *Die Menschenlawine: der Bevölkerungszuwachs als weltpolitisches Problem* (Stuttgart, 1956). Nazi eugenics and biopolitics could be "reeducated" into environmentalism.
21. For views similar to Weber's, see Ulrich Cürten, *Europäische Amerikakritik seit 1945. Ihr Bild vom Wandel des amerikanischen Weltverständnisses* (Clausthal-Zellerfeld, 1967), esp 167ff.
22. Willy Hellpach, *Pax Futura: Die Erziehung des friedlichen Menschen durch eine konservative Demokratie* (Braunschweig, 1949), 258, 260ff.
23. For Kennan's worries about American influence, see John Harper, *American Visions of Europe* (New York and Cambridge, UK, 1994), 204ff.
24. Thomas Reuther, *Die ambivalente Normalisierung. Deutschlanddiskurs und Deutschlandbilder in den USA, 1941-1955* (Stuttgart, 2000), 396.
25. Clay quoted in Hansjörg Gehring, *Amerikanische Literaturpolitik in Deutschland, 1945-1953: ein Aspekt des Re-education-Programms* (Stuttgart, 1976), 20-21. Clay argued that the "new nationalism" of 1948 that many American observers were branding as resurgent neo-Nazism was a "natural love of country" that did not jeopardize democratization. Ibid.
26. John Hilldring, "Amerikas Absichten in Deutschland," *Die Amerikanische Rundschau* 4, no. 19 (1948): 8.
27. Richard Merritt, *Democracy Imposed: U.S. Occupation Policy and the German Public, 1945-1949* (New Haven, 1995), 34ff.
28. See Hans Georg Betz, "The German Model Reconsidered," in *German Studies Review* 29, no. 2 (May 1996): "Germany was significantly closer to the corporatist northern European welfare states than to some of its more immediate neighbors." (307)
29. See A.J. Nicholls, *Freedom with Responsibility: The Social Market Economy in Germany, 1918-1963* (Oxford, 1994).

30. See Hans Zbinden, *Um Deutschlands Zukunft* (Heidelberg, 1947). Also Hans Zbinden, *Wither Germany?* (Chicago, 1948).
31. Oskar Nell-Breuning, "Unsere Gesellschaft und ihr kulturelles Gesicht," in *Untergang oder Uebergang*, proceedings of the Internationaler Kulturkritikerkongress, ed. Burghard Freudenfeld (Munich-Graefeling, 1959), 137.
32. Quoted in Hermann Glaser, *Bundrepublikanisches Lesebuch: drei Jahrzehnte geistiger Auseinandersetzung* (Munich, 1978), 358.
33. Wilhelm Röpke, *Die Lehre von der Wirtschaft* (Erlenbach-Zürich, 1961), 190. Translated as *Economics of the Free Society* (Chicago, 1963).
34. "Song of the Managers—by an Entrepreneur 1956," quoted in Alexander Rüstow, *Ortsbestimmung der Gegenwart. Eine universalgeschichtliche Kulturkritik*, vol. 3: *Herrschaft oder Freiheit?* (Erlenbach, 1957), 149-50.
35. Jürgen Habermas, "Notizen zum Missverhaltnis von Kultur und Konsum," *Merkur* 10, no. 97 (1956): 212ff., and esp. 220.
36. Rudolf Pechel, "Trilogie der Vernunft," *Deutsche Rundschau* 70, no. 8 (August 1947): 84-85.
37. Volker Berghahn and Paul Friedrich, *Otto A. Friedrich, ein politischer Unternehmer: sein Leben und seine Zeit 1902-1975* (Frankfurt and New York, 1993), 281. Friedrich was reluctant to use the term "Vorbild" for the American system even though it was to be emulated in many respects. Ibid.
38. Jean Amery, *Teenager-Stars. Idole unserer Zeit* (Rüschlikon, 1960), 97ff., 102ff, 104ff, and 108.
39. Norbert Frei, "Die Besatungsherrschaft als Zäsur?" in *Politische Zäsuren und gesellschaftlicher Wandel im 20. Jahrhundert*, ed. Mattias Frese und Michael Prinz (Paderborn, 1996), 787.
40. Joachim Radkau, "Wirtschaftswunder ohne technologische Innovation?" in *Modernisierung im Wiederaufbau: die westdeutsche Gesellschaft der 50er Jahre*, ed. Axel Schild and Arnold Sywottek (Bonn, 1993), 154.
41. Anneliese Poppinga, Konrad Adenauer, *Geschichtsverständnis, Weltanschauung und politische Praxis* (Stuttgart, 1975), 171; also 279, note 102. See Joachim Radkau, *Das Zeitalter der Nervosität* (Munich, 1998), 454.
42. Rudolf Pannwitz, *Der Übergang von Heute zu Morgen: Aufsätze und Vorträge* (Stuttgart, 1958), 20; for similar positions see also 39ff., 74ff., and 90. Thirty years earlier Pannwitz had written along parallel lines, calling for a "European 14 Points" to counter Wilson's vision for the world; see *Die deutsche Idee Europas* (Munich, 1931).
43. Radkau in Schild and Sywottek, *Modernisierung im Wiederaufbau*, 146.
44. Mark Landler, "Chancellor Schröder Strives to Increase His World Power," The New York Times, 4 October 2003. "Chancellor Gerhard Schröder said Friday that Germany had been right to oppose the American-led war in Iraq, driving home his defiant message by repeatedly using the German word for power, which leaders here have long eschewed because of its associations with the Nazi era." Ibid.
45. Richard Müller-Freienfels, "The Americanization of the Soul," in *Mysteries of the Soul* (New York, 1929), 292.

SAIGON, NUREMBERG, AND THE WEST
German Images of America in the Late 1960s

◆ ◆ ◆

Bernd Greiner

Fantasies of Revenge

"You, Mr. Chairman, and your cronies are just a bunch of criminal mobsters. I've certainly not come here to subscribe to your dirty aims, not to a single one." These were the words of Karl Dietrich Wolff, a renowned student activist and former head of the German SDS, the Socialist German Students' Association, before the US Senate Committee on Internal Security in March 1969. Wolff had traveled to the United States to meet civil rights workers and his counterparts from the American SDS. Yet this was not his first visit to the New World. Years earlier, he had enrolled in a high school exchange program. Ever since, he nourished the idea of a double America—the America of the oppressed and racially exploited, whose tactics of fighting back with civilian disobedience he admired and recommended as a role model for other nations. On the other side was the America of the bosses and generals eager to undermine and, if need be, abolish democracy altogether.[1]

The fact that a handful of FBI-agents had been detailed to observe Wolff's activities fit perfectly into his preconceived notions. When, above all, he was summoned to the Senate Committee on Internal Security, Wolff saw his chance to attack from within the "heart of the beast" and indict America's ruling class as a reincarnation of the Nazis: as the Jewish people in Germany, blacks were deprived in the United States of their language and culture; dissidents suffered from terrorist oppression; and like its German predecessor, the American political and military elite had become a threat to world security. "This is not only a private opinion of mine," Wolff lectured. "I'm here to represent all mankind."[2]

Notes for this section begin on page 61.

There are certainly many ways to interpret Wolff's outburst. One might see him as a frustrated maverick, or as an activist whose political heyday was over and who was desperately looking to gain a few more minutes of media fame. But the point is missed if we do not consider the larger picture of Germany's political discourse. In the late 1960s, both East and West Germany were in the process of redefining their images of America. A long history of similar debates suggests that emotions run high when the New World is debated against the backdrop of upheavals in the Old World. The year 1848, the turn of the century, World War I, the Weimar years, and last, but not least, 1945 provide well-known cases in point. All of them stand for times of deep social and political crisis—and so does the watershed year of 1968. First, the shadow of the Nazi past again loomed large over German social and political life. Just think of the rise of the right wing National Democratic Party of Germany (NPD), whose bid for seats in parliament was blocked at the eleventh hour. Think of the revolt of the young against the generation of their fathers or of the rivalry between a former Nazi holding the office of chancellor and a former emigrant challenging him. Second, cracks in the Cold War system indicated that the postwar period had come to an end. After Prague, Soviet hegemony over the Eastern bloc was no longer a given. The American war in Vietnam provoked unsettling questions about the United States' leadership of the Free World. The year 1968, therefore, was a year of collision. Unresolved questions of the German past met with issues of an uncertain future.[3]

As witnessed before, America again became a sounding board in Germany's quest for itself, kindling a host of contradictory fantasies and expectations. Therefore, images of America should primarily be interpreted as images of Germans about themselves and their own country. More than anything else, these images shed light on the mentality and state of political affairs in both West and East Germany.

The protest movement at the time was quick in associating Nazism with American politics and society. For all his outspokenness, Karl Dietrich Wolff was not an exception. From late 1965 to the early 1970s, demonstrators carried banners with double-images of Lyndon B. Johnson and Adolf Hitler, and equated the supposed "barbarism" of America's "cultural industry" with the barbarism of war. Slogans such as "USA-SA-SS" became a ritualized given—attractive even among the Social Democrats' youth organization, which in 1973 published its vision of the world's political future and without much ado marked the year 1984 as the beginning of a fascist dictatorship in the United States. At times political meetings—like the 1972 "Angela Davis Conference"—resembled a remake of the Nuremberg tribunal in reverse, with white America in the dock and Germany's revolutionary avant-garde on the bench, assisted by Jewish intellectuals like Herbert Marcuse. Such examples are myriad.[4]

Bestselling authors of the time readily supplied ideological ammunition. Recall Reinhard Lettau's book *Daily Fascism* about the United States, Rolf Hochhuth's homage to America's gravediggers entitled *Guerillas*, or L.L. Matthias's argument that America's terminal fall was inevitable given the dramatic rise of living standards in the Soviet Union. Any fancy idea seemed welcome as long as it fit into an intellectual straitjacket of rigid anti-Americanism; which is to say, American society and its way of life were portrayed as a cancer in the world's body politic in urgent need of removal. This was even more so because this rotten system, incapable of reform, could only survive by exploiting or eliminating others. Again, the Nazi rule was insinuated as a role model. Both systems allegedly cultivated the same rhetoric and policy of extermination and the same deadly dedication to become masters of the universe. Again, the slogan USA-SA-SS carried the day.[5]

In many cases, West German critics sounded like subscribers to an eastern propaganda machine. Since the early 1950s, media in the German Democratic Republic spread the word about the "Wall Street International of terrorist killers" directing a "beastly" and "criminal imperialism" only kept at bay by the sacrifice of vigilant socialists. Modern America became former Nazi-Germany's double. For many years, Reclam Books in Leipzig printed a licensed edition of Lettau's *Daily Fascism*. The trademark of East German propagandists, however, was to invoke a thinly veiled anti-Semitism on top of it all, blaming Germany's division on the revenge of America's omnipotent Jewish community and their successful manipulation of Washington's foreign policy. The stubborn refusal to recompense American citizens for confiscated property and to engage in financial help for Nazi-victims living in the United States was rooted in the same mindset. Its rigid logic offered a catchall exit-option: To charge the west and its leading power for a criminal foreign policy meant to lift the shadow of the past from the east.[6]

In late 1969, a similar relief spread across West Germany. Hardly had the truth about the My Lai massacre been uncovered when major media broke loose from their otherwise pro-American standards. In retrospect, it seems as if an outlet for long suppressed emotions had been opened and segments of the West German public felt a need to pay the United States back for their role in the Nuremberg tribunal. A wide array of articles in conservative and liberal newspapers used terms traditionally linked with Nazi policy to characterize American warfare in Vietnam: "Final solution," "totalitarian degeneration," "doctrine of salvation," "war of extermination," "scorched earth." Few other topics invited so many letters to the editor, and hardly ever did editors print so many of them. *Der Spiegel* is a telling example. Lidice, Oradour, and My Lai could not be equated, some readers maintained, because German perpetrators allegedly showed mercy for babies and children, or because their rage had been provoked by the locals. A good 50 percent of these letters showed relief about the loss of American moral integrity and the downfall of the "white giant." Those who had spoken a harsh verdict about the German "master race" in Nuremberg unmasked themselves as a replica in democratic disguise. In other words, Germany had every right to bid judges Jackson and Kempner a final farewell.[7]

Traditional German anti-Americanism had a brief, albeit remarkable, comeback. Not only the radical left fringe but journalists and readers from all walks of life denounced the United States as a society prone to violence and genetically deficient in basic cultural standards. The old-style verdict setting German "culture" apart from Western "civilization" again carried the day, featuring the well-known vocabulary describing the United States: money-driven shallowness, arrogance, ignorance, naiveté, primitive crudeness, moral-blind patriotism, self-righteousness. An endless list of charges paved the intellectual ground for two equally damning assumptions. First, such a state of social affairs was easy prey for totalitarian forces, as *Der Spiegel* stated in his renowned cover story about the Angela Davis trial. The headline "Fascism in America" still carried a question mark. But the term "fascist" was so freely used in the report as to leave no doubt what the answer actually should be. Second, the United States was seen as a society beyond the point of return, incapable of mobilizing the moral and intellectual strength required to correct its wrongs. In other words, America had finally disgraced its claim to being a worldwide role model for democracy.[8]

Monologues

It would be all too easy to confront these judgements with American realities and to add a new chapter to an already lengthy history of German misperceptions and deliberate distortions of life and politics in the United States. A different approach, however, is much more rewarding. Once we interpret German images of America not as approaches to life in the New World but as reflections of German life, we are much closer to the mark. Seen from this perspective, we witness a confrontation of Germany with itself. At issue is an inner monologue of Germans—foremost an attempt to straighten out the legacy of one's own history. More than anything else, America is used as an intellectual and emotional crutch. In other words, for historians, German images of America provide a stepping-stone to decipher the psychological dimension of German postwar history.

On the one hand, we witness a compulsive urge to break away from the stigma of Nazism. Time and again, American warfare in Vietnam is interpreted as a denial of German exceptionalism—in other words, as final proof that German atrocities are manifestations of a universal evil. Any country can fall victim to this maelstrom of history at any time, democracies no less than dictatorships. To blame Germans for their lack of resistance and civil disobedience seemed equally beside the point. What could you expect of a people under the heel of a ruthless maniac, if even a freedom loving people like the Americans failed to stem the tide of barbarity?[9]

This indeed seems to have been the heart of German self-assurance at the time—to declare acts of violence immune to political or moral interventions. Legal regulations after the event were seen at best as naive Monday morning quarterbacking, if not as highbrow judgements by ignorant victors rubbing the nose of the looser in the dirt. Be it *Der Spiegel*, the *Frankfurter Rundschau*, *Süddeutsche Zeitung*, or *Die Welt*, most commentators agreed on this notion: no line can be drawn between legal and illegal acts of killing, there is no way to contain or civilize warfare. And yesterday's prosecutors always were tomorrow's defendants. Not only by implication did commentators launch a head-on assault on the Nuremberg code and an equally uninhibited demand to finally vindicate Germany for the wrongs suffered in the 1945 trials. In the jungles of Vietnam, the postwar policy of degrading Germany had lost its legitimacy.[10]

The opposition movement was equally beset to dramatize the German past, albeit from a different perspective. Radical students and other activists saw their country as a land of opportunists and hypocrites unfamiliar with a citizen's political responsibility, and more than anything else prone to cultivate moral indifference—attitudes that in former times had opened the door for the Nazis and that in the 1960s accounted for the blind eye on the war in Vietnam, the rise of the neo-Nazis, and the Emergency Law passed by parliament. Any provocation, any confrontation, and any incitement seemed justified as long as it disturbed this leaden silence. Hans Magnus Enzensberger called for an outright revolution as the only way out. Members of the notorious Commune 1 in Berlin had their bodies not only photographed in the nude but posed in a way reminiscent of the Nazi victims on their way to the gas chambers. Many were the examples, but the message was only one: to make, as Karl Marx had once said, the stones dance by constantly playing their own melody (which, of course, was meant to be a fascist melody). No matter which topic was on the agenda, everything looked like a reincarnation of Nazism: modernity, the "culture industry," the world of commodities. And the United States continued to provide a convenient target; to attack the crusader against communism as the anti-Christ was always a recipe for scandal.[11]

Fascism and Nazism were around any corner, equally pervasive and beyond place and time. Declaiming this litany became an indispensable device to find oneself in the heroic posture of saviors—doing good for the tragic shortcomings of the parents' generation. Like in the 1930s, the world had to choose between an all-or-nothing option, between survival or ultimate destruction, between final victory or terminal defeat. With only one difference: the wizards of Armageddon resided no longer in Berlin but in Washington. Such was the rhetoric of the movement's political pacesetters. In its wake, the real history of Nazism lost what was left of its already hazy contours. The distorted image of the United States, however, stood out in every colorful and apocalyptic detail. Like an intellectual black hole, it absorbed all the disturbing assets of German history, assets hard to account for and therefore still unbearable. Here the protest movement shared common ground with the mainstreamers who considered the Nazi period closed—another irony of its history.[12]

Images of America therefore shed an unusual light on the late 1960s in Germany. Beyond the troubles and frictions displayed in public, it was also a time of hidden consent between the generations, between the old establishment and the young hotheads. What they had in common was a desire to withdraw from the legacy of history—be it out of ignorance, bad conscience, complicity, or just a feeling that it was all too much to handle. America was made to play the part of the defendant, the accused, who by sheer magic attracted negative passions of all sorts. More than anything else, this debate reflects helplessness. On both sides of the barricades, the trauma of Auschwitz was not addressed, but buried under a dissonant discourse about Vietnam. The net result was intellectual and moral self-paralysis, a silent void voiced over by a noisy confrontation on the surface.[13]

The year 1968, however, would not be 1968 if the story ended here.

Robinson Satchmo

The same students who bellowed "USA-SA-SS" while demonstrating in the streets in daytime could not get enough of American music after returning home at night. They wore cowboy boots and jeans, knew the lines of Hollywood movies by heart, were more familiar with Andy Warhol than Albrecht Dürer, devoured books by Jack Kerouac, Tennessee Williams, and Thornton Wilder, and introduced American slang into the German language. Never before had a social group or generational cohort been so open to the wares of American culture. Moreover, no earlier generation had a similar wealth of personal experience at its disposal, accumulated in years of exchange programs or in the course of overseas travels affordable to a well-to-do middle class since the 1960s. The dreamland America, which ever since the Romantic period had occupied youthful minds, was replaced by an America of real people and authentic events. Even more, its political landscape offered a variety of things unknown— not the least an agenda to break loose from the petty bourgeois misfits and authoritarian coating of German life.

The drive for freedom opened hearts and minds for the history of the American civil rights and protest movement. Sit-ins, teach-ins, civil disobedience, direct, nonviolent action, and a calculated disregard for rules and regulations—the itinerary of Selma and Berkeley looked like a remedy for an ailing democracy in Germany and a blueprint for a participatory model of democracy. Tolerance, transparency, open dialogue, and rationality were its principles, individuals styled after the self-enlightened "citizen" its dominant actors. The new German citizen was called upon to use the traditional American distrust of the state and any other powerful hierarchies as his guideline in personal and political life. Instead of Fichte, Hegel, or Marx, Henry David Thoreau became the spiritual godfather of a free association of individuals. The larger-than-life image of Thoreau as founder of American democracy was widely off the mark. In one respect, however, German activists read the textbooks of American democrats accurately: to challenge state, law, and order by way of "direct action" was certainly legitimate, but only as long as the constitution was respected and with it the legitimacy of the legal order.[14]

It seems safe to assume that a solid majority within the German protest movement accepted these rules and regulations, and subscribed to the legal limits of militant opposition. Rudi Dutschke's call for a revolutionary guerilla force remained mostly a Berlin-based sideshow. In other words, the American efforts at the political reeducation of German citizens had remarkable effects in the late 1960s—of all people, among those who proudly labeled themselves "anti-Americans." The political textbooks of German protesters offer a similar surprise. Their close reading reveals the decline of traditional anti-Americanism. Fundamentalist objections against life, politics, and culture in the United States, once popular with Germans irrespective of class and political status, lost their grip on hearts and minds.[15]

The widely read study on the origins of the Vietnam War by Jürgen Horlemann and Peter Gäng provides a case in point. It is a matter-of-fact analysis focusing on the politics of policy making in the Johnson administration. Interestingly enough, the authors do not engage in loose talk about desperados fighting imperialism's last bloody battle. Instead of being lectured about war mongering as the core of American foreign policy, we learn a great deal about misperception and lack of information as driving forces of decision making. Anti-Americanists of old would have jumped at the chance to denounce the United States as a whole. But this is not so of Horlemann and Gäng. They appreciate the strength of the constitutional order and a liberal democracy's capacity to keep militarism in check. Other popular books about Vietnam shared the same perspective.[16]

But what about images of America in German society at large? Is the awakening of students part of a larger picture? Does it stand for a broader "cultural turn" and—as some authors have claimed—a "shift to maturity"? Sound empirical data on this issue are in short supply. In the 1950s and 1960s, social scientists all but ignored the topic and left the field to opinion pollsters. The latter did indeed collect a vast amount of material. However, in the early postwar period, their profession was still in its infancy, and therefore pertinent findings should be treated with caution. Today's historians thus find themselves deadlocked in their judgement about the late 1960s. Some—like Dan Diner—assume a still profound impact of anti-American prejudices; others—to name Horst-Eberhard Richter as the most prominent—suggest a solid majority of "pro-Americans." Both judgements appear overly opinionated. The evidence at hand rather suggests a gradually shifting frame of mind beset by a mix of conflicting attitudes.[17]

On the one hand, newspaper reports on foreign and military policy still echo a host of prejudiced and distorted images of America. Some journalists stretched their Cold War–solidarity to the limit and shied away from any critical inquiry. Others tended to intone nationalistic *ressentiment* whenever feasible, as in the case of war crimes and My Lai. Nevertheless, the thrust to play down or dramatize superseded a balanced judgement. The mainstream press of the day provides a goldmine through which this point can be illustrated.[18]

And yet the overall picture is more complex. For there are, on the other hand, examples of nuanced reflections on the United States—of journalists throwing preconceived notions overboard and trying to understand the peculiarities of American society and politics. Thus, *Der Spiegel* pointed to the inner strength of an open society and the capacity to open up to intricate questions about its own history and self-image. Has it ever before been the case, asked *Die Zeit* and the *Frankfurter Allgemeine Zeitung*, that a war-waging society sits in judgement of itself? And that soldiers, of all people, stand up and publicly admit acts of criminal warfare committed by themselves?[19]

Opinion polls taken at the time also reflect diversified perceptions. American mass culture still aroused disapproving and outright negative comments, partly reminiscent of traditional stereotypes about the culturally inferior New World. But these images had obviously lost their driving ideological force. Otherwise, the majority could not have claimed stronger emotional and political bonds to the United States than to any other country. To criticize the American government for its foreign or military policy was accepted as a matter of course as long as it did not question transatlantic solidarity and German-American friendship. The case of this friendship was not argued for on emotional grounds but with a rational appreciation of liberal democracy and the freedom it represented. Such findings are even more remarkable when seen in light of the letters to the editor in *Der Spiegel* after My Lai. These letters undoubtedly represented a not-to-be neglected current in German political life. Yet they seem less significant than their prominent venue of publication suggests. We may assume that the days of images of America painted in black or white were over and that German society was on its way to uprooting a Manichean style of political thinking deeply entrenched in its past.[20]

For obvious reasons it is much harder to track down East German images of America. It is obvious, however, that the party leadership could not help but dampen its militancy in the wake of détente and after the exchange of ambassadors with the United States in 1974. One finds much more matter-of-fact reporting in the press; book publishers and educators could move more freely; and representatives of churches and universities were allowed to travel abroad—all changes and chances unheard of in former days. Last, but not least, the historian Fritz Klein flooded the trenches of hardboiled ideologues when he publicly praised imperialist powers for their will and capacity to live in peace. Various examples of this are available. How the public felt and thought, though, is an altogether different question.[21]

Available research suggests that, ever since the early 1950s, private images of America remained resistant to official propaganda. For all we know, anti-Americanism was not popular in East Germany. On the contrary. People nourished a naive sympathy and idolized America as a wonderland beyond the monotony and meagerness of life under socialism. Rainer Schnoor even talks about a "counterculture" alive with American music and literature, and irresistibly attractive to the younger generation. Like in West Germany, this impact gnawed at the authoritarian tradition and helped stimulate nonconformist attitudes—a sea change in the history of German mentalities, as Hannah Arendt put it. It might even be interpreted as a harbinger of the civil rights movement in the 1980s.[22]

The author Ulrich Plenzdorf caught this political potential in his 1973 novel *Die neuen Leiden des jungen W.*, an ironic comment on Goethe's *Die Leiden des jungen Werther*. He might just as well have titled his book *Progress and Freedom, Thy Name is America*. The New World is omnipresent in the life of the protagonist, Edgar Wiebeau. Plenzdorf's book epitomizes a youthful and rebellious lifestyle and individualism; most of all, it shows that happiness and material riches may be achieved, not in a distant future, but in your own lifetime. Edgar Wiebeau cherishes the idea that Socialist propagandists have every right to loathe America—because it stole their utopia by making it come true. Such are his thoughts in his jazz-inspired daydreams. When he wakes up, he feels like Robinson Crusoe and Satchmo in one. "Robinson Satchmo."[23]

Go West

Hans Magnus Enzensberger identified German images of America in the late 1960s as part of a political crisis of adolescence. The images bear witness to a time in which old notions were too weak to uphold their traditional roles, whereas new insights had not yet gained enough strength to dominate. Enzensberger, it should be recalled, was a unique observer. In January 1967, he made a dramatic point in hastily leaving the United States. He renounced his scholarship with the Center for Advanced Studies in an open letter to the president of Wesleyan University and castigated America's ruling class as the "Number One enemy of the world" because of its allegedly undeclared war against a billion people and its reckless drive for political, economic, and military world domination. The natural choice for proceeding with his studies was therefore Cuba. Seventeen years later, he explained the episode as a spin-off of the Vietnam War. Up to that time, America for him and his generation had been a country of almost dreamlike qualities, revered for its role in liberating Germany from Hitler. With Vietnam, adoration was replaced by an equally simple-minded rejection, staged in a flamboyant manner and a moralist's aggressive rhetorical overdrive. When the party was over, the United States had ended the war and driven a power-abusive president out of office. Enzensberger and his friends were left behind with a political hangover, as well as a surprising insight: that America had not lost the capacity to readjust itself in times of crisis, and that, under pressure, it does a better democratic job than most other societies. For the Enzensberger of today, totalitarian forces like the SA or SS do not match with the United States. In his view, America is safe from this challenge.[24]

Enzensberger's individual experience is part of a larger story: the time of extreme political mood swings is over. Opinion polls and other studies in the history of mentalities since the 1970s attest to a steadfast and high esteem for Americans and their political system among a sound majority of German citizens. At times, more than 33 percent favor neutrality between east and west. Even these findings, however, do not fit into old patterns. They do not go along with anti-American or nationalist fits, not even during heated disputes about Washington's political or military strategy. The intervention in Grenada and the Gulf War provide well-documented cases in point. Claims to the opposite—frequently made by authors Dan Diner, Richard Herzinger, or Hannes Stein—rest on poor empirical evidence.

The late 1960s can therefore be portrayed as a landmark of political change in Germany. The images of America salient ever since indicate a historically unique link with Western culture. At its core is an undisputed reverence for human and civil rights backed up by an unconditional support for international law with its binding character for all nations. In other words, after a detour via Saigon, Nuremberg and the legal code it represents found their way back into Germany.[25]

Notes

1. K.D. Wolff, quoted in Wolfgang Kraushaar, ed., *Frankfurter Schule und Studentenbewegung. Von der Flaschenpost zum Molotowcocktail, 1946-1995*, Vol. 1: *Chronik*, Hamburg *1998*, 408-9.
2. Ibid.
3. Cf. Manfred Henningsen, *Der Fall Amerika. Zur Sozial- und Bewusstseinsgeschichte einer Verdrängung* (Munich, 1974).
4. On the Young Socialists' view of "American Fascism," see Henningsen, *Der Fall Amerika*, 52.
5. Reinhard Lettau, *Täglicher Faschismus. Amerikanische Evidenz aus 6 Monaten* (Munich, 1971); (originally published in 1970 in *Nordamerikanische Zustände, Kursbuch* 22). Rolf Hochhuth, *Guerillas* (Munich, 1970); L.L. Matthias, *Die Kehrseite der USA* (Reinbek bei Hamburg, 1964); in the early 1970s, this book was published in its sixth edition).
6. Rainer Schnoor, "Das gute und das schlechte Amerika: Wahrnehmungen der USA in der DDR," in *Die USA und Deutschland im Zeitalter des Kalten Krieges. Ein Handbuch*, vol.1, 1945–1968, Detlef Junker, ed. (Stuttgart/Munich, 2001), 932–43; see 934ff; Christian Ostermann, "In Bonns Schatten: Die Beziehungen zwischen Washington und Ost-Berlin," in *Handbuch*, vol. 2, 1968–1990, Detlef Junker, ed. (Stuttgart, Munich, 2001), 152–62, see 153; Bernd Greiner, *Die Morgenthau-Legende. Zur Geschichte eines umstrittenen Plans* (Hamburg, 1995), 14–29.
7. *Frankfurter Rundschau*, "Die erste Niederlage," 13 December 1969; *Der Spiegel* 49, "Vietnam–Kriegsverbrechen: Wenn du sie killst," 1 December 1969, 120–36; *Der Spiegel* 51, "Briefe–Kriegsverbrechen," 15 December 1969, 8, 10, 11; *Der Spiegel* 52, "Briefe–Friede auf Erden," 22 December 1969, 12.
8. *Der Spiegel* 52, "Briefe–Friede auf Erden," 12; *Der Spiegel* 51, "Briefe–Kriegsverbrechen," 7; *Frankfurter Rundschau*, "Erschütterte, Ungläubige und Unbelehrbare," 9 December 1969; *Frankfurter Rundschau*, "Die erste Niederlage"; cp. *Frankfurter Rundschau*, "Zerstörter Mythos," 1 December 1969; *Der Spiegel* 46, "Rettet Angela vor dem Justizmord!", 8 November 1971, 128–47.
9. *Der Spiegel* 51, "Briefe–Kriegsverbrechen," 8; *Der Spiegel* 52, "Briefe–Friede auf Erden," 11. Cf. Gesine Schwan, *Antikommunismus und Antiamerikanismus in Deutschland. Kontinuität und Wandel nach 1945* (Baden-Baden, 1999), 54, 69ff; Dan Diner, *Verkehrte Welten. Antiamerikanismus in Deutschland. Ein historischer Essay* (Frankfurt/M., 1993), 131ff.
10. *Der Spiegel* 49, "Vietnam–Kriegsverbrechen: Wenn du sie killst," 124–28; *Die Welt*, "Das Blutbad von Song My lastet schwer auf Amerikas Gewissen," 28 November 1969. Cf. *Süddeutsche Zeitung*, "Verbrechen im Kriege," 25 November 1969. *Frankfurter Rundschau*, "Zerstörter Mythos"; *Der Spiegel* 51, "Briefe–Kriegsverbrechen," 8, 10, 11. Cf. Rolf Schörken, *Jugend 1945. Politisches Denken und Lebensgeschichte* (Frankfurt/M., 1995), 177ff; Bernd Greiner, "Bruch-Stücke. Sechs westdeutsche Beobachtungen nebst unfertigen Deutungen," in *Eine Ausstellung und ihre Folgen. Zur Rezeption der Ausstellung 'Vernichtungskrieg. Verbrechen der Wehrmacht 1941 bis 1944'*, Hamburger Institut für Sozialforschung, ed. (Hamburg, 1999), 15–87.
11. Cf. Martin Walser, "Praktiker, Weltfremde und Vietnam," in *Kursbuch* 9 (June 1967): 168–76; Peter Schneider, "Aufforderungsrede auf der Vollversammlung aller Fakultäten der FU, 5 May 1967," in *1968. Literatur in der antiautoritären Bewegung*, Klaus Briegleb, ed. (Frankfurt am Main, 1993), 156-57; Hans Magnus Enzensberger in Briegleb, *Literatur*, 228.

12. Peter Weiss in Briegleb, *Literatur*, 164; cp. ibid, 69, 194; Henningsen, *Der Fall Amerika*, 142; Diner, *Verkehrte Welten*, 141; Briegleb, *Literatur*, 217.
13. Briegleb, *Literatur*, 217.
14. Cf. Wolfgang Kraushaar, "Die transatlantische Protestkultur. Der zivile Ungehorsam als amerikanisches Exempel und als bundesdeutsche Adaption," in *Westbindungen. Amerika in der Bundesrepublik*, Heinz Bude and Bernd Greiner, eds. (Hamburg, 1999), 261–67, 274–76, 280–82.
15. Cf. Wolfgang Kraushaar, "'Der große Katalysator': Die Radikalisierung der Studenten in der Bewegung gegen den Vietnamkrieg," in *Vorgänge. Zeitschrift für Bürgerrechte und Gesellschaftspolitik* 155 (September 2001): 325–27; Ingo Juchler, *Die Studentenbewegungen in den Vereinigten Staaten und der Bundesrepublik Deutschland der sechziger Jahre* (Berlin, 1996).
16. Jürgen Horlemann, Peter Gäng, *Vietnam. Genesis eines Konflikts* (Frankfurt am Main, 1966), 152–88. Contemporary books on America published by Wagenbach, Rowohlt, Fischer, and Heyne also argue along these lines.
17. David B. Morris, "Auf dem Weg zur Reife: Amerikabilder in der westdeutschen Öffentlichkeit," in *Handbuch* 2, Junker, 761ff. For the early postwar period, see Anna J. Merritt and Richard L. Merritt, eds., *Public Opinion in Occupied Germany. The OMGUS-Surveys, 1945-1949* (Urbana, 1970).
18. Cf. Otto Köhler, "Mordet nicht die USA," in *Der Spiegel* 49, 1 December 1969, 132; Walser, "Weltfremde und Vietnam," 175f.; Briegleb, *Literatur*, 82; Gudrun Kruip, *Das "Welt"-"Bild" des Axel Springer Verlags. Journalismus zwischen westlichen Werten und deutschen Denktraditionen* (Munich, 1999).
19. Cf. *Der Spiegel* 49, "Vietnam—Kriegsverbrechen: Wenn du sie killst," 122, 134; *Die Zeit*, "Schlüssel zum Frieden?" 5 December 1969; *Frankfurter Allgemeine Zeitung*, "My Lai und die Folgen," 28 November 1969.
20. Cf. Morris, "Weg zur Reife," in *Handbuch* 2, Junker, 762ff, 771ff; Schwan, *Antikommunismus und Antiamerikanismus*, 206ff.
21. Günter Kunert, *Der andere Planet. Ansichten von Amerika* (Berlin/Weimar, 1974), 23. Cf. Rainer Schnoor, "Zwischen privater Meinung und offizieller Verlautbarung: Amerikabilder in der DDR," in *Handbuch* 2, Junker, 775ff.; Ostermann in Junker, *Handbuch* 2, 161ff.
22. Rainer Schnoor, "Das gute und schlechte Amerika," in *Handbuch* 1, Junker, 932ff.; "Meinung und Verlautbarung," in *Handbuch* 2, Junker, 780. Cf. Ina Merkel, "Eine andere Welt. Vorstellungen von Nordamerika in der DDR der fünfziger Jahre," in *Amerikanisierung: Traum und Alptraum im Deutschland des 20. Jahrhunderts*, Alf Lüdtke, Inge Marßolek, and Adelheid von Saldern, eds., (Stuttgart, 1996), 245–54; Ronald Galenza and Heinz Havemeister, eds., *Wir wollen immer artig sein ... Punk, New Wave, HipHop, Independent-Szene in der DDR 1980–1990* (Berlin, 1999); Hannah Arendt, "Ziviler Ungehorsam," in *Zur Zeit. Politische Essays*, Marie Luise Knott, ed. (Berlin, 1986), 119–59.
23. Ulrich Plenzdorf, *Die neuen Leiden des jungen W.* (Rostock, 1973); in the west published as licensed edition by Suhrkamp, Frankfurt am Main, 1976; see ibid, 37, 15, 16, 27, 30. Ralf Dahrendorf and Manfred Henningsen suggested the idea that America deprived the radical European left of their socialist ideas. Cf. Henningsen, *Fall Amerika*, 14, 204, 223ff.
24. Hans Magnus Enzensberger, "Warum ich Amerika verlasse," in *Die Zeit*, 1 March 1968. Reprinted in *Über Hans Magnus Enzensberger*, Jürgen Schickel, ed. (Frankfurt, 1970), 233–39. Cf. Bernd Greiner, "Of Love and Hatred. Five Observations on German Intel-

lectuals' View of America," in *Englisch-Amerikanische Studien* 2 (1988): 207-12. Hans Magnus Enzensberger, "Politische Brosamen," in Heinz D. Osterle, *Bilder von Amerika. Gespräche mit deutschen Schriftstellern* (Muenster, 1987), 42, 44f., 47; cp. 74. Cf. Erich Fried, "Über Krieg und Frieden," in *Bilder von Amerika*, 79ff. Marcel Reich-Ranicki also charged German writers of the time for their retreat into puberty fantasies; cf. *Der Spiegel* 12, "Männchen in Uniform. Über Reinhard Lettau: 'Feinde'," 17 March 1969, 164ff.

25. Cf. Schwan, *Antikommunismus und Antiamerikanismus*, 206ff.; Peter Krause, "Amerikakritik und Antiamerikanismus in der deutschen Presse am Beispiel der Berichterstattung zur Grenada-Intervention und zum Golfkrieg," in Schwan, *Antikommunismus und Antiamerikanismus*, 248ff.; Günter C. Behrmann, "Geschichte und aktuelle Struktur des Antiamerikanismus," in *Aus Politik und Zeitgeschichte. Beilage zur Wochenzeitung Das Parlament*, 21 July 1984, 3–15; Philipp Gassert, "Mit Amerika gegen Amerika: Antiamerikanismus in Westdeutschland," in *Handbuch* 2, Junker, 750ff.; Gerda Lederer, *Jugend und Autorität. Über den Einstellungswandel zum Autoritarismus in der Bundesrepublik Deutschland und den USA* (Opladen, 1983), 22ff, 97ff, 110ff; Gunter Hofmann, *Abschiede, Anfänge. Die Bundesrepublik Deutschland, eine Anatomie* (Munich, 2002). Dan Diner has serious reservations about the thesis of Germany's "arrival" in the west: cf. *Feindbild Amerika. Über die Beständigkeit eines Ressentiments* (Berlin, 2002).

Part 2

POPULAR CULTURE

Resisting Boogie-Woogie Culture, Abstract Expressionism, and Pop Art
German Highbrow Objections to the Import of "American" Forms of Culture, 1945-1965

◆ ◆ ◆

Jost Hermand

Anyone who expected that, after 8 May 1945, not only the German economy but also German culture would hit rock bottom was quite mistaken. As soon as the late summer and fall of that year, well-attended performances of dramas, operas, and concerts began to take place in the midst of the bombed-out cities—whether in the few theaters left standing, in concert halls set up as provisional theater spaces, next to the ruins of destroyed churches, or in less damaged parks. At this time the works that dominated in all four occupation zones were the masterpieces of the Christian or humanistic cultural heritage, such as Bach's *Matthäuspassion* (St. Matthew's Passion), Lessing's *Nathan der Weise* (Nathan the Wise), Goethe's *Iphigenie*, Mozart's *Zauberflöte* (Magic Flute), Beethoven's *Fidelio*, or Hofmannsthal's *Jedermann* (Everyman). Certainly the common goal here was to recall the "different, better Germany" that had not been totally destroyed even during the years of the Hitler dictatorship. Yet three ideological tendencies can be observed among artists; there were (1) those who wanted to secure a denazification certificate (*Persilschein*) for themselves by performing such works, after their involvement in the Nazi regime; (2) those who wanted to make a cultural contribution to the democratic renewal of Germany through the spirit of Christianity or the humanistic works of the Age of Goethe; or (3) those "once burned, twice shy" children of German fascism who wanted to retreat into a safe

---

Notes for this section begin on page 76.

cultural preserve because they hoped for consolation from such works in the "dark times" of the postwar era.

But no matter what the motivations behind these cultural beginnings, the activities in this area were enormous. Since nothing else remained to acquire, educated circles wanted at least to satisfy their hunger for higher things with culturally significant works—given that they were living in a world not yet flooded with all the subsequent media offerings. After returning to Frankfurt in 1949, for example, Theodor W. Adorno, who was disgusted by commercial US-American culture, wrote the well-known essay entitled "*Auferstehung der Kultur in Deutschland*" ("Resurrection of Culture in Germany"). Here he stated that, although he had expected to find a "barbaric" situation in postfascist Germany, what he actually encountered was a "humanistic intellectuality" that pleased him greatly, in spite of some misgivings.[1] To be sure, in contrast to other well-educated cultural critics of the first postwar years, he found fault with this "cultural hunger" for its blatant failure to deal with fascism, exile art, and the avant-garde works of the Weimar Republic.[2] But in the end even he was glad that many bourgeois intellectuals remained in Germany who still needed works of high culture, instead of simply yielding to the easy enjoyment of mass culture after the sufferings of World War II. Accordingly, almost no one from these circles found it inappropriate or strange that the famous historian Friedrich Meinecke seriously suggested at the conclusion of his 1946 book *Die deutsche Katastrophe* (*The German Catastrophe*) that "Goethe Societies" of like-minded "friends of culture" should be founded in all German cities. In his opinion, the goal of such groups should be to resist the "pressure of the masses" with the ideal of "personal, totally individual cultivation."[3] Meinecke was thinking of associations that would meet every Sunday afternoon for "ceremonies" featuring the performance of great works by German composers and the declamation of masterpieces by classical and romantic German authors. One heard similar thoughts expressed not only by West German humanists such as Ernst Robert Curtius but even by East German socialists such as Johannes R. Becher. After the 1945 founding of the Cultural League for the Democratic Renewal of Germany,[4] Becher repeatedly used the slogan "Forward to Goethe!" in addressing all Germans committed to high culture.

* * *

Such pronouncements were well received by the cultured middle classes in the immediate postwar period. In the midst of the general malaise of these years, many people tried to compensate for the lack of luxury and consumer goods with cultural products. Therefore, when these circles dealt with art, they almost always fell back on the "most noble" works of the German cultural heritage. Accordingly, they directed their cultural criticism primarily against two things: (1) art that was merely amusing, trivial, superficial entertainment; and (2) the "modernism" that had developed since the turn of the century. Because of the widespread need for consolation and compensation in the midst of general misery, they found such modernism too cold, too intellectual, and thus too inconsequential and flat.[5] In this context, hardly any differences existed initially among the four occupation zones. In particular, eastern and western intellectuals shared for a long time their rejection of ideologically "trivial" entertainment. The cultural theoreticians who saw themselves as representatives of the "other, better Germany" rejected most contemptuously and decisively the boogie-woogie culture propagated by the US-American occupation forces. Indeed, even young people seldom supported this American cultural import at first. The same was true for the widespread dislike of so-called modern art, particularly nonrepresentational painting along the lines of US-American abstract expressionism or the atonal music performed in the America Houses in Germany. Everyone from former Nazis to the groups belonging to the Inner Emigration in east and west rejected these forms of modern art as too "inexpressive" and even marginal, and instead advocated works from the older German cultural tradition or nonmodernist artists suppressed by the Nazis such as Carl Hofer, Ernst Barlach and Käthe Kollwitz.

Only in the course of the developing Cold War, which began to unfold in the late fall of 1947, did somewhat different assessments begin to be formulated about the culture industry as well as the often-apostrophized modernism. On the one hand, most theoreticians of high culture in all four occupation zones continued to reject both German and US-American commercial art by using the same arguments. After 1947/48, however, it became gradually possible to discern somewhat varying opinions with respect to art described as modern. Individuals on both sides continued to defend forms of higher culture in the same way. But after this time, Christian arguments in the west and socialist-humanistic arguments in the east intensified against the modernism of the day. Along these lines, for example, leading West German cultural critics such as Karl Scheffler and Wilhelm Hausenstein frequently maintained, as some representatives of the Inner Emigration had done before, that only a renewed emphasis on the God-given dignity of man could lead to a significant reorientation in the arts. Probably the most influential voice in these circles was that of Hans Sedlmayr. From his programmatic 1948 statement *Verlust der Mitte* (The Loss of the Center) to his 1955 book *Die Revolution in der modernen Kunst* (Revolution in Modern Art), he repeatedly maintained—recalling the Friedrich Schlegel of his late, Catholic phase—that since the Enlightenment modern art had found itself in a deep "crisis of faith." Therefore, he claimed, it had become unacceptably "godless," that is, "autonomous" or even "decadent." In his opinion, the most extreme forms of this type of modernism were *poesie pure*, atonal music, and nonrepresentational painting. Since these forms were "bereft of all meaning," he argued, they violated the religiously grounded idea that man was made in the "image of God."[6]

In the Soviet Occupation Zone, by contrast, those who continued to insist that art should still create noble images of humanity relied for the most part on the humanism of the Age of Goethe. This point of view was propagated above all by Johannes R. Becher, who frequently referred to Thomas and Heinrich Mann. By doing so, he wanted to block from the outset all "undignified, modernistic" artistic excesses, which were beginning to be associated more and more strongly with the "west" in the wake of Soviet cultural politics as formulated by Andrei Zhdanov. Especially later, in the context of the so-called formalism debate of the early 1950s, the state no longer tolerated any form of high culture that seemed elitist and thus incomprehensible to the masses, or any form of low culture that seemed trivial and thus escapist. Rather, the state only encouraged cultural expression and forms thought to "build up" socialism in an anticapitalist and thus anticommercial sense. Therefore, beginning in the late 1940s, state socialist concepts of "progressive" culture recognized only those works embracing the ideals of humanistic socialism proclaimed by the Socialist Unity Party. These ideals revolved around peace, friendship among nations, commitment to the socialist collective, and working to fulfill the economic plan for the welfare of the population as a whole. In the area of literature, state cultural functionaries, in praising German Classicism, generally relied on the writings of Georg Lukács.[7]

* * *

After the German Democratic Republic (GDR) was founded in 1949, the cultural theoreticians of East Germany continued to defend the older bourgeois culture of the era from 1750 to 1848. Indeed, their stance became even more rigid in certain respects in the course of the anti-Western campaign of the early 1950s. This is seen most clearly in the debates about painting and music. After 1950, for example, it became virtually impossible to exhibit nonrepresentational art in the style of US-American abstract expressionism or other similar trends. Anyone who tried to do so was labeled a Western "cosmopolitan," that is, someone who was disregarding all national particularities. Even stronger attacks were leveled against the popular music being broadcast into the GDR by West German and US-American radio stations. Eastern cultural politicians claimed that this music amounted to nothing but sentimental kitsch, crude eroticism, or chauvinistic tunes, and thereby contributed to the "artistic impoverishment" of the broad masses.[8] Along these lines, Ernst Hermann Meyer wrote in his 1952 book *Musik im Zeitgeschehen*

(Contemporary Music) that the "American amusement industry" was trying as hard as it could to undermine the "cultural independence" of other countries with its "boogie-woogie cosmopolitanism."⁹ A few years later, Georg Lukács used almost the same words to attack the "rock 'n' roll fad" as one of the "worst manifestations of music from the capitalist West."¹⁰ Similarly, GDR critics accused Western elitist music composers of "creating without a mission." They viewed this situation as leading to the "isolation of the artist" from society and amounting in many cases to nothing but a *"l'art pour l'art"* music alienated from all "humanistic" goals.¹¹ To illustrate their point, they cited the works of Schönberg and his school, which they characterized as formalistic and as "denying any type of national roots." Therefore, they viewed such works as based on the same "imperialism" as US-American pop music.¹²

The concept of cultural politics behind all these reproaches was the hope cherished by Johannes R. Becher and his compatriots that, by eliminating all trivial and modernistic elements from art, the entire population could be "put on track to becoming a united, highly cultivated nation." In such a nation, artists would not have to serve a culture industry that shamelessly exploited their talents. At the same time, they would not be forced to withdraw into an elitist, self-chosen isolation. In the same vein, other GDR cultural functionaries continued to hope in the 1950s that a generally accessible culture serving the entire population could be created. They imagined that the socialist form of production would enable such artists to distance themselves from all profit-making trivialities or modernistic extravagances in favor of concentrating on the humanistic goals of general popular enlightenment and aesthetic education.

* * *

A different development occurred in West Germany during the so-called economic miracle of the 1950s. In spite of widespread criticism from the highly cultivated elites, polarization intensified between the rapidly developing mass media and an elitist culture of modernism that was generally oriented around supposedly "international" Western trends. In this context, two main directions can be distinguished with respect to modernistic styles of art: (1) an obsessive emphasis on all technological achievements in art, which was related to the accelerated economic expansion rate during the "economic miracle"; and (2) connected to this, an elitist attitude that thoroughly approved of the newly available creature comforts, but preferred to withdraw into the realm of an *ars reservata*. À la Adorno, these circles continued to idealize concepts of artistic genius rooted in the latest stages of the bourgeoisie and unrecognized in both socialist and capitalist mass societies.

During this period the United States wanted to build up West Germany into a bulwark against Eastern communism by encouraging the rapid growth of economic production. Therefore, both of the above-mentioned directions in West German modern art evidenced specifically US-American elements of style, along with other Western, international elements. For example, as many recent studies have proven,[13] the exhibits of US-American abstract expressionism promoted by the CIA contributed greatly—along with French *art informel*—to the success of nonrepresentational painting, which celebrated its initial triumph at the first Kassel Documenta in 1955. This marked the prelude to the veritable dictatorship of "bars, circles, and lines" that predominated at the second Kassel Documenta in 1959.[14] The same is true in the area of elitist music that claimed to be "new" or "modern." Its unmelodic and inharmonic style was influenced above all by Schönberg and his school, as well as by the aleatoric compositions of the US-American John Cage. In particular, many West German music critics held up this latter method of composition as an expression of "Western freedom" in contrast to the music of the Eastern Bloc, which they denigrated as still subject to the supposed "dictatorship" of melody.[15]

But the areas of nonconformism within the various elitist arts were eventually superseded by a so-called Americanization, which in the final analysis amounted to an alignment with the cultural practices of the "Western" ideology of affluence. This development demonstrated the enormous influence of the US-American "culture industry," which Adorno had already repeatedly attacked from an elitist standpoint. The consequences of this development were not long in coming. The economic expansion rate finally accelerated so much during the 1950s in West Germany that the broad masses, and even some intellectuals, became more and more fixated on consumerism. With respect to culture, this meant they developed ever stronger desires to enjoy things that were mass-produced and thus easy to buy. Of course strong German traditions still existed in this area that went back to the 1920s and the Nazi period. These included hit songs, dance music, the film industry (especially its *Heimat* films), popular literature à la Heinz Günther Konsalik, and pulp fiction about romance, doctors, or the local German milieu.[16] But at the same time, US-American products entering West Germany were also conquering larger and larger shares of the market. This was especially true for jazz, pop music, the rock music of Elvis Presley, James Dean's films, western movies, and US-American posters and comics.

These imported or imitated art forms from the United States led to a clear division in the cultural behavior of the West German population. On the one hand, many young people warmly welcomed these popular cultural forms because of their lowbrow character, their emphasis on sensuality rather than intellect, and their infantilism that appealed to a teenage mentality. On the other hand, older people (particularly highly cultivated ones) decisively rejected what they perceived to be Americanization as "pleasure-seeking," "kitschy," or "unethical,"[17] as the Coca-Cola colonization of Germany. In these years, names such as Louis Armstrong, Duke Ellington, or Elvis Presley still made them see red. Young people, however, were especially enthusiastic about swing and jazz (especially so-called Negro jazz) as well as about early rock 'n' roll music,[18] and so they were increasingly less interested in radio performances of operas, symphonies, or chamber music.[19] Because of this development, sales of records increased about 50 percent every year after the mid-1950s. US-American popular music was the primary beneficiary of this, for West German young people loved its sensuality, rapid tempo, high volume, raw vocals, and vulgarity. Consequently, during this period every US-American hit song also became a hit in West Germany, whether on the radio, on records, in the movie theaters, or on television.

Nevertheless, the highly cultured middle classes in West Germany did not immediately allow themselves to be overtaken by this flood of mass media from the culture industry. Rather, they continued stubbornly to defend what Peter Bürger later termed the "institution of art."[20] Therefore, following a period directly after the war when high culture generally prevailed, quite a number of subcultures developed over the course of the 1950s that were connected to specific social groups and needs.[21] Either out of idealistic conviction or out of the capitalist desire to make a profit, the representatives of these subcultures attempted to stake a claim for themselves in a finely differentiated aesthetic supermarket. Here, along with an overwhelming selection of inexpensive mass-produced goods and even cheaper bargain basement commodities, they also arranged a gourmet counter for the more fastidious lovers of high culture.

In the course of this development, it became more common in West German publications on art theory to use the concepts of E-culture (serious or elitist culture) and U-culture (entertaining or popular culture), while the concept of an A-culture (generally understandable or educational culture) was hardly discussed any longer. In the area of U-culture—that is, in pulp and magazine fiction, bestsellers, popular movies, comic strips with figures such as Superman, Donald Duck, and Mickey Mouse, soap operas, detective stories, and hit music—the content was lowered to the comprehension level of people with only an elementary school education, who at that time made up 84 percent of the total population of West Germany.[22] On the other hand, art forms such as opera, drama, art films, lyric poetry, serious novels, classical music, and art in galleries and museums were directed primarily at the upper 16 percent of the population who had completed secondary school or the Gymnasium.

This situation hardly changed in the Federal Republic at the beginning of the 1960s. By contrast, the GDR continued to reject brusquely both bourgeois modernism as well as the West German/US-American culture industry and to promote state-sponsored high culture. Indeed, the only Western art that GDR cultural theoreticians exempted from this blanket condemnation was that deemed to have a "socially critical" thrust. For after all, these Eastern critics wanted to continue upholding the postulate of the "one united cultured nation." In the same period in the west, however, obvious shifts were occurring in the cultural scene. Well-educated people began to appreciate not only the high culture of the past but also the classical modernism of the early twentieth century and the neomodernism of the 1950s as equally important forms of high art. Indeed, after this point these same circles began to tolerate even some subcultures of youth art as "contemporary," meaning above all jazz, but also rock 'n' roll music and US-American films. In any event, increasingly fewer protests were heard from this quarter against what was perceived at the time to be the sensual, loud, and raw aspects of these art forms.[23]

Only one phenomenon led once again at the beginning of the 1960s to a short-lived wave of protest from West German high culture devotees: namely, US-American Pop Art. To be sure, this style had initially also encountered opposition in the United States from older "art mandarins" such as Peter Selz, Henry Geldzahler, and John Canady. They preferred the neomodernism of the 1950s and viewed the Pop Art of Andy Warhol, Claes Oldenburg, Roy Lichtenstein, and Robert Rauschenberg as "a giant put-on," "gag art," and "dimestore art," in other words, as "mass-produced vulgarity."[24] They tried to counter this trend by praising the art of, for example, Paul Klee or Jackson Pollock. Similar voices could be heard shortly thereafter in West Germany as well. For example, in 1964 the neomodernist journal *Das Kunstwerk* (*The Work of Art*) attacked US-American Pop Art as "supermarket art" or "non-art" based on mere "unimaginative banalities" in contrast to the elitist art of non-representational painting.[25] Such protests subsided in the second half of the 1960s, however. In the United States at that time, an enormous pride developed in New York Pop Art, which American critics believed would finally end the dominance of European painting. Accordingly, in the United States the aficionados of Pop Art or pop music groups took to labeling anyone who criticized these trends a "stuffed shirt" or a "Mr. Adorno." In West Germany, it became common either to admire US-American Pop Art or classify it in art historical terms as "Neo-Dada" or "Dada-Pop" in the framework of sequencing art's traditional "isms." In the final analysis, however, this West German reception of US-American Pop Art was only one manifestation of an increasing cultural synchronization within the framework of the Western alliance.

Already in the late 1960s, then, the trend toward the one-dimensional was becoming established that has since become so characteristic of the entire Western art scene—that is, the postmodern or US-American globalized art scene. In the course of this development, the intellectual elite gradually ceased to criticize lower forms of art from a perspective rooted in high culture, preferring instead to promote the slogan "anything goes." The result has been the growth of that aesthetic supermarket that still features a number of noncontradictory subcultures but in which every critical voice of those advocating high culture is rejected immediately as prescriptive or authoritarian. In recent decades, then, the relationship between E-art and U-art has shifted more in favor of the unchecked spread of the entertainment media produced and distributed by the corporations of the culture industry. Such media have no use for any kind of idealistic, didactic concepts. Rather, they rely on the principles of "electronic distraction," which generally tries to appeal to the lowest aesthetic common denominator with respect to social and educational ideals. In many areas, this trend can be seen as confirming what H. L. Mencken stated in the 1920s: "No one ever went bankrupt in the United States by underestimating the taste of the general public."[26]

Anyone who still places hope in the "critically activating character" of higher culture must necessarily question whether these developments really move in the direction of a truly democratic art that represents the interests of the broad masses. Nevertheless, it would be totally uncalled for to blame only the United States for this state of affairs. After all, this development, which led to the marginalization of older E-culture in favor of profit-making entertainment not only resulted from an increasing "Americanization." Rather, it also relates to the triumphal march of the capitalist culture industry, which is based solely on the principles of supply and demand. This culture industry simply developed somewhat more quickly in the United States than in Europe, because US practitioners and patrons did not need to overcome barriers arising from the traditions of aristocratic feudalism or the highly cultivated bourgeoisie. Therefore, influenced by or following in the footsteps of the United States, the current culture industry has developed in all highly industrialized countries. It employs all the social engineering strategies at its disposal to increase the impact of its advertising. In the end, the goal of this culture industry is to bring about an ideological synchronization of the majority of the population that will maximize its economic profits.

Translated by Carol Poore

Notes

1. Theodor W. Adorno, "Auferstehung der Kultur in Deutschland?" *Frankfurter Hefte* 5 (1950): 469-77.
2. See my article "Revolution und Restauration. Thesen zur politischen und ästhetischen Funktion der Kunst-Ismen nach 1918 und 1945," in *Konsequenzen der Inflation*, ed. Gerald Feldman (Berlin, 1989), 331-49.
3. See Jost Hermand, *Kultur im Wiederaufbau. 1945-1965* (Munich, 1986), 71.
4. On this see the programmatic statement of the "Cultural League" in *ibid.*, 104.
5. See, for example, Paul Höffer, "Neue Wege der zeitgenössischen Musik," *Aufbau. Kulturpolitische Zeitschrift* 2 (1946): 381-83.
6. Hans Sedlmayr, *Die Revolution in der modernen Kunst* (Hamburg, 1955), 49-64. See also the study by Axel Schildt, *Zwischen Abendland und Amerika. Studien zur westdeutschen Ideenlandschaft der 50er Jahre* (Munich, 1999).
7. As a representative of this point of view see Georg Lukács, "Skizze einer Geschichte der Neueren deutschen Literatur" (1944/45), which he published in 1955 as a book (Berlin, 1955).
8. Ernst Hermann Meyer, *Musik im Zeitgeschehen* (Berlin, 1952), 140-69.
9. *Ibid.*, 162ff.
10. Georg Lukács, *Die Eigenart des Ästhetischen* (Darmstadt, 1963), II, 400.
11. Meyer, *Musik im Zeitgeschehen*, 140ff.
12. This was Helmut Holtzhauer's view in "Gegen den Formalismus in der bildenden Kunst," in *Sächsische-Zeitung*, 25 April 1950. See also my article "Auf andere Art so große Hoffnung. Ansätze zu einer sozialistischen Musikkultur in der sowjetischen Besatzungszone und der frühen Deutschen Demokratischen Republik (1945-1965)," in *Poesie als Auftrag. Festschrift für Alexander von Bormann*, ed. Dagmar Ottmann (Würzburg, 2001), 199.
13. See among other things Jost Hermand, *Zuhause und anderswo. Erfahrungen im Kalten Krieg* (Cologne, 2001), 127.
14. See my article "Die restaurierte 'Moderne.' Zum Problem des Stilwandels in der bildenden Kunst der Bundesrepublik Deutschland um 1950," in *Stil und Gesellschaft*, ed. Friedrich Möbius (Dresden, 1984), 279-302.
15. See Jost Hermand, "Die restaurierte 'Moderne' im Umkreis der musikalischen Teilkulturen der Nachkriegszeit," in *Musikpädagogische Forschungen*, vol. 4, *Musikalische Teilkulturen*, ed. Werner Klüppelholz (Laaber, 1983), 172-93.
16. See my article "Bestseller und Heftchenromane in der Bundesrepublik seit 1945," in *Literaturszene Bundesrepublik*, Ferdinand van Ingen and Gerd Labroisse, eds. (Amsterdam, 1988), 79-104.
17. For examples of this, see the statements in *Frankfurter Hefte* 7 (1952): 775; 11 (1956): 248; and 13 (1958): 376.
18. See *Melos* 28 (1961): 42; and Fritz Eberhard, *Der Rundfunkhörer und seine Programme* (Bonn, 1962), 126-32. See also Uta G. Poiger, *Jazz, Rock, and Rebels: Cold War Politics in a Divided Germany* (Berkeley, 2000).
19. See Hermand, *Kultur im Wiederaufbau*, 56f.
20. Peter Bürger, *Theorie der Avantgarde* (Frankfurt am Main, 1974).
21. Hermand, *Kultur im Wiederaufbau*, 312-85.
22. See Jost Hermand, *Pop International. Eine kritische Analyse* (Frankfurt am Main, 1971), 23.

23. See Ulrich Kurth, "Als der Jazz 'cool' wurde," in *Musik der 50er Jahre*, Hanns-Werner Heister and Dietrich Stern, eds. (Berlin, 1983), 103-123. Compare in this context also Michael Geyer, "America in Germany: Power and the Pursuit of Americanization," in *The German-American Encounter: Conflict and Cooperation between Two Cultures, 1800-2000*, Frank Trommler and Elliot Shore, eds. (New York, 2000), 121-44.
24. Hermand, *Pop International*, 47f.
25. See Hans Platschek, "Tautologie der Gegenstände," *Merkur* 18 (1964): 37-38; Otto Schrag, "Pop-Un-Art," *Das Kunstwerk* 19 (1965): 101; and Katharina Scholz-Wanckel, *Pop Import* (Hamburg, 1969).
26. See my article "Die falsche Alternative. Neue Wege zum Verhältnis von E- und U-Literatur in den USA und der BRD," in *Literatur in den Massenmedien*, ed. Friedrich Knilli (Munich, 1976), 200-207.

From Nightmare to Model?
Why German Broadcasting Became Americanized

❖ ❖ ❖

Kaspar Maase

There is hardly a concept I find more complicated than that of Americanization. The more I work on this question, the harder it becomes for me to use the A-word, because in the German context, it still connotes a discourse of conquest by foreign infiltration. On the other hand, in the academic context, this term is generally used in a descriptive sense; it serves to denote a working consensus about the fact that, somewhere in the world, the situation is beginning to take on a marked similarity to American circumstances. The term is neither explanatory nor normative. And truly, the growing resemblance of German society to American society in the course of the twentieth century is so obvious, and the assumption that it has to do with the United States' dominant position in so many fields, from military to marketing, so plausible,[1] that it would be impossible to ask someone to refrain from using the tried and true A-word altogether.

It is from this point of view that I have chosen the subject of my paper, the German television and radio broadcasting system. At first sight, it appears to represent in exemplary fashion the fundamental transformation of German culture in the twentieth century. After World War I, it was dominated by a bourgeois, *bildungsbürgerlich* educative paradigm. The new medium was conceptualized in virtually obsessive opposition to what was understood to be American mass culture. And with the advent of the twenty-first century, a popular culture has become dominant in Germany in which American imports play a central role. For broadcasting professionals, the landmarks of American radio and television production are like signposts providing orientation for the future of broadcasting[2] in Germany.

Notes for this section begin on page 99.

The current "dual system" of competition between public and commercial networks developed from the originally state-controlled system. The experts agree: if the policymakers continue to define freedom of broadcasting in the sense of free enterprise (as in the United States), then there will be no stopping the marginalization of public broadcasting (as in the United States).

Not only the structure of broadcasting has changed; the same is true for the programming itself. In the 1920s, it was unthinkable for the vast majority of radio executives to orient this cultural instrument toward the desires of the majority of "educationally unwilling" listeners. Today, even public radio bows and scrapes almost slavishly before the wizards of "audience research" and cedes to the listeners' taste for entertainment above all else. Many observers also attribute this development to the effects of "Americanization."[3]

In this article, I will address the question, what role did the model and influence of the United States play in this transformation? Of course, I will have to reduce the complexity of the historical developments. My narrative identifies the pressure exerted by the broad audience, which is generally not oriented toward education, as the decisive transforming factor, in other words, the "masses" of mass culture.[4] In order to gain them as an audience, programming and structures were changed. This approach is not based on a simplistic model of consumer democracy; rather, I wish to explore the political, economic, and technological constellations in which pressure from the majority could effectively bring about changes.[5]

Finally, I would like to place my empirical findings in the context of more general theories of the Americanization of culture. My point of view is expressed well in the following quotation by Winfried Fluck: "We are not being Americanized. We are Americanizing ourselves."[6] And we are doing it because mass art *à l'americaine* attracts us to this day with offerings of exquisite aesthetic pleasure, permeated by popular modernity's promises of liberation.

Organizational Forms: From State Control to the Dual System

In the beginning, there was America. The experts may continue to argue about whether "radio for everyone" began on 2 November 1920 in the United States; in any case, radio arrived there several years before it did in Europe. In Germany, the American experiences were thoroughly evaluated, because, as the *Reichspostministerium*[7] declared in June 1922, "[t]he development ... which in America, due to the lack of legal restrictions, has no obstacles of any kind in its path and which has thus already led into chaos, is now encroaching upon Europe."[8] In Germany it was decided, as in Great Britain, to organize this technology differently. If radio for everyone could not be hindered, then it should at least be developed in a controlled fashion, "without bringing about conditions such as those in the United States."[9] Such were the words of Hans Bredow, who as a high official in the *Reichspostministerium* exercised great influence on the organization of German broadcasting. Two years later, he said in retrospect, "America was the guinea pig, but we European countries can be glad that we did not imitate the American path."[10]

What exactly did the political fathers of German broadcasting want to avoid at all costs? It was not the entanglement with the commercial sector that they rejected—on the contrary. The German broadcasting companies were run with private capital, and they proved to be quite profitable investments for private investors.[11] As early as 1924, radio advertising began, and soon it acquired its own congenial setting with light music from records. The *Reichspost* also earned money on the nascent medium through the fees they charged broadcasting companies and through the state-owned subsidiary company that held the monopoly for radio advertising. Because of this potential economic boon, members of the government who had categorically rejected the notion of "entertainment broadcasting" (as it was known at that time) were finally convinced.

Public criticism of radio advertising was not aimed at commercialization but rather at the putative injury to good taste that "broadcasted ads" brought into a cultivated and cultivating program. Thus, the American model of sponsored shows was recommended repeatedly, as it was considered much less obtrusive.

In 1922, when German officials began exploring the situation in America,[12] broadcasting in the United States was not yet dominated by profit-oriented businesses. Instead, a great variety of broadcasting entities existed: amateurs, universities, newspapers, religious organizations, department stores.[13] The lack of regulation of the new medium was the actual challenge. I began this chapter by saying that, in the beginning, there was America. A more precise characterization of German broadcasting policies would have to be that, in the beginning, there was the revolution. It was only with great effort that power could be wrested from the soldier's council of 190,000 military radio operators, the *Zentralfunkleitung*. Since then, "the highest principle of the development of broadcasting [was] that it not fall into the 'wrong hands'."[14] The fear of transmitters and receivers outside of state control led to the German model: privately owned broadcasting companies, in which the *Reichspost* held the majority of stock and therefore wielded decisive influence, as well as funding through fees paid by the listeners (in the first years, it was even required that they obtain official permission to own a radio receiver). In 1926, governmental control was increased through the creation of oversight commissions entitled to censorship as well as government-appointed *Kulturbeiräte*, or advisers in cultural affairs, whose function was to monitor all stations.[15] Nationalization of the broadcasting companies, which took place in 1932 under the Papen government and completely removed private capital from them, was not at all illogical to the organizational principles up to that time, and it prepared the way for *Gleichschaltung*—conforming with the National Socialist line—in 1933.

Mutatis mutandis, the model of a centralized state broadcasting system remained valid after World War II in the Soviet occupation zone and the German Democratic Republic (GDR).[16] In the western occupation zones, however, the reestablishment of the broadcasting system after the war meant a major break with the old model. Under the considerable influence of the American military government, the course was set toward a regionalized broadcasting system free of government influence.[17] In the face of a crushed economy, a commercial system was hardly thinkable, so it was decided that a public, self-run institution with controlling bodies in which all major social interest groups were represented would be the best solution. In the end, the BBC and its self-conception of broadcasting as a public service provided the model for the German system. The basis for journalistic independence would be provided by technical and economic independence (through the collection of listeners' fees).

From the first, the German contribution to this process consisted mainly of stubborn and generally successful attempts to dilute the clear principles of the western Allies. The political parties were able to exert influence on the broadcasting stations, especially with regard to hiring policies, by putting people loyal to them into the controlling body. Although this was not tantamount to government- or state-run broadcasting, a government worker mindset and bureaucratic mentality was (and is) prevalent in the various stations, as well as a norm of giving equal coverage to all parties (*Ausgewogenheit*) that impeded (and impedes) critical journalism and artistic creativity.

The second fall from grace came with the reintroduction of advertising on the air. In the prosperous years, it brought extra income with which cultural institutions and activities were financially supported. But as early as the late 1950s this changed dramatically; the development of television programming devoured such enormous amounts of money that the stations became dependent on advertising income.[18] When, in 1956, there was public debate over the issue, a station director (*Intendant*) warned that "firms buying commercial time will exert pressure on the standards of those parts of the programming in which they appear."[19] Nevertheless, the broadcasting stations pressed forward with their self-commercialization. It was the obvious thing to do, considering that politicians kept their funding to a minimum; but the consequences were considerable.

Although it was run by the same companies, television presented considerable competition for radio stations since the mid-1950s, which forced them to think more carefully about what programming would attract and hold listeners. To generalize a bit: the notion that, until privatized commercial broadcasting was legalized, the public stations had a monopoly on the market is more polemical than substantial. In 1983, each and every West German could view two national television programs and one regional station and listen to one national and at least three or four regional radio stations, each with different program styles. Furthermore, millions of Germans in borderland areas could even choose between the programs of more than one regional station due to the overlapping of broadcasting radii, allowing reception of two television stations, instead of only one, and six to ten or more radio stations. And listeners did just that, very selectively.[20]

Nevertheless, the development of the so-called dual system with the 1984 legalization of commercial television and radio networks[21] constituted an undeniable change of the whole system. Public broadcasting is obliged by law to secure a balanced supply of information, education, and entertainment; all owners of televisions and radios must pay fees regardless of which programs they choose. With the introduction of the dual system, public stations had to compete with private channels, which are financed solely by advertising and thus free for the users. The commercial networks were able to capitalize on entertainment programs, which public channels regarded as too trivial, sensational, violent, or erotic to be broadcast. The commercial strategy was successful with the audience; the public networks have been forced to adapt to the new patterns of programming in order to maintain their audiences, to compete for advertising income, and to secure general support for the arrangement that everybody has to pay a fee in order to finance public broadcasting. The presence of public broadcasting has been guaranteed by law, but it is possible that it will play only a marginal role in the near future.

It is understandable that many experts describe this development as Americanization. But in fact it was a purely internal political affair, a decision made in the interest of the political power of those parties who hoped for better representation in the new system—namely, the conservative Christian Democratic Union (CDU) and its Bavarian sister, the Christian Social Union (CSU).[22] It is one of the ironies of history that these very conservatives tried to gain support before and after 1984 with warnings against cultural Americanization and the proliferation of detrimental depictions of sex and violence particularly present in commercial television; this did not affect the dynamic initiated by the transformation of broadcasting from a public service into a commercial product for a market weakly regulated and aggressively vied for.

In 2003, the ratings of public television are clearly less than 50 percent, and even lower among viewers under the age of forty. Continued decline is expected—not to mention the new developments in the area of subscriber-media such as premium cable channels, video-on-demand, and so on. Regarding the social organization of broadcasting, one thing is very clear: Americanization did not come from the outside, it was asked for from within. German politicians dismantled the public service system established by the western Allies. Since the beginning of the debates over an alternative to public broadcasting, however, the "system changers" were always able to count on a majority of the population who did not want "cultural programming" and were of the opinion that "they should go along with what people like."[23]

Programming: From Education to Entertainment

Political circumstances have no doubt left their mark on the ups and downs of German broadcasting history. Yet listening has always been a voluntary decision; even under dictatorship, no one could be forced to do it. The topography of broadcasting history shows very different contours when seen from the perspective of the audience and the wishes they developed as their experience with the media increased. As so often from the point of view of everyday life, great political turning points appear of secondary importance. This is true not only for the daily routines of the "masses" but also for the patterns of those responsible for programming. Looking at their professional self-definition since the 1920s, it appears that they were mainly occupied with one central task: finding the right mix of education and entertainment.[24]

In other words, professional broadcasters were all concerned with elevating the knowledge and taste of the many from the beginning; the debate was about how much entertainment had to be conceded to the listeners in order to achieve this goal. The vast majority of the audience resisted the mass-educatory strategy of offering intellectually laborious programs and refusing light, cheerful, exciting, sensational programs. To put it in terms provocative to educated Germans: the tug-of-war that had been going on for decades was finally won by the majority with the advent of the dual system and its commercial programming.

In 1924, a poll among readers of a radio program guide revealed the following programming preferences:[25]

Operetta	83.3 %	Scholarly lectures	47.5 %
Daily news/current events	72.6 %	Humor	43.0 %
Chamber music	63.8 %	Cabaret	40.5 %
Mixed concert	63.5 %	Political news	39.4 %
Weather	53.6 %	Sports news	38.4 %
Dance music	48.7 %	Entertaining talks	35.8 %
Opera	48.2 %	Choral music	33.3 %

Light entertainment is at the top of the list, but "chamber music" and "opera" indicate a clear orientation toward high culture. The overall preference for music is also conspicuous even among the supporters of classical genres who represent the educated and well-to-do middle-class audience; music of all kind required less concentration and intellectual work than the spoken word, which clearly takes a back seat. The limited interest in political news is also striking; perhaps it expresses a longer-term constant in the expectations all classes had from the media, beyond the bourgeois contempt of the time for politics in the form of party politics.

The broadcasting company in Silesia took a broad poll in 1926 that confirmed the preference for the "feel-good factor" in radio programming and at the same time revealed a polarization in expectations.[26]

	Greatest Interest	No Interest
Music		
Light music	905	83
Military concerts	952	189
Marches	831	207
Folk songs	612	211
Operettas	570	210
Orchestral concerts	608	349
Recorded concerts	566	356
Opera	615	424
Dance music	539	538
Lieder/arias	365	418
Chamber music	419	510
Choral music	282	539
Spoken word		
Humorous recitation	845	220
Comedy	842	273
Radio plays	838	270
Local dialect	548	378
Cabaret	544	436

In 1931, a poll was taken among members of the Worker's Radio Club (*Arbeiterradiobund*) and readers of its magazine. Their programming preferences turned out to be quite unequivocal, as seen in the following results.[27]

Light music concerts	99.2 %
Recordings (mostly light music)	98.7 %
Marches	91.4 %
Orchestral concerts (medium heavy)	91.2 %
Cheerful, light talks/lectures	85.9 %
Radio plays	85.7 %
Lieder	80.1 %
Dance music (approx. half old and half new dance music or jazz)	77.4 %
Operettas	76.8 %
Choirs	62.8 %
Serious lectures	59.2 %
Scholarly lectures	54.4 %
Symphony orchestral concerts	22.2 %
Opera	6.0 %

In terms of their political and intellectual interests, the respondents tended to be from the upper level of the working class, and it is likely that, as members of a political organization, they were mostly male. The growing number of female listeners, on the other hand, liked to listen to the radio while doing their housework and appreciated light music, in addition to the advisory function of the radio. Advertising was targeted toward them, which combined catchy recorded tunes with commercials.[28] This supports Inge Marßolek's thesis that women were the "more modern audience" in that they made radio "as early as the 1920s into the background medium that it still is today."[29]

What the majority of the audience wanted (and what those responsible for programming did their best to minimize) has changed considerably in the course of eighty years. One constant audience trait has been the refusal to concentrate for longer stretches of time and exert oneself intellectually. Step by step, musical hits of the day moved into the foreground; since the 1960s, international pop music has dominated on the airwaves. From the 1920s well into the 1960s, the "ideal radio program" included a musical mix of "traditional/popular music" (brass bands, marches, and folk music) and "medium light entertainment" (salon music, operettas, "light classical," and "ballroom dance music"),[30] catchy radio plays and humorous recitations, the acoustic variety show known as the *Bunte Stunde*, and variety shows with comedic hosts. One also heard increasingly more reporting from sports events, and from the 1950s onward, elaborate quiz and game shows were introduced into the mix. These preferences bore a distinctly middle-class character; these listeners distinguished themselves from the upper classes by rejecting "serious" music and the "decadent" enthusiasm for jazz, and from the lower classes by rejecting current music hits and international pop music, which was increasingly dominated by American music, from swing to Tin Pan Alley.[31]

In the 1960s, of course, television replaced radio as the leading household medium. The light music and evening variety shows on the radio were replaced by the narrative genres (movies and series), as well as spectacular shows featuring top entertainment stars in a glamorous and costly setting:[32] the epitome of the attractive forms of broadcasting that the majority of the audience desired and for which public broadcasting—and this was a conviction that ran deep—had only pedantic contempt.

The change in the public's taste in entertainment was doubtlessly a generational phenomenon. The introduction of international commercialized popular music was also connected, however, with the altered social constitution of the audience, that is, with the growing number of blue-collar and lower-end white-collar listeners. In the first two decades after its introduction, the radio was a luxury item, and therefore largely limited to the more affluent (and because of limitations in the early transmitters, to inhabitants of urban areas).[33] To this day, the programming of private stations, with their considerably larger portions of light entertainment, attracts a segment of the audience with generally lower education levels (compared to public channels).[34] The success of commercial stations among young people of all socioeconomic levels shows, however, that a higher level of education does not necessarily translate into a preference for educational programming and distaste for pure entertainment.[35] Yet the continuity from the 1920s into the 1980s is obvious: the mass audience demanded "more entertainment" from public broadcasting.

This expectation collided with those of the "fathers of broadcasting," all of whom were from the educated classes and dedicated to the notion of "educating the masses." Their creed was that the medium should be used as a cultural and educational instrument.[36] There was considerable distance between this clear philosophical declaration of their goals, however, and the actual programming. Certainly one can agree with the historians' judgement that those responsible "tried to use broadcasting in the fight against Americanized mass culture and in favor of the education of those groups supposedly most susceptible to mass culture."[37] However, among aesthetic educators of the people (so-called *Volkserzieher*), a readiness for innovation and a search for new forms of instruction[38] were always part of their habitus, which had developed in Germany in the eighteenth century with the popularization of the Enlightenment. They made serious efforts to draw the "educationally unwilling"[39] into the process of taste elevation. In the 1920s, still, "education of the people" was more than just a euphemistic label for arrogance and discrimination.

Two types have been defined among the broadcasting executives of the Weimar Republic.[40] Besides those who regarded education and entertainment as mutually exclusive,[41] there were those who looked for a middle ground between both; this group was doubtlessly better equipped for the new medium. A detailed description of these executives' thoughts on how to use entertainment in order to make listeners more discriminating is beyond the scope of this article; nor can I adequately discuss the creativity with which, in the first decade of radio, stimulating, interesting, entertainingly educational programming was developed. Some of these programs may have exceeded the realistic intellectual capabilities of the audience; but in any case, a generalized characterization of Weimar broadcasting as a bourgeois medium that, in an educationally elitist manner, plainly ignored the recreational and amusement needs of the majority,[42] is too simplistic.

Two observations are important. First, the sections of programming defined as entertainment increased steadily until 1933.[43] From the beginning, music represented more than 50 percent of all programs,[44] and among this sector again, light tunes increased. This development affected the evening programming the least, however, which was understood as the central ingredient and flagship of broadcasting as a cultural factor. Second, station directors and their editorial personnel were pushed into this change more than they autonomously created it. From the start, they had faced pressure from listeners' organizations who accused the medium of overemphasizing the spoken word, information, education, and the canon of high culture. In 1931, the *Funk-Verband Ostsachsen* (Radio Club of East Saxony), for example, demanded "more light, particularly rhythmic instrumental music, less talk, the latter especially only in short presentations and great music only for certain festival evenings."[45] These words expressed precisely the feelings of many listeners, who wanted less demanding programming and more that cheered them up after a hard day's work.

This kind of criticism had an effect. If the programming began to distance itself from the ideal of the universalized concert and lecture hall and to approach the listeners who mostly played the radio in the background and only for short periods listened with full attention, then it did so because the listeners could exert a certain amount of economic pressure with their fees. At an internal meeting, the general manager of the *Reichsrundfunkgesellschaft* warned his program managers in no uncertain terms that the recreational needs of the audience formed the "economic backbone of broadcasting."[46]

Finally, the specific characteristics of the new medium also affected the form it eventually took. Technology (of transmitting and receiving), programming, and listener (situation) formed a constellation that differed from that of all other media—from that of the book, the course at the community college, the theater, or the concert hall. In order to realize its full potential and to offer the audience the highest possible consumer value, it required and made possible new communicative genres. Casual listening at home with the family was just as much part of this specific dispositive[47] as the playing of recorded music, the live report, the widely dispersed audience, the same programming broadcast to all homes in the country, and its one-way character. Within this framework, conventional ways of conveying information and participating in high culture became cumbersome relics. The new medium was characterized by timeliness, mobility, going to the edge of auditory possibilities, and the potential for rolling out carpets of sound capable of generating a pleasant mood. These possibilities increasingly influenced the expectations of the audience. They listened very attentively to what they were being offered in the way of useful information, as well as in the way of worldview and sensory and emotional arousal; the latter point can be summarized by saying that they appreciated the aesthetic experiences offered.

World War II: The Hour of Popular Entertainment

Although German broadcasting did, in fact, change in the course of its first decade, by 1933 the paradigm of mass education was still dominant. From the users' perspective, the few hesitant concessions to entertainment enlarged even further the gap between expectation and actual offerings; the above-mentioned demographic changes in the listening audience also contributed to this perception. We have seen thus far that the desire for entertainment-oriented broadcasting, which many observers considered and still consider, to indicate Americanization, became increasingly manifest since the 1920s. Among the reasons for why this was so, there is no direct or indirect American influence worth mentioning. The polarization of physical and intellectual work, as well as long-established patterns of taste and recreational preferences among the audience sector that does not work in the intellectual field, must be considered reason enough.

At this point, a more general question should be asked: which constellation made it possible for the manifest wishes of the audience (which for simplicity's sake I will refer to as "entertainment")[48] to influence programming in a qualitatively new way? The quick answer that comes to mind is total war and the free market. But in addition to sounding somewhat cynical, this answer is not totally accurate. However, it is hard to deny that under Joseph Goebbels' rule, broadcasting changed its character in two regards. First, it was transformed into a centralized instrument of propaganda adhering to the party line.[49] Second, the programming reform of 1941-1942 garnished the main dish of ideological mobilization with all the ingredients of "folksy/popular entertainment broadcasting."[50] The musical portion increased by 1943 to almost 90 percent, the amount of light music was almost 70 percent.[51] The melodies were to sound just as "light, lively, and cheerful" as the considerably shortened introductory remarks of the "merry" radio host. According to reports by the *Sicherheitsdienst*, the new programming was "practically totally accepted" among the populace, especially the switch "to almost exclusively cheerful and light programs," "liveliness ... and more air time for humor."[52] During evening prime time, the *Reichsprogramm* broadcast entertainment shows on 24 out of 28 days in October of 1942.[53]

In Great Britain, an interesting parallel development took place. In early 1940, the BBC started a second full-time channel called the Forces Programme, which complemented its original Home Service channel. [54] Whereas the original channel had a large proportion of spoken word (62 percent in 1942), music dominated the Forces Programme with a proportion of 63 percent; the entertainment character of spoken word as well as music was also considerably higher on the Forces Programme. The name points to the reasons: the idea was to lift the morale of the combatants, and that meant meeting first and foremost the taste requirements of young men, manual laborers, and office workers. That was more important to the leadership of the BBC than all highbrow principles; it was important for the war effort. This goal was also more important to Goebbels and his crew than the ideological dispute over "German dance music versus Jewish nigger jazz." If soldiers wanted "relaxed, strongly rhythmic music,"[55] then the radio of their own country had to broadcast it; due to the propaganda war, real competition existed on the airwaves. Moreover, the majority of the other listeners, who were also subject to great burdens on the "home front," enjoyed the new policy no less than those serving on the front lines.

The result was, from today's perspective, forced modernization; according to the radio historian Konrad Dussel,[56] Nazi entertainment broadcasting during the war corresponded to what had been developed on the basis of private capital in the 1920s in the United States and then transferred to Europe in the 1930s via Radio Luxembourg and similar commercial stations. The war served as a catalyst for the secular trend. During the Nazi dictatorship, the preferences of certain demographic groups considered especially sensitive became a decisive factor in the development of broadcasting, which was supported by the incipient scientific field of listener research.

Of course, this could not continue after 1945. Nazi broadcasting, whose ample entertainment offerings proved successful among the listening audience, fit perfectly into the interpretive scheme of cultural critique that so elegantly removed blame from the educated German classes: the Third Reich had been the rule of the rabble, the barbaric nadir of catering to the masses. More than ever, they believed, it was necessary to uphold the educative values of Western culture. Along with the creation of a nongovernmental, decentralized, noncommercial broadcasting structure came a zealous push for mass education, a change that represented an emphatic distancing by those now responsible from the wishes of the broad listening audience.

The Turnabout:
"The Worm Has to Be Tasty to the Fish, Not the Fisher"

Fewer than three decades later, by the mid-1970s, the educational objective of radio and television had been marginalized. A development had become irreversible, which—due to its fundamental orientation toward entertainment and its marked dependence on advertising income—historians of broadcasting have labeled Americanization.[57] The course was set long before open commercialization was introduced; the private networks appear to be nothing less than the logical consequence of a dynamic that had begun earlier. The factors that brought about the change were complex; I believe, however, that the crux can be described thus: a constellation had developed in which the responsible figures in public broadcasting felt the need to seek the acceptance of the broad audience. And for the standards of the viewers and listeners, popular culture from the United States played a growing, sometimes determining, role.

I cannot present the changes in programming itself in detail. The main concern in this article is the causal chain: how and why did German broadcasting Americanize itself? Several findings of recent broadcasting historiography will have to suffice. In the realm of radio, the idea of an integrative program "for everyone" was abandoned in the 1960s; the audience was increasingly perceived as being composed of various target groups, which were to be attracted by program offerings specific to them. The public networks developed parallel channels, each with a special emphasis on *Kultur* or entertainment.[58] Programming that put high culture (classical music, theater, radio essays, reports on exhibitions, etc.) and political information in the forefront was heard by at most 4 percent of listeners,[59] usually far less. The popular programs reduced the amount of spoken word dramatically and favored extensive *Magazinsendungen* (music shows with short inserts of news features), which offered "entertaining music at all possible times"[60] and casual, cheery hosts.

The introduction of the radio channel Bayern 3 in April 1971 can be seen as typical—a reaction to the radio station Ö 3 from the Austrian network, which Bavarian listeners switched to in droves. Bayern 3 was explicitly declared a "service program" whose standard did not reflect the "ideal intentions" of the program editors but rather the listeners' preferences. "Here there will be no demands made of them, rather, they will be served with that which they want, and not what a program plan has in mind." News was to be presented briefly and to include "besides the most important events of the day, things that interest the man on the street: scores from sporting events, major accidents, crime, society, and local news."[61] The other public stations followed with comparable "service channels," and it is no exaggeration to say that, with them, they started irrevocably down the path that led to, had to lead to, an open orientation toward the US model of radio format.

Television was given new momentum with the establishment of a second national network called *Zweites Deutsches Fernsehen* (ZDF); it began broadcasting in April 1963. The new channel was to be funded in large proportion by income from commercials, and that demanded a more entertainment-oriented emphasis compared to the *Arbeitsgemeinschaft der Rundfunkanstalten in Deutschland* (ARD).

Thus, the path was clear, but the speed with which the public stations took it proved too slow. In the early 1980s, as the conservatives pushed heavily for a change in the system, the population was not manifestly dissatisfied with the state of programming. The Christian Democratic Union and the Christian Social Union pursued their political objectives; they did not act as the mouthpiece for a grass-roots movement for private radio and television. But the resistance was limited for the most part to intellectual circles; the majority of the audience saw no reason to defend the status quo. And the fact that the commercial channels were quickly able to win over a significant portion of the listeners and viewers cannot be disqualified (with all due criticism of the problem of excessive portrayals of sex and violence) as dupery or taking perfidious advantage of lower instincts. These people compared programming and found that the private channels fulfilled their wishes somewhat better.

Thus far, I have argued that the educational paradigm had been replaced by the entertainment paradigm[62] as early as the mid-1970s, that is, well before the structural caesura of 1983-1984. Why and under what conditions did such "Americanization" take place? If we consider the audiences' preferences an independent variable, then the truly new or revolutionary factor was the emergence of a situation in which relatively autonomous networks could no longer ignore the wishes of an "educationally unwilling" audience without worrying. Dissatisfaction with educative radio was automatically discredited in public debate in the Weimar era. It was not just the broadcasting executives who could ignore the vote of the masses; no party would have taken up the cause.[63] The adaptation of Nazi radio to widely held desires for distraction and cheer had nothing to do with respect for the majority; it remained a dictatorial act. Well into the 1950s, audience preference had no independent authority; it was considered legitimate that media administrators proceeded as they saw fit.

To begin with, change was based on the fact that public radio lost its monopoly in the daily lives of people. During the 1950s, it could still be characterized as the "hegemon of leisure time in the home";[64] by the end of the decade, it was only one of several suppliers of information and entertainment. As previously mentioned, competition existed between the various public stations themselves; and radio hardly stood a chance against television, which, to top it off, switched to color transmissions starting in the fall of 1967. Radio found its special niche as a comfortably consumed medium, suitable as background during the day, with music and information: current, regional, helpful for daily life with weather and traffic reports, health, and consumer tips.

But in the arena of music, there was competition for public radio, particularly among younger listeners, from other stations (American Forces Network, British Forces Network/British Forces Broadcasting Service, the English-language programming on Radio Luxembourg), which played international, primarily English-language pop music. This kind of music was not broadcast on German public radio until 1965 (in a legendary show called Beat Club on Radio Bremen). The better the media equipment the youth owned (with turntables and tape recorders that allowed them to record and copy their hits), the more independent from radio music fans became and the more intensely the ARD stations felt the competition from the commercial music market.

A study on listener behavior in the broadcasting area of *Westdeutsche Rundfunk* (WDR) in 1970 provides a picture of the extent of the loss of their monopoly.[65] In that year, the two WDR stations were heard by 51 percent of all listeners. The radio station broadcast from over the border, Radio Luxembourg, reached 36 percent, and they listened for much longer stretches of time. However, the success of the commercial station was not the result of an interest in international (Americanized) pop music. What the listeners found there, in a quantity and atmosphere not offered by the ARD stations, were operetta melodies, German *Schlager* (light lyrical songs), evergreens, folk music, and light instrumental music, far more than foreign-language hits and beat music. The traditional German entertainment pattern still reigned on this station. That is, American influences played only a minor role in the programming shifts of the 1960s.

The quickly expanding audience research conducted by the public stations reported the loss of listeners to the executives; adaptation was inevitable. At the same time, in retrospect, more extensive listener research itself is clearly an indication of the emergence of a new definition of the relationship between broadcasting professionals and the mass audience. Well into the 1980s, it still could not be claimed that listener preferences were considered the most important criterion for program planning, much less that they dictated it. But the duty to respect their wishes became a part of media self-conception—a clear difference from the 1950s. This transformed approach among intellectual media executives was described, a bit cynically, by the long-time director of a private network, RTL, Helmut Thoma: "The worm must be tasty to the fish, not the fisher."

In my view, the change in norms of broadcasting journalism can be seen as part of West German democratization. The change also took place in the political arena at the same time, or even in advance. Since the 1960s, it was not possible simply to ignore poll results showing that the broadcasting being financed by all listeners did not reflect the preferences of large sections of the population. Certainly, it was often political parties, motivated by their own interests, that made these poll results into public scandals. But the final outcome was that the judgement and wishes of the absolute majority acquired the status of an institution in media policy, which, in principle, deserved respect in a democracy.

Another reason, much less lofty, for the acceptance of this point of view in the public networks was the dependence on income from advertising. The readiness to accommodate the wishes of potential customers for programs that promised high ratings and a consumer-friendly ambience was accordingly high. In this regard, the early evening programming in ARD and ZDF are quite revealing.[66] In a word, one could characterize the process that had taken place in television since the 1960s as Americanization—the self-Americanization of the viewers. The public networks were only allowed to broadcast commercials between 6 and 8 P.M., and the broadcasting of American series increased parallel to the expansion of advertising. The series proved cheaper for the public networks than producing original shows; they offered a balance between recurring, familiar figures and atmosphere on the one hand and constantly new adventures in a far-away world on the other, which made them particularly suited to casual viewing. Additionally, after all, they emphasized family values in a world that remained ideal and intact, even as its exciting problems had to be solved by the action of the series' heroes and their best friends (from Lassie to a chimpanzee named Charlie). Such shows were considered to offer a congenial advertising environment for products that also promised to solve life's problems. By the mid-1980s, around three-quarters of US series were broadcast in the afternoon and early evening; during prime time, they remained marginal.

The crucial point is that, from the beginning, the early evening programming was very popular among the viewers.[67] They could compare this bridgehead of commercialization with other blocks of programming and different types of shows over a long period—and many concluded that this segment came closer to their idea of television than others. Not only were American series broadcast in the early evening on ARD and ZDF. These stations also created successful productions of their own and imported shows from other countries, but they were the same type of feel-good productions with terrific people and solvable problems that US media corporations had popularized in the world market.

Americanization—Economic or Cultural Reading?

Isolated findings should not be overinterpreted. The success of the early evening programming, that ideal type of Americanization (according to the critics), demonstrates something that can be seen at many junctures of German broadcasting history: to explain the movement toward American models and the resonance for US imports, an economic reading is not enough. It misses the cultural realities—at least, if one understands culture in Ernst Cassirer's sense as the world of meanings.

Using the example of the Hollywood film on television, Irmela Schneider[68] has convincingly demonstrated that complex cultural changes *in Germany* were the starting point of so-called Americanization. First, the reevaluation of the artistic quality of classic American cinema by German filmmakers and cineastes in the 1960s and early 1970s led to such films being broadcast on television channels. That in turn helped pave the way for the mass success of present-day US films, a success that most Hollywood movies of the 1950s and 1960s did not enjoy.[69]

It was not just a question of familiarizing German audiences with Hollywood patterns of conflict, narrative style, and imagery. Behind this success lay a generational change. A new cohort among the educated classes, intellectuals, and artists dismissed the traditional bourgeois fixation on high culture and opened itself to the "unclassical" aesthetic qualities of the popular arts.[70] Thus, the experiences and values that in the 1950s had been limited to a few youthful fans of rock 'n' roll and American genre films became constitutive elements of a new common culture shared by all classes in modernizing West German society.[71] Because of a far-reaching change of values, which took place in Germany some two decades later than in the United States, Hollywood's narrative patterns and genre conventions were able to fulfill a new desire for self-realization among Germans—this is Schneider's argument.

I do not deny that the fact that American popular culture took root in German common culture benefited powerful protagonists in the United States (even if they sometimes recognized very late that successful popular culture of which they were not particularly fond, such as jazz, rock 'n' roll, and rap, nourished the overwhelming American mythology). Overt and covert strategies of power-wielding, economic expansion, and proselytizing to the world contributed strongly to this development. But does this explanation suffice, as if someone had said "push the Hollywood hits in the cinemas and make sure that the radio stations play American songs, and in a few years the Germans won't want to hear or see anything else anymore"? Such an argument would simply ignore decades of research in cultural studies that have shown that the users of mass culture are unpredictable protagonists who select and interpret what they consume in creative ways. When a product of popular culture has reached its *economic* endpoint, the consumer, its *cultural* existence is only beginning. As a symbolic good, it enters a new process of circulation in which its meanings are negotiated.

How do the findings presented here fit into more general models of cultural Americanization?[72] I prefer a reading that follows a modernization approach that has been stripped of normative and teleological implications.[73] The basic idea is that Western European societies share elementary commonalities with the United States in their economic logic and mental configuration within the framework of a western "capitalist culture."[74] Congruencies in social structure and the patterns of social problems—in the sense of a common matrix of development that, nevertheless, can lead to divergent national or regional paths—are based on these commonalities. Structural kinship with Europe is characteristic of American offers of goods, strategies in social policy, and lifestyles, which, after all, have already been tested under similar (western capitalist) conditions.

This kinship is also characteristic of the European "demand," if we call to mind values such as affluence, progress, security, or basic patterns of work and leisure time, which make congruent expectations of entertainment probable. It might be hard today to find a European who would argue that the United States is taking the ideal path of modernization, but many do see a superior position of American popular culture as a result of specific resources and head starts in development.

Cultural appropriation always takes place as change, as a transformation through and for the patterns of perception, value systems, norms of taste, and taboos of the borrowing culture. But the reception of North American models in developed capitalist industrial states was facilitated by commonalities among these societies. US models offered solutions to problems that were structurally congruent. This argument is not intended to play down contingent influences. If modernization does not require a unified path of development, then the implementation of elements from the US supply always means orientation toward a specific direction that is by no means "objectively necessary"; there is always an alternative. In this way, the chances for other paths of development are cumulatively reduced: needs and aesthetic norms become shaped such that they are more susceptible to the next transatlantic offers.

However, this is no reason to reactivate the discourse of cultural imperialism. Americanization is essentially based on the ability to offer practical and symbolic-aesthetic tools for the lives of hard-working people in industrialized and postindustrial societies. The transatlantic offers, as has been recognized in Germany since the 1920s, had already proved themselves in the everyday life of the working masses; they "fit" and appeared attractive and useful at first sight. And the framework of common, or at least compatible, cultural orientation facilitated the integration of American imports into the life of the "old world."

Thus, the wish for more entertaining broadcasting in Germany, which had remained unsatisfied for decades, led to developments that, at each point in time, meant a movement toward US practices; in World War II, however, it also led to an approach between *Reichsrundfunk* and the BBC's Forces Programme.[75] On the other hand, it is no surprise that, to an audience who felt frustrated since the 1950s, American television series and shows simply seemed superior in terms of entertainment.

Simply the Best?

Like many studies of popular culture in twentieth century Europe, the history of German broadcasting points to the close interplay between the rise of a commercialized popular culture strongly oriented toward American models and fundamental processes of cultural democratization—or, to use a term of Max Weber's that is perhaps more precise, mass democratization.[76] In a sort of zero-sum game, the deconstruction of educatory paternalism and the authoritarian regulation of cultural offerings for the masses in Germany was inseparably linked with the quantitative and qualitative expansion of options on the market of cultural goods and services. I am talking about democratization in a rather pragmatic sense, about the availability of experiences and pleasures and about the recognition of popular taste—and just that is important to the protagonists of everyday life. The theoretical question of the quality of the freedom of masses so poorly supplied with cultural capital must be discussed separately.

Recently, the intercultural transfer processes[77] between Germany and the United States in the fields of popular culture and everyday knowledge have repeatedly been referred to as "Americanization from below." The term, however, has taken on a different meaning than the one I intended when I introduced it.[78] Detlef Junker, for example, means with it "the influence of non-governmental *American* actors,"[79] whereas I would like to illuminate especially non-elite Germans as agents of their own self-Americanization.[80] Out of diverse offerings, they increasingly chose and choose American or Americanized popular art. In broadcasting history in particular, it is striking that they did so for a long time in situations in which US imports in no way dominated the market. At first, swing, boogie-woogie, rap, or even the first American series in commercialized early evening programming were controversial and supported only by a minority,[81] sometimes even stigmatized as oppositional or subcultural.

This means that the decision to "self-Americanize" must be considered well founded and that the reasons for it must be seriously sought. A question has to be asked that many European intellectuals find hardly thinkable: is American or Americanized popular art perhaps truly superior, and if so, in what way? The high standards of the craft and the creative expertise of the US culture industry are well known, after all. Here, I cannot discuss the attractiveness of the imports and their value for European users in this regard because this would require concrete product analyses. However, one can reflect on the general conditions for the success of American popular art, for the attractiveness of its semiotic potential.

In recent research, one approach has emerged that is interesting among other things because scholars from different disciplines, with different cultural backgrounds and different research goals developed it. At its core lies the argument that specific "American" characteristics of popular culture from the United States uniquely offer aesthetic pleasure and enjoyable imagination to different recipient groups throughout the world. Successful US mass art always links the great democratic, modernist promises of Americanism with special qualities of structure and performance of the popular. This view has been developed with different, sometimes opposing, accents, by Victoria de Grazia, Miriam Hansen, Berndt Ostendorf, Arjun Appadurai,[82] Winfried Fluck, and others. Underlying this approach is a paradigm according to which the products of mass culture, from streamline design to the "Madonna" phenomenon, are inscribed with fundamental characteristics of the American self-conceptualization, characteristics that have experienced propagandistic concentration and missionary export zeal in the ideologies of Americanism and exceptionalism.

De Grazia points out that the global appeal of mass culture from the United States is based on the fact that "the American experience was transformed into a universal model of business society based on advanced technology and promising formal equality and unlimited mass consumption."[83] Looking at the recipients of American exports, I have been able to show for West German society of the 1950s how the American way of life and entertainment attracted popular projections of long dreamed-of affluence and comfort, of glamour and democratic recognition of ordinary people.[84] Ostendorf demonstrates systematically how, since the nineteenth century, the basic features of the "American creed" shaped a popular culture and its performance that is adopted by socially disadvantaged groups in the entire world as an "individualized promise of liberation."[85] Others emphasize that, in the development of American popular culture, an artistic know-how has accumulated that is especially capable of accommodating the receptive competence and aesthetic expectations of non–middle-class audiences. Winfried Fluck mentions deconstruction of hierarchy and democratization, too; most of all, however, he demonstrates to what extent American popular art represents a unique store of elements for "imaginary self-staging and self-empowerment"[86] that more and more people strive for in modernizing societies. Miriam Hansen sees the aesthetic language of a globally understood "vernacular modernism" displayed in classic Hollywood films; it works via the development of a complex sensual sensibility and "as a powerful matrix for modernity's liberatory impulses—its moments of abundance, play, and radical possibility, its glimpses of collectivity and gender equality."[87]

These interpretations do not romanticize the AOL-TimeWarnerization of the world. They keep in mind that not just one modernity exists and that the global success of the American way always includes the marginalization of alternatives. But they do not deny, for the sake of the critique of capitalism, an experience that probably most European intellectuals have had: the enormous aesthetic power with which works of American popular art overwhelm the senses and emotions again and again, leaving lasting, standard-setting impressions—even in those cases in which a critical mind struggles to resist the messages of hypocritical or self-righteous Americanism.

Explaining success does not mean crowning it with the laurel wreath of inevitability. Rather, whereas since 1989 many have preached the danger of utopias, in these approaches survives the same sensibility for popular utopias called for by Ernst Bloch in his studies on the revolutionary potential of *colportage*.[88] In my view, this sensibility is indispensable if we want to offer complex answers to the question of the causes and meaning of global tendencies toward Americanization.

But let us return to the sober routine of historiography: this article presents a narrative of the Americanization of German broadcasting, in which the desire of the masses for stimulating entertainment played the main role. In the search for an explanation for it, a focus on the alluring qualities of American popular art seems to me more productive than notions of an overpowering cultural imperialism or the deliberate import by elites.

Notes

The text is based on a translation from German by Monique Scheer.

1. See for example Volker Berghahn, "Deutschland im 'American Century,' 1942-1992. Einige Argumente zur Amerikanisierungsfrage," in *Politische Zäsuren und gesellschaftlicher Wandel im 20. Jahrhundert*, Matthias Frese and Michael Prinz, eds. (Paderborn, 1996), 789-800; Volker Berghahn, "Conceptualizing the American Impact on Germany: West German Society and the Problem of Americanization," paper presented at the conference of the German Historical Institute, Washington, D.C., March 25-27, 1999. Available at <http://www.ghi-dc.org/ conpotweb/westernpapers/berghahn.pdf>, accessed on 17 October 2003.
2. I use the term "broadcasting" to mean both radio and television.
3. See Winand Gellner, ed., *Europäisches Fernsehen—American Blend? Fernsehmedien zwischen Amerikanisierung und Europäisierung* (Berlin, 1989); Irmela Schneider, ed., *Amerikanische Einstellung. Deutsches Fernsehen und US-amerikanische Produktionen* (Heidelberg, 1992); Harald Wenzel, ed., *Die Amerikanisierung des Medienalltags* (Frankfurt am Main, 1998).
4. I refer here to the findings of Knut Hickethier, "Dispositiv Fernsehen, Programm und Programmstrukturen in der Bundesrepublik Deutschland," in idem, ed., *Geschichte des Fernsehens in der Bundesrepublik Deutschland*, vol 1. (Munich, 1993), 171-244; and Konrad Dussel, "Der Streit um das große U. Die Programmgestaltung des öffentlich-rechtlichen Rundfunks und der Einfluss der Pulikumsinteressen 1949-1989," in *Archiv für Sozialgeschichte* 35 (1995): 255-89. However, while according to Hickethier (182f.) the "principle of constant conformity to viewer behavior" affects the compatibility between structures of programming and those of everyday life, yet not the actual contents of programming, Dussel (258, 288) extends this principle to include the assertion of the entertainment paradigm.
5. A further study would have to investigate which elective possibilities were in fact available to the majority of the audience in different situations. Historical course-settings should in no way be regarded as identical with an ideal of modern democratic culture. Instead of presuming to know what people were actually supposed to want, the historian must ask which options were excluded and why, and which structural limitations were part of the choices made.
6. Winfried Fluck, "'Amerikanisierung der Kultur,' Zur Geschichte der amerikanischen Populärkultur," in *Die Amerikanisierung des Medienalltags*, ed. Wenzel, 13-52; quote from 49. This touches more generally on a point of view according to which westernization, democratization, and modernization of Germany "should not at all be interpreted as 'Americanization', but rather as a cultural and social synthesis in the Federal Republic of Germany in which American influence has flowed and is stored [aufgehoben]." Detlef Junker, "Politik, Sicherheit, Wirtschaft, Kultur und Gesellschaft: Dimensionen transatlantischer Beziehungen," in *Die USA und Deutschland im Zeitalter des Kalten Krieges 1945-1990*, vol 1., ed. Detlef Junker (Stuttgart, 2001), 17-56; quote from 50.
7. In Germany, the postmaster general was responsible for communication over the airwaves.
8. Report published by the *Reichspostministerium* on the 21st meeting of the *Reichsfunkkommission* (RFK) on 9 June 1922. Quoted in Winfried B. Lerg, *Die Entstehung des Rundfunks in Deutschland. Herkunft und Entwicklung eines publizistischen Mittels* (Frankfurt am Main, 1965), 367.
9. Minutes of the 21st meeting of the RFK, ibid., 127.

10. Staatssekretär Dr. Bredow über den Rundfunk, *Der Radio-Amateur* 2, no. 33 (1924): 880-84; quote from 881. The public debate over whether something could be learned from broadcasting in the United States—and if so, what—was quite varied; there were the prejudices of cultural anti-Americanism, objective discussions, and switching between pro and con depending on one's own interests. See Dagmar Regul, "Konservative Kritik am Medium Rundfunk in den ersten zehn Jahren seines Bestehens (1923-1933)" (Master's thesis, University of Münster, 1976); Lothar Walter, "Die Entstehung des Rundfunks in Deutschland im Spiegel der zeitgenössischen Tagespresse" (Master's thesis, Freie Universität Berlin, 1979); Daniela Tosch, "Der Rundfunk als 'Neues Medium' im Spiegel der Münchner Presse 1918-1926" (Munich, 1987). See also the evidence presented by Christian Maatje, *Verkaufte Luft. Die Kommerzialisierung des Rundfunks. Hörfunkwerbung in Deutschland (1923-1936)* (Potsdam, 2000), 220, 222, 237, 240, 249f., 256, 323.
11. See Karl Christian Führer, *Wirtschaftsgeschichte des Rundfunks in der Weimarer Republik* (Potsdam, 1997).
12. In the spring of 1922, the Reichspost sent a team of experts to the United States. They were very impressed by the great demand for radios; however, they adopted critical American opinions warning of "wild development" without legal regulations and demanding a ban on radio advertising (Lerg, *Die Entstehung des Rundfunks in Deutschland*, 199f.; on the British parallel example, ibid., 122f.).
13. See Ralph Engelman, *Public Radio and Television in America. A Political History* (Thousand Oaks, 1996), 11ff.; Susan Smulyan, *Selling Radio. The Commercialization of American Broadcasting, 1922-1934* (Washington, 1994); Erik Barnouw, *A History of Broadcasting in the United States. Vol. 1: A Tower in Babel* (New York, 1966), 96ff.
14. August Soppe, "Die Einführung des Rundfunks in Deutschland," in *Massen/Medien/Politik [= Argument-Sonderband AS 10]* (Karlsruhe, 1976), 115-49, quote from 123; cf. Konrad Dussel, *Deutsche Rundfunkgeschichte. Eine Einführung* (Konstanz, 1999), 22ff.; Lerg, *Die Entstehung des Rundfunks in Deutschland*, 45ff.
15. Winfried B. Lerg, *Rundfunkpolitik in der Weimarer Republik* (Munich, 1980), 372ff.; Horst O. Halefeldt, "Sendegesellschaften und Rundfunkordnungen," in *Programmgeschichte des Hörfunks in der Weimarer Republik*, vol. 1, ed. Joachim-Felix Leonhard (Munich, 1997), 23-245, 278-350, esp. 165-245; Theresia Wittenbrink, "Beratungsgremien mit beschränktem Einfluss: die Kulturbeiräte," ibid., 246-77.
16. Dussel, *Deutsche Rundfunkgeschichte*, 127ff.; Wolfgang Mühl-Benninghaus, "Rundfunk in der SBZ/DDR," in *Rundfunkpolitik in Deutschland*, vol. 2, ed. Dietrich Schwarzkopf, 795-873, here 795ff.; Adelheid von Saldern and Inge Marßolek, eds., *Zuhören und Gehörtwerden. Vol. 2. Radio in der DDR der fünfziger Jahre - Zwischen Lenkung und Ablenkung* (Tübingen, 1998), esp. 11-170; Peter Hoff, "Organisation und Programmentwicklung des DDR-Fernsehens," in *Geschichte des deutschen Fernsehens*, ed. Knut Hickethier (Stuttgart, 1998), 245-88, here 245ff.
17. In the year 2003, 10 public broadcasting stations exist that form the *Arbeitsgemeinschaft der Rundfunkanstalten Deutschlands* (ARD), the German Broadcasting Cooperative. In addition to their altogether 60 regional radio programs, they cooperate in the nationwide programming for "Channel One" (*das Erste Fernsehprogramm*) as well as eight regional stations each known as "Channel Three" (*das Dritte Programm*) and four other nationwide television channels with more specific programming. In addition, there is the public television station known as "Channel Two" (ZDF: *Zweites Deutsches Fernsehen*), two nationwide public radio stations and the government-run *Deutsche Welle*, which broadcasts outside Germany.

18. See Joan Kristin Bleicher, "Institutionsgeschichte des bundesrepublikanischen Fernsehens," in *Geschichte des deutschen Fernsehens*, ed. Hickethier, 67-134, esp. 100ff. In 1970, the income from radio and TV advertising made up about one third of the amount of income from listeners' fees for ARD and about one half of that for ZDF —figured according to *Media Perspektiven. Daten zur Mediensituation in der Bundesrepublik Deutschland* (Frankfurt am Main, 1979), 2f. See also Günter Giesenfeld and Prisca Prugger, "Serien im Vorabend- und im Hauptprogramm," in *Geschichte des Fernsehens*, vol 2., Helmut Schanze and Bernhard Zimmermann, eds. (Munich, 1994), 349-88, here 361; Hickethier, *Dispositiv Fernsehen*, 210; Angela Krewani, "Amerikanisierung am Nachmittag. Amerikanische Serien in ARD und ZDF," in Schneider, *Amerikanische Einstellung*, 172ff., here 176, n. 10.
19. Quoted in Dussel, *Deutsche Rundfunkgeschichte*, 226.
20. See Dussel, "Der Streit," 265ff.
21. In the year 2003, the commercial television market is still evolving. Seven regular channels and five or six special-interest channels as well as one subscriber-TV channel are considered relevant. Most households receive further national and international channels via cable and satellite dish, on the average about 30, sometimes many more. In addition to approximately 50 private radio stations with a middle-range broadcasting radius, there are innumerable ones broadcasting short-range, for a very localized area.
22. See Dietrich Schwarzkopf, "Die 'Medienwende' 1983," in idem, *Rundfunkpolitik in Deutschland*, vol. 1, 29-49; Dussel, "Der Streit," 282f.
23. "Kein so kulturelles Programm" and "Man soll sich nach dem richten, was den Leuten gefällt"—statements in a poll in 1958 with which 58% of the population agreed (Dussel, "Der Streit," 277f.).
24. See Leonhard, *Programmgeschichte*, vol. 2; Carsten Lenk, *Die Erscheinung des Rundfunks. Einführung und Nutzung eines neuen Mediums 1923-1932* (Opladen, 1997), 183ff.; documents 4-7, 21, 22 in *Quellen zur Programmgeschichte des deutschen Hörfunks und Fernsehens*, Konrad Dussel and Edgar Lersch, eds. (Göttingen, 1999).
25. Quoted in Ludwig Stoffels, "Kulturfaktor und Unterhaltungsrundfunk," in Leonhard, *Programmgeschichte*, vol. 2, 623ff., here 635. The question was "What do you want to hear on the radio?" The regular announcement of the time of day was in third place with over 70%. Between 30% and 20% were Esperanto, instructional programming, language courses, reports from the stock market, and speeches for the youth. Between 20% and 15% were political speeches, fashion, fairy tales, and theater. In last place were sermons, with 9%.
26. Ibid., 635f. (numbers correspond to answers given).
27. Arbeiterfunk 1931, no. 43; cited in Thomas Penka, *"Geistzerstäuber" Rundfunk: Sozialgeschichte des Südfunkprogramms in der Weimarer Republik* (Potsdam, 1999), 258f.
28. Maatje, *Verkaufte Luft*, 326, 336f.
29. Inge Marßolek, "Radio in Deutschland 1923-1960. Zur Sozialgeschichte eines Mediums," in *Geschichte und Gesellschaft* 27, no. 2 (2001): 207-39, quotes from 214, 237. Cf. also Uta C. Schmidt and Monika Pater, "'Adriennes Hochantenne': Geschlechtsspezifische Aspekte medialer Durchsetzungsprozesse am Beispiel des Rundfunks," in *Feministische Studien* 15, no. 1 (1997): 21-33.
30. See Michael Stapper, *Unterhaltungsmusik im Rundfunk der Weimarer Republik* (Tutzing, 2001).
31. On Weimar radio as a "middle-class gadget," see Lenk, *Die Erscheinung des Rundfunks*, 128ff. More generally on the confrontations against "modernism" and "Americanism" in Weimar culture, see Adelheid von Saldern, "Massenfreizeitkultur im Visier. Ein Beitrag

zu den Deutungs- und Einwirkungsversuchen während der Weimarer Republik," in *Archiv für Sozialgeschichte* 33 (1993): 21-58; Adelheid von Saldern, "Überfremdungsängste. Gegen die Amerikanisierung der deutschen Kultur in den zwanziger Jahren," in *Amerikanisierung. Traum und Alptraum im Deutschland des 20. Jahrhunderts*, Alf Lüdtke, Inge Marßolek, and Adelheid von Saldern, eds. (Stuttgart, 1996), 213-44.

32. See Irmela Schneider, "Ein Weg zur Alltäglichkeit. Spielfilme im Fernsehprogramm," in *Geschichte des Fernsehens*, vol. 2, Schanze and Zimmermann, 227-302; Giesenfeld and Prugger in *Geschichte des Fernsehens*, vol. 2, Schanze and Zimmermann; Gerd Hallenberger, "Vom Quiz zur Game Show: Geschichte und Entwicklung der Wettbewerbsspiele des bundesrepublikanischen Fernsehens," in *Geschichte des Fernsehens*, vol. 4, Hans Dieter Erlinger and Hans-Friedrich Foltin, eds. (Munich, 1994), 25-68; Werner Faulstich, "Fernsehgeschichte als Erfolgsgeschichte: Die Sendungen mit den höchsten Einschaltquoten," in *Geschichte des Fernsehens*, vol. 5, ed. Werner Faulstich (Munich, 1994), 217-36; Werner Faulstich and Ricarda Strobel, "Prominente und Stars: Fernsehgeschichte als Stargeschichte," in *Geschichte des Fernsehens*, vol. 5, Faulstich, 93-118.

33. Karl Christian Führer, "Auf dem Weg zur 'Massenkultur'? Kino und Rundfunk in der Weimarer Republik," in *Historische Zeitschrift* 262 (1996): 739-80, here 766ff.; Lenk, *Die Erscheinung des Rundfunks*, 126ff., 288ff.; Penka, *"Geistzerstäuber" Rundfunk*, 437f.; Uta C. Schmidt, "Radioaneignung," in *Zuhören und Gehörtwerden. Vol. 1. Radio im Nationalsozialismus. Zwischen Lenkung und Ablenkung*, Inge Marßolek and Adelheid von Saldern, eds. (Tübingen, 1998), 243-360, here 268ff.

34. See Uwe Hasebrink and Friedrich Krotz, "Fernsehnutzung im dualen System," in *Medien-Transformation. Zehn Jahre dualer Rundfunk in Deutschland*, Walter Hömberg and Heinz Pürer, eds. (Konstanz, 1996), 359-73; Udo Michael Krüger, "Tendenzen in den Programmen der großen Fernsehsender 1985-1995," in *Media Perspektiven* (August 1996): 418-40; Udo Michael Krüger and Thomas Zapf-Schramm, "Die Boulevardisierungskluft im deutschen Fernsehen," in *Media Perspektiven* (July 2001): 326-44; Christa-Maria Ridder and Bernhard Engel, "Massenkommunikation 2000: Images und Funktionen der Massenmedien im Vergleich," in *Media Perspektiven* (March 2001): 102-25, esp. 112ff.

35. For a broader analysis of the development, see Kaspar Maase, "Spiel ohne Grenzen. Von der 'Massenkultur' zur ‚Erlebnisgesellschaft': Wandel im Umgang mit populärer Unterhaltung," in *Zeitschrift für Volkskunde* 90, no. 1 (1994): 13-36; idem, "'Gemeinkultur'. Zur Durchsetzung nachbürgerlicher Kulturverhältnisse in Westdeutschland 1945 bis 1970," in *Die januskōpfigen 50er Jahre*, Georg Bollenbeck and Gerhard Kaiser, eds. (Wiesbaden, 2000), 170-89.

36. Succinctly shown in Horst O. Halefeldt, "Das erste Medium für alle? Erwartungen an den Hörfunk bei seiner Einführung in Deutschland Anfang der 20er Jahre," in *Rundfunk und Fernsehen* 34 (1986): 23-43, 157-76, esp. 35ff.

37. Marßolek, "Radio in Deutschland," 234.

38. See Kaspar Maase, "Krisenbewußtsein und Reformorientierung. Zum Deutungshorizont der Gegner der modernen Populärkünste 1880-1918," in *Schund und Schönheit. Populäre Kultur um 1900*, Kaspar Maase and Wolfgang Kaschuba, eds. (Cologne, 2001), 290-342.

39. In 1929, the director of the broadcasting station in Munich made a distinction between the "großen Masse der aus Unvermögen und dauernd bildungsunlustigen Hörer" [great mass of listeners unable and constantly unwilling to be educated] and a considerable percentage of those exhausted from work and therefore only "vorübergehend bildungsunlustiger Hörer" [temporarily educationally unwilling listener]. Cited from Dussel and Lersch, *Quellen zur Programmgeschichte*, 40.

40. Stoffels, *Kulturfaktor*, 623.
41. "Die ... Forderung, des Nachmittags ... leichte Unterhaltungsmusik für die zu Hause gebliebenen Frauen und Kinder und des Abends ... ein ... an den Aufnehmenden nur geringe Ansprüche stellendes Programm für die ganze Familie zu senden, ist ... überhaupt nicht zu diskutieren" [The call for broadcasting light music in the afternoon for the women and children at home and for evening programming for the entire family, which does not ask too much of them, is utterly out of the question]. Cited from Dussel and Lersch, *Quellen zur Programmgeschichte*, 38.
42. As, for example, Führer, "Auf dem Weg," 776f. argues.
43. Penka, *"Geistzerstäuber" Rundfunk*, 44ff., 138ff., 443ff.; Stoffels, *Kulturfaktor*, 637ff.; Renate Schumacher, "Radio als Vermittlung von Gegensätzen," in Leonhard, *Programmgeschichte*, vol. 2., 1196-1208, here 1196ff.; Dussel, *Deutsche Rundfunkgeschichte*, 66f.
44. Projektgruppe Programmgeschichte, "Hörfunk als neues Medium. Vor einer Programmgeschichte des Rundfunks in der Weimarer Republik," in *Materialien zur Rundfunkgeschichte*, vol. 2, ed. Deutsches Rundfunkarchiv (Frankfurt am Main, 1986), 153-251; see 211.
45. Cited from Stoffels, *Kulturfaktor*, 635.
46. Cited from ibid., 630.
47. For the concept of media dispositives, see Lenk, *Die Erscheinung des Rundfunks*.
48. I understand entertainment in modern popular culture to be a practice of aesthetic experience in John Dewey's sense of the term. See John Dewey, *Art as Experience* (New York, 1958); Richard Shusterman, *Pragmatist Aesthetics. Living Beauty, Rethinking Art* (Cambridge, Mass., 1992). For a stimulating definition of the aesthetic qualities of entertainment, see also Hans-Otto Hügel, "Ästhetische Zweideutigkeit der Unterhaltung. Eine Skizze ihrer Theorie," in *montage/av* 2, no. 1 (1993): 119-41.
49. See Ansgar Diller, *Rundfunkpolitik im Dritten Reich* (Munich, 1980).
50. Konrad Dussel, "Kulturkonzepte im Konflikt. Britische, deutsche und schweizerische Hörfunkprogramme während des Zweiten Weltkriegs," in *Vierteljahreshefte für Zeitgeschichte* 49 (2001): 441-63, quote 441; idem, *Deutsche Rundfunkgeschichte*, 89ff.
51. See Nanny Drechsler, *Die Funktion der Musik im deutschen Rundfunk 1933-1945* (Pfaffenweiler, 1988), 33, 44.
52. Heinz Boberach, ed., *Meldungen aus dem Reich 1938-1945. Die geheimen Lageberichte des Sicherheitsdienstes der SS*, vol. 8 (Herrsching, 1984), 2931; quotes from the instructions for programming after Dussel, *Deutsche Rundfunkgeschichte*, 102.
53. Dussel, "Kulturkonzepte im Konflikt," 450.
54. See Asa Briggs, *The War of Words. The History of Broadcasting in the United Kingdom*, vol. 3 (London, 1970), 46f., 126ff., passim; Dussel, "Kulturkonzepte im Konflikt."
55. Hans Hinkel (head of the programming committee of the *Reichsrundfunk*), letter of 30 March 1943, quoted in Drechsler, *Die Funktion der Musik*, 131.
56. Dussel, "Kulturkonzepte im Konflikt," esp. 460f.
57. See for example Konrad Dussel, "Rundfunkgeschichte—Mediengeschichte—Zeitgeschichte. Der Rundfunk und die Entwicklung der westdeutschen Gesellschaft," in *Radiozeiten. Herrschaft, Alltag, Gesellschaft (1924-1960)*, Inge Marßolek and Adelheid von Saldern, eds. (Potsdam, 1999), 39-56; Marßolek, "Radio in Deutschland"; Hans J. Kleinsteuber and Barbara Thomaß, "Der deutsche Rundfunk auf internationaler Ebene," in Schwarzkopf, *Rundfunkpolitik*, vol. 2, 1008-1071.
58. The BBC, which started a third channel with a clear focus on high culture in the 1950s in addition to their "Light Programme" (which had developed out of the "Forces Pro-

gramme"), provided important impetus for this development (Dussel, *Deutsche Rundfunkgeschichte,* 209ff.).
59. Manfred Jenke, "Hörfunk im Wettbewerb," in Schwarzkopf, *Rundfunkpolitik,* vol. 2, 643-700, see 650.
60. Henning Wicht (radio director, or *Hörfunkdirektor,* of Hessian Broadcasting), "Der Hörfunk im Zeitalter des Fernsehens," in ARD-Jahrbuch 1969, 63-70; reprinted in Dussel and Lersch, *Quellen zur Programmgeschichte,* see 288.
61. Walter von Cube, "'Bayern 3'. Ein Hörfunkprogramm für Autofahrer," in ARD-Jahrbuch 1972, 63-65; reprinted in Dussel and Lersch, *Quellen zur Programmgeschichte,* see 294, 296.
62. Konrad Dussel, "Deutsches Radio, deutsche Kultur. Hörfunkprogramme als Indikatoren kulturellen Wandels," in *Archiv für Sozialgeschichte* 41 (2001): 119-44, here 141. Hickethier (*Dispositiv Fernsehen,* 225, 236; *Geschichte des deutschen Fernsehens,* 341) also notes a long-term reorientation toward entertainment and fiction in public television; however, he sees the point at which it switches over at the end of the 1970s and emphasizes the anticipation of commercial competition.
63. The closest any one came were a few voices in the Social Democratic party with understanding for the wish for lighter material; cf. Penka, *"Geistzerstäuber" Rundfunk,* 305f.
64. Axel Schildt, "Hegemon der häuslichen Freizeit: Rundfunk in den 50er Jahren," in *Modernisierung im Wiederaufbau. Die westdeutsche Gesellschaft der 50er Jahre,* Axel Schildt and Arnold Sywottek, eds. (Bonn, 1993), 458-76.
65. See Dussel, "Deutsches Radio," 139.
66. For the following, I rely primarily on Krewani, "Amerikanisierung am Nachmittag."
67. Heike Klippel, "'Von Grund auf dumm'. Zur Kritik amerikanischer Serien in den Fachkorrespondenzen," in Schneider, *Amerikanische Einstellung,* 224-44, see 241. Spot checks among the data of audience polls taken by "Infratestest" and "Infratam" from 1961 to 1965 seem to confirm the attractiveness of American television series.
68. Schneider, "Ein Weg zur Alltäglichkeit," 272ff.
69. See Joseph Garncarz, "Hollywood in Germany. Die Rolle des amerikanischen Films in Deutschland: 1925-1990," in *Der deutsche Film. Aspekte seiner Geschichte von den Anfängen bis zur Gegenwart,* ed. Uli Jung (Trier, 1993), 167-213.
70. See Albrecht Göschel, *Die Ungleichzeitigkeit in der Kultur. Wandel des Kulturbegriffs in vier Generationen* (Stuttgart, 1991).
71. Maase, "'Gemeinkultur'"; idem: *Grenzenloses Vergnügen. Der Aufstieg der Massenkultur 1850-1970* (Frankfurt am Main, 1997), 248-69.
72. Good overviews of this topic in Anselm Doering-Manteuffel, "Dimensionen von Amerikanisierung in der deutschen Gesellschaft," in *Archiv für Sozialgeschichte* 35 (1995): 1-34; Philipp Gassert, "Amerikanismus, Antiamerikanismus, Amerikanisierung. Neue Literatur zur Sozial-, Wirtschafts- und Kulturgeschichte des amerikanischen Einflusses in Deutschland und Europa," in *Archiv für Sozialgeschichte* 39 (1999): 531-61; Bernd Greiner, "'Test the West'. Über die 'Amerikanisierung' der Bundesrepublik Deutschland," in *Westbindungen. Amerika in der Bundesrepublik,* Heinz Bude and Bernd Greiner, eds. (Hamburg, 1999), 16-54; Axel Schildt, "Sind die Westdeutschen amerikanisiert worden?" in *Aus Politik und Zeitgeschichte* 50 (2000): 3-10; Heide Fehrenbach and Uta G. Poiger, "Introduction: Americanization reconsidered," in *Transactions, Transgressions, Transformations. American Culture in Western Europe and Japan,* Fehrenbach and Poiger, eds. (New York, 2000), XIII-XL; Rob Kroes, *If You've Seen One, You've Seen the Mall* (Urbana, 1996).

73. I understand modernization here to be a complex of social changes triggered by the striving toward a more effective industrial-capitalist economy within the sphere of influence of "occidental rationalism" (Max Weber).
74. Dieter and Karin Claessens, *Kapitalismus als Kultur. Entstehung und Grundlagen der bürgerlichen Gesellschaft* (Duesseldorf, 1973).
75. Whereas in indubitably western capitalist Switzerland the conventional "European" educational paradigm was maintained; see Dussel, "Kulturkonzepte im Konflikt."
76. Cf. studies from very different perspectives: Dussel, "Deutsches Radio"; Kerstin Barndt, *Sentiment und Sachlichkeit. Der Roman der Neuen Frau in der Weimarer Republik* (Cologne, 2001); Panajotis Kondylis, *Der Niedergang der bürgerlichen Denk- und Lebensform. Die liberale Moderne und die massendemokratische Postmoderne* (Weinheim, 1991); D.L. LeMahieu, *A Culture for Democracy. Mass Communication and the Cultivated Mind in Britain between the Wars* (Oxford, 1988); Jim Cullen, *The Art of Democracy. A Concise History of Popular Culture in the United States* (New York, 1996). Kaspar Maase, "Establishing Cultural Democracy: Youth, 'Americanization', and the Irresistible Rise of Popular Culture," in *The Miracle Years: A Cultural History of West Germany, 1949–1968*, ed. Hanna Schissler (Princeton, 2001), 428-50; Maase, *Grenzenloses Vergnügen*.
77. See Johannes Paulmann, "Internationaler Vergleich und interkultureller Transfer. Zwei Forschungsansätze zur europäischen Geschichte des 18. bis 20. Jahrhunderts," in *Historische Zeitschrift* 267 (1998): 649-85.
78. See for example Junker, "Politik, Sicherheit, Wirtschaft," 48, and Axel Schildt, "Vom politischen Programm zur Populärkultur: Amerikanisierung in Westdeutschland," in Junker, *Die USA und Deutschland*, 955-65, here 960ff.; Schildt, "Sind die Westdeutschen." See in comparison Kaspar Maase's *BRAVO Amerika. Erkundungen zur Jugendkultur in der Bundesrepublik der fünfziger Jahre* (Hamburg, 1992), 19, 231, passim, and "Amerikanisierung von unten. Demonstrative Vulgarität und kulturelle Hegemonie in der Bundesrepublik der 50er Jahre" in Lüdtke, Marßolek, and Saldern, *Amerikanisierung*, 291-313.
79. Junker, "Politik, Sicherheit, Wirtschaft," 48, emphasis mine.
80. See Kaspar Maase, "'Americanization,' 'Americanness' and 'Americanisms': Time for a Change in Perspective?" Paper presented at the conference of the German Historical Institute, Washington, D.C., March 25-27, 1999. Available at: <http://www.ghi-dc.org/conpotweb/westernpapers/maase>.
81. Not until the 1980s did the professional critique begin to deal with US television series in a less prejudiced, and aesthetically and analytically more appropriate, manner; see Klippel, "Von Grund auf dumm," in Schneider, *Amerikanische Einstellung*.
82. Appadurai points out the new role that imagination plays as a medium of social orientation in a globalizing world. The masses use the cultural flow of emerging "mediascapes" without concrete location. Here, "the United States is no longer the puppeteer of a world system of images, but is only one node of a complex transnational construction of imaginary landscapes"; Arjun Appadurai, "Disjuncture and Difference in the Global Cultural Economy," in *Public Culture* 2, no. 2 (1990): 1-24, quote from 4.
83. Victoria de Grazia, "Americanism for Export," in *Wedge* (July/August 1985): 74-81, quote from 74; thanks to Maria Höhn for the copy of the article. See also idem, "Mass Culture and Sovereignty: The American Challenge to European Cinemas, 1920-1960," in *The Journal of Modern History* 61, no. 1 (1989): 53-87, esp. 53ff.
84. Maase, *BRAVO*.
85. Berndt Ostendorf, "Why Is American Popular Culture so Popular? A View from Europe," in *Amerikastudien / American Studies* 46, no. 3 (2001): 339-66, quote from 345.

86. Fluck, "'Amerikanisierung der Kultur,'" 44. On the development of an aesthetic "universal language" in American series and movies linked to an internationally widespread knowledge of schemes and patterns of narration and narrative patterns of expectation, see Irmela Schneider, "Vom Sunset Strip zur Southfork Ranch. Wege der amerikanischen Serie zum deutschen Publikum," in *Amerikanische Einstellung*, ed. Schneider, 96-135, here 102f.; Schneider, "Ein Weg zur Alltäglichkeit," 276ff.
87. Miriam Bratu Hansen, "The mass production of the senses: classical cinema as vernacular modernism," in *Reinventing Film Studies*, Christine Gledhill and Linda Williams, eds. (London, 2000), 332-50, quote from 341.
88. Ernst Bloch, "Über Märchen, Kolportage und Sage," in idem, *Erbschaft dieser Zeit* [1935], (Frankfurt am Main, 1962), 168-86; cf. Gert Ueding, *Glanzvolles Elend. Versuch über Kitsch und Kolportage* (Frankfurt am Main, 1973).

LEARNING FROM AMERICA
Reconstructing "Race" in Postwar Germany

◆ ◆ ◆

Heide Fehrenbach

Over the past few decades, a vast historical literature has grown up around the attempt to understand various dimensions of the state-sponsored program of murderous racism enacted in National Socialist Germany. In view of the intense scrutiny that historians have devoted to the racist ideology and policies of the Third Reich, it is striking that more attention has not been devoted to the postwar *devolution* of the Nazi "racial state"—particularly given the recent boom in the study of its successor states.[1] Historical studies of the postwar Germanys tend not to be conceptualized around the general category of "race" but rather explore the more narrowly defined phenomena of anti-Semitism or state policies towards, and social experiences of, specific minority groups, such as Jews, ethnic German refugees, migrant ("guest") workers, or asylum-seekers. This tendency, I would argue, is largely unrelated to the current critical practice of dismissing the scientific basis—if not the historical and social salience—of race by positing it as a fictional, if intensely ideological, construct. Rather, it is the more direct result of historical inquiry responding to the language contained in the primary sources. During the Nazi period, racial difference was expressed through terminology such as "*Rasse*," "*Blut*," "*Erbe*," and historians have organized their research around the exploration of such conceptual categories. While postwar references to these concepts were not completely absent, especially in the first decade or so after the war, the public invocation of race became taboo. Over the course of the 1950s, there was a gradual shift away from public discussions of *Rasse* in favor of *Andersartigkeit* (difference) and more recently *Andersaussehen* (looking different) in the Federal Republic.[2] In the Democratic Republic, socialist

---

Notes for this section begin on page 121.

ideology declared *Rasse* an extinct category of social classification and excised it from official rhetoric. Each Germany declared the concept inconsistent with their founding documents (the Basic Law in the west) or doctrines (socialism in the east). Strikingly, this erasure of race has been echoed in the historical scholarship on the period.

Racialist thinking, however, did not disappear with the Nazi regime. The language and ideology of race underwent fundamental changes after 1945, yet the social landscape and national imaginary of both postwar Germanys remained highly racialized, if in ways distinct from the interwar and wartime years. The postwar years mark a period of crucial transition, as military defeat, occupation, and the Cold War mandated a rethinking of the fit between race and nation in the emerging democratic and socialist societies of West and East Germany.

At the level of political and governmental institutions, the issue is straightforward: the National Socialist state ceased to exist by Allied dictate. But the fact of the Nazi state's demise tells us nothing about the social and cultural dimensions of racial reconstruction after 1945. What were the specific processes by which the notion of race was reformulated and enacted in social policy, scientific studies, media representations, or even in informal social encounters? Historical research into these issues remains in its infancy.[3]

This essay examines responses to black "occupation children" (the so-called *farbige Besatzungskinder, farbige Mischlingskinder,* or *Negermischlingskinder*) in western Germany in order to explore some specific ways that race was rearticulated after 1945. Although the offspring of white German women and Allied occupation soldiers of color numbered only 3,000 in 1950, they were cast as a significant minority and social problem in an incessant stream of press coverage, scholarly studies, social welfare and education reports, and two official censuses in the Adenauer period. As a result, the children were accorded a symbolic significance in West Germany far out of proportion to their small numbers.[4] In this essay, I examine why this was the case. My intention is not merely to chronicle a discrete, if interesting, episode in postwar German history. Rather, I want to suggest that postwar responses to black German children played a crucial role in racial reconstruction after 1945 precisely because they helped constitute postwar understandings of the fit between race and national belonging and did this with strategic and sustained reference to the United States.[5]

Zones of Contact

The military zones of occupation were, from their very beginnings, zones of social and cultural contact between occupiers and occupied, and as such constituted informal sites of racial reeducation. German commentators were quick to criticize German women's fraternization with occupation troops as dishonorable and disloyal to Germany and its former soldiers. But the most vociferous condemnation was targeted at interracial sex and reproduction between Allied troops of color and white German women. The victims of coercive sex were forgiven and during the first year of occupation were extended the possibility of abortion.[6] Rape narratives entered the postwar public culture as allegories of collective German victimization.[7] Consensual interracial sex, however, was a different matter. With its increasing incidence (even after the worst of the "hunger years"), German women were denounced as willful traitors—the dregs of German femininity who selfishly indulged their transgressive sexual pleasures and materialist cravings at the expense of German men, German honor, and the German nation.[8] Women who fraternized with black troops were assumed to be prostitutes and from the lowest social classes (although the majority were not) and therefore, by definition, outside of the boundaries of respectable German femininity. In a period characterized by nonpartisan commitment to normalized gender relations and the restoration of the (white) patriarchal family, the mothers of interracial children were denounced as the unacceptable and immoral anti-norm.[9]

Of course, one can attribute such responses to a continuation of German racism from the pre-1945 period, which no doubt they were. But of interest to this discussion is the fact that antiblack racism was reinforced by the parallel responses of white American occupation troops to interracial dating and reproduction in defeated Germany. Ample evidence suggests that many white US soldiers overtly resented fraternization between their own black troops and white German women—and sometimes expressed their displeasure with violence. Antiblack racism, moreover, was condoned, and indeed institutionalized, by the US military and its officers in segregated troop and work assignments, as well as living quarters, mess halls, and leisure facilities—but also more informally in commanding officers' marked reluctance to approve black soldiers' requests to marry white German women (once marriage was permitted between occupation personnel and native Germans) after 1947.[10] Such racist displays were noticed by Germans, who commented on the irony of being democratized and reeducated by a nation with a Jim Crow army and a host of antimiscegenation laws at home.[11]

This is not to suggest that postwar Germans learned antiblack racism from American occupiers, since Germans already had a long tradition of such bigotry that predated, and was intensified by, Germany's short stint as a colonial power prior to 1918. Rather, the point is that, at the level of the street, Germans were absorbing the postwar lesson (inadvertently taught by their new masters) that democratic forms and values were consistent with racialist, and even racist, ideology and social organization. During the occupation, then, white supremacy—one might even say white Christian supremacy—informally emerged as a shared value of mainstream American and German cultures.[12]

Black Americans, of course, had long since learned the unhappy lesson of their subordinate status in the United States. But one of the surprises of intercultural contact in occupied Germany was reserved for African-American soldiers, who generally experienced their stay in this formerly fascist country as unexpectedly liberating. They commented upon the striking absence of racism in German society: the relative friendliness of the German population and their ability to move about without undue restriction and to socialize with anyone they pleased without the imminent threat of lynching. As a 1946 report in the African-American magazine *Ebony* put it:

> Strangely enough, here where once Aryanism ruled supreme, Negroes are finding more friendship, more respect and more equality than they would back home either in Dixie or on Broadway.... Race hate has faded with better acquaintance and interracialism in Berlin flourishes. Many of the Negro GIs in the German capital are from the South and find that democracy has more meaning on Wilhelmstrasse than on Beale Street in Memphis.[13]

Of course much of this German response can be attributed to African-American soldiers' stature as representatives of a victorious occupying power. But their reception in defeated Germany nonetheless departed significantly from their social position and experience in the United States, and was a happy novelty for many of the men—some of whom expressed their intention to stay in Germany after their tours of duty ended. In fact, Germany's reputation as a desirable place to be stationed spread among African-American troops, and it remained a sought-after assignment throughout the American civil rights era.[14]

Such assessments are relative, of course, and therefore implicitly critical of the comparatively more dangerous ways that racism was mobilized and expressed in the United States than in occupied Germany. In his book *Desegregation of the U.S. Armed Forces*, for example, historian Richard Dalfiume quoted a letter written in 1946 to Dwight D. Eisenhower by an "indignant former national commander of the American Legion" after he saw a photo of a black GI fraternizing with a white German woman:

> My dear General, I do not know ... where these negroes come from, but it is certain that if they expect to be returned to the [U.S.] South, they very likely are on the way to be hanged or burned alive at public lynchings by the white men of the South.[15]

African-American soldiers' positive response to Germany does not indicate that Germany had been transformed overnight into a racial paradise; it was not. Rather, the soldiers indicated a heightened sense of personal safety and freedom of movement and association. One might also add that, as members of a well-paid US military, they enjoyed an elevated economic status and sociopolitical power vis-à-vis ordinary Germans. Yet these benefits had their downside as well, and during the occupation years, African-American soldiers attracted the resentment of white German men and white American soldiers as competitors for white German women, precisely because they had the opportunity and the means to attract and court them.

Thus, "blackness" became a significant referent for postwar German definitions of race in the first decade and a half after the war and, for various reasons, this focus on "blackness" echoed the simplified black-white binary that had emerged in the United States over the course of the 1940s and came to characterize American definitions of race in the postwar period. In making this point, I am not arguing that a wholesale "Americanization" of German racial ideologies and race relations took place between 1945 and 1960. Rather, I want to suggest that various West Germans of the period quite consciously worked to Americanize the postwar German problem of race in order to pursue specific strategic political and social agendas.

The disproportionate German focus on blackness in the postwar period was tied first and foremost to the fact of foreign occupation and to the presence and heightened social profile of black Allied, and especially African-American, troops. It was also connected to the consequent postwar increase in interracial (black-white) relations and reproduction and to the progeny of such unions, which resulted in a small postwar population of black German children.

Mischlingskinder and the Postwar Taxonomy of Race

Part of a larger group of "occupation children" ("*Besatzungskinder*") born to German mothers and Allied soldiers after 1945, interracial children were widely characterized in official and popular parlance as "*Mischlinge*" or "*Mischlingskinder.*" The use of this term is significant. It was employed as a legal classification during the Third Reich to demote German citizens to subjects on the basis of race. The uncontested retention of this term after 1945 was surprising; nonetheless, its meaning had changed. First, it was stripped of legal significance and returned to its pre-1935 use as social marker. Second, while it was earlier applied primarily to the children of Christian-Jewish unions, after 1945 this usage was dropped, and *Mischling* was employed exclusively to designate German children of colored foreign paternity, usually African or African American, but also occasionally Puerto Rican or French Indochinese. Thus the term marked the children's racial and national difference from white German children.

There was, however, one hitch: the children were not foreign. Because of their out-of-wedlock births, black German children inherited their mothers' German citizenship.[16] Their nationality was legally unambiguous. However, continued attention to their paternity and putative phenotypical foreignness fueled discussions regarding their social identity and national belonging throughout the 1950s.

An important factor accounting for black German children's significance after 1945 is that this was a juvenile population of German citizens subject to the control, and in some cases under the legal guardianship (*Vormundschaft*) of West German authorities. In this way, they differed from the majority of the postwar Jewish population in West German territory, who, as displaced persons, were subject to Allied supervision. In the case of the offspring of occupation soldiers, Allied officials made it clear that care of the children was a German responsibility. In the American zone, paternity suits were not entertained. As a result, German official and academic response to the children differed in kind from their response to other minorities and especially Jews. The children—as a subgroup of "occupation children"—were the subject of two official censuses (by the West German *Länder* in 1950 and the federal Ministry of the Interior in 1954/55) and were singled out for a series of anthropological, psychological, and educational studies of the sort that would be unimaginable if conducted on Jews, Slavs, or so-called Gypsies—groups, that is, who had been targeted for sterilization or extermination on the basis of race under the Nazi regime.[17]

After 1945, black/colored (*Neger/farbige*) heredity, rather than Jewish heredity, was labeled, understood, and investigated in racial terms. In official and semiofficial discourses of social policy and scientific study, the notion of race became inscribed as blackness/color.[18] This is not to say that anti-Semitism disappeared from West German life or that Jews and other "white" European minorities were not still perceived as distinct races by postwar West Germans. Ample evidence exists to suggest that they were.[19] Rather, West German social policy and academic scholarship of the 1950s did not authorize defining those differences as racial. In this sense, postwar West German definitions of race paralleled those of the postwar United States, where, during the 1940s, social scientists "softened" the differences among whites of European origin (including, in particular, Jews) to a cultural one and conceived of these groups in terms of "ethnicity." Race, as a concept, continued to be employed but was reduced to the radically simplified terms of the black-white binary—or at its most articulated, the black-white-yellow triad—thus redrawing the lines of meaningful difference according to a stereotypical phenotype. One finds, then, at least in the 1950s, a confluence of the broad forms of racial taxonomy in both West Germany and the United States.

Within a few years of the creation of the West German state, moreover, the increased attention to postwar *Mischlingskinder* created a certain typology, or better said, mythology. As censuses by state and federal interior ministries established the statistical dominance of American paternity among occupation children, *Mischlingskinder* were increasingly discussed as the offspring of African-American soldiers. This had the effect of erasing the range of national and ethnic affiliation of the individual fathers (who hailed from such diverse places as Morocco, Senegal, French Indochina, Chicago, Alabama, and Puerto Rico), both in the domain of media coverage and also increasingly among state officials and social workers who dealt with youth issues. Two important consequences of this genealogical imprecision was that, as race in West Germany became identified with blackness (rather than Jewishness), blackness became identified with African-American paternity, and the children were assigned a homogenous racialized group identity. The problem of race came to be embodied by the *Mischlingskind* and linked to America.[20] As a result, contemporaries actually made the astounding claim that the "*Rassenproblem*"—by which they meant both racial difference and racial prejudice—were postwar imports of US origin. By 1952, as the oldest of their cohort were entering West German schools, black occupation children were singled out in official and scholarly discourses as posing a historically unique social challenge to the recently democratized German state. Both the children and the postwar problem of race had been literally "Americanized" in West German official and media representations. Not surprisingly, perhaps, with the end of military occupation, West German officials and social workers began to advocate that the postwar race problem be solved by "returning" the children to the United States via international adoption to black American families there.

Learning from America

These reformulations of notions of race after 1945 did not happen in a vacuum; rather, they were shaped by transnational impulses and interactions between Americans and Germans. While I cannot address the full range and complexity of transnational influences in this short essay, I would like to locate some important "contact points" between Americans and Germans in order to give some indication of the processes by which racial reconstruction occurred.

I have already indicated that white Germans quickly extended to interracial occupation children a symbolic significance that greatly outweighed their small numbers. This was because they were viewed as the physical manifestation of a humiliating defeat and occupation, displaced German masculinity and weakened German patriarchy, and the offspring of traitorous German women, who, through their fraternization with black troops, transgressed national and racial boundaries, as well as the deeply held moral values upon which these were based.[21] Within narrow national history and mythology, the children were negative signifiers of loss, trauma, and pollution.

What was unexpected for West German officials and social workers after 1949 was that the children would have heightened symbolic value for segments of the American population as well. After all, during the occupation, American military government officials had prohibited German state youth and welfare offices in their zone from surveying the numbers of occupation children, regardless of race. The reasons for this policy included a determination to avoid embarrassing negative publicity regarding the moral behavior of American troops abroad as well as an unwillingness to recognize paternity and child support suits when sexual relations resulted in out-of-wedlock births.[22] Despite official reticence to draw attention to such issues, the American press prominently featured articles on occupation children, including the so-called brown babies, in popular magazines like *Newsweek, The Survey, U.S. News and World Report,* and *Ebony*.[23]

More central for this discussion, however, is that direct institutional contacts were forged between American organizations and West Germans. A significant example of this in the postwar period was the creation of the *Gesellschaft für Christlich-Jüdische Zusammenarbeit* (Society for Christian-Jewish Cooperation), which was modeled on the National Council of Christians and Jews founded in the interwar United States to fight anti-Semitism and the racist violence of the Ku-Klux-Klan. After World War II, in response to the murderous racism of National Socialist Germany, the initiative was exported, and the International Council of Christians and Jews was founded in 1946 and 1947 in England, France, and Switzerland. By mid-1948, a US representative of the National Council of Christians and Jews, Minnesota minister Carl Zietlow, with the official support of Lucius Clay and the US military government, recruited Germans to establish branches in Munich, Wiesbaden, Frankfurt, Stuttgart, Berlin, and other German cities in order to lead the fight against racial discrimination and anti-Semitism, and to foster tolerance and interconfessional understanding in postwar Germany. Over the course of the next two years, the American patrons of the *Gesellschaft* pushed the German branches to broaden their aims, encouraging them to counter all forms of prejudice and to cultivate a broad sense of humanism and brotherhood among all peoples of the world. By 1950, the American president of the National Council of Christians and Jews, Everett Clincy, founded the international organization World Brotherhood, headquartered in New York City, in order to further these goals by centralizing what had been nationally based initiatives under American leadership. This organizational and ideological refashioning appears to have been a strategy for transmitting American values and enhancing US influence abroad in response to the new challenges posed by decolonization and Cold War. Some of the German branches of the *Gesellschaft* affiliated themselves with World Brotherhood, while others, including the West German *Koordinierungsrat* (Coordinating Council), resisted surrendering their autonomy.[24]

Despite the varied responses by German branches after 1950, one notes several noteworthy consequences of the *Gesellschaft*'s founding. First, it transferred to the Federal Republic the American model of "intergroup relations" that had first emerged in the United States in the 1930s and that sought to counter racism by building viable educational and activist communities across confessional, ethnic, and racial lines. Second, it introduced into West Germany the reigning American social-scientific tool for investigating racism, namely, "prejudice studies," which had important consequences for how race was discussed and understood in the postwar German context.[25]

In fact, the "prejudice studies" approach is evident in the *Gesellschaft*'s engagement with the topic of the *Mischlingskind*. In 1952, the year that postwar black German children began entering German schools, the organization sponsored the publication of a pedagogical pamphlet called *Maxi, unser Negerbub*, which became recommended reading for all West German teachers, and organized a national conference in Wiesbaden for state officials and educators on the "problem of postwar *Mischlingskinder*."[26] These initiatives proved crucial in shaping state and school policies regarding the children and in establishing the ways they would be presented to the public at large as they made their way from the privacy of home to the classroom. Furthermore, they pioneered the principles upon which a liberal discourse of race would be constructed in West Germany.

A primary goal of both the conference and the pamphlet, *Maxi*, was to domesticate postwar interracial children by recasting them as a German problem (rather than an American import) that would require German compassion and solutions. In order to facilitate that aim, German participants of the Wiesbaden conference focused in part on language—what the children should properly be called—and resolved to reject the term "*farbige Besatzungskinder*," which they felt emphasized their foreign paternity, in favor of "*farbige Mischlingskinder.*" While this may have served to nativize the children in terms of nationality, it certainly reproduced earlier taxonomies of essentialized racial difference; nonetheless, it was consistent with American practices of categorizing individuals on the basis of any black heredity (according to the so-called one-drop rule). Additionally, and also consistent with contemporary American practices, German conference participants (and the pamphlet *Maxi*) marked a departure from the German tradition by psychologizing the race problem. Thus, racism began to be understood as a virulent psychological malady that, when acted upon, had serious effects—both for the psychological and emotional health of its target and for society's well-being as a whole.²⁷

Although the stated goal of the *Gesellschaft*'s conference was to facilitate the social acceptance and integration of black German children into West German society, the psychological approach to race and racism could as easily authorize a policy of segregation—something that had in fact been proposed for the children's care and education within West Germany—and their ultimate emigration. German segregationists professed to be motivated by concern for the well-being of the children, who were considered too vulnerable, sensitive, or maladjusted to deal in healthy ways and on a daily basis with their difference from white classmates. As blacks in a fundamentally white society, the children were considered at risk for developing more severe emotional problems, which, it was feared, would culminate in future social alienation or socially pathological behavior, such as licentiousness or criminality, once they approached puberty.²⁸

If the psychological approach to racism and its effects was an American import, it was one of the few popular ones in the 1950s, precisely because of its value in denationalizing the postwar German problem of race. In other words, this explanation construed racism as a function—and a pathology—of human, rather than German, psychology. Racism was universalized as an ahistorical human malady that had plagued all people at all times. So, for example, in the pedagogical pamphlet, *Maxi unser Negerbub,* as the fictional teacher of a black German child researches the problem of prejudice, he finds to his relief:

> a scientific explanation: how prejudice has always existed in the world, how it typically arises, how it functions, what one can do about it. He likes the fact that the many examples that make the book so readable are drawn from outside of Germany. That others can also make mistakes can only reassure us.²⁹

When historical examples were offered, they were situated in the land of Jim Crow. The United States was inscribed as the leading postwar site of racial problems, and racism was reformulated as a problem common to modern Western democracies.³⁰

It seems plausible to argue, then, that postwar reformulations of race assisted in the moral rehabilitation of the West German state and, consequently, in facilitating an emerging identity of interests that coalesced into an Atlantic alliance. As postwar evolved to Cold War, understandings of race were mobilized, at least from the American side, in ways to integrate, rather than isolate, West Germany vis-à-vis the Western allies. This is consistent with the findings of scholars like Mary Dudziak, whose book *Cold War Civil Rights* demonstrates that race was employed strategically by the US government during the Cold War to consolidate spheres of influence at the international level. At the same time, Cold War considerations conditioned official American responses to domestic race relations. Increasingly, concerns about international opinion—how domestic US issues would "play" abroad and whether they could effectively be mobilized as negative propaganda by Cold War enemies—encouraged a more receptive official posture toward civil rights initiatives at home.[31]

Perhaps the most interesting intervention in German debates about postwar *Mischlingskinder* came from the National Association for the Advancement of Colored People (NAACP) and the black American press (such as the glossy monthly *Ebony*, as well as newspapers like *The Chicago Defender*, Baltimore's *Afro-American,* and the *Pittsburgh Courier*). Their attention to the fate of black German children appears initially to have surprised West German officials in federal and state ministries. As had many Germans in the early 1950s, the African-American press and NAACP representatives expressed concern about the fate of black German children in this historically white land and advocated their adoption to the United States. In January 1951, for example, the NAACP (along with representatives of the US Displaced Persons Commission, the Urban League, Child Welfare League, and a variety of American Christian social welfare organizations) formed a committee "to consider … the immigration of … German orphans of Negro Blood."[32] The African-American press also publicized the existence and plight of "Negro German children" and covered the efforts of African-American organizations and individuals to have them adopted in the United States.[33] Such attention resulted in more international contact, as West Germans involved in the care of black German children began appealing to the NAACP and black press directly to seek financial support for the children or assistance in facilitating the children's emigration to the United States.[34]

While concern for the children's welfare was no doubt genuine in most cases, both German officials and African-American activists realized that such international contact and cooperation could also benefit their distinct political agendas. Serving as lobbyists for black German children's interests at home and abroad permitted African-American activists to voice trenchant observations regarding comparative race relations in the postwar United States and West Germany. What is more, these comparisons played to a national, and international, audience of officials and publics. In a press release distributed by the Associated Press in September 1952, for example, Walter White of the NAACP argued that the problem of the black "occupation" child was created by discriminatory official US policies toward their African-American fathers:

> Where other factors were favorable, white soldiers were not only permitted but encouraged to marry the mothers of their children. In the case of Negro soldiers, every

possible obstacle [including the outright refusal of commanding officers] was placed in the path of would-be couples.[35]

The year before, another NAACP representative made a similar point, stating that black occupation children were

> a political problem ... created by the [U.S.] Government's refusal to allow soldiers to marry.... [T]he Government has some responsibility ...[for] these children ... The Negro community would like to know what responsibility would be taken by the Government, and if any effort has been made for a project to bring them to this country.[36]

Expanding the criticism to include popular attitudes, *Ebony* magazine in 1952 pointed to the corrosive international effects of American racism abroad when it noted that "More than one German child has been taught to shout 'nigger bastard' by American soldiers who neglect to tell them the meaning of the words."[37]

From the early 1950s, some representatives of African-American organizations also began to express doubts about the wisdom of encouraging the children's adoption to the United States, given the state of race relations in American society at the time:

> there is a question as to whether German children rejected in their own country because of their color would be any better off in this country. ... There [are] colored children in this country, in Georgia for example, who probably were much worse off than the colored children in Germany.[38]

Writing several months after black German children began entering German schools in 1952, Walter White cast the comparison in even starker terms:

> What is ... immensely significant in view of the racist doctrines of the Nazis is what is now being done in Germany to assimilate these children. ...It was most interesting, in light of the impending argument in the U.S. Supreme Court dealing with segregation in education, that the German teachers who had lived under Hitler voted unanimously that the only right, just, and sensible way to handle the situation is on a basis of full integration and without any kind of segregation based on race. The Bavarian Minister of Education has issued a law to all school superintendents, ... principals, and teachers that Negro children must be fully integrated into the schools, and any practice of segregation based upon race are contrary to policy and will be dealt with accordingly. Somewhat similar steps are beginning to be taken in Japan...
>
> It is significant that these two nations which have recently undergone violent indoctrination in racism appear to have recovered from the virus of racial supremacy to a greater extent than some sections of the United States.[39]

Thus the NAACP's analysis and international engagement on behalf of black occupation children, which was echoed by the African-American press, was grounded in a social critique of racist American culture and practices. By focusing on the comparative national responses to the children and their fathers, moreover, prominent African-American organizations and media exposed the Achilles heel of American race relations and advertised their own just cause of racial equality and black civil rights—along with the pressing need for America's *own* postwar democratization. What is more, they did this in a way that inadvertently highlighted the West German state's impressive moral progress when compared to that of the United States.

By the mid-1950s, West German officials in the federal interior, family, and foreign ministries also began discouraging the adoptions of black German children by families in the United States because of the negative psychological and emotional impact of racial segregation on the children. That is, they began to attend to some of the disturbing issues raised by the NAACP in their consideration of the children's national placement and to investigate the experience of black German children who had been adopted in the United States.[40] While West German officials never convinced themselves that the children were unproblematically German, they did decide that they were more European than American. In the process, they consciously assumed the role of state protector of the postwar *Mischlingskind* and in the process instrumentalized their plight to facilitate the rehabilitation of the West German state. While West German federal and state officials stopped short of engaging in explicit social criticism of their Cold War patron, their actions suggested that the United States had been tested and found wanting on the very principles with which it had come armed to reeducate and democratize Germany. In the short decade since Hitler's defeat, a chastened nation appeared to have surpassed its tutor in the lessons of democracy—and was "credentialed" to that effect by the favorable reviews of African-American organizations and the press.

In the second half of the 1950s, West German commentators continued to discuss the children's integration into West German society, as the oldest black German children approached puberty and graduation from secondary school. But, by the turn of the 1960s, the issue of the children's integration was narrowed to a myopic focus on job placement. Thanks to a strong economy and low unemployment, municipal and state offices reported the ready acceptance of black German youth into apprenticeships and, ultimately, the national workforce by West German employers—thereby conveying the image of a stable and prosperous nation whose bureaucrats and employers operated according to the precepts of social justice and economic rationality. As a result, the specter of racist irrationality was declared banished, but only because "integration" was defined in exclusively economic, rather than broadly social, terms. After judging the integration of *Mischlingskinder* an overwhelming success, official and media attention to the children, as well as the postwar problem of race, sharply subsided in the Federal Republic. The early 1960s initiated a shift in West Germany away from the domestic discussions of race and national belonging that had characterized the 1950s.

Some Reflections on Americanization

In conclusion, I would like to draw three broad lessons from this West German story regarding historical approaches to the problem of Americanization. First, the intense focus on interracial fraternization and reproduction in occupied Germany suggests the central importance of race for evaluating interactions with "America" abroad. This applies not only to the cultural realm, which has been a favorite topic of scholarly investigation, but also at the level of social policy, social criticism, and social change. Informal contacts between occupier and occupied—along with the discriminatory policies of the US military toward its minorities and the tense relations among occupation soldiers of differing ethnicities—affected the ways Germans perceived and received American political and social values after 1945. German understandings of the *content* of "democratization," I would argue, were conditioned by the implicitly racialized *context* within which it was delivered. The transmission of American ideas, values, social policies, and social behaviors was often organized around race-based notions and practices, and this needs more careful investigation by scholars of Germany and Europe more generally, particularly for the period after 1945.

Second, in investigating or invoking the term "Americanization," scholars must guard against treating America, and by extension its cultural, social, political, ideological exports, as unitary or homogenous entities; both of the terms "America" and "Americanization" need to be de-essentialized.[41] As this essay has demonstrated, a productive first step in this process would be to shift analytical attention from the realm of the national (the false unity of America) to the level of the subnational (e.g., the international politics of a self-identified African-American activist community) and the transnational (which would examine not only official US-German interactions in this case, but also informal and semiofficial ones between various constituencies on each side of the Atlantic). The virtue of this approach is to show how complicated and ideologically complex the flow of influences across the Atlantic was: these traveled in both directions at a multiplicity of levels in pursuit of a discernible set of discreet political and social agendas in both the United States and West Germany. Equally significant, this approach shows that the impact of mutual influence was felt in German and American societies: it held out transformative possibilities for both.

Finally, it follows that notion of America needs to be conceptualized as a fluid and evolving—rather than a stable and static—range of influences, projections, and self-understandings. As societies and subnational social groups outside the United States variously absorbed, debated, or decried American influences and exports, Americans at home were simultaneously debating, defending, or challenging the reigning cultural perceptions and social/political practices underlying their country's democracy and the American way of life. In other words, the production and content of America derive from an ongoing social dynamic within the United States and as such are ever open to dispute and revision. The challenge for scholars of Americanization is to recognize this fact and to investigate international engagement with things American in ways that takes into account the fundamental dynamism of America as a referent.

Notes

1. The term "racial state" is borrowed from Michael Burleigh and Wolfgang Wippermann, *The Racial State: Germany, 1933-1945* (New York, 1992).
2. See Tina Campt and Pascal Grosse, "'Mischlingskinder' in Nachkriegsdeutschland: Zum Verhältnis von Psychologie, Anthropologie, und Gesellschaftkritik nach 1945," *Psychologie und Geschichte* 6, no. 1-2 (1994): 48-78; Jeffrey Peck, "Turks and Jews: Comparing Minorities in Germany after the Holocaust," *German Cultures, Foreign Cultures: The Politics of Belonging*, ed. Jeffrey Peck, AICGS Report No. 8, Humanities Program, 1997; and Ruth Mandel, "Turkish Headscarves and the 'Foreigner Problem.' Constructing Difference through Emblems of Identity," *New German Critique* 46 (1989).
3. Some examples of recent scholarship are Frank Stern, *The Whitewashing of the Yellow Badge: Antisemitism and Philosemitism in Postwar Germany* (New York, 1992); Tina Campt, "'Afro-German': The Convergence of Race, Sexuality, and Gender in the Formation of a German Ethnic Identity, 1919-1960" (Ph.D. diss., Cornell University, 1996); Tina Campt, Pascal Grosse, and Yara-Colette Lemke-Muniz de Faria, "Blacks, Germans, and the Politics of the Imperial Imagination, 1920-60," Sara Friedrichsmeyer, Sara Lennox, and Susanne Zantop, eds., *The Imperialist Imagination: German Colonialism and its Legacy* (Ann Arbor, 1998), 205-29; Uta G. Poiger, *Jazz, Rock and Rebels: Cold War Politics and American Culture in a Divided Germany* (Berkeley, 2000); Maria Höhn, *GIs and Fräuleins: The German-American Encounter in 1950s West Germany* (Chapel Hill, 2002); Katrin Sieg, *Ethnic Drag: Performing Race, Nation, Sexuality in West Germany* (Ann Arbor, 2002); and Heide Fehrenbach, "Of German Mothers and 'Negermischlingskinder': Race, Sex, and the Postwar Nation," Hanna Schissler, ed., *The Miracle Years* (Princeton, 2000), 164-86.
4. Although the children comprised only a tiny minority of postwar births, contemporary estimates inflated their numbers to between 10,000 and 950,000, indicating the disproportionate symbolic significance accorded them.

5. In West Germany, the postwar reformulation of race was conditioned in important respects by intense interaction with "America." This took the shape of official and unofficial encounters between Germans and US personnel and organizations, through scholarly contacts and intellectual impulses, through social models, media imports, and cultural consumption. Recent scholarship on these encounters include Volker R. Berghahn, *America and the Intellectual Cold Wars in Europe: Shepard Stone between Philanthropy, Academy, and Diplomacy* (Princeton, 2001); Frank Trommler and Elliott Shore, eds., *The German-American Encounter: Conflict and Cooperation between Two Cultures, 1800-2000* (New York, 2001); Heide Fehrenbach and Uta Poiger, eds. *Transactions, Transgressions, Transformations: American Culture in Western Europe and Japan* (New York, 2000); Jessica C. E. Gienow-Hecht, *Transmission Impossible: American Journalism as Cultural Diplomacy in Postwar Germany, 1945-1955* (Baton Rouge, 1999).

6. Staatsarchiv Augsburg, Nr. 30: Gesundheitsamt Sonthofen, memo from the Bürgermeister des Marktes Sonthofen, regarding "Schwangerschaftsunterbrechung," 7 June 1945; and memo of the Reichsministerium des Innern, "Unterbrechung von Schwangerschaften," 14 March 1945. By 1950/51, Bavarian doctors were ordered to report all miscarriages so that officials could investigate whether the affected women were attempting to pass off an intentional abortion as an "act of God." Staatsarchiv Augsburg, Gesundheitsamt, File 19: Neuberg; and File 91: Nördlingen. For historical background, including interwar attempts to repeal Paragraph 218, see the following two works by Atina Grossmann: *Reforming Sex* (New York, 1995) and "A Question of Silence: The Rape of German Women by Occupation Soldiers," Robert G. Moeller, ed., *West Germany Under Construction: Politics, Society, and Culture in the Adenauer Era* (Ann Arbor, 1997), 33-52. For a discussion of abortion policy in East Germany, see Donna Harsch, "Society, the State, and Abortion in East Germany, 1950-1972," *American Historical Review* 102, no. 3 (February 1997): 53-84.

7. Rudolf Albart, *Die letzten und die ersten Tagen: Bamberger Kriegstagesbuch 1944/46* (Bamburg, 1953); and Hans Rommel, *Vor zehn Jahren. 16.-17. April 1945. Wie es zur Zerstörung von Freudenstadt gekommen ist* (Freudenstadt, 1955). See also Regina Mühlhauser, "Vergewaltigung in Deutschland 1945. Nationaler Opferdiskurs und individuelles Erinnern betroffener Frauen," Klaus Naumann, ed., *Nachkrieg in Deutschland* (Hamburg, 2001), 384-408.

8. For a discussion of how images of women were utilized for postwar German reconstruction see Elizabeth Heinemann, "The Hour of the Women: Memories of Germany's 'Crisis Years' and West German National Identity," *American Historical Review* 101, no. 2 (April 1996): 354-95; Erica Carter, *How German Is She? Postwar West German Reconstruction and the Consuming Woman* (Ann Arbor, 1997); and Fehrenbach, "Of German Mothers"; see also Fehrenbach, *Cinema in Democratizing Germany: Reconstruction National Identity after Hitler* (Chapel Hill, 1995), 92-117, 148-68, and 194-210. On the construction of German masculinity in the 1950s, see the forum on "The Remasculinization of Germany in the 1950s," *Signs: Journal of Women in Culture and Society*, 24, no. 1 (autumn 1998): Robert G. Moeller, Introduction, 101-6; Robert G. Moeller, "'The Last Soldiers of the Great War' and Tales of Family Reunions in the Federal Republic of Germany," 129-45; Uta G. Poiger, "A New 'Western' Hero? Reconstructing German Masculinity in the 1950s," 147-62; and Heide Fehrenbach, "Rehabilitating *Fatherland*: Race and German Remasculinization," 107-28. See also Frank Biess, "Survivors of Totalitarianism: Returning POWs and the Reconstruction of Masculine Citizenship in West Germany, 1945-1955," Schissler, *The Miracle Years*, 57-82; and Frank Biess, "'Pioneers of a New Germany': Returning POWs from the Soviet Union and the Making of East Ger-

man Citizens, 1945-50," *Central European History* (1999); and Uta G. Poiger, "Krise der Männlichkeit: Remaskulinisierung in beiden deutschen Nachkriegsgesellschaften," Klaus Naumann, ed., *Nachkrieg in Deutschland* (Hamburg, 2001), 227-63.
9. For an expanded discussion of this point, see Fehrenbach, "Of German Mothers."
10. Sherie Mershon and Steven Schlossmann, *Foxholes and Color Lines: Desegregating the U.S. Armed Forces* (Baltimore, 1998); Höhn, *GIs and Fräuleins*; National Archives, College Park, Maryland, RG 260: OMGUS circular 18.
11. American occupation officials were not unaware of this irony. The treatment of African-American troops was the subject of media coverage by the black press in the US; in addition, Walter White, as head of the NAACP, toured the European theater of operations and the American zone of occupied Germany in order to meet with black troops and review their living and work conditions first hand, but also to lobby for improvements and for desegregation with occupation officials. See Walter White, *A Rising Wind* (New York, 1945) and "Report of Walter White" to the NAACP Office and Board regarding his trip to Paris and Germany, September-October, 1948. Library of Congress, NAACP Papers, Reel 8: Group II, Series G, Veterans Affairs Files: G11 Folder 1, 1948, July-December 1948.
12. On early American occupation policy regarding Jews, and on postwar German responses to Jews, see Stern, *The Whitewashing of the Yellow Badge;* Julius H. Schoeps, ed., *Leben im Land der Täter. Juden im Nachkriegsdeutschland* (Berlin, 2001); Leslie Morris and Jack Zipes, eds., *Unlikely History: The Changing German-Jewish Symbiosis, 1945-2000* (New York, 2002); and Juliane Wetzel, "An Uneasy Existence: Jewish Survivors in Germany after 1945," in Schissler, *The Miracle Years*, 131-44.
13. "Germany meets the Negro Soldier," *Ebony*, October 1946, 5-10.
14. Historian Lary May mentioned that West Germany was the preferred destination for African-American soldiers he knew in the 1950s (conversation with author, May 1996). See also "Germany meets the Negro Soldier," *Ebony*, 6; David Brion Davis, "The Americanized Mannheim of 1945-46," *American Places: Encounters with History—A Celebration of Sheldon Meyer,* William E. Leuchtenburg, ed. (New York, 2000), 79-91; and Maggi M. Morehouse, *Fighting in the Jim Crow Army: Black Men and Women Remember World War II* (New York, 2000), esp. chapters 5 and 6. For a fictional account of an African-American soldier's experience in occupied Germany by a 21-year-old African-American novelist who served in the military there, see William Gardner Smith, *Last of the Conquerors* (New York, 1948). For discussions of the "African American diaspora" in postwar Europe, and especially Paris, see Tyler Stovall, "Harlem-sur-Seine: Building an African American Diasporic Community in Paris," *Stanford Electronic Humanities Review* 5.2 (1997), available at <www.standord.edu/group/SHR/5-2/Stovall.html>; and James Campbell, *Exiled in Paris: Richard Wright, James Baldwin, Samuel Beckett, and Others on the Left Bank* (New York, 1995).
15. Richard Dalfiume, *Desegregation of the U.S. Armed Forces: Fighting on Two Fronts, 1939-1953* (Columbia, Mo., 1969), 133.
16. While some German state officials informally protested this legal resolution, Allied military government officials made it clear that they would neither entertain paternity suits nor readily grant citizenship to their troops' illegitimate offspring abroad.
17. Walther Kirchner, "Untersuchungen somatischer und psychischer Entwicklung bei Europäer-Neger-Mischlingen im Kleinkindalter under Berücksichtigung der sozialen Verhältnisse," *Studien aus dem Institut für Natur- und Geisteswissenschaftliche Anthropologie*, 1. Berichte (1952): 29-36; W. Kirchner, "Eine anthropologische Studie an Mulattenkindern in Berlin unter Berücksichtigung der sozialen Verhältnisse" (Phil. diss., Freie

Universität Berlin, 1952); Erna Maraun, "Zehn kleine Negerlein," *Der Rundbrief. Fachliches Mitteilungsblatt des Hauptjugendamtes Berlin* 3, no. 1 (1953): 2-6; Rudolf Sieg, *Mischlingskinder in Westdeutschland. Festschrift für Frederic Falkenburger* (Baden-Baden, 1955); Erhard Schneckenburger, "Das Mischlingskind in der Schule," *Neues Beginnen* 1 (1957).

18. On shifts in US understandings of race, see Matthew Frye Jacobsen, *Whiteness of a Different Color: European Immigrants and the Alchemy of Race* (Cambridge, Mass., 1999).
19. I am not addressing popular attitudes in this argument. For a discussion of some of these issues at the grassroots level, see Höhn, *GIs and Fräuleins*.
20. Bundesarchiv Koblenz (referred to hereafter as BAK), B189: Akten des Bundesministeriums für Jugend und Familie, 6858, 6859, 6861; and BAK, B153: Bundesministerium für Familien- und Jugendfragen, File 1335, I-II; also Hauptstaatsarchiv Stuttgart (referred to hereafter as HStAStg), EA2/007, Akten des Innenministeriums Baden-Württemberg, Nr. 1177: "Jugendwohlfahrt: Statistik und Unterhalt der unehelich geborenen Kinder..., 1951-55"; HStAStg, EA2/008, Akten des Innenministeriums, Nr. 1176, "Jugendwohlfahrt: Unterhalt für uneheliche Kinder - Unterhaltsverpflichtung von Mitgliedern ausländischen Streitkräfte (1955-70)"; and Bayerisches Hauptstaatsarchiv (BayHStA), Ministerium des Innerns (MInn) 81087, "Verfolgung von Unterhaltsansprüchen gegen Angehörige von ausländischen Streitkräften - Pariser Verträge, 1955-57."
21. See Fehrenbach, "Rehabilitating Father*land*" and "Of German Mothers."
22. HStAStg, EA2/007: Akten des Innenministeriums Baden-Württemberg, memo dated 14 January 1947, also "Vorbemerkung" from 7 February 1947.
23. For example, James P. O'Donnell, "Occupation: The GI Legacy in Germany," *Newsweek*, 16 June 1947, 48-50; Vernon W. Stone, "German Baby Crop left by GIs," *The Survey*, November 1949, 579-83; "Unsolved Problem of War – 400,000 Babies Left Behind," *U.S. News and World Report*, 23 November 1955, 10-11; Erich Lissner, "We Adopted a Brown Baby," *Ebony*, May 1953, 37-45; "Children Nobody Wants," *Ebony*, May 1959, 59-61; "Big Brother to Brown Babies," *Ebony*, October 1959, 34-37; "Brown Babies Go to Work," *Ebony*, November 1960, 97-108.
24. Josef Foschepoth, *Im Schatten der Vergangenheit. Die Anfänge der Gesellschaft für Christlich-Jüdische Zusammenarbeit* (Göttingen, 1993), 155-203.
25. For discussions of these developments in the United States, see Stuart Svonkin, *Jews against Prejudice: American Jews and the Fight for Civil Liberties* (New York, 1997).
26. Alfons Simon, *Maxi, unser Negerbub* (Bremen, 1952). For an analysis of the pamphlet *Maxi*, see Fehrenbach, "Of German Mothers." For a general discussion of the *Gesellschaft*'s activities in the early postwar period, see Stern, *The Whitewashing of the Yellow Badge*, 310-34, and Foschepoth, *Im Schatten der Vergangenheit*.
27. For a discussion of this phenomenon in the US, see Svonkin, *Jews against Prejudice*; Daryl Michael Scott, *Contempt and Pity: Social Policy and the Image of the Damaged Black Psyche, 1880-1996* (Chapel Hill, 1997); and Ruth Feldstein, *Motherhood in Black and White: Race and Sex in American Liberalism, 1930-1945* (Ithaca, 2000).
28. See for example Wilhelmine Hollweg, "Ohne Ansehen der Rasse...," *DPWV-Nachrichten* 5, no. 6 (June 1955): 2-3, a clipping of which was filed in BAK, B153/342. Also "Zur Frage der Aufnahme farbiger Kinder in Heimen," *Unsere Jugend* 5, no. 8 (August 1953): 376-77; Hans Pfaffenberger, "Farbige Kinder im Heim—ein Prüfstein," *Unsere Jugend* 5, no. 12 (December 1953): 533-36; and the anthropological studies by Kirchner and Sieg.
29. Simon, *Maxi, unser Negerbub*, 18.
30. Simon opens the book by having his fictional teacher, Herr Schmidt, reflect on race, which he first associates with Jews. When his mind settles on the "*Negerfrage*," or "Negro

problem," his first thoughts are of the American South and reading newspaper reports of yet another "negro lynching." Simon, *Maxi, unser Negerbub*, 7.
31. In October 1947, in fact, the NAACP presented a petition to the United Nations titled "An appeal to the world." In it, the NAACP denounced US race discrimination as "barbaric" and asserted that it was "not Russia that threatens the U.S. as much as Mississippi." See Mary Dudziak, *Cold War Civil Rights* (Princeton, 2000), 44-45.
32. "Meeting of the Committee to consider … the Immigration of…German orphans of Negro Blood," 29 January 1951, NAACP papers, Reel 8: Group II, Box G11, "Brown Babies, 1950-58."
33. In 1951-1952, the Baltimore newspaper *Afro-American* advertised and covered the facilitation of adoptions of black German children to African-American families. See also "German War Babies," *Ebony* (January 1951): 35-38; Allan Gould, "Germany's Tragic War Babies," *Ebony* (December 1952): 74-78; Pearl S. Buck, "Should White Parents Adopt Brown Babies?," *Ebony* (June 1958): 26-34.
34. Letters from Frau Dilloo, founder of the "Albert Schweizer Kinderheim" and from Frau Maya Angowski, head of the "Hilfsorganization 'Das Besatzungskind,'" e.V. in Munich from 18 May 1954, who later founded the first German Branch of the NAACP there. NAACP papers, Reel 8: Group II, Box G11, "Brown Babies, 1950-58."
35. Walter White Press Release, NAACP Papers, Reel 8: Group II, Box G11 "Brown Babies 1950-58."
36. "Meeting of the Committee to consider … the Immigration of … German orphans of Negro Blood," 29 January 1951, NAACP papers, Reel 8: Group II, Box G11, "Brown Babies, 1950-58."
37. Allan Gould, "Germany's Tragic War Babies," 74-78; this quotation from 78.
38. Ibid.
39. Walter White Press Release, NAACP, Reel 8: Group II, Box G11 "Brown Babies 1950-58." Similar points were made in Allan Gould, "Germany's Tragic War Babies."
40. BAK, B153: Bundesministerium für Familien- u. Jugendfragen, file 1335; HstAStg, EA2/007, Nr. 1750: "Vermittlung der Annahme an Kindesstaat—Allgemeines," Band II, 1955-66.
41. See Fehrenbach and Poiger, eds., *Transactions, Transgressions, Transformations*, esp. xiii-xxix.

Part 3

FILM

CINEMATIC AMERICANIZATION OF THE HOLOCAUST IN GERMANY
Whose Memory Is It?

❖ ❖ ❖

David Bathrick

The Americanization of the Holocaust is a subject that has clearly grown into a major sub-industry within Holocaust Studies. This essay seeks to address the issue of cinematic Americanization of the Holocaust as perceived and in some cases contested within a once divided and now united Germany. The choice of the word "contest" seeks to encompass both the verbal articulations on this topic as well as attempts on the part of artists to respond in the form of medial representations. My task more specifically will be to explore the discourse around Americanization of the Holocaust in the light of US films about that event as they have impacted Germany at three junctures between 1945 and 1980. In doing so, I shall focus on the following questions: what have been the salient theoretical issues emerging from critical responses to some of these works? How do they compare to the discussions in the United States? Is there another way of configuring the issue about America's impact on Holocaust representation in Germany?

In mapping out the so-called Americanization of the Holocaust within the framework of the United States, several issues emerge that have been central to the discussions since 1945 and that will also impinge on our treatment of the process in Germany. The first, and perhaps most consuming, set of problems concerns the tensions, contradictions, and even competing narratives that have arisen around this subject among Americans, Jews, and non-Jews alike. On the one hand, we find the destruction of European Jewry under Nazism increasingly being recognized as the defining moment of Jewish-American identity, as a unique event that has helped forge communal mem-

---

Notes for this section begin on page 145.

ory for post-Holocaust generations living in the United States. Sometimes linked to such a view are a whole set of caveats and taboos: concerning the impenetrability of the Shoah as a *mysterium tremendum*; of the impossibility or even impropriety of claiming to understand or represent visually the experiences in the death camps.

Parenthetically, and not always in conflict with the claim for Jewish centrality, is a notion of the Shoah as containing universal meanings beyond the singularity of the event itself; of its Americanization "as having contributed to making the history of this genocide far more accessible and transparent to increasingly larger audiences."[1] In the words of Michael Berenbaum, the US Holocaust Museum's former research director, "the museum will take what could have been the painful and parochial memories of a bereaved ethnic community and apply them to the most basic of American values."[2] Berenbaum appears optimistic about negotiating a balance between Jewish particularism (his term is "parochialism") and the universalist (some say relativist) need to extend the Holocaust discourse to include many different forms of genocidal evil. Alvin H. Rosenfeld, in an article entitled "The Americanization of the Holocaust," is less so, as he wonders how, simply at a narrative level, "any story of the crimes of the Nazi era can remain faithful to the specific features of those events and at the same time address contemporary American social agendas."

A second set of issues, not unrelated to the first, is concerned more specifically with problems of representation. When Paddy Chayesky responded to the scandal surrounding NBC's miniseries *Holocaust* with the single declarative sentence "television is trivialization," he did not do so with the hope of upgrading the aesthetic standards of American television; nor was he thinking only about television as a medium.[3] The trivialization argument concerns itself at a broader level with all that transpires when a subject such as the Holocaust is turned into just another product of American mass consumption. For the selling of the Holocaust, we are told, is more than just the reduction of sacred values to the vulgarities of the market place; it is at the same time, by virtue of its explicit and implicit claim to be able to know and represent, a violation of the experience and memory of those who survived.

Sanctification versus popularization, trivialization, profanation; authentic collective memory in light of its potential erasure through the ideological and economic tenants of the culture industry: such are the discourses that have come to define conceptually some of the debates carried out under the rubric of the Americanization of the Holocaust within the United States. What a treatment of such a topic demands above all is a focus on the changing nature of the issues and their rearticulation: the evolving forms of representation and the role of the viewer; the heightened emphasis upon memory together with fears about its erosion in the contemporary situation; the gradual demise over the years of a primary, survivor generation; the changing notion of regional, national, and global identities. To what extent finally does the rubric "the Americanization of the Holocaust" refer to elements unique to the culture of the United States or the ethnic identity of certain American Jews? Or are we talking about processes of globalization, in which cultural meanings can no longer be meaningfully contained within or limited to discretely national discourses (where, as already in the Germany of the 1920s, the signifier "Americanism" often becomes a stand-in for much that was either problematic or reinvigorating about processes of industrial, social, and cultural modernization in the early stages of the twentieth century)?

The Holocaust before the "Holocaust": 1945

While the word "Holocaust" was not firmly a part of public discourse until the NBC miniseries in 1978, the role of the United States in defining the meaning of the genocide of European Jewry had already begun in 1945. The documentary photos and films of camps such as Buchenwald, Dachau, Bergen-Belsen, Mauthausen, and Ohrdruf by amateur and professional cinematographers fighting with or accompanying the invading allied armies, had a lasting impact on the way the event has been remembered, as well as repressed. While the employment of such materials as part of pedagogical, juridical, and political discourses has been debated over the years, in a broader epistemological sense these camp films have also helped shape questions and issues at the very core of representing this event.[4]

Important to keep in mind as we assess medial representations of the Holocaust is the notion that the photographic image has always been a doubly coded one. On the one hand, we have its function as *index*, which attributes to filmic representation "a material, physical, and thus extremely potent connection between image and referent"[5] As media of technological duplication, photography, and cinema participated in a tradition of nineteenth-century mechanically reproduced mimesis, which would claim for itself the legitimacy of documentary, empirical verisimilitude. In this vein, the early pictures from the camps were seen by many to provide unquestioned factual corroboration of a truth that "spoke for itself." They stood at once as a trace of the real and its self-evident interpretation; they were seen to provide information and witness, while at the same time accusing, reeducating, and even convicting.

Yet as much as these shocking camp images served an evidentiary and prosecutorial function within a specific historical venue, the increased narrowing over the years of this "public archive" to a smaller selection of ever repeated images transformed their status from witness into icon. Being limited in number and thereby universally legible, they achieved the status of a universal language. Iconic images express an aura of timelessness and a lack of spatial specificity. They claim implicitly to tell the whole story. The "atrocity films," as they were called at the Nuremberg Trials, gradually came to stand as symbols for Nazi crimes in toto—emblematic of a system conflating *concentration* and *death* camps, of an Auschwitz in extremis—at once the absolute telos of Nazi ideology and its practice of total annihilation.

One scholar who already in the early 1950s was concerned about the loss of historical specificity through the reception of these images was Hannah Arendt. In her book *The Origins of Totalitarianism*, she addresses what she calls "misleading" impressions imparted by many of the allied photos during the immediate postwar period. The films mislead us, she writes, because they depict almost exclusively concentration camps in Germany (Buchenwald, Bergen-Belsen, and Dachau) at a particular moment of chaos and disintegration in the final days of the war. Such depictions, she continues, do not impart how these camps functioned for most of the years prior to that time. For Arendt, the mountains of dead and half-dead bodies discovered by the Americans and British in liberating the camps in the west were transformed photogenically into *the* camp experience in toto, despite the fact that none of them were extermination camps.[6] Thus as iconic images, they served as a self-evident indictment of the seemingly medieval dimension of the crimes committed by Nazi perpetrators, while at the same time shielding their viewers from the enormity of mass industrial death found in such extermination camps in the east as Auschwitz, Majdanek, Treblinka, and Sobibor.

Arendt's stress upon a particularist reading of photographic and cinematic representations of Nazi genocide points to tensions and difficulties that will play themselves out in each of the ensuing encounters between American films about such events and various German viewing publics. In the case of the camp films, we find from the very outset competing hermeneutic agendas, which explains why this period as a whole came to represent both a remembering and a forgetting, an acknowledgment of crime and a disavowal of some victims. Thus, this discussion of the cinematic Americanization of the Holocaust must of necessity begin with a consideration of the documentary films to emerge from this period, at least two of which, *Nazi Concentration Camps* and *Death Mills,* were brought to fruition under the guidance of leading Hollywood filmmakers.

The film *Nazi Concentration Camps* was commissioned specifically by the supreme commander of the allied expeditionary forces, General Dwight D. Eisenhower, to be used in the Nuremberg trials in the prosecution of Nazi War Criminals. Produced by the well-known director, Lieutenant Colonel George C. Stevens, *Nazi Concentration Camps* is a fifty-nine minute compilation film based on over thirteen hours (80,000 ft.) of documentary and newsreel footage shot in the concentration camps of Western Europe by liberating American and British forces in April of 1945. In written affidavits introducing the film, Stevens, along with Navy cameraman E.R. Kellogg (a former "director of photographic effects" for 20th Century Fox), certify that to the best of their knowledge "these motion pictures constitute a true representation of the individuals and scenes photographed" (Stevens) and that the "images of these excerpts have not been retouched, distorted, or otherwise altered in any respect" (Kellogg).[7] While credited with the film's direction, it is clear from the disparate nature of its evolution that Stevens would have had little control and virtually no oversight of its initial evolution. The original footage was shot by numerous Army photographers with varying levels of expertise and drawn from over thirty concentration camps covering a geographic area stretching from Breendonck prison in Belgium to the concentration camp in Mauthausen in northern Austria.

Yet despite the ad hoc nature of its genesis, *Nazi Concentration Camps* does articulate a set of coherent responses to the horrors it represents. The film's most forceful enunciation emerges from its call to witness—a cinematic evocation to *view*, with shock, rage, and disbelief, the tens of thousands of tortured and murdered human beings. Its evocation is realized by means of a camera that cannot get enough of the myriad piles of beaten, half-starved corpses strewn across the landscape and through the eyes of officers and infantry of the US Army, together with members of the United States Congress, as they bear witness at the Ohrdruf camp.[8] The images are meant for an American audience, but also interpellate others who ought pay them heed: immediately available, onsite perpetrators—suspected SS officers, Nazi Party members, doctors who, we are told, carried out death-producing experiments; and various other male and female camp personnel, forced in close to the stench as they carry the rotting remains to a final burial ground; or, finally, as forced to be seen by German civilians living in the immediate vicinity of the camps. In one case, a thousand unsuspecting citizens from the town of Weimar are shown being taken on a spring day outing by foot to Buchenwald, suddenly to be confronted with atrocities in the form of lampshades made out of human skin, shrunken heads, and teeming corpses.[9] What we are presented with are scenes of a crime after the fact; delivered with an onslaught of evidence suggesting various levels of criminal involvement.[10]

How does *Nazi Concentration Camps* seek to verify the reliability, the objectivity of its visual representations? One primary medium employed is that of verbal and written forms of edification. The affidavits shown on the screen at the outset are also read aloud in stentorian tones by two voice-overs, as though to counter any inclination on the part of viewers to disbelieve the authenticity of the images that follow. These oaths also serve to allay any juridical concerns that might arise from the fact that *Nazi Concentration Camps* had at least officially been "authored" by two members of the Hollywood entertainment industry. However, such promises of visual, that is, imagistic, authenticity can guarantee very little, since in the editing down of so much raw footage, selections are made that ultimately do amount to "tampering" with material—a shaping of data into narrative coherence and even argument, a honing of effect and impact, the establishment of emotional rhythms.

Also imbuing this film with an air of authority is the manner of its continued use of voice-over narration: summing up what we see; casting judgements about individuals and events; offering (in some cases inaccurate) information about the differing functions and purposes of individual camps.[11] To be sure, the occasionally ironic, often accusatory, and understatedly omniscient tone of that voice-over (there are actually three different voices heard on the soundtrack) must be seen contextually as an immediate reflection, but also as an attempted containment, of the shock, confusion, and increasing helplessness on the part of Allied forces, faced as they were with a situation for which they were ill prepared. The unarticulated dissonance between the surfeit and extremity of its overwhelming imagistic display, on the one hand, and the continuing efforts on the part of the various narrative strategies (voice, editing, etc.) to get on top of it, to render meaning and coherence in the face of potential breakdown and chaos, is but one of the formal means by which this film unwittingly addresses the mayhem, bordering on hysteria, in which it operates.

Certainly the raw "documentary" power of its images, framed within the juridical authority of an international trial for which it was intended, lent the film a powerful aura of verisimilitude concerning the enormity of the crime portrayed. This authority led the film to serve a pivotal role in the Nuremberg trial, which began on 20 November 1945. In the eyes of Robert L. Jackson, the American chief counsel for the prosecution, for example, *Nazi Concentration Camps* would stand as proof that, in the words of his opening address to the court, "the wrongs which we seek to condemn and punish have been so calculated, so malignant, and so devastating that civilization cannot tolerate their being ignored because it cannot survive their being repeated."[12]

The role of this film within the trial itself was from the outset multi-inflected. Some assessments of its emotional and political impact tend to situate it as a turning point in the proceedings. The officially appointed psychologist, Gustav M. Gilbert, describes how several of the defendants broke down during and subsequent to the screenings; how they were moved sufficiently by them to distance themselves from the controlling influence of Hermann Goering and acknowledge their own responsibility for the crimes.[13] Other commentators stressed the film's broader impact on world opinion, which was in turn seen to help create a climate of retribution lending support ultimately to the severity of the punishments. Indeed, it was precisely the horror of the bodies that ultimately enabled the prosecution to stage the trial as a threat to the notion of law itself.[14]

Yet as much as the films did play a significant role in condemning perpetrators and articulating the extremity of the perceived atrocities, the legal and visual metadiscourses created to do so also helped in eliciting three moments of *silence*. Within the juridical proceeding itself, the silence consisted in allowing the films to stand self-evidently as proof of criminal behavior: there was no cross-examination follow-up to the screenings, either by the defense or the prosecution, concerning the relevance of the material in relation to specific crimes committed by or linked to the twenty-two defendants. As suggested above, *Nazi Concentration Camps* itself by no means points a finger of guilt definitively at any one group within the SS, Gestapo, Nazi Party, Wehrmacht, or other larger governing hierarchies, suggesting instead a more inclusive notion of culpability closer to what Carl Jaspers was to define within the category of collective guilt.

Beyond the prosecutorial silence concerning the film's meaning as evidence (as opposed to witness) was the larger silence regarding the victims of these crimes so dramatically highlighted in these pictures; a silence that impacted how people viewed the event itself subsequent to 1945. Jackson's emphasis upon the universal, in his terminology "civilizational" aspects of the crime, underscores the extent to which the trial itself, even at its outset, already subordinated the destruction of European Jewry to merely one of an "endless list of war crimes committed by the Nazis."[15] In the judgement documents concluding the trial, only three of the 226 pages deal specifically with Jewish extermination.[16]

In this regard, the film itself could be seen as basically confirming the prosecution's tendency to universalize the murdered inmates as victims of war crimes or crimes against humanity, thereby denying them any specific ethnic, political, sexual political, or racial identities that might in turn require a more differentiated treatment both of the victims themselves and the Nazi exterminist and racialist policies developed in relation to them. The word "Jew" is only spoken once in the film in the sentence "The 4,000 Ohrdruf victims are said to include Poles, Czechs, Russians, Belgians, Frenchman, German Jews, and German political prisoners." Whether Stevens or the many authors of the film script knew that due to Soviet advances, beginning already in November of 1944, significant numbers of Jewish prisoners had been relocated from Auschwitz and other eastern European death camps to Mauthausen, Dachau, Bergen-Belsen, and Buchenwald is beside the point. Important is the fact that the victims of these "atrocities" were seen largely in relation to war crimes, political resistance, and the needs of slave labor, not primarily as victims of ethnic or racial genocide.[17]

The theme of the universal victim (as opposed to the specific perpetrator) finds a particularly powerful visual articulation in the cinematography patterns of *Nazi Concentration Camps*. In the footage taken in Mauthausen and Dachau in particular, but apparent as well throughout the film, one notes the frequent tendency to lengthen the takes and retard the pans when photographing the stacked or tangled bodies of dead victims. Here the camera seems to linger, almost surrealistically, as it slowly reframes what seem in their concatenating reception like interchangeable frozen images of bleached and emaciated body parts, heads with holes for eyes and mouths, etc. The intention here is an obvious effort to provide empirical, corporeal evidence of torture, starvation, and death as the ultimate realistic/documentary testimony of the horrors at hand. Yet the very freezing of these black and white images into icons—bodies in endless rows, heads tilted back—lends them a kind pictorial abstraction, one is tempted to say with Adorno aestheticization.

A third silence attributed to the camp films was on the part of the German public at large. The forced showings in January of 1946 of a twenty-two minute compilation documentary called *Death Mills*, edited by the Hollywood director Billy Wilder, was met with a mixture of revulsion, a growing refusal to accept such accusations, and the beginnings of a long-term disavowal regarding the crimes committed in their name; a disavowal and silence, I must briefly add, which was sustained and encouraged by the Allies themselves.

From Documentary to Fiction: *The Diary of Anne Frank*

Certainly the reception process of the immensely popular *Diary of Anne Frank*, as book, play, and film in the 1950s, represented a very different form of Americanizing the Holocaust from that of the atrocity films. The interpretive authority for this text was not constituted through governmental policies and juridical proceedings of the occupying powers, but rather slowly emerged as part of a process centered within the publishing and entertainment industries of Europe and the United States. Also important here was a shift of focus. Where the atrocity films, both juridically and as instruments of forced enlightenment, directed their investigative focus, if not their lenses, mostly at the perpetrators, the Anne Frank story dealt almost exclusively with the victims.

Much as been written about the evolution and evisceration of the diary on its journey from book to movie: how the original story was adapted by Albert Hackett and Francis Goodrich, a husband and wife scriptwriting team from MGM studios, into an award-winning Broadway play directed by Garson Kanin in 1955, which in turn served as the screenplay for George Steven's equally acclaimed film of 1959;[18] how the Americanizing (also universalizing) of Anne Frank included what many have referred to as a de-judification of the heroine and her surroundings: the toning down of her growing sense of Jewish identity (and hate for the Germans) in the wake of increased Nazi incursions.[19] A passage in the original diary that reads "we're not the only Jews that have had to suffer, right down the ages there have been Jews and they have all had to suffer" becomes "we are not the only people who have had to suffer, there have always been people who suffer, sometimes one race sometimes another."[20]

Perhaps the most controversial emendation occurred around the Hanukkah scene where it was decided that the songs would not be sung in Hebrew but in English. The Hacketts offered the following justification: "It would set the characters in the play apart from those people watching them ... for the majority of our audience is not Jewish. And the thing we are striving for, toiled for throughout the whole play is to make the audience understand and identify themselves; to make them feel that "there for the grace of God might have been I."[21]

Finally, there is the narrative transformation of the Anne Frank story itself in accordance with the play and film's basic theme that good triumphs over evil. The diary's structure is characterized for the most part by countless repetitions, lacking, in accordance with its genre, any sense of purposeful development. Anne's initial optimism that the captivity would be short-lived, the girls soon back in school, the allied invasion quick and successful gives way to debilitating bickering and backbiting as things unravel perceptively into periods of gloom and uncertainty about the future. The narrative logic at the center of the Hacketts' "story"/plot reorganizes those redundancies—the growing isolation and tension among all the members of the secret annex— into a tale of uplifting, ultimately life affirming value and meaning. This sense of redemption is particularly apparent in the film's almost overbearing move to a feel-good ending.

Such are the bare outlines of the Americanization argument that have developed in numerous revisionist readings, mostly emanating in the United States since the 1980s.[22] The present study poses two related questions: To what extent can we attribute the extraordinary popularity and meaning of this story, its universalization if you will, to processes and national characteristics unique to the United States? Related to this, how might one sustain a reading of the German reception of Anne Frank in the Federal Republic that would point to what is particular to the context of that society's coming to terms with its past?

One finds in much of the more recent writing about the *Diary* a focus on what was left out of its more "popularized" versions; or, in more incriminating terms, the extent to which the "original" was bowdlerized in the move to stage and screen. Within this strategy, the reinvention of Anne Frank by the Hacketts has often been portrayed as uniquely driven by needs of universalization and happy resolution intrinsic to the Hollywood aesthetic and deeply endemic to the American imagination. In his book *Selling of the Holocaust*, Tim Cole stresses that when Anne Frank was "exported" to the United States she underwent changes that had a major impact on our memory of her, "as it was in America that what may be termed as the 'Myth of Anne Frank' was created…[Here] a diary in which the Holocaust provided the context rather than the central theme was made into a play and a film which reflected the concerns of 1950s America much more than it reflected the Holocaust."[23]

Lawrence Langer is particularly harsh in lumping the play and the film with a number of other commercially successful American media representations of the Holocaust (*The Wall, Incident at Vichy*, Stanley Kramer's *Judgement at Nuremberg*, and Gerald Green's *Holocaust* for NBC) that "permit the imagination to cope with the idea of the Holocaust without forcing a confrontation with its grim details," that are spoon fed to audiences who in turn "would find little to threaten their psychological or emotional security."[24] "The American imagination" he concludes, seems reluctant to take "the non Kirkegaardian leap into unfaith" that might reveal a vision of the Holocaust in which the sources of human dignity are "poisoned" beyond the point of recognition (217). Finally, in a controversial article in the *New Yorker*, Cynthia Ozick railed against the way the diary has been "bowdlerized, ….infantilized, Americanized, homogenized, sentimentalized; falsified, kitschified, and, in fact, blatantly and arrogantly denied," suggesting that it would have been better were it "burned, vanished, lost."[25]

This bleak picture of collective projection and national denial stands as a heavy indictment of the American imaginary's seemingly congenital inability to deal straightforwardly with the horrors of such an event as the Holocaust. Yet what its powerful polemic fails to account for is the larger social and cultural contexts that had already shaped the *Diary*'s processes of editorial genesis and public reception well before the Hacketts got their hands on it in 1955.

The first such context concerns more narrowly the publication history of the book itself. A closer examination of its evolution before and after the Broadway play and Hollywood film reveals a considerably more complicated narrative of re-and cross-appropriation than is encompassed in the one-sided story of Americanization. As is well known, the Hacketts were not the first to bowdlerize Anne's diary, nor was the text they worked with even the "original." The very first edition was published in Dutch, the language in which it was written, in 1947, edited by Anne's father Otto Frank. However, already in 1946, Frank had organized a German translation by Anneliese Schutz for Anne's grandmother, which in turn became the basis for the first German edition by the Lambert Schneider Verlag in 1950.

In his editing of the Dutch edition, Frank made a number of significant changes, starting with an expurgation of Anne's highly critical depiction of her mother and moving to out and out censorship of her confessions of budding sexuality: Anne's description of her vagina; her erotic dreams and fantasies, her unfolding sexual relationship with Peter. A third invasion of the text, one absolutely pivotal for the story's move toward universalization, involved the father's cutting out any mention by Anne of her growing anti-German sentiments, phrases such as "there is no greater hostility than that which exists between Germans and Jews," or "speak softly, all civilized languages are permitted, therefore no German allowed." These erasures were justified by Otto Frank as his concern for the feelings of their many German friends and later by *Der Spiegel* on the grounds that "a book intended for sale in Germany ... cannot abuse the Germans."[26] Thus, all of these revisions could be seen to have contributed significantly to the image of Anne Frank as one of wholesome teenage innocence and boundless forgiveness toward her tormentors.

The points to be made about the text's evolution then are the following: first, there was and is no "original" text. Even the manuscript that Otto Frank received upon his return from the camps had already been partly "reworked for publication" by Anne Frank herself. Hence from the very beginning he was forced to work with two versions. Second, by effacing the specifically Jewish dimension of Anne's experience in the initial publication, Anne's father also helped shape the image of his daughter as that of a universal victim of Nazi war crimes rather than as someone who had been murdered as a part of systematic Nazi genocide of European Jewry.

Thus, while it is clear that the Broadway and Hollywood Anne Frank is not the Anne of the book version of the *Diary*, let alone the Jewish victim who died of sickness in the overcrowded filth of Bergen-Belsen, her eventual elevation to what one critic has called "a patron saint of liberalism"[27] was not simply the product of one national culture or the work of two Broadway scriptwriters and a Hollywood director. In one regard, Peter Novick is quite right when he argues that "the *Diary* was not twisted into an optimist and universalist document by the Hacketts, Garson Kanin, George Stevens or anyone else. It *was* such a document, and it was that fact which commended it to Americans in the 1950s, including most of the organized Jewish community."[28] What Novick's remark fails to account for is the fact that the *Diary* attains its universalist status as an ongoing process of rewriting, re-reading, and remediatizing. Anne's own decision to revise came after she heard a BBC broadcast calling for accounts by the Dutch people of their own experiences under German occupation. Otto Frank in turn made selections from both her first "private" version and the one for "imagined publication" in putting together the first edition.[29]

With the appearance of the American translation in 1952, Anne Frank arrived on US shores an unknown European victim of Nazi war atrocities.

Four years later, following exceptional book sales in America and Japan,[30] together with its theatre success on Broadway, the play version moved back to Europe and on to the Americas, Asia, Israel, and elsewhere—as much a world as an American phenomenon.

If not simply the Americanization of Anne Frank, what is it that we are talking about when we speak of the iconization of this figure into an emblem of universal suffering? What issues are being enacted, and what was being achieved? Within the context of the first postwar decade, it must be recognized that little or no public discussion or medial representation of the concentration camps took place in either Europe or the United States. As mentioned above, attempts by the Allies to confront the "Germans" with what they saw as war atrocities were so ineptly carried out that the occupiers soon gave up in despair.[31] In addition to failures of communication at the level of propaganda and "re-education," along with an adamant refusal on the part of the vanquished to accept in any way responsibility for the crimes in question, the Allies soon came to realize that their need to make Germany a central bulwark against Communism would only be disrupted by forced efforts to work through the past.

The reception of Anne Frank in West Germany in the 1950s must be seen in light of the silence about the Holocaust up until this period. The success in 1956 of the American version of the play, with simultaneous productions in five major cities, led to a breakthrough of the diary as a bestseller. Within the next five years, eighteen new editions of the book sold over 700,000 copies. In addition, the subject of Anne Frank was included in primary school instruction, and the large number of medial treatments in film and television culminated in the 1960 George Stevens film.

What was significant for German audiences about the diary, play, and film (they came to be read as one and the same, i.e. the play and then the film succeeded in folding the diary into their message) was the fact that, in contrast to their confrontation with the camp films, the figure of this young girl and her story offered the possibility of access: contact with this highly idealized victim as a point of identification; access through an implied forgiveness and reconciliation to a larger international community.[32] "It was an act of exculpation, that Anne Frank in the play and film versions put the emphasis upon the positive in life, instead of speaking accusingly about her torturers."[33]

Seen only from the present, such attitudes must rightly be seen as escapist, avoidance, denial. Universalization in this regard means individualizing the fate of this one person and thereby removing it from the historical context of an entire people. On the other hand, set in the context of an absolute condition of nationally and internationally sanctioned denial, not only in the land of the perpetrators, the universalist response to the Anne Frank complex can also be understood as a first, tentative, collective step toward acknowledging a fate and responsibility that heretofore had not been publicly visible at all. In short: the universalization of Anna Frank shielded German audiences from facing the horror of the crime just as it provided for the first time, at a larger national level, emotional access to the victims—however defined. Returning to the concentration films, the abstract icons of horror montaged so brutally in the panning cameras of the Army Corps had become in the iconic Anne Frank the palpable figure encompassed in the phrase "there for the grace of God might have been I."

Holocaust as Soap Opera?

Certainly one of the defining moments in the expansion of Holocaust awareness in the United States and in West Germany was the NBC miniseries Holocaust. Its broadcast on German television in January of 1979, eight months after its phenomenal reception in the United States, was preceded by extremely heated debates as to whether it should be shown at all, and if so nationally or just regionally. The decision to proceed with the broadcast resulted in a national event that far exceeded anyone's speculations. Over a four-night stretch, an estimated 20 million viewers watched each showing. In addition, a phone-in service established by the Westdeutscher Rundfunk and operated by trained professionals—scholars, counselors, psychotherapists—was virtually overwhelmed by the caller response, which averaged 5,000 calls a night. While some voiced strong criticism, ranging from pleas to stop denigrating German national pride to disapproval of the perceived desacralization of the Holocaust, the majority of the responses came from viewers wanting more specific historical information or simply wanting to share their feelings of shock and shame.

The initial media response to "Holocaust" in Germany was in some ways similar to the critique leveled by American Jews such as Elie Wiesel. His article in the *New York Times* entitled "Trivialization of the Holocaust" set the tone in the United States for a radical rejection of the series on moral and aesthetic grounds. In an article in *Der Spiegel* entitled "Gaskammern a la Hollywood," several directors of regional television networks denounced the program as "a cultural commodity ... not in keeping with the memory of the victims."[34] Other critics, some writing even before it was shown in Germany, argued that this "soap opera" amounted to a commercial horror show, and accused the WDR of opportunistically importing a cheap commodity. "It may be that such a sloppily made film can still offer people in the USA, so very far away, some information.... We and our European neighbors know better. In France, Denmark, Sweden, Switzerland, Austria, *Holocaust* for that reason is met with rejection or at the very least skepticism."[35] In an article entitled "The Extermination of the Jews as Soap Opera," appearing in the *Frankfurter Allgemeine Zeitung* months before the broadcast in Germany,[36] Sabine Lietzmann is incensed at the notion of combining the fictional with the factual, or of even locating the depiction of such monstrous crimes within the realm of the "private sphere," that is, as a family soap opera. She concludes her piece by quoting Wiesel to the effect that "the Holocaust must remain in our memory, but not as a tv show."[37]

The many references to Elie Wiesel in the German discussions, as well as the reprinting of his article from the *New York Times* in a West German anthology of pieces on the Holocaust debate,[38] raise a number of issues that I want to keep in the foreground during the rest of this discussion. The first concerns, of course, the question of Americanization. At one level, Wiesel's assault upon this televisualization, which he called "untrue, cheap, offensive, and an insult," was much more extreme than anything the German left-liberals and conservatives had to say. By extreme, I do not mean rhetorically or politically. Rather I refer to what it suggests in regards to issues of aesthetics and epistemology. When Wiesel expresses shock that the program "transforms an ontological event into a soap opera," the thing to note is not the phrase "soap opera" but rather the word "ontological." For Wiesel, as for other proponents of a pristine collective memory belonging only to the survivors themselves, there is *no* art form or mode of representation that would enable one to capture the enormity of this experience: in his own words, "a film about Sobibor is either not a film or it is not Sobibor." This is certainly a legitimate position—others like George Steiner, and to a certain extent, even Theodor Adorno, have maintained similar views.

Those German discussants citing Wiesel, however, were doing so in part because he was an American Jew who was launching what they wished to see as an attack similar to their own; one that, while open to cooptation, arose ultimately from a very different set of epistemological assumptions. Here I differ to a certain degree with Jeffrey Herf when he says the following: "I must confess that even if the climate of resistance to discussing and or doing something about facing the Nazi past had been different, I would still view objections to *Holocaust* on aesthetic grounds made by West Germans in a different light than *identical objections* made by a Jewish novelist of the Holocaust such as Elie Wiesel. This blatant double standard often turned out to be an accurate gauge of hypocrisy posing as a defense of culture."[39]

While I would agree with Herf that the aesthetic rejections by the German left of what they viewed as Holocaust a la Hollywood certainly involved some hypocrisy, or better yet disavowal, I would nevertheless argue that the positions are not "identical" and that the differences underlying Wiesel's project and that of the German critics tell us much about the varying meanings denoted by the phrase "Americanizing the Holocaust" within the two national cultures.

Take the inflationary use of the word trivialize. For Elie Wiesel, the problem of trivialization was ultimately less a media issue, less a matter merely of aesthetics, than it was a question of whose memory it is. Wiesel sees himself as empowered to represent the Holocaust in his written testimonies by virtue of the fact that as a survivor he is uniquely qualified to do so. In so arguing, he seeks to counter two trends within the contemporary American scene: first, the claim on the part of any number of artists and media producers that they as non-survivors do indeed have the right to know and represent what they have not experienced; second, the tendency in the United States of late to expand the relevance of the Holocaust experience to include any number of other historical forms of genocide or persecution. In both these cases, Wiesel's status as a survivor becomes the lynchpin of an argument claiming sole priority of representation, regardless of his secondary, somewhat hackneyed assault upon television as a genre.

In the German discussion of *Holocaust*, we are of course also dealing with questions of memory and representation, but here the issue is much more one of a perceived crisis of aesthetic failure called forth by the emotional response of the German public to this television miniseries. The key question that had to be faced in the light of *Holocaust*'s success in Germany was precisely why this series opened up an understanding of the Holocaust that all the enlightened, rational, objective discourses and aesthetic representations of prior decades had failed to produce. Underlying the vehemence of the seemingly anti-American attacks upon the validity of a Hollywood-style fictionalization of the Holocaust—posed in the name of documentary film, political theater, and a modernist aesthetic—was the whole history of attempts by German writers, artists, and filmmakers to come to terms with the past. The showing of *Holocaust* did indeed raise questions about that history, questions that had, in Andreas Huyssen's words, "remained buried in the false dichotomies of high versus low, avant-garde versus popular, political theater versus soap opera,"[40] critical audience response versus identification. And the questions arising here were absolutely central for a left-wing cultural politician in the 1970s. "To what extent," Huyssen continues, "did *Holocaust* seem to invalidate earlier attempts at *Vergangenheitsbewältigung*, either in theater and television productions or by intellectuals and educators in their fight against the social amnesia characteristic of the post-war decades in the Federal Republic?" (119) Here we think of films by artists such as Alexander Kluge, Rainer Fassbinder, Werner Schlöndorff, Hans Syberberg, and others; or political theatre with plays such as Max Frisch's *Andorra*, Rolf Hochhuth's *The Deputy*, Peter Weiss's *The Investigation*, or Heinar Kipphardt's *Joel Brand*.

These are a few of the deeper issues at the heart of the debate around the television miniseries *Holocaust* that take us beyond what sometimes feels like compulsive repetitions about the inevitable and inexorable powers of the

American culture industry to rob other people's culture and memory. In making that point, I in no way wish to dismiss the profound problems involved in articulating and developing specifically regional or national forms of cinematic expression within the framework of global capital and its control of markets and the imagination.

In an essay entitled "Independent Film after *Holocaust*", filmmaker Edgar Reitz quite poignantly sums up the difficulties of independent filmmakers worldwide to assert themselves in the face of a dominant Hollywood.

> If we look throughout the world at countries with independent film cultures—India, Brasil, Spain, France, the Federal Republic, yes even the United States—then what we find are film auteurs with the same basic problems: their concern is the individuality, the representation (*Wiedergabe*) of experiences that are uniquely bound to one specific region. In order to do so, they must develop a cinematic language to narrate these experiences. … In just this way filmmakers all over the world are struggling to take possession of their own history, and thereby the history of the group to which they belong. Yet they often experience that their history is being ripped out of their hands. The deepest kind of expropriation imaginable is the expropriation of a human being from his own history (*die Enteignung des Menschen von seiner eigenen Geschichte*). With *Holocaust* the Americans have taken away our history from us.[41]

I would like to make two points about the above quotation that will also serve as this chapter's conclusion. First, it should be mentioned that Reitz's critique of *Holocaust* must be seen in relation to the making of his own 16-hour television film, *Heimat*, which he saw as an answer to the predatory features of the Hollywood-style television series *Holocaust*. In his film, he hoped to offer a counter notion of memory rooted in the language, culture, and memory of a specific region, one that would allow German viewers to see themselves and their own experiences. While the series was indeed a success in many ways, its narrowness of focus and detail, in terms of projected audience, the scope of its memory, and its sense of history reveals precisely the limits of such an aesthetic for dealing with a world epochal phenomenon such as the destruction of European Jewry.

Which brings us back to the question: whose memory is it? Clearly, the memory and history of something like the Holocaust cannot and will not, by the very nature of its global, nonterritorial locus, be contained or represented within the epistemological borders of the national or the regional. The social memory that Reitz calls for is limited to a specific place and time, to events and symbols within a shared culture and common experience. The staggering scope in time, space, and catastrophe of an event like the Holocaust blows asunder the very possibility of pristine regional remembrances nestled unencumbered within it. Such an event calls for a different notion of historical memory, one mediated by the technological and aesthetic languages of global communication. In this regard, Thomas Elsaesser is absolutely right when he notes that "in spite of his diatribe against Hollywood, Reitz is clearly aware that in our century to talk about memory is to talk about audio-visual representations of events. None of us can escape the force of the images that always already exist, and to build a counter-memory from scratch is as heroic as it is impossible."[42] In the case of the Holocaust, of course, one set of images that "already always exist," are the photographs and films from the camps. To that extent, any film about the destruction of European Jewry will always be at some level a rescreening of those camp films and of films that have been made since then, evoking memories that necessarily belong to all of us.

Notes

1. Anson Rabinbach, "From Explosion to Erosion: Holocaust Memorialization in America since Bitburg," *History and Memory* 9, no. 1/2 (fall 1997): 230.
2. Ibid. Cited in Rochelle G. Saidel, *Never Too Late to Remember: The Politics behind New York City's Holocaust Museum* (New York and London, 1996), 219.
3. Cited in Ilan Avisar, *Screening the Holocaust: Cinema's Images of the Unimaginable* (Bloomington, 1988), 130.
4. See Dagmar Barnouw, *Germany 1945* (Bloomington, 1996); Cornelia Brink, *Ikonen der Vernichtung* (Berlin, 1998); and Barbie Zelizer, *Remembering to Forget* (Chicago, 1998). Where Barnouw focuses on the impact of these images on attitudes of Americans toward the Germans, Brink concentrates on their impact upon the Germans, in particular those living in the Federal Republic.
5. Marianne Hirsch, "Surviving Images: Holocaust Photographs and the Work of Postmemory," ed. Barbie Zelizer, *Visual Culture and the Holocaust* (New Brunswick, 2001), 223.
6. Hannah Arendt, *Elemente und Ursprünge totaler Herrschaft* (Frankfurt am Main, 1962), 654.
7. The Trial of the Major War Criminals before the International Military Tribunal (hereafter IMT), Eighth Day: Thursday, 29 November 1945, 433. Available at <www.yale.edu/lawweb/avalon/imt/proc/11_29_45.htm>.
8. Ohrdruf was a sub-unit of Buchenwald lying south of the city of Gotha that had carried out Hitler's personal order "for the liquidation of all prisoners who could not be evacuated to prevent them from falling into the hands of the allies." See Michael R. Marrus, *The Holocaust in History* (New York, 1987), 197. This resulted in 4,000 deaths and the devastation discovered by the allies when they arrived at the camp on April 4, four days before the liberation of Buchenwald. The fact that Ohrdruf was the first concentration camp within Germany to be liberated by the allies is also the reason why Generals Eisenhower, Omar Bradley, and George Patton made a special visit to the camp, followed by other American dignitaries.

9. This somewhat gruesome affair was thought up by General George Patton, who contacted the mayor of Weimar asking that he put together a delegation "of at least 1000 Weimar citizens, half men and half women, a third of which would be from the common people and two thirds from the wealthier classes and with as many Nazi Party people as possible." Guido Knopp, *Holokaust* (Munich, 2000), 339.
10. For an excellent and already canonical article on *Nazi Concentration Camps* and its relationship to the trial see Lawrence Douglas, "Film as Witness: Screening *Nazi Concentration Camps* Before the Nuremberg Tribunal," *The Yale Law Journal*, 105 (1995-1996): 449-81. I am greatly indebted to this article for many points in my discussion of this film.
11. We are informed by William Donovon, chief and founder of the OSS and a prosecutor at the Nuremberg trials who offered the *Nazi Concentration Camps* in evidence, that "its accompanying narration had been taken directly from the reports of the military photographers who filmed the camps." Certainly this would explain the differing styles and emphases offered in narrations of the twelve camps.
12. IMT.
13. See Gustav M. Gilbert, *Nuremberg Diary* (New York, 1947), 45ff.; see also Joseph Persico, *Nuremberg: Infamy on Trial* (New York, 1995), 142ff., 256f.
14. Douglas, "Film as Witness," 449.
15. Daniel Levy and Nathan Snaider, *Erinnerung im globalen Zeitalter: Der Holocaust* (Frankfurt am Main, 2001), 68.
16. IMT.
17. This was not simply because the word "genocide" had been recently coined.
18. The film won three Oscars at the Academy Awards.
19. See Tim Cole, *Selling the Holocaust* (New York, 1999), 30ff., for a detailed discussion of the differences between the diary, on the one hand, and the play and screen versions, quoting at length passages that were left out or eviscerated.
20. *The Diary of Anne Frank*, dramatized by Frances Goodrich and Albert Hackett (New York, 1954), 96.
21. Letter from Hacketts to Otto Frank (3 July 1956) cited in Judith E. Doneson, "The American History of Anne Frank's Diary," *Holocaust and Genocide Studies* 2, no. 1 (1987): 152.
22. Major texts in this regard are Alvin H. Rosenberg, "Popularization and Memory: The Case of Anne Frank," in ed. Peter Hayes, *Lesson and Legacies: The Meaning of the Holocaust in a Changing World* (Evanston, 1991): 243-78; Sander L. Gilman, *Jewish Self Hatred* (Baltimore, 1986); James E. Young, "Das Anne Frank Haus," in ed. James E. Young, *Mahnmale des Holocaust* (Munich, 1993), 107-113; Lawrence Langer, "The Americanization of the Holocaust on Stage and Screen," in ed. Sarah Blacher Cohen, *From Hester Street to Hollywood: The Jewish-American Stage and Screen* (Bloomington, 1993), 213-30; Cole, *Selling the Holocaust*, 23ff.
23. Cole, *Selling the Holocaust*, 29, 33.
24. Langer, "The Americanization of the Holocaust," 214.
25. Cynthia Ozick, "Who Owns Anne Frank?" *New Yorker*, 6 October 1997.
26. *Der Spiegel*, 1 April 1959.
27. Cole, *Selling the Holocaust*, 33.
28. Peter Novick, *The Holocaust in American Life* (Boston, 1999), 120.
29. See the Forward to Anne Frank, *Diary of a Young Girl*, Otto H. Frank and Mirjam Pressler, eds. (New York, 1997) for a discussion of the different versions and editions.
30. It is estimated that over 100,000 copies were sold in each country the first year alone.
31. See Barmouw, *Germany 1945*, and Kornelia Brink, *Ikonen der Vernichtung*.

32. Alvin H. Rosenfeld, in "Popularization and Memory," emphasizes that what is appealing to German readers about the Anne Frank book is "the tone of forgiveness in which it appears that the murdered are forgiving the murderers." (265)
33. Levy and Snaider, *Erinnerung im globalen Zeitalter*, 74.
34. "Gaskammern a la Hollywood," *Der Spiegel*, 15 May 1979, 230
35. Peter Schulze-Rohr, "Keine Frage von rechts oder links," *Die Zeit*, 23 June 1978, reprinted in *"Holocaust": Eine Nation wird betroffen*, Peter Märthesheimer and Ivo Frenzel, eds. (Frankfurt am Main, 1979), 46-48.
36. Sabine Lietzmann, "Die Judenvernichtung als Seifenoper," *Frankfurter Allgemeine Zeitung*, 20 April 1978), reprinted in Märthesheimer and Frenzel, *"Holocaust": Eine Nation wird betroffen*, 35-39.
37. Elie Wiesel, "Trivializing the Holocaust: Semi-Fact and Semi-Fiction," *New York Times*, 16 April 1978.
38. Ibid.
39. Jeffrey Herf, "The Holocaust Reception in West Germany: Right, Center and Left," *New German Critique* 19 (winter 1980): 36. Emphasis added by author.
40. Andreas Huyssen, "The Politics of Identification," *New German Critique* 19 (winter 1980): 118.
41. Edgar Reitz, *Liebe zu Kino: Utopien und Gedanken zum Autorenfilm: 1962-1983* (Cologne, 1984), 102. This essay first appeared in the May 1979 issue of *medium* with the title "Let's work on our memories."
42. Thomas Elsaesser, "Memory, Home and Hollywood," *Monthly Film Bulletin* (February 1985); reprinted in *New German Critique* 36 (fall 1985): 13.

ANTI-AMERICANISM AND THE COLD WAR
On the DEFA Berlin Films

❖ ❖ ❖

Sabine Hake

Sustained by well-established anti-American stereotypes and clichés, the romance between German and American culture has been a key ingredient of German cinema since its inception. The encounter with American mass culture produced compelling stories of infatuation and seduction, but also of conquest and surrender. Almost always, this encounter is coded in gendered terms, with the provocation of Otherness thematized through the generic conventions of musical comedy, social drama, and, most frequently, heterosexual romance. Two basic scenarios seem to predominate, with the German-American coupling leading either to the regeneration of German *Kultur* through American optimism and vitality or to the corruption of German *Innerlichkeit* by American materialism. The characters identified with the American way of life may initially antagonize their families and friends but eventually convince them to accept mass culture and consumer culture as indispensable parts of any modernized middle-class society, German style.

From the 1910s to the 1940s, German filmmakers responded to the continuing process of Americanization with alternately humorous and serious treatments that, no matter how difficult the initial process of adaptation and incorporation, always allowed for the assertion of local, regional, and national differences against the powerful forces of modernization. After 1945, the dissemination of American mass cultural products and the permeation of everyday life by American tastes, attitudes, and sensibilities gave rise to more complicated scenarios that reflected the changing balance of political power in postwar Europe.[1] As Marshall Plan aid brought economic and political reconstruction, the filmic responses to postwar Americanization became at once more antagonistic and more ambivalent. On and off the

---

Notes for this section begin on page 00.

screen, the myth of "America" began to infiltrate many areas of youth culture, from fashion styles, consumer products, and recreational activities to the habitually evoked trinity of jeans, jazz, and rock 'n' roll. Through stock characters like the rebellious young man and oversexed young woman, the phenomenon of Americanism assumed a highly symptomatic function in the spheres of mass entertainment as well as political debate—and did so primarily through interpretative patterns developed during the Weimar phenomenon of *Amerikanismus*.[2] But whereas the cultural and political elites denounced Americanization as an agent of social disintegration and cultural leveling, the young generation enthusiastically embraced all things American as an agent of social mobility and cultural opposition, thus also confirming the underlying antagonisms as a struggle among competing definitions of sexual, social, and national identity.

The controversy over American mass culture during the postwar period revolved around specific consumer products and the attitudes, values, and personalities acquired through them. The provocation of the American way of life typically took place on three levels: in the form of specific products associated with Americanization (e.g., jeans, jazz, rock 'n' roll); through the representation of American culture in German and American feature films (e.g., most famously, in the rebel films); and as part of more complicated discursive processes that turned Americanism from a reaction to cultural products into a cultural production with its own independent rules of engagement. Directly or indirectly, the negative qualities attributed to American mass culture and consumer culture articulated more pervasive concerns about the crisis of traditional middle-class society and the future of national culture and identity. Serving largely symptomatic functions, the phenomenon of anti-Americanism represented both a response to Americanization and a function of that very discourse. It would therefore be shortsighted, if not misguided, to read the symbolic practices associated with "America" merely on the level of surface phenomena and to dismiss any critique of mass consumption as a predictable contribution to the high versus low culture debate in its various elitist, racialist, and nationalistic manifestations. In particular, the widespread fears about the corruption of bourgeois individualism by possessive individualism (McPherson) can only be understood through their strategic function as part of the political antagonisms of the Cold War and in relation to the new collectivities organized under the opposing systems of capitalism and communism.

In almost all films from the postwar period, the narrativization of Americanization involves a process of successfully adapting and incorporating American elements into German texts and contexts. Rarely are rejection and expulsion of the other considered—except in the well-known Berlin films produced by the East German DEFA studio during the height of the Cold

War.³ Their radical difference from standard (western) accounts of German cinema and postwar Americanization is reason enough in my opinion to take a closer look at the central role of anti-Americanism in the mapping of ideological differences across the divided topographies of the 1950s. Three guiding principles should inform such an undertaking. First, the causes, mechanisms, and effects of anti-Americanism extend from actual cultural *and* political differences to the structure of their mutual instrumentalization in the rhetoric of Cold War cinema; understanding these differences requires close textual analysis. Second, a critical assessment of the contribution of cinema to the articulation of political anti-Americanism cannot be achieved through traditional definitions of politics alone but must extend to the role of fiction, narrative, and fantasy in constructing identities, especially those related to gender and sexuality. And third, the attraction of the American way of life can be reconstituted most effectively through a closer look at the highly politicized contemporary dramas made during the early 1950s, a period of considerable uncertainty and instability in all areas of culture and ideology. Accordingly, anti-American positions are found not only in DEFA's famous antifascist dramas but also in the contemporary dramas that focus on the reorganization of public and private life, the changing relationship between work and leisure, the emergence of new forms of association and community, and the gradual transformation of cultural tastes and preferences in accordance with an emerging socialist culture.

In the following pages, I intend to show how these films relied on highly gendered divisions to first problematize the pursuit of individual happiness under capitalism and then enlist the same libidinal structures in proclaiming socialism as the only valid alternative. The underlying struggle over of the place of individual desire in socialist societies was typically articulated through the romantic yearnings, artistic ambitions, and consumerist needs of the female main protagonists. In tracing the central role of anti-Americanism in this (gendered) conceptualization of the individual under socialism, I focus on Kurt Maetzig's *Roman einer jungen Ehe* (1952, Story of a Young Couple), Slatan Dudow's *Frauenschicksale* (1952, Women's Destinies), and Gerhard Klein and Wolfgang Kohlhaase's *Eine Berliner Romanze* (1956, A Berlin Romance), three films that captured both the optimism of the reconstruction years and the paranoia of the emerging Cold War. Unlike the Berlin films made after 1962 to justify the building of the "anti-imperialist protective rampart," these early contributions used the Americanization of cultural and social life as a negative foil for the emergence of the New Socialist Man. Their highly didactic narratives described—or, rather prescribed—the obligatory journey to be made by ordinary people from the false promises of individual self-realization in capitalist societies to the convergence of individual and collective desire in socialist societies. Maetzig and Dudow relied on the old gendered scenarios of Americanization for formulating the new oppositions of individualism versus collectivism, consumerism versus productivism, materialism versus idealism—in short, of capitalism versus communism. Articulating the question of gender through the aesthetics of socialist humanism and socialist realism, respectively, allowed these two famous DEFA directors to redefine the relationship between public and private sphere in accordance with the overlapping ideologies of antifascism, antimilitarism, and anti-Americanism. But the equation of Americanization with feminization, though not necessarily with women, also perpetuated a uniquely German pattern—that is, a bourgeois reaction formation—in the public response to modern mass culture that, in the end, helped to subordinate the building of socialism to the demands of Cold War politics and cultural nationalism.

Since the end of the Cold War, the divided topographies of postwar culture have attracted growing attention as a subject of critical inquiry. Under the influence of new approaches in cultural studies, scholars have used the category of gender to shed new light on the official cultural policies implemented in the name of Americanization and Sovietization and to examine the various strategies of aesthetic resistance and adaptation developed in the context of high culture, folk culture, and, most importantly, popular culture. Recent studies by Heide Fehrenbach, Erica Carter, and Uta Poiger on the society of the *Wirtschaftswunder* (Economic Miracle) have drawn attention to the highly gendered nature of popular and critical responses to American mass culture and consumer culture.[4] The alternately paranoid and hysterical fantasies about a feminization of postwar culture have allowed these scholars both to connect the crisis of masculinity to the emergence of mass consumption as a new cultural paradigm and to examine the return to traditional gender roles and family structures as a rather problematic solution to the perceived crisis. However, as Poiger has implied in her comparative studies on youth culture, and as I will argue in my analysis of the DEFA Berlin films, the equation of Americanization with consumerism and of consumerism with feminization arguably served very different functions in the GDR because of its heightened ideological significance within the Cold War.

At first glance, a comparison of East and West German postwar cinema would yield remarkable similarities in the filmic representation of American mass culture. These extend from the close attention to the problems of women in postwar society to the eroticizing of consumer products and the equation of consumption with feminization. Such female-dominated narratives and gender-specific forms of identification can be explained through two related factors: the large number of women in the audience and growing concerns over sexual mores and gender roles in a society with a significant *Frauenüberschuß* (surplus of women). On the level of narrative structure and character development, the elevation of women to symbols of community on both sides of the Iron Curtain follows very similar strategies of narrative containment known from classical Hollywood cinema. These include a shared preference for moralistic endings that transform rebellious young women into responsible members of society, whether as wives, mothers, or working women. Even the identification of strong women with the rebuilding of postwar society and of weak men with the corrupting effects of German class society and American-style capitalism can be found in East and West German productions; the same holds true for the demonizing of an Americanized youth threatening to destabilize all social and sexual hierarchies. The differences became most apparent in the narrative resolution of this kind of gender trouble. While the West German versions substitute the romance of the nuclear family for the eroticized spectacle of the commodity, the East German versions end up offering a political alternative in the fantasy of the socialist collective. Even more important, the conflation of cultural and political arguments in the east motivates very different strategies of division and exclusion aiming at a political rather than social or cultural solution to the threat of Americanization. The resultant discursive effects on the level of fantasy production can only be understood through an acute awareness of the different function of American mass culture as signifier and as signified in the depoliticized responses to Americanization in the west and the highly politicized responses to the same phenomena in the east.

The gendered division between the capitalist west and the socialist east did not remain limited to the products and rituals of modern mass culture but extended to the divided topography of Berlin as the center of the Cold War. Allowing for the uncontrollable movements of goods, tastes, and ideas across borders, West Berlin provided East Berliners with the public settings—train stations, department stores, nightclubs, and the infamous border cinemas—for indulging in escapist fantasies and succumbing to consumerist pleasures. Taking advantage of these transgressions, the Americans openly used mass cultural products in their own political offensive, for instance through the many Hollywood films shown to East German youth in the cheap border cinemas; the American-financed radio stations and various cultural events taking place in West Berlin, and the Berlin Film Festival founded in 1951 as a showcase for western film production.[5] The various efforts by the East German regime to control this dangerous traffic in ideologies began with the 1949 Blockade and culminated in the 1961 building of the Berlin Wall. In the interim years, the contemporary urban dramas instructed East German audiences in the importance of political vigilance, responsibility, and commitment. The filmmakers achieved this goal by showing "the divided city of Berlin as reflected in the emotional world of the protagonists," to cite one influential critic.[6]

In articulating the east-west romance in spatial terms, DEFA films present the decadent west and its mindless diversions through well-known attractions from Kurfürstendamm, including the Hotel am Zoo, Cafe Kranzler, and Astoria-Kino. As the capital of the GDR, East Berlin remains identified both with the historical center around Unter den Linden and Gendarmenmarkt and with the first monuments to an emerging socialist identity, Alexanderplatz and Stalinallee. Whether juxtaposing the meeting of lovers near Friedrichstraße station with the gatherings of criminals at the Zoo station in West Berlin or moving from the peaceful movement of workers across Warschauer Brücke to the threatening presence of American soldiers at Checkpoint Charlie, all of these films end up confirming politics as the determining factor in the organization of contemporary life. To underscore this point, the successful integration of mass cultural practices into socialist cultural practices is promised, if not already achieved, through the inclusion of official events such as the 1950 Whitsun Meeting of the Free German Youth (FDJ), the 1951 World Youth Festival, and, in an extensive documentary sequence from a much later Berlin film, the 1962 May Day Parade.

Through the double crisis of urban space and gender identity, the specter of Americanism provides a convergence point for two very different discourses within postwar cinema: the ideological divide introduced by the Cold War and the cultural divide among the generations opened up by postwar Americanization. In this context, anti-Americanism functions above all as an instrument for connecting the formation of the romantic couple to that of the work collective and enlisting both in the larger project of socialist nation building. This triangulated affair involves three participants—the German Democratic Republic, the Federal Republic, and the United States—and three corresponding paradigms of culture: East German proletarian culture, West German bourgeois culture, and American mass culture; the Soviet Union remains an absent fourth referent. Central to all negotiations are the processes of identity formation, and of identification, structured around gender and sexuality. Both operate as transmission belts, as it were, in the making of a socialist identity beyond traditional bourgeois individualism and American-style individualism. These libidinal investments around the category of gender and sexuality offer a point of departure for new desires and fantasies within the highly contested terrain defined by traditional working-class culture, an emerging socialist culture, and the actually existing Americanized mass culture.[7]

In *Roman einer jungen Ehe*, director Kurt Maetzig turned to the standard Marxist critique of autonomous art in order to uncover the alliances that linked the representatives of bourgeois culture both to the legacies of the Third Reich and to the forces of US imperialism. In focusing on the story of a young couple, he relied on well-tried dramatic conventions—first tested in the German-Jewish pairing from *Ehe im Schatten* (1945, Marriage in the Shadows)—of narrating the antagonisms of German history in marital terms.

In the director's own words, the film collective aimed at an artistic treatment of "one of the greatest problems for all true Germans today, the division of our fatherland and the possibility of its reunification."[8] Characterizing the protagonists as actors allowed the director furthermore to thematize the relationship between art and society through explicit references to then-ongoing debates on socialist literature and film that articulated the project of democratic socialism in aesthetic terms. At the same time, the many economic references took up anticapitalist positions articulated first in the critically acclaimed *Rat der Götter* (1950, Council of the Gods), a documentary drama about the wartime collaboration between Standard Oil and IG Farben.

Told from the woman's perspective, the flashback story recounts the personal and professional difficulties of two aspiring young actors during the early reconstruction years. The confrontation of capitalism and socialism, as well as its resonance in competing definitions of art and politics, almost destroys their marriage. Agnes and Jochen fall in love during a production of Lessing's *Nathan der Weise* at the Westend Theater in West Berlin. But disagreements over the social responsibility of the individual artist soon threaten their happy union. Their opposing views become clearly identified with three prominent colleagues: an idealistic theater owner who still believes in the autonomy of art; an opportunistic producer who espouses an American business approach to art as entertainment; and a communist director who advocates the transformation of art into a political weapon. The stereotypical greedy producer functions mainly to establish an elective affinity between antifascism and anti-Americanism, for instance by showing his willingness to support both the political goals of the Marshall Plan and the artistic plans of an old UFA director, referred to in the film as the director of *Jud Süss* (i.e., Veit Harlan). As a stand-in for Maetzig, the idealistic theater director from the east performs the opposite role by overseeing the political education of Agnes from naive actress into socialist activist. Already during their first film shoot, he responds to her characterization of art as a distraction from daily life with his utopian dream of art as "a bright torch on the difficult path to the future."

The highly didactic narrative can be summarized through its stark ideological oppositions. The Cold War first enters the couple's life in the form of wedding gifts, including a large CARE package and a smaller package from, in the words of the communist director, "our Russian friends." These external influences become more noticeable after the NWDR broadcast of a radio play based on Anna Segher's *Das siebte Kreuz* that coincides with the announcement of Marshall Plan aid and the currency reform. Agnes is outraged by the introductory commentary that reclaims this famous antifascist novel as an anticommunist work and, for the first time, sides with the communist against her apolitical husband and their bohemian friends. She becomes even more aware of the close connection between bourgeois art and imperialist aggression after Jochen defends his stage appearance as a Nazi officer in Zuckmayer's *Des Teufels General* as a great artistic challenge. Indignantly, Agnes rejects the offer of a lead role in Sartre's *Les mains sales*, calling its existentialism "cold and heartless ... disgusting." Thus while Jochen still recites love poems for RIAS Berlin, Agnes already prepares for her lead role in the East German *Aufbaufilm, Die ersten Jahre*. And while he reads freedom poems during an American-financed cultural event at the Titania-Palast in Steglitz, she enthusiastically performs Kuba's (i.e., Kurt Barthel's) infamous ode to Father Stalin during a celebration at the construction site on Stalinallee.[9] When Jochen cruelly dismisses her first film as "an abuse of art" and then defiantly declares that "the arts are my only party," their political differences can no longer be ignored. "In the struggle between east and west, my marriage has been destroyed irrevocably," is how Agnes explains their hopeless situation to a paternal friend.

But just as Jochen's stubborn adherence to the myth of bourgeois individualism involves three elements (the relationship between autonomous art and the culture industry, the relationship between capitalism and bourgeois culture, and the relationship between fascism and imperialism), his conversion to the socialist cause takes place in three phases. The closing of the Westend Theater due to financial difficulties and the producer's dubious film project with the Harlan figure at last force Jochen to recognize the capitalist foundation of bourgeois art and to acknowledge the continuities between fascism and imperialism. Scheduled to appear in a Hollywood film about "the dark [criminal] East Berlin around Alexanderplatz," he makes the all-important move from theory to praxis and decides not to take part in such blatant anti-communist propaganda. Then, on his way to the divorce hearing, he sees plainclothes men attack a group of ordinary citizens distributing leaflets against remilitarization. His spontaneous decision to guide some of the protesters to safety eliminates all remaining obstacles to the reconciliation of the couple who, to complete the happy ending in the spirit of anti-Americanism, have a new apartment already waiting for them on Stalinallee.

As my discussion has shown so far, the specter of American mass culture in the Berlin films of the early 1950s brought together a number of ideological concerns: the advance of global capitalism and its steady companions, militarism and imperialism; the leveling effects of modern mass culture on bourgeois high culture and traditional working class culture; and the debates about the future of German national unity and identity in the new geopolitical order. In *Roman einer jungen Ehe*, the gender dynamics of the east-west romance established a framework for articulating these developments and debates through the simplistic binaries of strong versus weak, and of true versus false, that confirmed socialism as the only truly humanizing force. The divided narratives of mass culture and modernity associated with the Economic Miracle in the west and with the building of socialism in the east relied on particular forms of gendering that combined older German arguments about massification and commercialization with specific postwar anxieties about the crisis of masculinity and the threat of cultural colonization. Reflecting the emerging ideological divisions of the Cold War, the danger of Americanization and the necessity of anti-Americanism were narrated within a love triangle, with capitalist ideology presented as an obstacle not only to the formation of the socialist couple and, by extension, society but also to the preservation of peace and democracy in all of Germany and Europe. To what degree the success of this fantasy of anti-Americanism hinged on the identification of Americanization with feminization becomes even more apparent in my next example, *Frauenschicksale*.

By infusing socialist realist conventions with modernist flourishes, Slatan Dudow used *Frauenschicksale* to reveal the connection between capitalism and bourgeois individualism and, through the equation of erotic desire and consumerist desire, to unmask the individual pursuit of happiness as a founding myth of American capitalism. The director possessed considerable experience in the gendering of ideological conflicts, from his collaboration with Bertolt Brecht on *Kuhle Wampe* (1932, Whither Germany?) to the early DEFA *Aufbaufilm*, *Unser täglich Brot* (1949, Our Daily Bread). All three films focus on young working-class women to show the close connection between the personal and political and to confront the underside of American-style consumerism with the promise of true happiness under socialism. In all cases, the movement of woman's desire from degradation to deliverance serves two equally important goals: to highlight the destructive impact of commodity fetishism on sexual and social relations and, in so doing, to demonstrate the superiority of the socialist ethos of collectivism and productivism.[10]

A widely acknowledged problem in postwar society sets into motion all dramatic complications in the 1952 production, the large number of single, widowed, and divorced women and the (real or imagined) threat they pose to traditional notions of femininity, masculinity, and, perhaps most disconcertingly, normative heterosexuality. Dudow largely ignores the long-term consequences of the *Frauenüberschuß* for the organization of the socialist public sphere.[11] Instead, he utilizes the excess of erotic desire and its substitute, consumerist desire, as a device in mapping the exchangeability of goods and people in capitalist societies. Addressing the female spectator through strategies of identification known from the romance novel, the narrative first reenacts the attractions of the west—in other words, it acknowledges the legitimacy of women's desire for love—but then redirects this desire toward the socialist collective. In typical socialist realist style, the film suggests two ways of resisting the lure of the decadent west: through the ideology of productivism, with its protestant work ethic a powerful shield against consumerist sloth and sexual debauchery, and through the ideology of collectivism, with its ethos of social responsibility and self-sacrifice an equally effective weapon against the excesses of possessive individualism.

The romantic longings of three single women establish the libidinal structure in which the American way of life finds programmatic expression in the personal motto of a small-time womanizer known as Conny: "You only live once." Personifying the lure of capitalism, Conny is repeatedly proven wrong by the women's choices of a second life under socialism. During her brief affair with this man about town, Barbara, an otherwise mature law student, becomes distracted, irritable, and withdrawn. She even neglects the political responsibilities formerly so evident in her work for the communist resistance during the Third Reich. Yet after a traffic accident—and sufficient time spent in the hospital reading up on dialectical materialism—she recognizes her mistakes and, newly committed to the socialist state, is rewarded with a judgeship and marriage to a colleague. Anni, a naive young seamstress who lives and works in the western sector, falls for Conny's superficial charms only to end up alone, pregnant, and unemployed. Responding to the many wanted ads by the new state-owned companies, she eventually moves to East Berlin. There the young mother not only enjoys free childcare but also has the opportunity to design attractive but inexpensive dresses, a small concession to women's consumerist needs despite the general push toward industrialization.

Renate, the last woman to be seduced by Conny, lives in a small East Berlin apartment with her widowed mother and younger brother. Selfish, unfeeling, but also extremely needy in her interactions with others, she requires the most reeducation; this is already apparent in her rude indifference toward her female coworkers in a radio factory. Desperate to keep the man interested, she develops an obsession with an expensive baby-blue dress, a rather obvious device (via the Blue Flower of Romanticism) for the projection of human longing into the commodity form. Caught stealing money from her mother, she accidentally kills her brother. Even during the ensuing trial, Renate insists on her inalienable right to be happy, a direct reference to the quintessentially American pursuit of happiness. Far for condemning her "feverish lust for life," the defense attorney reminds the socialist collective of its responsibility to all members, including those traumatized during the war and early postwar years. Working in a scrap metal factory as part of the conditions of her prison terms, Renate eventually learns to appreciate the rewards of hard physical labor. After her release, she is welcomed back into society with the promise of a romantic relationship to a fellow worker and the gift of a new blue dress manufactured, incidentally, by her predecessor Anni. In the film's propagandistic closing sequence, all three women happily join the celebrations during the World Youth Festival with a renewed commitment to "world peace and friendship among all nations."

If the three women stand for all those "dazzled by the false glitter of a doomed social system," what are we to make of the man at the center of such libidinal investments? Conny's parasitic existence and manipulative demeanor bring together a number of anticapitalist clichés. His black market connections implicate him in the inequities of the so-called free market economy and its exploitative system of supply and demand. His affected American phrases—"darling," "wonderful," and "bye-bye"—attest to the infiltration of postwar Germany by American tastes and attitudes. All of these allusions culminate in the close attention to elegant clothes and affected mannerisms that suggest strong effeminate, if not homosexual tendencies. Apart from the silk robes and scarves that function as a code for homosexuality, it is above all his complete lack of sex appeal to the women themselves that confirms this character's largely symbolic function.

Conny's identification primarily with bourgeois lifestyles and secondarily with American-style consumer culture culminates in a West Berlin nightclub scene distinguished from the rest of the film by its extensive rapid editing and visual symbolism. Confirming the earlier diagnosis of decadence, the spectacle of nouveau riche patrons dancing rock 'n' roll recalls imagery of social decline from the roaring twenties (via George Grosz and Otto Dix). Even more disconcertingly, the wall drawings of cigar-smoking apes closely resemble the racist iconography from Nazi propaganda campaigns against "Negro" jazz. By being associated with all social classes (i.e., the aristocracy, bourgeoisie, and petty bourgeoisie) except the one that brings about his downfall (i.e., the proletariat), Conny serves an important double role in the gendered scenarios of the Cold War. For by acting out what was often denounced as the feminizing effects of Americanization on the German male, the figure links older traditions of anti-Americanism to the new political rhetoric of anticapitalism and anti-imperialism. Significantly, the ubiquitous serial seducer is expelled from the socialist narrative by a young woman in a FDJ uniform, a highly significant scene that takes place under an advertisement for *Neues Deutschland* at the Friedrichstraße station. The political conclusions to be drawn from this last romantic encounter between east and west are spelled out clearly in the Hanns Eisler song performed during the film's triumphant finale, "Happiness is worth fighting for," which means, by building a unified front against Americanization in all of its social and cultural manifestations.

Thus, the rhetoric of anti-Americanism in the early Berlin films took two forms, exposing autonomous art as a function of bourgeois ideology and, by extension, of US imperialist aggression (in *Roman einer jungen Ehe*) and exposing the pursuit of happiness as a function of bourgeois individualism and, in its latest manifestation, of American consumer culture (in *Frauen-*

schicksale). These narrative solutions made Maetzig's humanist antifascism and Dudow's socialist realism part of a larger Cold War topography of demarcation, exclusion, and containment. On the one hand, both directors gave their female protagonists unprecedented narrative agency. Because of their association with the collective, these socialist heroines did not have to be punished with the kind of masculinization or hyperfeminization found in most West German women's films from the same period. On the other hand, the women's personal and political choices were shown to derive from their female nature, which manifested itself either instinctively, as in the virginal heroine of *Roman einer jungen Ehe,* or after a period of trials and tribulations, as in the reformed female sinners of *Frauenschicksale* and the naive young girl of *Eine Berliner Romanze.* Only through the simultaneous articulation and transformation of female desire, these films seemed to suggest, could East German identity be simultaneously conceived of as German (i.e., national) and non-German (i.e., international) and the problem of gender and sexuality be absorbed within the larger project of nation building.

During the second half of the decade, the connection between bourgeois individualism, the ethos of socialism, and the filmic imagination became increasingly politicized as these early conversion stories gave way to more aggressive cautionary tales that left no doubt about the political measures necessary to stop the continuing traffic in consumerist fantasies between East and West Berlin. In the process, strong female characters gradually disappeared from the grand narratives of building socialism, only to be reconfigured in the parallel projects of masculinization and militarization that, in the real metropolis, culminated in the building of the Berlin Wall. In the remaining pages, I want to sketch this line of argumentation by looking at the critically acclaimed Berlin films written by Wolfgang Kohlhaase and directed by Gerhard Klein, *Alarm im Zirkus* (1954, Alarm in the Circus), *Eine Berliner Romanze* (1956, A Berlin Romance), and *Berlin Ecke Schönhauser* (1958, Berlin at the Corner of Schönhauser).[12] Their neorealist style has been hailed as innovative, if not subversive, in much of the critical scholarship. However, in terms of their political commitments, these films cannot be separated from the anti-American arguments of the early 1950s, with the tone becoming increasingly antagonistic in light of the continuing dissemination of mass culture and consumer culture into East Berlin. Moreover, their male-dominated narratives introduce a decidedly dogmatic tone by conflating the crisis of (East German) masculinity, the provocation of female sexuality, and the influence of American mass culture, as well as by blaming the problems in postwar families on the weakening of authoritarian structures in public and private life.

Focusing on children, adolescents, and, in the case of *Eine Berliner Romanze,* young adults, Klein and Kohlhaase's Berlin trilogy takes advantage of the earlier tradition of east-west romances but depicts the resulting ideological conflicts with greater attention to the differences between the parent generation—that is, the founders of the GDR—and the children growing up during the 1950s.[13] *Eine Berliner Romanze* comes closest to the standard romantic pattern that places a young East Berlin woman, Uschi, between two young men from West Berlin. Whereas the more superficial of the two tries to participate in the Economic Miracle, the other, more thoughtful fellow recognizes the increase in poverty, unemployment, and housing shortages as part of a larger pattern of exploitation in capitalist societies. By moving in with the girl's solid working-class family, he consciously decides in favor of the socialist ethos of "work, struggle, and love." Whereas *Roman einer jungen Ehe* and *Frauenschicksale* treat female emancipation as a prerequisite for the building of socialism, the gendered representation of the Americanized youth culture in *Berliner Romanze* leaves little room for a strong female presence. The pretty HO salesgirl and aspiring model enables the filmmakers to present their critique of Americanization as part of a broader reflection on capitalism and modernity. In Uschi's misguided words, "In the west, everything is more modern"—that is, more fashionable, exciting, interesting, and desirable. But in leftist (and rightist) critiques of capitalism, modernity also means atomization, dislocation, and alienation; above all, it means the victory of the culture industry and the cult of the commodity. Rejecting this American model of democratization through mass cultural practices, the film's happy ending again relies on the young woman, now reduced to a mere object of male desire, to show the attractiveness of a third socialist alternative: the acceptance of modernization in the program of productivism and the rejection of individualism in the ethos of collectivism.

In typical neorealist fashion, Klein and Kohlhaase evoke the Americanization of East Berlin youth through their relationship to modern mass culture. In the case of Berlin *Ecke Schönhauser*, this means fashion choices like leather jackets, status objects like portable radios, favorite movies like "Devil in Blond," and English nicknames like Lord, Jimmy, and Charlie. Emulating their screen idols Marlon Brando and James Dean, these disaffected young men cultivate the aggressive masculinity of the working class, but in the commodified terms established by Hollywood. Their Americanization leads them to reject traditional family values for the fellowship of all-male groups; but their oppositional stances also functions as a vehicle for sexist attitudes and misogynist tendencies. Like the West German *Halbstarke* in the films by Georg Tressler, the East German *Rowdys* respond to the feared feminization of German men by retreating into homosocial structures and homoerotic situations. In both cases, the male-male attraction revolves around a shared obsession with consumer objects as convenient means of individual self-expression and, by extension, resistance to prevailing norms of sociability.[14] As in the West German *Die Halbstarken* (1956, The Hooligans), this defiant identification with American objects and practices takes place on the level of symbolic behavior. In the words of Dieter from *Berlin Ecke Schönhauser*, "When I stand on the street corner, I am a hooligan. When I dance boogie-woogie, I am American. When I wear my shirt tucked in, I am politically suspect."

The German rebel films make clear to what degree the attraction of American mass culture for these young men lies in its provocative effect on parent and authority figures. Yet what in the original context is directed against the social conformity of suburban middle-class America becomes, in the very different setting of Cold War Germany, a gesture with broader political implications—because it challenges the official ideology of economic prosperity in the west and of socialist nation building in the east. The obligatory denunciation of American mass culture (by priests or teachers in the west and by party members or policemen in the east) takes place in the name of a more authentic German culture, which of course means working-class culture in the east and middle-class culture in the west. In the process, the transformation of women into objects of male sexual desire and the subordination of the female perspective to the conflicts between rebellious sons and authoritarian father figures become important stabilizing elements in the intensifying conflict between two political systems. Cognizant of the inherent dangers in such an arrangement, *Berlin Ecke Schönhauser* thus closes with a call for greater vigilance: "Our enemies are everywhere where we are not."

In assessing the contribution of DEFA cinema (and, more generally, GDR culture) to the bifurcated narratives of postwar Americanization, we would have to take into account two additional factors that, because of limitations of space, can only be mentioned briefly here. After all, Americanization as a cultural model is thematized both through the form of specific representations (e.g., of American consumer products) and through the search for alternatives to the classical narrative models of Hollywood and the old UFA studio. First, a more thorough discussion of the critique of American mass culture and consumer culture would have to consider the aesthetic and ideological trajectory from the humanism of the early socialist melodramas (e.g., in the work of Maetzig) and the codification of a socialist realist style (e.g., in the work of Dudow) to the new visual sensibilities introduced through references to Italian neorealism (e.g., in the films of Klein and Kohlhaase). The more hidden patterns of anti-Americanism would also have to be connected to the official attacks on modernism—typically denounced as formalism—and the conflicting positions on the relevance of national traditions (e.g., expressionism) and international movements (e.g., existentialism) for the development of socialist art and entertainment.[15] Second, the highly gendered narratives of Americanization should ideally be analyzed as part of larger cultural configurations that include the relationship of genre cinema to the classical heritage in literature and the other arts; the contribution of socialist cinema to working-class culture and popular culture; and the enlistment of modern mass media in a multi-layered attack on American capitalism and imperialism that, among other things, serves to hide vestiges of German nationalism and cultural elitism. A critical assessment of this gendered topography of Cold War cinema would not be complete without at least some reference to the significant shifts in the self-understanding of the GDR from the antifascist socialism of the early reconstruction years to the continuing strategic adjustments within the entire Eastern Bloc captured in the rhetoric of freezes and thaws. Any detailed analysis of the gendering of anti-Americanism would ultimately have to extend to comparative perspectives not only between East and West German cinema but also among other East and West European cinemas similarly affected by postwar Americanization. Obviously such an enormous task cannot be accomplished on a few pages. Thus it might be more useful to conclude this discussion of Cold War cinema by calling for a reexamination of the very discourse of Americanization and anti-Americanism.

The current reassessment in German studies of postwar Americanization is structured around the West German master narrative from reconstruction to reunification. According to this hegemonic account, "America" during this period functioned as Germany's Other, and the prevailing stereotypes and clichés are to be read not as images of America but as images of self. Within such a system of projections and incorporations, America always signified difference, not just ordinary foreignness. Implicated in the difficult process of self-definition and self-representation, "America" provided a narrative of change and transformation, with Germany posited defensively at the receiving end of industrialization, mechanization, standardization, and rationalization—in short, of modernization. At the core of these reaction formations, most scholars conclude, was a deep-seated ambivalence toward modernity that found expression in various scenarios of Americanization and self-Americanization.[16]

My discussion of the DEFA Berlin films has shown that this western model cannot fully account for the complicated triangulation of politics, culture, and identity during the Cold War. After all, from the East German perspective of the 1950s, America did remain the radical Other that could not be integrated in any dreams of daily life under socialism, especially as regards its very different forms of identity formation and fantasy production. Kaspar Maase's notion of Americanization as cultural democratization may have moved the scholarly debates beyond the all-too-familiar conservative complaints about homogenization and commercialization of German culture during the Adenauer era.[17] However, the coupling of capitalism and democracy that has sustained the utopian, or fantastic, aspects of "America" for so long has, since the Third Reich and throughout the Cold War, also given rise to very different models of selective inclusion and exclusion in which repressive political systems have repeatedly enlisted American cultural and social phenomena in their very different projects of nation building. In light of recent political developments, the relationship between Americanization and anti-Americanism and, more specifically, between political and cultural anti-Americanism can no longer be explained through any simple binaries or affinities but must finally take into account the triangulated ideological configurations and the highly gendered fantasies of attraction and rejection that first developed during the Cold War.

Notes

1. Assuming the sentimental perspective of American tourists, many West German films continued in the tradition of *Heidelberger Romanze* (1951, A Heidelberg Romance) and *Königliche Hoheit* (1953, His Royal Highness), an adaptation of the eponymous Thomas Mann novella. Among the productions that included references to the American occupation, very few underscored the benefits to be gained from the kind of cultural exchanges depicted in the fraternization comedy *Hallo Fräulein!* (1949). More serious treatments could be found in *Toxi* (1952), where the appearance of the Afro-German child forces a middle-class family to confront their racist attitudes, and *Die goldene Pest* (1956, The Golden Plague), where the corrupt dealings of the village folk expose the deep moral crisis of postwar society. In the Hollywood films about the Allied occupation, the gendered division of labor between German *Geist* and American *Tat* that had characterized the American love affair with European culture until this point became taken over by hostility and suspicion. Noirish occupation dramas like Jacques Tourneur's *Berlin Express* (1948), Billy Wilder's *A Foreign Affair* (1948), and *The Big Lift* (1950), about the Berlin Blockade, set the tone for the entire decade by warning about the dangers of German-American sexual encounters. But in the end, the feminization of the defeated enemy always allowed the United States to assert its political, economic, and, most important for my discussion, cultural hegemony. For a general overview of Hollywood and the Cold War, see Nora Sayre, *Running Time: Films of the Cold War* (New York, 1982) and Ronnie D. Lipschutz, *Cold War Fantasies: Film, Fiction, and Foreign Policy* (Lanham, 2001).
2. For an introduction to postwar cinema in the Federal Republic, see Claudius Seidl, *Der deutsche Film der fünfziger Jahre* (Munich, 1987), Ursula Bessen, *Trümmer und Träume: Nachkriegszeit und fünfziger Jahre auf Zelluloid: Deutsche Spielfilme als Zeugnisse ihrer Zeit: Eine Dokumentation* (Bochum, 1989), and Micaela Jary, *Traumfabriken made in Germany: Die Geschichte des deutschen Nachkriegsfilms 1945-1960* (Berlin, 1993). On the relevance of postwar cinema for a reconceptualization of German film, see the excellent essay by Tassilo Schneider, "Reading Against the Grain: German Cinema and Film His-

toriography," in *Perspectives on German Cinema*, Terry Ginsberg and Kirsten Moana Thompson, eds. (New York, 1996), 29-47.

3. On the early years of DEFA, see Heinz Baumert and Hermann Herlinghaus, eds., *20 Jahre DEFA-Spielfilm von "Die Mörder sind unter uns" bis "Solange Leben in mir ist"* (Berlin, 1969). For general overviews, see Ralf Schenk, *Das weite Leben der Filmstadt Babelsberg: DEFA 1946-92* (Berlin, 1994), and Seán Allan and John Sanford, eds., *DEFA: East German Cinema, 1946-1992* (New York, 1999). On the representation of daily life in DEFA films, see Joshua Feinstein, *The Triumph of the Ordinary: Depictions of Daily Life in the East German Cinema* (Chapel Hill, 2002). On the present difficulties (and future possibilities) of placing DEFA cinema within German and East European cinema, see Barton Byg, "Introduction: Reassessing DEFA Today," 1-23, and Katie Trumpener, "DEFA: Moving Germany into Eastern Europe," 85-10, both in *Moving Images of East Germany: Past and Future of DEFA Film*, Barton Byg and Bethany Moore, eds. (Washington, D.C., 2002).

4. On gender as a central category in the study of postwar culture, see Erica Carter, *How German Is She? Postwar West German Reconstruction and the Consuming Woman* (Ann Arbor, 1997), especially "Film, Melodrama, and the Consuming Woman," 171-201; and Uta G. Poiger, *Jazz, Rock, and Rebels: Cold War Politics and American Culture in a Divided Germany* (Berkeley, 2000), especially "The Wild Ones: The 1956 Youth Riots and German Masculinity," 71-105.

5. On this later point, see Heide Fehrenbach, *Cinema in Democratizing Germany. Reconstructing National Identity after Hitler* (Chapel Hill, 1995), 234-53.

6. Wera and Claus Küchenmeister, review of *Eine Berliner Romanze*, rpt. in *Spielfilme der DDR im Urteil der Kritik*, Lissi Zilinski, et al., eds. (Berlin, 1970), 127. Citation modified, with "the protagonists" substituted for "Hans and Uschi."

7. For competing definitions of socialist culture during the 1950s, see Thomas Heimann, *DEFA, Künstler und SED-Kulturpolitik: Verständnis von Kulturpolitik und Filmproduktion in der SBZ/DDR 1945 bis 1959* (Berlin, 1994) and Dagmar Schittly, *Zwischen Regie und Regime: Die Filmpolitik der SED im Spiegel der DEFA-Produktionen* (Berlin, 2002). For a general overview, also see Manfred Jäger, *Kultur und Politik in der DDR 1945-1990* (Cologne, 1995).

8. Kurt Maetzig, "Unsere Absicht" (1950), rpt. in *Kurt Maetzig—Filmarbeit: Gespräche, Reden, Schriften*, ed. Günter Agde (Berlin, 1987), 218.

9. The Titania-Palast episode refers to the June 1950 founding of the Congress for Cultural Freedom (CCF), a CIA front organization. On the propagandistic role of Radio Free Europe (RFE) and Radio in the American Sector (RIAS) during the Cold War, see Walter L. Hixon, *Parting the Curtain: Propaganda, Culture, and the Cold War, 1945-1961* (New York, 1998), 29-55.

10. For an introduction to Dudow, see Hermann Herlinghaus, *Slatan Dudow* (Berlin, 1965). On the representation of working women in the DEFA film, see Uta Becher, "'Packen wir es an'—Die Darstellung der Arbeitswelt als Feld der Selbstverwirklichung von Frauen," in *Der geteilte Himmel: Arbeit, Alltag und Geschichte im ost-und westdeutschen Film*, Peter Zimmermann and Gebhard Moldenhauer, eds. (Constance, 2000), 381-97.

11. Nonetheless, the press attacked the 1949 production for failing to show typical figures in typical situations, a key requirement of socialist realist cinema. On the problem of the *Frauenüberschuß*, see Elizabeth D. Heineman, *What Difference Does a Husband Make? Women and Marital Status in Nazi and Postwar Germany* (Berkeley, 1999).

12. On this point, see Annette Kaminsky, *Wohlstand, Schönheit, Glück: Kleine Konsumgeschichte der DDR* (Munich, 2001). For a comparative West German perspective, see

Jennifer A. Loehlin, *From Rags to Riches: Housework, Consumption, and Modernity in Germany* (New York, 1999).

13. The protagonists from East Berlin belong to the generational cohort of 1949 described by Dorothee Wierling as being socialized into an identity markedly different from that of West Germans, given the prevalence of working mothers, the emphasis on collective settings, and the ubiquitous politicization of private life. See "Mission to Happiness: The Cohort of 1949 and the Making of East and West Germans," in *The Miracle Years*, 110-25. On youth culture in the Berlin films, see Horst Claus, "Rebels with a Cause: The Development of the *Berlin-Filme* by Gerhard Klein and Wolfgang Kohlhaase," in *DEFA: East German Cinema*, 93-116. On the films' gender politics, also see Julie Gregson, "East or West—A Straight Choice? Representations of Masculinity and Constructions of National Identity in Wolfgang Kohlhaase and Gerhard Klein's 'Berlin-Ecke Schönhauser,'" in *Millennial Essays on Film and Other German Studies*, Daniela Berghahn and Alan Bance, eds. (Oxford, 2002), 63-78.

14. In a longer contribution, it might also be worthwhile to examine further the connection established by the DEFA rubble films—for example *Die Mörder sind unter uns* (1946, The Murderers Are among Us), *Irgendwo in Berlin* (1946, Somewhere in Berlin), and *Razzia* (1947, Raid)—between the crisis of German identity and the crisis of masculinity, as articulated through the figures of the missing or ineffectual father and of the (sexually or racially ambiguous) stranger preying on fatherless boys. On gendering in the rubble film, see Erica Carter, "Sweeping Up the Past: Gender and History in the Post-war German 'Rubble Film,'" in *Heroines without Heroes: Reconstructing Female and National Identities in European Cinema, 1945-1951*, ed. Ulrike Sieglohr (London, 2000), 91-110.

15. A brief discussion of East German anti-Americanism during the 1950s can be found in Ina Merkel, "Eine andere Welt. Vorstellungen von Nordamerika in der DDR der fünfziger Jahre," in *Amerikanisierung: Traum und Alptraum*, 245-54. On the bifurcated nature of postwar Americanziation, also see Michael Geyer, "America in Germany: Power and the Pursuit of Americanization," in *The German-American Encounter: Conflict and Cooperation between Two Cultures, 1800-2000*, Frank Trommler and Elliot Shore, eds. (New York and Oxford, 2001), 121-44.

16. On West German patterns of argumentation, including the defensive strategies of self-Americanization, also see Ermarth, "'Amerikanisierung' und deutsche Kulturkritik 1945-1965," in Jarusch and Siegrist, *Amerikanisierung*, 312-34.

17. Kaspar Maase, "Establishing Cultural Democracy: Youth, 'Americanization,' and the Irresistible Rise of Popular Culture," in *The Miracle Years: A Cultural History of West Germany, 1949-68*, ed. Hanna Schiessler (Princeton, 2001), 428-50. On "Americanization" as a critical category in debates on the Adenauer era, see "Amerikanisierung von unten. Demonstrative Vulgarität und kulturelle Hegemonie in der Bundesrepublik der 50er Jahre," in Lüdtke et al., *Amerikanisierung*, 291-313 and "'Amerikanisierung der Gesellschaft': Nationalisierende Deutung von Globalisierungsprozessen?" in Jarusch and Sigrist, *Amerikanisierung und Sowjetisierung*, 219-41. On the Americanization of cinema, also see his "'Halbstarke' and Hegemony: Meanings of American Mass Culture in the Federal Republic of Germany during the 1950s," in *Cultural Transmissions and Receptions: American Mass Culture in Europe*, R. W. Rydell et al., eds. (Amsterdam, 1993), 152-70.

GERMAN CINEMA FACE TO FACE WITH HOLLYWOOD
Looking into a Two-Way Mirror

◆ ◆ ◆

Thomas Elsaesser

The patterns of competing, cooperating, and contending with Hollywood and the American presence in the German film business from 1945 to 2000 can be outlined, I think, across three different phases and three types of narrative: the first one is broadly economic-political, the second is governmental-institutional, and the third is cultural-authorial. Depending on which narrative one prefers, the periodization will also slightly shift. The cultural and legal models often prefer the phases 1945 to 1962, 1962 to 1982, and 1982 to 2000, while the economic periodization is somewhat simpler: it knows two cycles that run from 1945 to 1971, and from 1974 to today. The first period marks the apparent apogee, but in fact reflects the gradual decline of Hollywood hegemony (what might be called "Dominance in Disarray"); the second period marks Hollywood redux ("Dominance through Dispersal"). Since I shall be mostly looking at the issues from a German rather than Hollywood perspective, I shall keep the triple period division. However, for reasons that I hope will become clear at the end, a fair amount of overlap and blurring of these boundaries is inevitable, since I also want to contrast an orthodox account with a "revisionist" account, where the latter takes a European perspective, in contrast to the primarily national—in our case, Germano-centric—emphasis of the canonical story.

Traditionally, the economic model has been applied mainly to the first phase, from 1945 to 1960: it is the story of how Hollywood attained hegemony in the German film market, through a policy of divide and rule. It focuses on the dismantling of the heavily centralized prewar film industry, the forced

---

Notes for this section begin on page 184.

regionalization of German production units, and the dumping practices of American distributors in order to saturate the market with Hollywood films.[1]

The second phase is generally given over to the cultural model, typified by strong governmental intervention and a legislative framework. It relies on the notion of the *Autorenfilm* and the New Waves: for Germany, this means the Young German Film, followed by the New German Cinema. It stands under the sign of oedipal revolt: *Papa's Kino ist tot*, long live the *Autor*, which is why the cultural model could also be called the oedipal-generational approach to succession, filiation, and transmission. As I have shown elsewhere, the New German Cinema's relation to Hollywood is largely a function of this generational revolt—with interesting consequences at the cross-cultural level of identification and projection, producing some of the strategies of othering and the mirroring-effects alluded to in my title. During these years between 1962 and 1982, Hollywood's presence on the German cinema screen, with one or two exceptions that I shall return to, is of relatively little consequence for the cultural model. By contrast, American-produced shows on German television, notably in 1977 and 1979, were to be of momentous consequence for the New German Cinema.

The third phase encompasses the period since the early 1980s, when Hollywood returned in force to the German big screens with its blockbusters and must-see "event" movies, changing both the priorities of production and the patterns of exhibition (urban multiplexes, the Cinemaxx chain), thus radically altering the cinema-going experience. At the same time, some of the brightest talents in filmmaking, production, and distribution—though not only there, but across the whole media sector—could not enter into business with Hollywood and US companies fast enough.

In this chapter, I shall attempt to nuance this picture somewhat, above all, by trying to apply the double focus—economic and cultural—to all three periods just outlined, in order to put up for discussion in what sense film relations with the United States are invariably both economic and cultural, mediated by the state more than by the market. That this has always been the case is one of my subtending contentions: I argue that the complex *cultural* relations in matters of moving images and visual icons between Europe and the United States since 1945, with Germany perhaps representing a special case, are actually a replay of the *economic* relations during the 1920s and early 1930s, so that US-German film relations show great continuities across the whole of the last century.

The question this raises for our present century, then, is whether the stereotypical binary divides, in which Europe stands for culture, and America for commerce, still hold, or if we can perceive, and conceive, of a somewhat different alignment. Here are, for quick reference, some of the implicit items of conventional wisdom, as they characterize not only the cinematic divide: Europe stands for art, and the United States for pop; Europe for high culture, America for mass entertainment; Europe for artisanal craft, America for industrial mass production; Europe for state (subsidy), Hollywood for studio (box office); European cinema for pain and effort, Hollywood for pleasure and thrills; Europe for the auteur, Hollywood for the star; Europe for experiment and discovery, Hollywood for formula and marketing; Europe for the film festival circuit, Hollywood for Oscar night; Europe for the festival hit, Hollywood for the blockbuster.

An additional interest in presenting this table is to ask whether in all this juxtaposition and polarization, there might be a hidden dialectic that we film scholars have not yet figured out, but where our colleagues from other disciplines, notably economic and political historians, might usefully offer suggestions.

But first, to flesh out briefly the economic history of Hollywood hegemony: the phase from 1945 to 1962 was characterized by the US State Department directives to prevent another Ufa empire from arising during the postwar reconstruction period of the *Wirtschaftswunder*, while fully benefiting from the boom in consumption and leisure, by keeping the enormously important German market wide open for American films.[2] In effect, an economic imperative (free market nonprotectionist film policy for US product) and an ideological-political imperative (reeducation and democratization of the German people) happily coincided, to the benefit of Hollywood, preventing postwar West German cinema from being more than a cottage industry operating in an assembly-line economic environment. This happened not without internal contradictions or resistance even in the United States. Let me cite two instances. In a famous speech from 1947, Spyros Skouras, head of 20th Century Fox, argued that

> it is a solemn responsibility of our industry to increase motion picture outlets throughout the free world because it has been shown that no medium can play a greater part than the motion picture industry in indoctrinating people into the free way of life and instil[ling] in them a compelling desire for freedom and hope for a brighter future. Therefore, we as an industry can play an infinitely important part in the world-wide ideological struggle for the minds of men, and confound the Communist propagandists.[3]

Thomas Guback has detailed how, despite these fine and patriotic sentiments, the Hollywood film industry was able to hold the Military Government to ransom over the use of American films for reeducation and propaganda purposes. Only when the Motion Picture Export Association, headed by its powerful and indomitable president Jack Valenti, was satisfied that its earnings on the German market could be converted into dollar-holdings and there were no restrictions on the free movement of capital did Hollywood follow its words with deeds. This happened when the United States Senate passed the

Information Media Guarantee Program in 1948, which effectively gave the go-ahead for the commercial exploitation of the German market:

> The reluctance of American companies to send films to West Germany ... was a result of concerns with revenue. Even the Military Government's objective, to re-educate Germany, was not sufficient incentive for the companies. The event which turned the trickle of American films into a torrent was, clearly, the initiation of guarantees by the American government. That the IMG program was lucrative to Hollywood was apparent when ... Congressman H.R. Gross attacked film industry lobby in Washington and the IMG, declaring that ... the "Motion Picture Export Association has been given a pretty good ride on the Informational Media gravy train...".[4]

By 1951, over two hundred American films were released annually in the three Western-occupied zones. For the German cinema, trying to reestablish indigenous film production out of the ruins of what had, from the 1920s onwards, been one of the most prosperous and technically advanced film industries, this saturation of the market proved a permanent handicap.[5]

However, in light of recent empirical research, this story needs revision. According to Joseph Garncarz, for instance, the German commercial cinema, despite several crisis cycles, actually survived and occasionally thrived during the years 1947 and 1970; it was economically viable, even if it had little critical prestige and virtually no export chances.[6] What kept it respectable was its domestic market share of spectators, with German films year-in, year-out outperforming Hollywood titles at the box office until 1970.

The still unanswered question is why West Germany could not develop the mixed model of an art cinema and a commercial cinema that Italy and France maintained throughout the 1960s and well into the 1970s, or develop along the British model by retooling its studio-capacity to provide US offshore production facilities, specialist craftspeople for Hollywood companies, as in the James Bond films or for the *Star Wars* saga, and exporting its popular culture (the Beatles films, swinging London comedies) to America's youth. Italy, it must be said, also experienced a collapse of its film industry similar to that in Germany around 1972-1973, when the spaghetti western—Italy's own coming to terms with Hollywood—ceased to attract audiences, and domestic comedies with Toto or Fernandel became relics of a bygone age.

As to Germany, was it new technologies, such as the videotape revolution, that killed off German genre cinema? Was it television? Was it the new marketing strategies of the Hollywood blockbuster? None would be specific to Germany, so an additional factor might have to come into play, such as the particular paradoxical and politically complicated generational transfer in West Germany. It would point to a cultural, rather than an economic, legacy that at least for a period seems to have inflected the US-German film axis, but it did so across an inter-German conflict situation.

With this we enter the second phase: the years from the Oberhausen Manifesto in 1962 to the Hamburg Declaration in 1977, and from the "German Autumn" of 1977 to the death of Rainer Werner Fassbinder in 1982, which coincided with the end of the social-liberal coalition of the Brandt-Schmidt years.

The Young and New German Cinema had very distinct attitudes toward Hollywood, ranging from total hostility to ambivalence, and from playing off one good auteurist America-Hollywood, against another, bad imperialist America-Hollywood. Despite some harsh words from directors like Wim Wenders about "the Yanks having colonized our subconscious," we know that Wenders in particular was probably the classical Hollywood cinema's greatest and most knowledgeable fan among New German directors. But Wenders already belonged to the second generation. The Young German Cinema of Alexander Kluge and Edgar Reitz—that is, those born ten years earlier—was more or less solidly anti-American from the start; their oppositional stance against commercial mainstream (German) cinema extended to Hollywood, probably under the double impact of seeing their entry into filmmaking blocked by ex-Nazi directors still dominating the industry, and seeing the entry of their independently made films into the German cinemas blocked by US distributors, who were of course supported by cinema owners, even where these were German-owned (their numbers dwindling as the 1970s wore on).

Also significant for shaping the image of Hollywood was the role of journalists and critics around the Munich-based monthly *Filmkritik*. Here, too, the second generation (among whom could be found future filmmakers such as Wenders and Rudolf Thome) proved more pro-Hollywood than the first and the third. After the initially exclusive aesthetics of neorealism (anti-Hollywood), there came to prominence, from the mid-1960s onwards, a faction who took over from the *Cahiers du cinéma* the reevaluation of the Hollywood director as auteur. These critics (including Enno Patalas and Frieda Grafe) made clear distinctions between the 1960's American productions they mostly detested, and the classic Hollywood of the 1930s and 1940s by American auteurs whom they celebrated: John Ford, Alfred Hitchcock, Howard Hawks. A special place was reserved for the Germans working in Hollywood: besides the 1920s émigrés Ernst Lubitsch and F.W. Murnau, they championed the political exiles Fritz Lang, Billy Wilder, Max Ophuls, and even such commercial contract directors like Robert Siodmak, or later, the Hollywood B-movie director Douglas Sirk (after the British had "rediscovered" him).

The ambivalences characterizing the New German Cinema directors vis-à-vis America (the label and thus the distinction "New German Cinema," incidentally, was also invented by Anglo-American critics and scholars) can be described by several mutually interdependent identity formations. I have called it the oedipal matrix, where I distinguish the colonial paradigm, the elective paternity paradigm, and the no-contest or "American friend" paradigm.[7]

Both the colonizing cliché and the oedipal dimension of conflict and contest come very directly out of the postwar German generation's experience of Hollywood hegemony and the reeducation effort, which had an impact not on the first but second generation. While their parents may have been obdurately high-culture in their tastes and outlook, preferring Sartre or Camus to Steinbeck and Reader's Digest while shunning the cinema altogether, the generation of Wenders, Fassbinder, and Werner Herzog not only grew up with but embraced American cinema, AFN radio, and Disney comics, finding in them a liberation and refuge from the stultifying, repressed, and dishonest atmosphere of the parental home during the Adenauer years. Wenders's perhaps over-quoted line about American colonization from *Im Lauf der Zeit* (released in English under the title *Kings of the Road*) needs to be balanced against his other famous remark, where he called rock and roll his "lifesaver" as an adolescent, at a moment in which American popular culture provided the antidote to "twenty years [of parental amnesia ...]; we filled it with Mickey Mouse, Polaroids and chewing gum." Thus, "the Yanks have colonized our subconscious" points in several directions at once, and in the narrative-filmic context in which it occurs, it functions both approvingly and critically: one of the two protagonists cannot get the lyrics of a pop song out of his head. Furthermore, the site of the scene is also important: an abandoned US patrol hut at the German-German border. Faced with this barbed-wire border, it seems preferable to have one's subconscious colonized by American rock music than to be an actual colony of the Soviet Union, like the other Germany the two young men can see from the US Army lookout. In other words, the protagonists allude to America at a juncture in their journey where they are forcibly reminded of the historical events that had brought the Americans to Germany in the first place, and in what role (as liberators from Nazism, and as buffer from Stalinism). Not unimportant for the structure and ideological work of the film is also the fact that the remark is made at a point in the two men's wary friendship, when a growing intimacy and regression to childhood threatens their sense of separate and (hetero-)sexual identity. It indicates in Wenders's oeuvre the homoerotic undercurrent, associated in his mind with American popular culture, which eventually became his way of resolving the oedipal confrontation with the fathers via the two-buddies-on-the-road or two-angels-in-the-city solution.

Without detailing here the discursive texture and filmic embodiments of these different positions among the leading figures of the New German Cinema, one can nonetheless observe that across the split between past Hollywood grandeur (of classic auteurs and maverick outsiders inside America) and the present—that is, the 1960s and 1970s imperialist US superpower, operating, as it was perceived, repressively outside its borders—the German directors tried to reconstruct their own national imaginary between the liberal traditions of the Weimar Republic and the totalitarian horrors of the Nazi period. Filmmakers regularly "adopted" good elective fathers, in order to reject their own bad (Nazi cinema or natural) fathers. One finds, for instance, very strong elective paternity suits by Wenders (Nick Ray and Sam Fuller) and Fassbinder (Douglas Sirk, Raoul Walsh, and Michael Curtiz). But one cannot help being disconcerted by the extraordinary anti-Hollywood diatribes of an Edgar Reitz and Hans Jürgen Syberberg. Thus, Hollywood came to function as a complex signifier—both catalyst and stick with which to beat the opposition—in the post-1968 German intergenerational confrontation, which culminated politically in the Red Army Fraction and cinematically in *Germany in Autumn*. The "return to history" among the art-cinema directors found its echo in the "Hitler Wave" of the popular media and the retro-fashion films from Italy, France, and Germany (Ingmar Bergman filming in Munich-Geiselgasteig), and yet this typically European or even German obsession with the recent past was itself not unaffected by the 1972 American hit movie *Cabaret*, with its stylish revival of 1930s fashion and iconography.

West Germany's cinephile identity formation around oedipal paradigms was broken up with the screening of the US-television series *Holocaust* in 1978 and 1979. Such was the shock at discovering American television "appropriating" *the* German subject par excellence that the New German Cinema "responded" with films by Volker Schlöndorff (*The Tin Drum*), Kluge (*The Patriot*), Syberberg (*Hitler - A Film from Germany*), Fassbinder (*The Marriage of Maria Braun*), Margarethe von Trotta (*The German Sisters*), Helma Sanders Brahms (*Germany Pale Mother*), culminating in Reitz's 1984 *Heimat*.[8] This so-called mastering-the-past debate gave the New German Cinema its internationally defining identity, but it left a notable gap: the whole debate around the television series *Holocaust* kept the issue of German-Jewish relations (i.e., anti-Semitism) prior to *Kristallnacht* and after Auschwitz out of the German directors' pictures. Excluding one or two of the films of Fassbinder, Kluge, and the little-known Herbert Achternbusch, the omission was hardly noticed as significant—except by American critics. How can you represent somebody or something whose disappearance you do not acknowledge, whose presence you do not miss?[9]

These, then, would be some of the markers or terms for reconstructing a particular cultural line of transfer and transmission, wherein Hollywood, time and again, played a role in catalyzing, exacerbating, or profiling German film culture's relation to its own identity. One could say that after denial and disavowal in the 1950s, and opposition and rejection in the 1960s, we find in the 1970s patterns of reverse identification with America and even over-identification with Hollywood. In other words, the coherence, purpose, and identity of the New German Cinema, during the brief period in which it was experienced as both new and German, was founded on a series of fantasies that involved Hollywood literally and metaphorically, materially and as the imaginary other. Furthermore, almost all the aesthetic debates as well as the film-politics—focused on German cinema as a national cinema during the 1970s and 1980s—were displaced versions of antagonism and competition, of oedipal rivalry and submission to Hollywood: perverse in Syberberg, disingenuous in Reitz, geographically dislocated in Herzog, disarmingly devious in Fassbinder, and filial-fraternal in Wenders.

In terms of a cross-cultural exchange, these fantasies are eminently readable: first, they belong to a very traditional German history in which America has so often served as the screen of self-projection and self-alienation.[10] But the fantasies of *Fernweh* and homecoming can also be read as a fairly precise account of acts of self-creation (by the *Autor*) in a specific film-historical conjunction, by a cinema that wants to be national and representative, but because it disavowed its own popular cinema (both *Papa's Kino* of the 1950s and the Ufa genres of the 1940s), had to go to Hollywood to legitimate itself. In the course of this, it staged a revolt as well as a submission, and then rewrote this dependency into a Kaspar Hauser foundling story (in Herzog, Wenders), an exile story (Herzog's Kinski figures), and into the return of the prodigal son (Wenders again, Syberberg, and the opening scene and repeated motif in Reitz' *Heimat*): both stories together made up West Germany's own myth of a "national" and "independent" cinema, in a movie business that by then had become global and interdependent or not at all.

Possibly realizing the artistically productive, but economically crippling, miscognitions in this self-understanding of a national or auteur cinema in a rapidly globalizing environment, a segment of Germany's filmmaking community turned away from such tormented love-hate relationships with Hollywood in the mid-1980s. Instead, they transformed the encounter with an imaginary America, mirroring an introspective and retrospective Germany still in thrall to its recent history, into a more or less straightforward exchange. Abandoning imaginary over-identification and virtual exile, these directors and directors of photography (Wolfgang Petersen, Michael Ballhaus, to name the two most prominent) practiced a deliberate and open emulation of Hollywood: their dream was to make films that either found a large popular audience or pleased an American distributor, in order then to set off and emigrate to New York and Los Angeles.[11]

If, for much of the 1980s, it was the multiply refractured, projected, and introjected Hollywood that gave the work of Wenders, Herzog, and Fassbinder its precarious German identity, the names associated with emulation and subsequent emigration are, besides Petersen (*In the Line of Fire, Out-*

break, Airforce One, The Perfect Storm), Roland Emmerich (*Stargate, Independence Day, Godzilla, The Patriot*), and Uli Edel (*Last Exit to Brooklyn, Body of Evidence*), all of whom have been making films in Hollywood itself, but for global audiences. Instead of the Lacanian mirror-phase, of "colonizing the unconscious," or acting out a Kaspar Hauser complex, the talk is now of tax shelters, package deals, talent scouts, product repurposing, and corporate synergies.

Considered from the German side, however, this third phase is not without its own mirroring effects. First, in some respects it repeats and mirrors the transatlantic movie trade of the 1920s, with German directors, such as Ernst Lubitsch, Fritz Lang, and F.W Murnau embracing Hollywood production methods and genres already when working in Germany (as did Petersen, Edel, and Emmerich in the 1980s when they started in Germany), in the hope of being offered Hollywood contracts. Petersen and company were joined by Michael Ballhaus, Fassbinder's former cameraman, who became the Karl Freund of his generation, with credits (besides working for Petersen) on films by Martin Scorsese and Francis Ford Coppola, such as *Goodfellas, The Age of Innocence, Bram Stoker's Dracula, Gangs of New York*. These German film people are singularly successful in adapting themselves, at least compared with their fellow filmmakers from the same generation, such as Schlöndorff, Percy Adlon, and Wenders, who also made films directly in the United States, but whose sojourns were brief and for whom Hollywood in retrospect appeared to be a career detour rather than the chosen destination.

Second, the mirroring effects extend to the films themselves, especially when one switches perspectives and looks at the mirror from the other side, that is, from Hollywood. The picture so far given implies that already during the second phase—from 1960 to 1980—Hollywood had let slip its dominant position not only in Germany but had lost its grip on audiences worldwide. To some extent, this is true. Although Hollywood experienced its deepest domestic crisis in the 1950s, as the Paramount decree demanded de-cartelization, and television took away its core clients (the family audience), the impact on foreign sales only manifested themselves fully in the 1960s. The old formulas no longer worked; not even new technologies such as Cinemascope, epic subjects, or lavish musicals could keep audiences or attract the younger generation, especially abroad. Thus, the springtime of the new waves all over Europe—not just in Germany, which was a latecomer when we think of Britain, France, Poland, and even Brazil—resulted in part not from the strength of the European auteurs but to the weakness of Hollywood itself.

Nonetheless, the long years of structural changes in America's audio-visual entertainment sector gave Europe breathing space. While Hollywood was in disarray, Europe made some inroads that have permanently changed the film cultural landscape. The 1960s, for instance, were the time of the growing importance of the film festival circuits, which emerged as a new force in European cinema, developing an alternative system of promotion, distribution, exhibition (and sometimes even an alternative production model), coexisting with Hollywood. The festivals—Cannes, Venice, Berlin, London, New York, Sundance—provided the launching pads for auteurs and national movements, not least for directors from Germany. The programming of these regular venues throughout the year became, together with the Goethe Institutes, the institutional base from which German independent directors benefited, especially during the 1980s.

While film festivals took on a new importance for art cinema auteurs and independent productions worldwide, the reorganization of the American film industry was also largely completed by the middle of the Reagan years. New ownership patterns in the production sector (Hollywood's old studio facilities turned over to making television series), a new business model of the delivery systems (the rise of cable and the prerecorded video tape market, for instance), and synergies in repackaging content (culminating in the Time Warner deal) were some of the economic changes that led to the remarkable revival of Hollywood as the world's premier provider of mass entertainment. The new cultural hegemony, on the other hand, was in part due to new branding and advertising methods, which in turn relied on the reorganization of Hollywood's global markets through distribution agreements among the studios, who formed cartels for their overseas distribution, by acquiring worldwide outlets and thus the ability to program thousands of first run cinema the world over for opening a film wide, which is to say, to schedule carefully coordinated release dates and thereby reap profits from theatrical release very quickly, within two to three weeks. The rise of the blockbuster as a new marketing concept (tie-ins, merchandising, the Disney and Dreamworks high-concept movies that now dominate popular entertainment) thus represents a gradual and complex story, based economically on reestablishing so-called vertical integration and culturally on the return of family audiences to the new multiplexes, the capturing of the youth market, notably with movies that appeal to young women as well as men. The blockbuster concept also racked up the cost of such movies to unprecedented levels, generating the need to suck in venture capital but also multiplying the risk to investors, with the not unwelcome side-effect of excluding most European countries (with their delicate balance of state-funding, television production money and weak box office for their audiovisual sector) from being able to afford a commercial film industry.

Important for our topic is that Hollywood in the age of the blockbuster is servicing global audiences, with often very different tastes. Just as it had done in the 1920s, it has thus been interested in recruiting filmmakers and film personnel from all over the world who can deliver these global audiences. Thus, the 1990s saw an unprecedented influx of foreign talent to Hollywood, among whom the German contingent forms a substantial but by no means exceptional part. Once one thinks of tiny Netherlands, which with Paul Verhoeven and Jan de Bont also supplied two top blockbuster directors, or remembers France, where Luc Besson and Jean Pierre Jenet have made the trip to Los Angeles (and back to Paris) several times, not to mention Finland (Rene Harlin), Spain (Alejandro Amenábar), and Ireland (Neil Jordan), then the success of the German directors mentioned above no longer seems exceptional. It is dwarfed, for instance, by the stream of talent from Australia (Peter Weir, Phil Noyce, Mel Gibson), New Zealand (Peter Jackson, Lee Tamahori), and Great Britain, where John Borman, Ridley and Tony Scott, Alan Parker, Adrian Lyne, Mike Figgis led the way in the 1980s, with a veritable invasion, and where a British producer, David Puttnam, actually occupied the position of studio head of a major Hollywood company (Columbia Pictures), albeit briefly.

This 1980s and 1990s influx of directors was itself the succession of an earlier migration or trickle, partly caused by the thaw in Eastern Europe in the late 1960s—Milos Foreman, Roman Polanski, but including also Louis Malle and even, briefly, Michelangelo Antonioni, the Wim Wenders of his generation in this respect, if you pardon the anachronism. The Russians, too, after the collapse of the Soviet Union, provided some new talent to Hollywood (Andrej Konchalowsky comes to mind), but many more continue to come to Hollywood from East Asia, India, Mexico.

An economic perspective thus sees the 1990s under the sway of the American model: providing global markets with entertainment by buying up international talent and content, while controlling distribution and exhibition, by exporting the multiplex cinema, complete with merchandising and popcorn. Across its three postwar phases—Hollywood hegemony, Hollywood in disarray, and Hollywood redux—the studio system with its constant striving for vertical integration has remained remarkably stable over a very long period. It proved adept at adapting itself to new technologies, to new demographics and business models, emerging as a global force, despite bankruptcies, takeovers by foreign interests, and other challenges, such as the video cassette, digitization, and the Internet. This American model of popular culture, as we know, is still making vast inroads, even in areas of the globe where other aspects of American values and especially American foreign policy agendas are sharply condemned or encounter violent and bloody resistance.

Europe—and especially Germany—was not able to either reverse-engineer the American model successfully (as did Hong Kong, for instance, and Bollywood, India's popular cinema) or to counter it with a film industry model of its own (as did Egypt in the 1980s and Iran in the 1990s). Within Europe, as indicated, France and Britain were much more successful than Germany.

France excelled in the area of what one might call cultural prototypes: French films have been remade in the United States, sometimes by another director (*Three Men and a Baby*), sometimes by the same one (*Nikita*). Yet thanks to journals such as *Cahiers du cinéma* in the 1950s and 1960s, France also provided much of the theory by which America now evaluates, celebrates, and appropriates its own cinematic heritage and the history of Hollywood. Britain was most successful in the area of popular music, playing back to US audiences their own ethnic and regional music: bands such as the Rolling Stones, the Beatles, and the Animals systematically repackaged as youth and rebranded as pop American rhythm and blues, rock and roll, country music, gospel music, and other forms of ethnic popular music.

Nothing of this kind can be said of Germany, whose impact on America's popular culture has only been in the area of automobiles: from the VW beetle, via the BMW, to the luxury division of Mercedes and Porsche. Compared to this, the New German Cinema—whether with commercial or art-house films—cut a very poor figure even in its heyday, and economically played no role at all.

However, this is where the broadly cultural parameters of my analysis may well offer some compensation and correction: what I earlier described as the generational or oedipal model, and which I here call the two-way mirror model of cultural transfer, applies (as I have just tried to indicate) also the other way round, namely, to America itself. The case of Britain and pop music, and of France and critical discourses, are both based on a sort of mirror function: Europe appropriates something from the United States, reprocesses or rearticulates it across a European sensibility and then plays it back to the United States, whose dissident intellectuals, maverick artists, and sometimes even popular audiences are happy to perceive themselves thus culturally upgraded and recognized in the mirror of their European fans and admirers. Just as the American novel of Faulkner and Hemingway after 1945 found itself accepted as serious literature by the appreciation of a Gide, a Sartre, or a Claude Edmonde Magny, so Martin Scorsese, Francis Ford Coppola, Paul Schrader, and Steven Spielberg learned to love their own past Hollywood cinema across the panegyrics penned by Francois Truffaut, Claude Chabrol, Jacques Rivette, and Jean Luc Godard. One might say that both the British and the French have, in their different ways, been playing at being American without losing their own distinctive cultural inflexion. As American signs, icons, and values are retranslated twice over, they produce not so much the Chinese whisper effect of surrealist *cadavres exquis*, nor the hybridization so vaunted by postcolonial theorists, but an amplification effect that knows its own noise and interference yet offers a sort of dialogue across the Europe-America divide that seems to have added cultural capital to the cinema rather than pushed it down-market.

The German case is somewhat different and more complex. It is different in that West Germany never had the popular culture appeal of working-class Britain: nothing to compare with the Beatles from Liverpool (who got their start in Hamburg), the Rolling Stones from suburban London, and the Animals from Newcastle. The best Germany could offer was the internationalization of the *Heimatfilm*, but that was *The Sound of Music*, a Hollywood production, of course, set in Salzburg, Austria. Nor did Germany have the high-culture discourse of Parisian cinephiles. On the contrary, its dominant postwar intellectual idiom, the Frankfurt School critical theory, was notoriously hostile to American popular culture, comparing it more than once to Nazism.

Yet precisely because of the legacy of Nazism, the situation is also more complex than in France or Britain. For Adorno and Horkheimer rightly recognized that Nazism had produced one of the most seductively modern and mediatized forms of populism, with a strong iconography of styling and design, the political equivalent of marketing a brand. I therefore may need to modify what I said about Germany only marketing its automobiles as popular culture. As already hinted at, its other export to the United States in the 1970s and 1980s were narratives and images of its national disaster. The New German Cinema became critically successful and culturally significant when it began to "represent" its terrible history in the form of stories about Nazism and the war. Virtually all the films still remembered from the New German Cinema have this twelve-year period and its aftermath as their direct or indirect topic (*The Tin Drum, Our Hitler, The Marriage of Maria Braun, Lili Marleen, The German Sisters, Germany in Autumn, The Patriot, The Power of Feelings, Germany Pale Mother, Heimat*, and *Wings of Desire*). We may think this is because of the quality of the films or the gravity of the subject matter, but in the United States it is Nazism that carried a special recognition value for the signifier "Germany" within popular culture. It has been and still is a taboo-breaking, transgressive signifier, emotionally, ideologically as well as libidinally, besides having—in these films—the high-culture appeal necessary to make some impact in the American public sphere. That a political and human disaster with unimaginable individual tragedies, where indescribable crimes and atrocities were committed by men of unremitting evil, should be a subject that "played well" in both the popular mass media and in high-brow culture may be an observation of egregious callousness. So let me phrase somewhat differently what seems to be at stake. Seen as another moment of cultural transfer and transatlantic transmission, two aspects of "fascinating fascism" and its cinematic representations call for comment: first, the construction of the meaning of Nazism and the Holocaust for Germans themselves and between Germany and the rest of the world; and second, the generic coding of heroes and villains in popular culture generally, where their function is generally the testing through transgressions of the social norms of a community, and the boundaries of what it means to be human.

The representability of the Holocaust and the interpretations of Nazism have remained to this day not only a topic among professional historians. They are probes for the state of public debate, and the possibilities of cultural dialogue, tested by unresolved issue of victims and perpetrators, survivors and the second generation, and of their mutual claims upon each other, their self-images and representational spaces. In this respect the somewhat embarrassing statements of Hans Jürgen Syberberg,[12] or the seemingly naive remarks of Edgar Reitz[13] in reply to Elie Wiesel,[14] were nonetheless tokens of a dialogue and an exchange, however truncated, just as the role of a Francis Ford Coppola in giving the films of Syberberg and Herzog American art-house and "special event" distribution greatly enhanced their visibility, not by bringing them to Hollywood but to San Francisco, the Bay Area, and Berkeley's Pacific Film Archive instead.

How this entrepreneurial activity of Coppola fits into his own self-image of the Shakespearean overachiever in love with grandiose failure is an aspect of my topic I cannot fully enter into here. But it helps me build a bridge to the second issue at stake, as well as to yet another two-way mirror effect, attached to my third phase, that of German-born filmmakers in Hollywood since the 1990s. For this emulation-emigration generation, I would venture that a similar pattern obtains, where reflections of Nazism are, despite appearances to the contrary, still an issue. Petersen made his name in the United States with *Das Boot*, an action film (i.e., a typically American genre) on a topic (war) and with a theme (male bonding under pressure) that for the post-Vietnam generation proved to capture the right mirror of otherness, while still servicing the image Americans associated with Germany: the war, Nazis, automotive machinery. Petersen, for his part, has admitted that he liked making films in Hollywood not only because of the state-of-the-art facilities and a worldwide public but also because it gives him the opportunity to make political-patriotic films of a kind he could never make in Germany. What is missing there are not the budgets as much as the ideological climate. His favorite topics—leadership, courage, and individual initiative—are still too sensitive in Germany, while they are the very stuff of the Hollywood hero.

Roland Emmerich profiled himself already in Germany as a sci-fi director. He, too, is an expert in terrestrial and extra-terrestrial disasters, making movies that could easily be said to reflect the legacy of war-like or emergency scenarios. In this sense, Petersen and Emmerich are true to an earlier pattern, where non-American Hollywood directors had to be both European in their view of America, and at the same time capable and willing to make 110 percent American films. With *Das Boot, Die Endlose Geschichte, Christiane F.-Wir Kinder vom Bahnhof Zoo, Das Arche Noah Princip* and *Joey,* Petersen,

Edel, and Emmerich proved that they were at home not so much in the American genres of sci-fi, fantasy, children's films, and action pictures, but that they have primed them for the myths, values, conflicts, and anxieties that power these genres in the media-event and prosthetic-memory culture of the American cinema of the 1990s. Defeat and rescue, childhood helplessness and omnipotence, man-made and natural disasters, wars and invasions, the legitimacy or corruption of power, innocent perpetrators and the guilty who get away with it: these are perhaps universal themes, but blockbuster cinema has given them such allegorical elaborations that their meanings can be extracted by audiences everywhere, while still referring unmistakably to an America between Vietnam and September 11. It is too early to tell what exactly the cultural significance is of Hollywood's dominant ideologies in the 1990s—Michael Rogin has tried to read Emmerich's *Independence Day* in this light[15]—but that non-American directors have made a major contribution to their visual feel as well as their narrative fabric seems already evident. Even the works of Verhoeven and de Bont can be said to belong to this genre of disaster films after disaster: Verhoeven, for instance, has had a lifelong obsession with Nazism, which goes back to his experience of German occupation of the Netherlands and its immediate aftermath when he was a child after the liberation. *Total Recall* or *Starship Troopers* make perfect sense against this historical foil. Their portrayal of action heroes and intergalactic disasters also fit into a postclassical Hollywood preoccupation with traumatized males and reactive automatons, with questions of power and sovereignty, obedience and legitimacy, or the fine line between demented heroism and dedicated patriotism.

Thus, the metamorphosed legacy of the war and Nazism in today's Hollywood can be seen as a form of cultural transfer, a manner for Europe and America each looking into a two-way mirror. With films like *Independence Day, Starship Troopers, In the Line of Fire, Air Force One, The Patriot*, and several others, it is as if the German and European directors mentioned are "reading" America for Americans, in a way not all that different (though in a different idiom and register) than how Lubitsch, Stroheim, or Hitchcock read Vienna, Paris, and London for Americans in the 1920s and 1930s, or how the German émigrés from the 1930s—Lang, Ophuls, Wilder, Siodmak, Bernhard, and Ulmer—helped create film noir by reading American nightmares of urban malaise and male insecurity across their experience of the feverish energy and dark excesses of the final days of the Weimar Republic. The compliment was returned some twenty years later, when French and German directors in the 1960s and 1970s used Hollywood gangster films and B-movies to read postwar France and Germany, while yet another twenty years later, a Quentin Tarantino would read his own Los Angeles suburban subcultures as if they were located in Godard's Parisian *banlieux*.

Without dwelling on all the paradoxes involved, I hope to have indicated just how layered the cultural factor can be when seen in the context of an industry such as filmmaking in the narrow sense, or popular culture in the wider sense. However, there is one paradox I do want to highlight, because it brings us back to our economic analysis. One of the reasons why these directors are in Hollywood, I argued, is that Hollywood needs to address global audiences, because it is now economically dependent on them, a fact that has not always been the case, certainly not in the 1950s. But another reason why especially the German directors are in Hollywood—beyond their choices as creative individuals and possibly auteurs with a personal thematic signature—is the vision and resolve of a single individual. He is, however, not a director in the usual sense, but the epitome of the entrepreneur, the impresario, and the producer, very much the German equivalent of, say, the more flamboyantly cigar-stomping David Puttnam who engineered the British invasion of Hollywood in the 1980s. His name is Bernd Eichinger, and outside specialist circles, he is relatively little known. Born in 1949 and thus roughly of the generation of Wenders and Fassbinder, Eichinger went to the Munich film school, directed some none-too-successful literary adaptations in the mould of Schlöndorff, and began his career as producer in 1978, by buying up the once prestigious but by then moribund distribution-cum-production business Constantin. Eichinger brackets as well as bridges the 1970s and the 1990s, and he furnishes all the ingredients for an alternative history of the New German Cinema in the 1980s. Standing apart from both the state-subsidized, television-funded author's cinema, and the old German film industry chiefs, like Atze Brauner, Horst Wendlandt, and Luggi Waldleitner, he produced the early films of Petersen (*Das Boot* and *Die Endlose Geschichte*), but also films by Doris Dörrie and Söhnke Wortmann. He is thus largely responsible for the much-derided turn of German cinema to comedies (*Beziehungskomödien*) and the building of German movie stars out of television personalities. Yet he always pursued a double strategy, servicing the German market and making European coproductions out of high-brow but popular novels, such *The Name of the Rose*, directed by a Frenchman, Jean Jacques Annaud and starring Sean Connery, ex-James Bond, or *The House of the Spirits*, directed by a Dane, Bille August, and starring Jeremy Irons and Meryl Streep. Eichinger's own brand of European internationalism was designed to get him into the American market, and from there back into Europe, Asia, and Latin America.[16]

However, Eichinger is not only a less visible David Puttnam, a successor to the Italian international producers Carlo Ponti, Dino de Laurentiis, or the Italo-American James-Bond franchise owner, Albert Broccoli. Eichinger epitomizes for me the economic equivalent of the two-way mirror, and of the various mutual interdependencies that come with Hollywood hegemony: he is what I would call the embodiment (or with respect to the film business maybe even a pioneer) of the principle of strategic "inward investment" in the United States, where what is invested is not only capital but cultural capital, and not only manpower but brainpower and talent.

In this sense, Eichinger fits into a wider set of shifts in the relations between Europe and the United States, after GATT, after protectionism and cultural exceptionalism of the French variety, and after state-funded filmmaking of the German sort. In Germany one can put him next to and following on from one of his rivals, Günter Rohrbach, the chief of Bavaria studios in the 1980s, a former television producer who tried to become a global player by building up a studio base—that of Munich-Geiselgasteig, one of the oldest production facilities in Germany. Eichinger, on the other hand, came into the business from distribution, and immediately adopted the post-studio system of the New Hollywood, based as it is on the package deal, on outsourcing and subcontracting, in short, on post-Fordist methods of flexible production and reduced plant and personnel overheads.

At the same time (and thus making up yet another internal German rhyme or mirroring effect), Eichinger pretty well followed the strategy and fulfilled the role in Germany in the 1990s that Erich Pommer had pioneered in the 1920s inside Ufa, when he created a Cinema Europe, while always also keeping one foot firmly planted in Hollywood. Pommer was pushed by Ufa twice, the second time in 1933 for racial reasons. Yet such is the irony, but also the logic, of the German film business in its dealing with America that Pommer came back in 1946, now in a US Army uniform, and as the US Government Chief Film Officer, entrusted with denazifying, rebuilding and relicensing the German film business, which he started to do in no other place than Munich's Geiselgasteig Studios. That Pommer eventually had to give up, vilified and sabotaged by the Germans he tried to help (but no less frustrated and disappointed by the Hollywood lobby in the State Department, who would not allow him to build up a centralized viable production base even in the American zones) is another story—well worth telling, because it, too, gives a more nuanced and revisionist account to the one I began with about Hollywood's "divide and rule" policy after 1945.[17]

But back to Pommer's historical double from the 1980s, Eichinger. The larger picture to which Eichinger belongs is not only the history of the German film industry face to face with Hollywood in 1925, 1933, 1945, and the 1990s, or of the European film industry since GATT and beyond. The associations I tried to invoke, by calling his method "strategic inward investment," is of course meant to call to mind also the likes of Jürgen Schremp, head of Daimler-Chrysler, Leo Kirch, founder of Kirch Media—until 2001 a global player with a film library, television interests, and publishing assets who modeled himself on Rupert Murdoch, Ted Turner, and Silvio Berlusconi—and Thomas Middenhoff, the now deposed CEO of Bertelsmann, whose rise and fall in turn mirrors that of Jean Marie Messier of Canal+ and Vivendi-Universal in France—the very company that, under the name of Compagnie Générale des Eaux, bought the old UFA/DEFA Studios in Neu-Babelsberg and hired none other than Volker Schlöndorff to be the new company's production head, which makes Schlöndorff, at least in this respect, a failed Bernd Eichinger.

What could be the moral of this story, or rather, what might be the hidden dialectic I was hoping would emerge out of shaking up the binaries and polarities of *Kunst* and *Kommerz*, art and show business, high-culture and pop? The first hidden dialectic is, of course, that there is no dialectic. At best, there are a set of differentials, of shifting terms and relations that have to be tracked individually and closely, if they are to yield any kind of reliable knowledge or illuminating insight. But in another respect, and despite the spectacular failures of the likes of Middenhoff, Messier, Kirch, and possibly even Eichinger, something suggests to me that a hidden dialectic becomes visible when—once more calling upon our mirror metaphor—we adopt the position of the Americans, but look through the mirror with our European eyes, namely the very European perspective of the avant-garde, experiment and prototype. Except that the avant-garde today is located in the United States and no longer in Europe, if one agrees (with Walter Benjamin) that a given artifact should be judged avant-garde only when it embodies the most (technically) advanced practice and employs the most experimental, risk-taking practitioners. Looked at from this avant-garde American point of view, we have another binary scheme, no longer based on the art versus commerce opposition, but structured around the terms we now associate with globalization: space/place, mobility/ubiquity, mapping/tracking, etc., but where the pairs do not line up on a positive/negative scale, and instead represent different modalities, aggregate states of varying intensities. In such a line-up, both Hollywood and Europe would no longer mark distinct territories, and more states of mind, or modes of thinking about the same practice or phenomena. Thus Hollywood would connote "differential," and Europe "dialectical," Hollywood would be inclusive, and Europe exclusive, Hollywood hybrid, relational, while Europe autonomous, essentialist, Hollywood multipurpose and mixed media, Europe specific and monomedia, Hollywood deterritorialized and rhizomatic, Europe territorial and hierarchical, Hollywood time is real time, Europe time is history, Hollywood space is site (access for all, from anywhere), European space is place (local, geographically, linguistically bounded).

While this new Hollywood hegemony probably implies that the United States operates politically as an empire, this too is a mirror that looks both ways. "It is a dangerous world out there," George Bush likes to warn his fellow

Americans, but there is an irony that may have escaped his speechwriters: the very success of America as an idea, and of Hollywood as a state of mind means that—at least as far as movies, popular culture, and mass consumption are concerned—there is no longer an "out there": all the world—for good or ill—is already "in here." Bush's threat to "America's enemies," in other words, also pertains to a promise. Hollywood spectators everywhere have a right to hold the president to that promise: they are part of "America" and they matter.

With this, I may have come to the end of the useful life of my two-way mirror metaphor. For what my revisionist account suggests is the possibility of inward investment extending beyond financial capital to a certain kind of cultural capital. Complementing the identity politics of marking boundaries would be the identity politics of cultural mimicry—of the always already "inside" of culture, after universalism, but also after multiculturalism. My look at film history has shown that almost as many Americans love to play at being European as Europeans love to play at being American. My hidden dialectic suggests that besides the discourse of anti-Americanism and of counter-Americanism, we may have to find the terms of another discourse: let me call it, in a provisional gesture of Euro-de-centrism, the discourse of karaoke-Americanism—that doubly coded space of identity as overlap and deferral, as compliment and camouflage.

Notes

1. Kristin Thompson, *Exporting Entertainment* (London, 1986).
2. Reinhold E. Thiel, "Was wurde aus Goebbels' UFA?" *Film Aktuell* 2 (February 1970).
3. Thomas H. Guback, *The International Film Industry* (Bloomington, Ind., 1969), 112.
4. Guback, 135.
5. See Klaus Kreimeier, *Kino und Filmindustrie in der BRD. Ideologieproduktion und Klassenwirklichkeit nach 1945* (Kronberg, 1973) and more recently Heide Fehrenbach, *Cinema in Democratizing Germany: Reconstructing of National Identity After Hitler* (Chapel Hill, 1995).
6. Quoted in Peter Krämer, "Hollywood in Germany, Germany in Hollywood," in Tim Bergfelder, Erica Carter, and Deniz Göktürk, eds., *The German Cinema Book* (London, 2002), 227-37, quoted here 236, note 35.
7. Thomas Elsaesser, "American Friends," in Geoffrey Nowell-Smith and Steve Ricci, eds., *Hollywood and Europe* (London, 1998), 142-55.
8. Peter Märthesheimer and Ivo Frenzel, *Der Fernsehfilm Holocaust. Eine Nation ist betroffen* (Frankfurt, 1979).
9. For a further elaboration of this seeming paradox in German postwar cinema, see Thomas Elsaesser, "Absence as Presence, Presence as Parapraxis," in Tim Bergfelder, et al., eds., *The German Cinema Book* (London, 2003).

10. "You have to go away in order to come home," Louis Trenker's old school teacher tells him in the 1934 film *The Prodigal Son*, before he leaves for New York, while Peter Handke noted that "America is for [my] story only a pretext, the attempt to find a distanced world in which I can be direct and personal. [...] At the same time, there is no other place except America which provokes in me such depersonalization and estrangement." Thomas Elsaesser, "Wim Wenders and Peter Handke," in ed. Susan Hayward, *European Cinema* (Birmingham, 1985), 31-52; quoted here 33.
11. Thomas Elsaesser, "German Cinema in the 1990's," in Thomas Elsaesser and Michael Wedel, eds., *The BFI Companion to German Cinema* (London, 1999), 4-5.
12. Hans Jürgen Syberberg, "The Syberberg Statement," *Framework* 6 (autumn 1977): 12-15.
13. Edgar Reitz, "Arbeiten an unseren Erinnerungen," *Medium* 5 (1979): 21-22.
14. Elie Wiesel, "Trivializing the Holocaust," *New York Times*, 16 April 1978.
15. Michael Rogin, *Independence Day* (London, 1998).
16. Elsaesser and Wedel, 73-74.
17. Ursula Hardt, *From Caligari to California* (Providence, 1996).

Part 4

EUROPEAN AND GLOBAL PERSPECTIVES

DOUBLE CROSSINGS
The Reciprocal Relationship between American and European Culture in the Twentieth Century

❖   ❖   ❖

Richard Pells

In the immediate aftermath of the attacks on the World Trade Center and the Pentagon, there was—as we all know—an outpouring of sympathy in Europe and elsewhere for the United States. But since the beginning of 2002, this international affection has been replaced by resentment at America's political "arrogance," its overwhelming economic and military power, and the Bush administration's apparent "unilateralist" foreign policy.

Americans like to think that "they" hate "us" because of who we are, rather than what we do. Yet neither formulation may explain the resurgence of global anti-Americanism. Dislike for the United States stems also from what foreigners consider America's cultural "hegemony." America's mass culture, in particular, inspires ambivalence, anger, and sometimes violent reactions, not just in the Middle East but all over the world.

There is no doubt that America often seems to be the elephant in everyone's living room. But the discomfort with America's cultural dominance is not new. In 1901, the British writer William Stead published a book called, ominously, *The Americanization of the World.* The title captured a set of apprehensions—about the disappearance of national languages and traditions, the decline of intellectual and artistic standards, and the obliteration of a country's unique "identity" under the weight of American habits and states of mind—that persists until today.

When people in other countries worried in the past, as they do in the present, about the international impact of American culture, they were not thinking of America's literature, painting, or ballet. "Americanization" has always meant the worldwide invasion of American movies, jazz, rock 'n' roll, mass-circulation magazines, best-selling books, advertising, comic strips, theme parks, shopping malls, fast food, television programs, and now the Internet. This is, in the eyes of many foreigners, a culture created not for patricians but for the common folk. Indeed, it inspired a revolution in the way we conceive of culture.

More recently, globalization has become the main enemy for academics, journalists, and political activists who loathe what they see as the trend toward cultural uniformity. Still, they typically regard global culture and American culture as synonymous. And they continue to insist that Hollywood, McDonald's, and Disneyland are eradicating regional and local eccentricities—disseminating images and subliminal messages so beguiling as to drown out the competing voices in other lands.

Despite these allegations, the cultural relationship between the United States and the world over the past 100 years has never been one-sided. On the contrary, the United States was, and continues to be, as much a consumer of foreign intellectual and artistic influences as it has been a shaper of the world's entertainment and tastes. What I want to emphasize, therefore, is how reciprocal America's cultural connections with other countries really are.

That is not an argument with which many foreigners (or even many Americans) would readily agree. The clichés about American's cultural "imperialism" make it difficult for most people to recognize that modern global culture is hardly a monolithic entity foisted on the world by the American media. Neither is it easy for critics of Microsoft or AOL Time Warner to acknowledge that the conception of a harmonious and distinctively American culture—encircling the globe, implanting its values in foreign minds—has always been a myth.

Nevertheless, the United States has been a recipient as much as an exporter of global culture. Indeed, immigrants from Europe, Asia, Latin America, and increasingly the Middle East, as well as African-Americans and the thousands of refugee scholars and artists who fled Hitler in the 1930s, have played a crucial role in the development of American science, literature, movies, music, painting, architecture, fashion, and food.

It is precisely these foreign influences that have made America's culture so popular for so long in so many places. American culture spread throughout the world because it has habitually drawn on foreign styles and ideas. Americans have then reassembled and repackaged the cultural products they received from abroad, and retransmitted them to the rest of the planet. In effect, Americans have specialized in selling the fantasies and folklore of other people back to them. This is why a global mass culture has come to be identified, however simplistically, with the United States.

There are other reasons, of course, for the international popularity of American culture. Certainly, the ability of America's media conglomerates to control the production and distribution of their products has been a major stimulus for the worldwide spread of American entertainment.

Moreover, the emergence of English as a global language has been essential to the acceptance of American culture. One billion people on the planet, at the beginning of the twenty-first century, speak some form of English. People who have learned English as a foreign language now outnumber those who are native speakers.

Yet more significant than its diffusion around the world is the effectiveness of English (unlike German, Russian, Chinese, or even French and Italian) as a language of mass communications. Its simpler structure and grammar, along with its tendency to use shorter, less abstract words and more concise sentences, are all advantageous for the composers of song lyrics, advertising slogans, cartoon captions, newspaper headlines, and movie and television dialogue. English is thus a language exceptionally well-suited to the demands of American mass culture.

Another factor contributing to the globalization of American culture is the size of the American audience. From the 1920s on, America's artists and entertainers have benefited from a huge domestic market. This market has provided an economic cushion for the producers of American mass culture, a cushion unavailable in many other countries. The possibility that American filmmakers and television executives could retrieve most of their production costs and make a profit within the borders of the United States in turn encouraged them to spend more money on stars, sets, special effects, location-shooting, and merchandising—the very ingredients that attract international audiences as well.

But the power of American capitalism, the worldwide familiarity with English, and the economic advantages of a large home market do not by themselves account for America's cultural ascendancy. American entertainment has always been more cosmopolitan than "imperialistic." It is this cosmopolitanism that helped make America's mass culture a global phenomenon.

In short, the familiar artifacts of American culture may not be all that "American." Americans, after all, did not invent fast food, amusement parks, or the movies. Before the Big Mac, there were fish and chips, wurst stands, and pizzas. Before Disneyland there was Copenhagen's Tivoli Gardens (which Walt Disney used as a prototype for his first theme park in Anaheim, a model later re-exported to Tokyo and Paris).

Nor can the roots of American popular culture be traced only to native entertainers like P.T. Barnum or Buffalo Bill. Its origins lay as well in the European modernist assault, in the opening years of the twentieth century, on nineteenth-century literature, music, painting, and architecture—particularly in the modernists' refusal to honor the traditional boundaries between high and low culture. Modernism in the arts was improvisational, eclectic, and irreverent. These traits have also been characteristic of, but not peculiar to, mass culture.

The hallmark of nineteenth-century culture was its insistence on defending the purity of literature, classical music, and representational painting against the intrusions of folklore and popular amusements. No one confused the work of Leo Tolstoy with dime novels, opera with Wild West Shows, the Louvre with Coney Island. High culture was supposed to be educational, contemplative, and uplifting—a way of preserving the best in human "civilization."

These beliefs did not mean that a Dickens never indulged in melodrama or that Brahms disdained the use of popular songs. Nor did Chinese or Japanese authors and painters refuse to draw on oral or folkloric traditions. But the nineteenth-century barriers between high and low culture were resolutely, if imperfectly, maintained.

The artists of the early twentieth century shattered what seemed to them the artificial demarcation between different cultural forms. They also questioned the notion that culture was primarily a means of intellectual or moral improvement. They did so by valuing style and craftsmanship over philosophy, religion, or ideology. Hence, they deliberately called attention to language in their novels, to optics in their paintings, to the materials in and function of their architecture, to the structure of music instead of its melodies.

And they wanted to shock their audiences, which they succeeded in doing. Modern painting and literature—with its emphasis on visually distorted nudes, overt sexuality, and meditations on violence—was attacked for being degrading and obscene, and for appealing to the baser instincts of humanity in much the same way that critics would later denounce the vulgarity of popular culture.

Although modernism assaulted the conventions of nineteenth-century high culture in Europe and Asia, it inadvertently accelerated the growth of mass culture in the United States. Indeed, Americans were already receptive to the blurring of cultural boundaries. In the nineteenth century, symphony orchestras in the United States often included band music in their programs, while opera singers were asked to perform both Mozart and Stephen Foster.

So, for Americans in the twentieth century, Surrealism, with its dreamlike associations, easily lent itself to the wordplay and psychological symbolism of advertising, cartoons, and theme parks. Dadaism ridiculed the snobbery of elite cultural institutions and reinforced instead an already-existing appetite (especially among the immigrant audiences in America) for "low-class," disreputable movies and vaudeville shows. Igor Stravinsky's experiments with atonal (and thus unconventional and unmelodic) music validated the rhythmic innovations of jazz. Writers like Ernest Hemingway and John Dos Passos, detesting the rhetorical embellishments of nineteenth-century prose and fascinated by the stylistic innovations of James Joyce and Marcel Proust (among other European masters), invented a terse and hard-boiled language, devoted to reproducing as authentically as possible the elemental qualities of personal experience. This laconic style became a model for modern journalism, detective fiction, and movie dialogue.

All of these trends provided the foundations for a genuinely new culture. But the new culture turned out to be neither modernist nor European. Instead, America transformed what was still an avant-garde and somewhat parochial project, appealing largely to the young and the rebellious in Western society, into a global enterprise.

This cultural metamorphosis is striking in literature. Hemingway, Dos Passos, and William Faulkner may have been captivated in the 1920s by European modernism. But the raw power of their prose and their ability to dramatize the sensation of living in a world of absurdity in turn became enormously popular with Italian novelists and literary critics in the 1930s who were disgusted with Mussolini's bombast, and with writers like Jean-Paul Sartre and Albert Camus after World War II who wanted to puncture the bourgeois stuffiness of French life. Thus, American literature, initially molded by European ideas, became a template for world literature in the second half of the twentieth century.

The propensity of Americans to borrow and alter modernist ideas, and transform them into a global culture, is even more visible in the commercial uses of modern architecture. The European Bauhaus movement—intended in the 1920s as a socialist experiment in working-class housing—eventually provided the theories and techniques for the construction of commercial skyscrapers and vacation homes in the United States. But the same architectural ideas were then sent back to Europe after World War II as a model for the reconstruction of bombed-out cities like Rotterdam, Cologne, and Frankfurt. Thus, the United States converted what had once been a distinctive, if localized, rebellion by Dutch and German architects into a generic "international style." Similarly, the American abstract expressionists of the 1940s were heavily influenced by European refugee painters, sculptors, and art dealers, yet their work became, at least for a time, the world's most dominant form of art.

But it is in popular culture that America's embrace and reshaping of foreign influences can best be seen. The American audience is not only large; because of the influx of immigrants and refugees, it is also international in its complexion. The heterogeneity of America's population—its regional, ethnic, religious, and racial diversity—forced the media, from the early years of the twentieth century, to experiment with messages, images, and story lines that had a broad multicultural appeal. The Hollywood studios, the mass-circulation magazines, and the television networks had to learn how to speak to a variety of groups and classes at home. This has given them the techniques to captivate an equally diverse audience abroad. The American domestic market has, in essence, been a laboratory, a place to develop cultural products that could then be adapted to the world market.

One important way that the American media succeeded in transcending internal social divisions, national borders, and language barriers was by mixing up cultural styles. American musicians and composers have followed the example of modernist artists like Pablo Picasso and Georges Braque by intermingling elements from high and low culture, combining the sacred and the profane. Aaron Copland, George Gershwin, and Leonard Bernstein incorporated folk melodies, religious hymns, blues and gospel songs, and jazz into their symphonies, concertos, operas, and ballets. Bernstein's *West Side Story*, for instance, transformed Shakespeare's *Romeo and Juliet* into a saga of juvenile gang warfare on the streets of New York, just as Alan Jay Lerner and Frederick Loewe converted George Bernard Shaw's *Pygmalion* into *My Fair Lady*—perhaps the most commercially successful, and certainly the wittiest, of all American musical comedies. Even an art as quintessentially American as jazz evolved during the twentieth century into an amalgam of African, Caribbean, Latin American, and modernist European music. It is this blending of forms in America's mass culture that has enhanced its appeal to multiethnic domestic and international audiences by reflecting their varied experiences and tastes.

Nowhere are these foreign influences more unmistakable than in the American movie industry. If movies have been the most important source both of art and entertainment in the twentieth century, then Hollywood, for better or worse, became the cultural capital of the modern world. But it was never an exclusively American capital. Like past cultural centers—Florence, Paris, Vienna, Berlin—Hollywood has functioned as an international community, built by immigrant entrepreneurs, and drawing on the talents of actors, directors, writers, cinematographers, editors, costume and set designers, from all over the world. The first American movie star, after all, was Charlie Chaplin, whose comic skills were honed in British music halls.

Moreover, during much of the twentieth century, American moviemakers thought of themselves as acolytes, entranced by the superior works of foreign directors. In the 1920s, few American directors could gain admittance to a European pantheon that included Sergei Eisenstein, F.W. Murnau, G.W. Papst, Fritz Lang, and Carl Dreyer. The postwar years, from the 1940s to the mid-1960s, were once again a golden age of filmmaking in Britain, Sweden, France, Italy, Japan, and India. An extraordinary generation of foreign directors—Ingmar Bergman, Frederico Fellini, Michelangelo Antonioni, François Truffaut, Jean-Luc Godard, Akira Kurosawa, and Satyajit Ray—became the world's most celebrated auteurs.

Of course, the French directors learned much of their craft by watching and analyzing Hollywood Westerns and gangster movies, copying the American tough-guy style in films like Godard's *Breathless* and Truffaut's *Shoot the*

Piano Player. Nevertheless, it is one of the paradoxes of the postwar European and Asian cinema that its greatest success was in spawning American imitations—another example of how these cultural transmissions and influences resemble a hall of mirrors.

After the 1967 release of *Bonnie and Clyde* (originally to have been directed by Truffaut or Godard), the newest geniuses—Francis Ford Coppola, Martin Scorsese, Robert Altman, Steven Spielberg, Woody Allen—were American. The Americans may have owed their improvisational methods and autobiographical preoccupations largely to Italian neo-Realism and the French New Wave. But who in any country needed to see another *La Dolce Vita* when you could now enjoy *Nashville*? Why try to decipher *Jules and Jim* or *L'Avventura* when you could savor *Annie Hall* or *The Godfather*? Wasn't it conceivable that *Seven Samurai* might not be as powerful or as disturbing a movie as *The Wild Bunch*?

It turned out that foreign filmmakers had become too influential for their own good. The Americans used the techniques they absorbed from the European and Asian auteurs to revolutionize the American cinema, so that after 1960s and 1970s it became harder for any other continent's film industry to match the worldwide popularity of American movies.

Still, American directors in every era have emulated foreign artists and filmmakers by paying close attention to the formal qualities of a movie and to the need to tell a story visually. Early twentieth-century European painters wanted their viewers to recognize that they were looking at lines and color on a canvas rather than at a reproduction of the natural world. Similarly, many American films—from the multiple narrators in *Citizen Kane*, to the split screen portrait of how two lovers imagine their relationship in *Annie Hall*, to the flashbacks and flash-forwards in *Pulp Fiction*, to the roses blooming from the navel of Kevin Spacey's fantasy dream girl in *American Beauty*—deliberately remind audiences that they are watching a carefully crafted, highly stylized movie, not a play or a photographed version of reality. Thus, American filmmakers (in the movies as well as on MTV) have been willing to use the most sophisticated techniques of editing and camera work, much of it inspired by foreign directors, to create a modernist collage of images that captures the speed and seductiveness of life in the contemporary world.

Hollywood's addiction to modernist *visual* pyrotechnics is particularly evident in the *nonverbal* style of many of its contemporary performers. The tendency to mumble was not always in vogue. In the 1930s and 1940s, the sound and meaning of words were important not only in movies but also on records and the radio. Even though some homegrown stars, like John Wayne and Gary Cooper, were famously terse, audiences could at least hear and understand what they were saying. But the centrality of language in the films of the 1930s led more often to a dependence in Hollywood on British actors (like Cary Grant) or on Americans who sounded vaguely British (like Katharine Hepburn and Bette Davis). It is illustrative of how important foreign (especially British) talent was to Hollywood that the two most famous Southern belles in American fiction and drama—Scarlett O'Hara and Blanche DuBois—were both played in the movies by Vivien Leigh.

Indeed, foreign voices of all types were in great demand. This is, in part, why Marlene Dietrich and Greta Garbo were such charismatic stars in the 1930s, and why, in one of the most famous Hollywood films, *Casablanca*, every actor except for Humphrey Bogart and Dooley Wilson (who played Sam the piano player) was an émigré or a refugee from Europe, including the Hungarian director Michael Curtiz.

But the verbal eloquence of pre-World War II acting, in the movies and the theater, disappeared after 1945. After Marlon Brando's revolutionary performance in *A Streetcar Named Desire*, on stage in 1947 and on screen in 1951, the model of American acting became a brooding, almost inarticulate, introspectiveness that one did not find in the glib and clever heroes or heroines of the screwball comedies and gangster films of the 1930s.

Brando was trained in the Method, an acting technique originally developed in Stanislavsky's Moscow Art Theater in prerevolutionary Russia, and then imported to New York by the members of the Group Theater during the 1930s. Where British actors, trained in Shakespeare, were taught to subordinate their personalities to the role as written, the Method encouraged actors to improvise, to summon up childhood memories, and to explore their innermost feelings, often at the expense of what a playwright or screenwriter intended. Norman Mailer once said that Brando, in his pauses and his gazes into the middle distance, always seemed to be searching for a better line than the one the writer had composed. In effect, what Brando did, in the movies even more than on Broadway, was to lead a revolt—carried on by his successors and imitators, from James Dean to Warren Beatty to Robert De Niro—against the British school of acting with its reverence for the script and the written (and spoken) word.

Thus, since World War II, the emotional power of American acting lay more in what was not said, in the unearthing of passions that could not be communicated in words. The Method actor's reliance on physical mannerisms and even on silence in interpreting a role has been especially appropriate for a cinema that puts a premium on the inexpressible. Indeed, the influence of the Method, not only in the United States but also abroad (where it was reflected in the acting styles of Jean-Paul Belmondo and Marcello Mastroianni), is a classic example of how a foreign idea, originally intended for the stage, was adapted in postwar America to the movies, and then conveyed to the rest of the world as a paradigm for both cinematic and social behavior. More important, the Method's disregard for language permitted global audiences, even those not well-versed in English, to understand and appreciate what they were watching in American films.

Just as American filmmakers borrowed modernist ideas and practices, and relied heavily on foreign talent, the notorious commercialism of Hollywood movies and of American popular culture in general is hardly peculiar to the United States. Picasso cared as much about the prices for his paintings, and Brecht about the number of people who came to his plays, as Louis B. Mayer did about the box office receipts for his movies and Walt Disney about the ratings of his television show or the profits at his theme parks.

On both sides of the Atlantic and Pacific, however, the hunger for a hit and the fear of commercial failure—and the effort therefore to establish an emotional connection with and enthrall an audience—have occasionally resulted in works that are original and provocative. No matter where they came from, the greatest directors—Charlie Chaplin, Orson Welles, Alfred Hitchcock, John Ford, Howard Hawks, Federico Fellini, François Truffaut, Francis Ford Coppola, Martin Scorsese, Steven Spielberg—have always recognized the intimate connection between art and entertainment. To quote Woody Allen, the American filmmaker who is supposed to have the most pronounced "European" sensibility: "The audience has a right, when they sit down, to be entertained. No matter how intelligent your message, no matter smart or wonderful [or] progressive your ideas are, if they are not entertaining they should not be in a movie."

In these instances, the requirements of the market and the urge to entertain have both served as stimulants for art. Hence, there may be no inherent contradiction between commerce and culture either in America or abroad. On the contrary, for the creators of high and mass culture alike, the relationship has often been symbiotic.

Finally, American culture has imitated not only the modernists' visual flamboyance but also their emphasis on personal expression rather than on the delivery of social messages. The psychological, as opposed to political, preoccupations of America's mass culture may have accounted, more than any other factor, for the worldwide popularity of American entertainment. American movies, in particular, have customarily focused on human relationships and private feelings, not on the problems of a particular time and place. They tell tales about romance, intrigue, success, failure, moral conflicts, and survival. The most memorable movies of the 1930s (with the exception of *The Grapes of Wrath*) were comedies and musicals about mismatched people falling in love, not socially conscious films dealing with the issues of poverty and unemployment. Similarly, the finest movies about World War II *(Casablanca)* or the Vietnam War *(The Deer Hunter)* linger in the mind long after these conflicts have ended because they explored their characters' deepest emotions instead of dwelling on headline events.

Such intensely personal dilemmas are what people everywhere wrestle with. So Europeans, Asians, and Latin Americans flocked to *Titanic* (as they once did to *Gone With the Wind*) not because these films celebrated "American" values but because audiences, no matter where they lived, could see some part of their own lives reflected in the stories of love and loss.

America's mass culture has often been witless, crude, and intrusive, as its critics—from American academics like Benjamin Barber to German directors like Wim Wenders—have always complained. In their eyes, American culture is "colonizing" everyone's subconscious, reducing us all to passive residents of "McWorld."

But American culture has never felt all that foreign to foreigners, not even in the Middle East. Just the opposite, at its best it has transformed what it received from others into a culture everyone everywhere could comprehend and embrace (if they did not always love), a culture that is, at least some of the time, both emotionally and artistically compelling for millions of people throughout the world.

So, despite the current hostility to America's policies and values, not only in the Middle East but in Europe and Latin America as well, it is important to recognize how familiar much of American culture seems to people abroad. In the end, America's mass culture has not transformed the world into a replica of the United States. Instead, the ethnic and racial pluralism of American society, together with its dependence on foreign cultural influences, has made the United States a replica of the world.

If Americans have mostly adopted and reshaped the artistic traditions of Europeans and others, if the cultural relationship between America and the rest of the world has not been as one-sided as foreigners usually insist, and if global entertainment is in fact an artistic and intellectual smorgasbord, are people outside the United States really losing respect for their native cultures?

There is no doubt that America's culture is visible everywhere. But the ubiquitous presence of Coca-Cola billboards and fast-food chains is only a superficial sign of America's global influence. None of this has affected how people actually live, shop, eat, think about the role of their governments, use their cities, or entertain themselves in neighborhood cafés or in the privacy of their homes.

In reality, the effect of America's culture and consumer goods has been more negligible than intellectuals, politicians, and parents worried about the malleability of their Nike-clad children are willing to admit. Eating a Big Mac, lining up for the newest Hollywood blockbuster, or going to Disneyland in Paris or Tokyo does not automatically mean that one has become either "Americanized" or a compliant inhabitant of the global village. The purchase of a Chicago Bulls t-shirt by a Brazilian adolescent or the decision of a German family to have dinner at the nearby Pizza Hut does not necessarily signify an embrace of the American or the global way of life. Sometimes, to paraphrase Freud, a hamburger is just a hamburger, not an instrument of cultural or ideological seduction. And neither the movies nor the Internet compel people to wear the same clothes, listen to the same music, idolize the same screen heroes, speak the same language, or think the same thoughts.

Nor are audiences, either adolescent or adult, a collection of zombies, spellbound by the images transmitted by the global media. Intellectuals often overestimate the power of mass culture to manipulate the masses. People in America and abroad are affected not just by the media but by their genes, their childhoods, their parents, their spouses and friends, by their experiences at work, and their problems at home. These varied influences enable people to resist or at least reinterpret the media's messages rather than silently submit. Hence, far from being docile, audiences have adapted global culture to their own tastes and traditions.

Still, the critics of globalization presume that unwary audiences, regardless of their dissimilar social backgrounds and life histories, will react to movies, television programs, and music in the same way. But given the volatility of the market and the shifting preferences of the audience, the American media has prospered by remaining competitive and eclectic, offering a multiplicity of icons and viewpoints that have different meanings for different groups at different times in different countries.

Dallas, for example, was the most popular television show in the world during the 1980s. But studies of audience reactions to the program demonstrated that people in Holland interpreted the melodramatic lives of the Ewings very differently than audiences in Israel—or in America. These divergent interpretations were shaped almost entirely by the distinctive cultural assumptions and expectations of viewers in disparate parts of the world. Such dissimilar responses to the same television soap opera suggest that global entertainment has produced not a homogenous or a monocultural world, but a reinforcement of cultural diversity.

If anything, the globalization of mass communications sometimes leads not to cultural uniformity but to cultural fragmentation. The shared cultural experience that came from watching one or two television channels, or seeing movies with hundreds of others in a movie theater, has given way to multiple choices among hundreds of television programs broadcast on satellite and cable stations, to family decisions about when to watch a movie or a television program on their VCRs or DVDs, and to more and more time spent by individuals on computers and the Internet. With these devices, we may be connected to the world, but often in our own way and at our own time, according to our own specific desires.

English, for instance, may have spread throughout the world but it has not thereby become a universal language, understood in the same way by everyone everywhere. Instead, millions of non-native speakers add their own words and meanings, creating a hybrid language that is less a reflection of British or American culture than one rooted in local needs.

Moreover, the critics of the international media conglomerates may have misjudged the ability of national, regional, local, and ethnic cultures to survive and even flourish in an age of globalization. The growth of regionalism, for example, is reflected not only in the Islamic resistance to and even hatred of "Western" values, but in the tendency of different countries to export their own culture to neighboring lands. Mexico and Brazil transmit their films and television soap operas to other countries in Latin America. Sweden remains the dominant culture in Scandinavia. Egyptian and Indian movies are popular in other parts of the Middle East and Central Asia. The Hong Kong film industry is a major force in the East Asian market. At the same time, Argentina can look to France, Brazil to Africa, Chile to Spain, Mexico to its indigenous Indian language and history, for cultural alternatives to the United States.

Australia is a classic example of these regional forces at work. Until 1945, the dominant "foreign" culture in Australia was British. Afterwards, American popular culture became increasingly influential. But in the last two decades, as Australia has developed closer economic ties with the countries of the Pacific rim, and admitted larger numbers of immigrants from Vietnam, China, and Japan, Australians have begun to see themselves increasingly as a multicultural society—part European, part British, part American, and part Asian. In fact, the Australian experience illustrates the degree to which global culture has been eclectic rather than homogeneous, a culture made up of elements from many different countries and continents.

Finally, the movie and television industries in other countries are starting once again to capture the attention of local audiences. German television viewers increasingly favor dramas and situation comedies made in Germany. In Poland, which was inundated with American movies after the collapse of the Communist regime in 1989, several locally produced films have attracted more ticket buyers than did *Titanic* or *Star Wars: The Phantom Menace*.

Nonetheless, filmmakers in Europe and Asia have justifiably grumbled since the 1970s that they cannot get their works shown in the United States. For this, they blame Hollywood's monopoly on distribution, and the alleged loathing of American audiences for movies that are subtitled or dubbed. Yet some foreign language films, particularly in the past decade, have been surprisingly successful and influential in the United States. These include Italian movies like *Cinema Paradiso, Il Postino*, and *Life Is Beautiful*; *Run Lola Run*, which was the most successful German film ever released in America; and *Crouching Tiger, Hidden Dragon*, which was the first foreign language film since Ingmar Bergman's *Cries and Whispers* in 1973 to be nominated for an

Oscar for best picture of the year. Meanwhile, box office receipts in the United States for French films (like *Amélie* and *Under the Sand*) reached $30 million in 2001, compared with just $6.8 million in 2000. The renewed popularity and profitability of foreign films among general audiences in the United States should remind us that it has never been just college students and elite film critics who admire works that come from abroad.

None of these tendencies point to globalism's imminent demise. Instead, they raise a dilemma for millions of citizens in every country. How do we live in a global culture (whose elements are not exclusively American) while at the same time preserving our attachments to a neighborhood, a town, a region, or a nation?

One answer is that people in the future might have to maintain a dual set of allegiances—one to their local or national traditions and institutions, the other to an international culture. These multiple identities and divided loyalties can be paralyzing. And they can also lead, as we have been recently and tragically reminded, to a fanatical and totalitarian rejection of modernity.

Yet they may also be liberating because people can decide which cultural influences they allow at any moment into their lives. Given the innumerable and often competing cultural influences with which we all live daily, we have no choice except to choose.

In the end, neither foreigners nor Americans have been passive receptacles for Hollywood movies or MTV; we are all free to choose what to embrace and what to ignore. Recognizing this may enable people in the twenty-first century to live more comfortably in what is, for all the arguments about "Americanization" and the fears of "globalization," still a decidedly pluralistic world.

Anti-Americanism and Anti-Modernism in Europe
Old and Recent Versions

◆ ◆ ◆

Rob Kroes

There are many varieties of anti-Americanism. They may arise in response to an overbearing American projection of power, political and military, and elicit a discourse that sees America as driven by the logic of imperialism. They may also be a reaction to America's economic power, relentlessly opening up foreign markets for the worldwide dissemination of American consumer products. The discourse in this case often blends into a discussion of globalization. Capitalism—in Joseph Schumpeter's famous words, a force of creative destruction—is truly the subtext; America only appears in such discourse as the locus from which this force centrally emanates. Yet a third variety of anti-Americanism takes aim at another relentless process affecting every part of the world, a process commonly referred to as modernization. Again, America appears as the force centrally driving this process, while casting it in a recognizably American mold. In a sense, this third variety conflates the other two. American global power, political and economic, is seen as providing the necessary leeway for modernization to proceed.

The European interbellum may have been the preeminent period for the articulation of an anti-Americanism that truly addressed issues of modernization as it affected Europe at the time. "The machine" is arguably the central trope in the way Europeans envisaged their recent past, their present, and prospects for the future. World War I had confronted them with the machine as a cold and dehumanized killing device, the 1920s showed the mechanization of entire areas of life as equally dehumanizing. An intellectual and cultural avant-garde of a certain stripe may have seen things differently,

---

Notes for this section can be found on page 220.

celebrating the machine, its pounding rhythm, its shapes, in short its aesthetics, as the perfect expression of a new world arising from the ruins of war and destruction, as the proper reflection of a stage of modernity where societies in the west had to adapt to the advent of the "mass" onto the historical stage. There were visions conflating the mass and the machine as equally responsive to human control and coordination. Examples abound, in music and painting of the time, in early Soviet film, in Busby Berkely's playful 1930's Hollywood choreographies, and, most famously or infamously, Leni Riefenstahl's *Triumph of the Will*. Charlie Chaplin's *Modern Times*, on the other hand, emphasized precisely the dehumanization brought by the machine. There are echoes of machine aestheticism in the way Chaplin rendered his view of modern times, turning into ballet the interplay between man and machine, yet unmistakably casting the machine as the partner leading the dance.

In that sense, Chaplin playfully reflected an anguished critique of contemporary culture prevalent on both sides of the Atlantic. Yet European critics tended characteristically to add one element to their diagnosis. In their eyes, America became the historical actor driving the mechanization of culture and society. As a group, irrespective of national origin, they tended to be highly explicit in singling out American agency in the transformation of the world. Their precise arguments may show individual and characteristic differences, yet as a body of interbellum anti-Americanism one sees remarkable consistency. In its central thrust, this variety of anti-Americanism is highly repetitive and familiar to a point where we now need to read just one line to recognize the genre. Yet overworked as it may be, the genre survives to the present day. We can find recent variations on an almost daily basis.

Yet, and this is the point of my argument, this particular indictment of "America" may have become so familiar that often critics of modernity no longer need to be explicit in their rejection of America as its central agent. Upon a closer reading of contemporary critiques of the forces transforming our world, we recognize the logical structure of an older, more explicit, anti-American discourse, yet America has turned into a subtext. It no longer needs to be explicitly mentioned in order for an audience unfailingly to pick up the implied assignment of agency. In the following pages, I intend to take the reader back in time, to the European interbellum, when America was explicitly cast in the role of agent of the more general and abstract forces transforming the world. Then in a leap across decades, I wish to give the reader a sense of the way in which America has become a subtext, but still stands indicted.

Interbellum Anti-Americanism

As indicated above, interbellum anti-Americanism in Europe centrally turned around the debate about the mechanization and standardization of culture. Due mainly to the fact that America was ahead of Europe in what the Dutch historian Johan Huizinga called the instrumentalization of life, many were wont to attribute these ominous trends to America. Hardly ever did people pause to consider whether these processes of mechanization and standardization might not have parallel effects in Europe and America, irrespective of their provenance, or whether they might not work out differently depending on historic context and prevailing cultural attitudes. Mostly people tended implicitly to take an intermediate position, assuming that the process of mechanization had already assumed a thoroughly American guise and Europe would only get to know it as such.

It is good, therefore, to recognize that many guardians of culture in America as well worried about the commercialization, mechanization, and standardization of American culture. There is Henry Adams, scion of one of the leading families in America, and his concern about the loss of spirituality in the culture of his homeland. He had a keen sense of decay and degeneration that he shared with many of his status and descent. Another "New England eccentric", Charles Ives, expressed himself in his diaries as follows: "But the Camp Meetings aren't the only thing that have gone soft. How about some of the seed of 1776? There are probably several contributing factors. Perhaps the most obvious if not the most harmful element is commercialism, with its influence tending towards mechanization and standardized processes of mind and life (making breakfast and death a little too easy). Emasculating America for money! Is the Anglo-Saxon going 'Pussy'?"[1] The quotation is redolent of a fear that the nation's proud Anglo-Saxon founders had become effete, due to the newly rising culture of consumption and its facile pleasures.

A chorus of concordant voices in Europe produced similar litanies. In 1927, the Frenchman André Siegfried had this to say: "For so much luxury brought within reach of every worker a heavy price is being paid: nothing less than the transformation of millions of workers into automatons. 'Fordism', i.e. the essence of American industry, results in the standardization of the worker-as-such. Craftsmanship … has no more place in the New World, and with it have gone certain conceptions of man that we in Europe do consider as the veritable basis of civilization."[2] What Ives still saw as the result of the process of mechanization alone assumes under Siegfried's hands the proportions of an American/European clash. Huizinga for that matter takes a larger view; he perceives in America the first signs of a process of civilization that is much more general in portent: "Organization becomes mechanization; that is the fatal moment of the modern history of civilization."³ His broader view, however, does not make his mood of cultural demise any less acute. Yet he is aware that without mechanization there will be no civilization at all: "The process of refining culture is inseparable from that of instrumentalization." The process, however, has two distinct effects; it has a power-to-bind and a power-to-liberate. And it would appear ("taking America as the most perfect example") as if the balance tends too much towards the first, toward the subservience and bondedness of the individual, rather than towards setting him free. Huizinga goes on to ponder the possibility of whether the instrumentalization of life in America might not work out differently than in Europe: "Organization in the sense of standardization means the establishing of a uniform and well-defined technical nomenclature ... to the American it constitutes not only an individual need rather than a necessary evil, it also constitutes a cultural ideal ... Everyone familiar with their sense of conformity and collective identity will realize this. The American *wants* to be equal to his neighbor. He feels spiritually safe only in the normatively ordained, not to mention the fact that the latter also implies 'efficiency'."⁴ Siegfried further sharpens this contrast: "As for the races that are individuals in their work— the Frenchman who insists on thinking for himself and by himself; the Mediterranean with his genius for gardening and love of the soil—they all aggressively assert their individuality as if they could not fit in into the American MACHINE."⁵ This takes us back again to one of those classical oppositions that Europeans tend to perceive between themselves and "America": individual heterogeneity versus the uniformity of the mass. The opposition here as in so many other cases is a tactical sleight-of-hand, intended to keep the American threat at a safe distance. Europe, according to this view, would simply not be amenable to the American way.

Georges Duhamel, for one, had long given up on this hope. America, as he saw it, was Europe's future. Mass society would manifest itself in Europe in the forms that it had already assumed in America; from America it would hurl itself like a devastating wave across the Old World. In his apocalyptic vision, *le machinisme* and *l' homme-outil* take center stage. He too would conceive of mechanization mostly in terms of the loss of human individuality and creativity.⁶

In the German view of the perils of mechanization, we find this same theme of the machine-man. *Chauffeurmenschen* they were occasionally called there. Yet the accent appears to be placed differently, on the preservation of the "folk spirit" (*Volksgeist*) and *Kultur*, on the collective rather than the individual. A well-known example from the 1920s is a book by Adolf Halfeld, *Amerika und der Amerikanismus*.⁷ It bears the highly charged subtitle, *Kritische Betrachtungen eines Deutschen und Europäers*. The publisher used the dust jacket of the book really to lay it on: "*Das Gegenstück zu Henry Ford. Wer dieses Buch gelesen hat, ist dagegen gefeit, den Amerikanismus zu predigen!*" ("The counterweight to Henry Ford. Those who will have read this book, will be safe-guarded against preaching Americanism!") The culture of Europe, he wrote, "German culture in particular," was destined for annihilation "at the hands of an America that is geared to materialism and the mechanization of life." Rationalization in the American vein was the order of the day, "regardless of whether it kills what is human in Man." The publisher presented the book as a counterblast to the much more positive view of America prevalent in German industrial circles, both among the entrepreneurs and organized labor, in which America was seen as the epitome of rational economic organization. Halfeld and other conservative critics of culture opposed this view, arguing the case of the many negative effects of mechanization and rational organization.

Halfeld, sported as "German and European," came up with the following contrast between Europe and America: "a European world of strong characters, of expressive symbols and of a communal spirit rooted in the folk" stands opposed to "an America of Machine people, which from the one guiding principle of success deduces a value system of the most offensive spiritual poverty and which robs life of its eternal mysteries."[8] ("[*Eine*] *Europäische Welt der Charaktere, der plastischen Symbole und des im Volkstum wurzelnden Gemeinschaftsgeistes*" stands opposed to "*ein Amerika der Maschinenmenschen, das aus dem einen Grundprinzip des Erfolges eine Wertordnung von beleidigendster Dürftigkeit ableitet und das Leben seinen ewigen Geheimnisse beraubt.*") Clearly it does not matter much that European observers, from Karl Marx to Max Weber, basing themselves solely on European developments, had designed their grand theories about the rationalization and the *Entzauberung* (the disenchantment) of the world. Halfeld still felt he could describe Europe as the continent where the luster and magic of life were still untouched. "Seen from the higher vantage point of our western development, Americanism appears as the straightforward attempt at realizing the synthesis of all social forces in a modern form—and it does this by setting a goal that is one-sidedly economic, in opposition to the mental reservations of the human spirit."[9] ("*Von der höheren Warte unserer abendländischen Entwicklung gesehen, erscheint der Amerikanismus geradezu als ein Versuch, die Zusammenfassung aller gesellschaftlichen Kräfte in moderner Form zu verwirklichen—und zwar durch eine gegen den Geist und seine stets wachen Bedenken gerichtete, einseitig wirtschaftliche Zwecksetzung.*")

Other German authors developed variations on this general theme of mechanization and economic rationality representing a threat to the European spirit. Once again the entire metaphoric repertoire of anti-Americanism is brought to bear. A contribution by Richard Müller-Freienfels to *Der Deutsche Gedanke* (*German Thought*) in 1927, for instance, makes it clear that to him the danger of Americanism for Europe lies not "in the introduction of American machines as such" but "in the leveling of the mind which they have produced in America" ("*in der Nivellierung des Geistes, die diese in Amerika selbst gezeitigt haben*"). He distinguishes a general Americanism as a developmental phase that Europe is experiencing as well, and a more specific Americanism that Europe would have to oppose. As elements of this latter form of Americanism, he sees, in addition to a spiritual leveling, the mindless pursuit of ever new records, the idolization of sports, the devaluation of man to a machine. That is what Europe should fend off; in opposition, Europe must stress "its valuation of quality as opposed to quantity, organic life versus mechanization, personality against uniformity."[10]

Yet another German contemporary, the philosopher Count Hermann Keyserling, a holist in the Carl Jung tradition, would found his critique of the mechanized society mainly on an ideal type of man-in-his-totality. But he did in fact connect his more general cultural critique to America, especially in his *Amerika: Der Aufgang einer neuen Welt* (*America: The Rise of a New World*), a book that would be published in France as *Psychanalyse de l'Amérique* and would influence the French image of America. Much like Huizinga he uses a stratagem intended to keep America at a distance: he acknowledges the existence among Americans of a natural socialism and attributes it to the fact that "the social inclinations do truly dominate the American soul." American ideals such as "normalcy," "like-mindedness," and "standardization" all testify to this. Yet in fact they constitute the relapse from a higher to a lower level of civilization. Given their cast of mind, which limits itself to "what the intellect can fathom," to the level of practical intelligence and common sense, Americans orient themselves toward the future, yet tend to ignore "the inseparable connections between the past, the present and the future."[11] The image of Man in America is cast in terms of mechanization and the physical control of the world. In the psychology of behaviorism—according to Keyserling a typically American view of Man—human beings appear as animals, rats in a treadmill. All human behavior can be reduced to acquired routines that, in turn, are fully determined by external factors and therefore open to external manipulation and control. Thus the American appears as a species that is uniquely in tune with the world of commerce, of mechanization, of manipulation through advertising, of rational organization. He is the perfect cog in the perfect American machine.

One notes remarkable consistency in the arguments as summarized above, almost to the point that their very validity seems reinforced more by their repetition in endless variations than by anything else. Yet at the hands of other authors, this same discourse can suddenly appear in a different light. What we have seen thus far, in the case of those Europeans who tended to connect America to secular trends of mechanization and industrialization, was their willingness to acknowledge the rationality and efficiency of America's economic organization (as Huizinga put it, "Your perfect organization"). Yet one finds examples illustrating the contrary view. Consider H.G. Wells, who after his arrival in New York had this to say: "Noise and human hurry and a vastness of means and collective result, rather than any vastness of achievement, is the pervading quality of New York. The great thing is the mechanical thing, the unintentional thing which is speeding up all these people."[12] One day later "the effect remained still that of an immeasurably powerful forward movement of rapid eager advance," but, due perhaps to a good night's sleep, he could also write that "the human being seemed less of a fly upon the wheels."[13] He was now able to perceive more clearly an element of human direction and control, of a collective exercise of will, in what only a day before had struck him as "the mechanical thing, the unintentional thing." The image of a machine world, without sense or purpose, in constant motion, yet without "vastness of achievement," may remind us of Henry Adams, who at about the same time projected his metaphor of entropy onto the American scene. Yet Wells was cut of different timber. He was the kind of socialist who saw the way of the future lying in large-scale technology wedded to an equally large-scale spirit of collective enterprise. Sentimentality and nostalgia were alien to him. At Niagara Falls, the power turbines impressed Wells the most: "They are will made visible, thought translated into easy and commanding things."[14] In Boston he had already encountered this sense of purpose, of planning and foresight, applied to problems of urban growth. He described his tour of the city as the exploration of "a fresh and more deliberate phase in this great American symphony, this symphony of Growth."[15] Growth excited him, "mechanical things" made him rave rapturously, as long as there was the attendant element of "deliberateness," of intentionality. In that sense he was closer to the enthusiasms of the Progressive Movement in America than to the sense of disinheritance and alienation that characterized aesthetes like Henry Adams and Henry James.

Thus, mechanization and its cultural effects could be seen from totally different perspectives: as a threat to tradition and individuality, especially in France; as undermining the *Volksgeist* and *Kultur* so valued in Germany; as a force of renewal that would bring prosperity and freedom, in the view of labor union leaders and socialists in a number of European countries; and finally as the carrier of a new aesthetics, more beautiful than Niagara Falls.

Contemporary Anti-Americanism: America as a Subtext

"*Nous sommes tous américains.*" We are all Americans. Such was the rallying cry of the French newspaper *Le Monde*'s editor-in-chief, Jean-Marie Colombani, published one day after the terrorist attack against symbols of America's power. He went on to say, "We are all New Yorkers, as surely as John Kennedy declared himself, in 1962 in Berlin, to be a Berliner." If that was one historical resonance that Colombani himself called forth for his readers, there is an even older use of this rhetorical call to solidarity that may come to mind. It is Jefferson's call for unity after America's first taste of two-party strife. Leading opposition forces to victory in the presidential election of 1800, he assured Americans that "We are all Federalists, we are all Republicans," urging his audience to rise above the differences that many at the time feared might divide the young nation against itself. Clearly, there would have been no need for such a ringing rhetorical call if there had not been at the same time an acute sense of difference and division. Similarly, in the case of Colombani's timely expression of solidarity with an ally singled out for vengeful attack, solely because, among allies, this particular one had come to represent the global challenge posed by a shared Western way of life. An attack against America was therefore an attack against common values held dear by all who live by standards of democracy and the type of open society that it implies. But, as in Jefferson's case, the rhetorical urgency of the call for solidarity suggests a sense of difference and divisions now to be transcended, or at least temporarily to be shunted aside.

As we all know, there is a long history that illustrates France's long and abiding affinity with America's daring leap into an age of modernity. It shared America's fascination with the political modernity of republicanism, of democracy and egalitarianism, with the economic modernity of progress in a capitalist vein, and with an existential modernity that saw Man, with a capital M and in the gender-free sense of the word, as the agent of history, the sculptor of his social life as well as of his own individual identity and destiny. It was after all a Frenchman, Michel Guillaume Jean de Crèvecoeur, who on the eve of American independence pondered the question, "What, then, is the American, this new Man?" A long line of French observers have, in lasting fascination, commented on this American venture, seeing it as a trajectory akin to their own hopes and dreams for France.[16] Similarly, French immigrants in the United States, in order to legitimize their claims for ethnic specificity, have always emphasized the historical nexus of French and American political ideals, elevating Marquis de Lafayette alongside George Washington to equal iconic status.[17]

But, as we also know, there is an equally long history of French awareness of American culture taking directions that were seen as a threat to French ways of life and views of culture. Whether it was Alexis de Tocqueville's more sociological intuition of an egalitarian society breeding cultural homogeneity and conformism, or later French views that sought the explanation in the economic logic of a free and unfettered market, their fear was of an erosion of the

French cultural landscape, of French standards of taste and cultural value. As I have argued elsewhere, the French were not alone in harboring such fears,[18] but they have been more consistently adamant in making the case for a defense of their national identity against a threatening process of Americanization. The very word is a French coinage. It was Charles Baudelaire who, on the occasion of the 1855 *Exposition Universelle de Paris*, spoke of modern man, set on a course of technical materialism, as "so Americanized that he has lost all notion of the differences that set apart the phenomena of the physical world from the moral world, the natural from the supernatural."[19] The Goncourt brothers' *Journal*, from the time of the second exposition in 1867, refers to "The Universal Exposition, the last blow in what is the Americanization of France."[20] As these critics saw it, industrial progress ushered in an era where quantity would replace quality and where a mass culture feeding on standardization would erode established taste hierarchies. There are echoes of Tocqueville here, yet the eroding factor is no longer the egalitarian logic of mass democracy but the logic of industrial progress. In both cases, however, whatever the precise link and evaluating angle, America had become the metonym for unfettered modernity, like a Prometheus unbound.

Europeans, French observers included, have always been perplexed by two aspects of the American way with culture, two aspects that to them represented the core of America's cultural otherness, one its crass commercialism, the other its irreverent attitude of cultural bricolage, recycling the culturally high and low, the vulgar and the sublime, in ways unfamiliar and shocking to European sensibilities. As for the alleged commercialism, what truly strikes Europeans is the blithe symbiosis between two cultural impulses that Europeans consider incompatible: a democratic impulse and a commercial one. From early on, American intellectuals and artists agreed that for American culture to be American it must be democratic. It should appeal to the many, not the few. Setting itself up in contradistinction to Europe's stratified societies and the hierarchies of taste they engendered, America proclaimed democracy for the cultural realm as well. That in itself was enough to make Europeans frown. Could democratic culture ever be anything but vulgar, ever be more than the largest common denominator of the people's tastes? Undeniably, there were those in Europe who agreed with Americans that cultural production there could not simply follow in the footsteps of Europeans, and who were willing to recognize an American Homer in Walt Whitman, America's poet of democracy. But even they were aghast at the ease with which the democratic impulse blended into the commercial. What escaped them was that, in order to reach a democratic public, the American artist found himself in much the same situation as a merchant going to market. If America was daring in its formation of a mass market for goods that it produced en masse, it was equally daring in its view that cultural production in a democratic vein needed to find its market, its mass audience. In the absence of forms of European cultural sponsorship, it needed to *make* its audiences, to create its own cultural market, if only with a view to recouping the cost of cultural production. Particularly in the age of mechanical reproduction when the market had to expand along with the growth in cultural supply, American culture became ever more aware of the commercial calculus. By that same token, it became ever more suspect in the eyes of European critics. Something made for profit, for money, could inherently never be of cultural value. This critical view has a long pedigree and is alive and well today.

The other repertoire of the European critique of American mass culture focuses on its spirit of blithe bricolage, of its anticanonical approach to questions of high versus low culture, or to matters of the organic holism of cultural forms. Again, some Europeans were tempted, if not convinced, by Whitmanesque experiments in recognizing and embracing the elevated in the lowly, the vulgar in the sublime, or his experiments in formlessness. They were willing to see in this America's quest for a democratic, if not demotic, culture. But in the face of America's shameless appropriation of the European cultural heritage, taking it apart and reassembling it in ways that went against European views of the organic wholeness of their hallowed heritage, Europeans begged to differ. To them, the collage or reassemblage attitude that produced Hearst Castle, Caesar's Palace, or the stylistic jumble of the European architectural vocabulary seen in some of America's high-rise buildings seemed proof that Americans could only look at European culture in the light of its being contemporaneous, as if it were one big mail-order catalog. It was all there at the same time, itemized and numbered, for Americans to pick and choose. It was all reduced to the same level of usable bits and pieces, to be recycled, reassembled, and quoted at will. Many European critics have seen in this an antihistorical, antimetaphysical, or antiorganicist bent of the American mind. When the Dutch historian Huizinga was first introduced, in the 1920s, to the Dewey Decimal System used to organize library holdings, he was aghast at the reduction of the idea of a library, an organic body of knowledge, to the tyranny of the decimal system, to numbers. Others, like Charles Dickens or Sigmund Freud, more facetiously, saw American culture as reducing cultural value to exchange value, the value of dollars. Where Europeans tend toward an aesthetics that values closure, rules of organic cohesion, Americans tend to explode such views. If they have a canon, it is one that values open-endedness in the recombination of individual components. They prefer constituent elements over their composition. Whether in television or American football, European ideas of flow and continuity become cut up and jumbled, in individual time slots as on television or in individual plays, as in football. Examples abound, and will most likely come to your mind, "even as I speak" (to use American television lingo).

Potentially, the result of this bricolage view of cultural production might be endless variety. Yet what Europeans tended to see was only fake diversity, a lack of authenticity. A long chorus of French voices, from Duhamel and François Mauriac in the interwar years, to Jean-Paul Sartre and more particularly Simone de Beauvoir after World War II, in the 1940s and 1950s, kept this litany resounding. At one point Beauvoir even borrowed from David Riesman, an American cultural critic, to make a point she considered her own. She referred to the American people as "*un peuple de moutons*" ("a nation of sheep"), conformist, and "*extéro-conditionnés,*" French for Riesman's "other-directed." At other points, she could see nothing but a lack of taste, if not slavishness, in American consumerism.

Such French views are far from dated. They still inform critiques of contemporary mass culture. Yet, apparently, the repertoire is so widespread and well known that often no explicit mention of America is needed anymore. America has become a subtext. In the following I propose to give two examples, one illustrating the dangers of commercialism in the production of culture, the other the baneful effects of America's characteristic modularizing mode in cultural production, its spirit of bricolage.

Commercialism and Culture

In our present age of globalization, with communication systems such as the Internet spanning the globe, national borders have become increasingly porous. They no longer serve as cultural barriers that one can raise at will to fend off cultural intrusions from abroad. It is increasingly hard to erect them as a cultural "Imaginot" line in defense of a national cultural identity. Yet old instincts die hard. In a typically preemptive move, France modernized its telephone system in the 1980s, introducing a communication network (the Minitel) that allowed people to browse and shop around. It was a network much like the later World Wide Web. The French system was national, however, and stopped at the border. At the time, it was a bold step forward, but it put France at a disadvantage later on, when the global communications revolution got under way. The French were slower than most of their European neighbors to connect to the Internet. And that may have been precisely the point.

At every moment in the recent past when the liberalization of trade and flows of communication was being discussed in international meetings, the French raised the issue of cultural protection. They have repeatedly insisted on exempting cultural goods, such as film and television, from the logic of free trade. They insist, most recently again in a book by France's minister of foreign affairs, Hubert Védrine,[21] on protective quotas for trade in this area and on the sovereign right of national governments to set national content criteria for television and film programming and to subsidize its production. They do this because, as they see it, France represents cultural "quality" and therefore may help to maintain diversity in the American-dominated international market for ideas. The subtext for such defensive strategies is not so much the fear of opening France's borders to the world but rather fear of letting American culture wash across the country. Given America's dominant role in world markets for popular culture, as well as its quasi-imperial place in the communications web of the Internet, globalization appears to many French people as a Trojan horse. For many of them, globalization means Americanization.

With the recent attempts at starting a new round for the further liberalization of world trade, France was up in arms again. The French minister of culture published a piece in the French daily newspaper *Le Monde*, again making the French case for a cultural exemption from free trade rule. A week later one of France's leading intellectual lights, Pierre Bourdieu, joined the fray in an article published in the same newspaper.[22] It was the text of an address delivered on 11 October 1999 to the International Council of the Museum of Television and Radio in Paris. He chose to address his audience as "representing the true masters of the world," those whose control of global communication networks provides them not political or economic power but what Bourdieu calls "symbolic power," that is, power over people's minds and imaginations gained through cultural artifacts—books, films, and television programs—that they produce and disseminate. This power is increasingly globalized through international market control, mergers and consolidations, and a revolution in communications technology. Bourdieu briefly considers the fashionable claim that the newly emerging structures, aided by the digital revolution, will bring endless cultural diversity, catering to the cultural demands of specific niche markets. Bourdieu rejects this out of hand; what he sees is an increasing homogenization and vulgarization of cultural supply driven by a logic that is purely commercial, not cultural. Aiming at profit maximization, market control, and ever larger audiences, the "true masters of the world" gear their products to the largest common denominator that defines their audience. What the world gets is more soap operas, expensive blockbuster movies organized around special effects, and books whose success is measured by sales, not by intrinsic cultural merit.

It is a Manichean world that Bourdieu conjures up. True culture, as he sees it, is the work of individual artists who view their audience as being posterity, not the throngs at the box office. In the cultural resistance that artists have put up over centuries against the purely commercial view of their work, they have managed to carve out a social and cultural domain whose organizing logic is at right angles to that of the economic market. As Bourdieu puts it, "Reintroducing the sway of the 'commercial' in realms that have been set up, step by step, against it means endangering the highest works of mankind."

Quoting Ernest Gombrich, Bourdieu says that when the "ecological prerequisites" for art are destroyed, art and culture will not be long in dying. After voicing a litany of cultural demise in film industries in a number of European countries, he laments the fate of a cultural radio station about to be liquidated "in the name of modernity," a victim to Nielsen ratings and the profit motive.

"In the name of modernity" indeed. Never in his address does Bourdieu rail against America as the site of such dismal modernity, yet the logic of his argument is reminiscent of many earlier French views of American culture, a culture emanating from a country that never shied from merging the cultural and the commercial (or, for that matter, the cultural and the democratic). Culture, as Bourdieu defends it, is typically high culture. Interestingly, though, unlike many earlier French criticisms of an American culture that reached Europe under commercial auspices, Bourdieu's defense is not of national cultures, more specifically the French national identity, threatened by globalization. Rather, as he argues, the choice is between "the kitsch products of commercial globalization" and those of an international world of creative artists in literature, visual arts, and cinematography, a world that knows many constantly shifting centers.

Yet blood runs thicker than water. Great artists, and Bourdieu lists several writers and filmmakers, "would not exist the way they do without this literary, artistic, and cinematographic international whose seat is [present tense!] situated in Paris. No doubt because there, for strictly historical reasons, the microcosm of producers, critics, and informed audiences, necessary for its survival, has long since taken shape and has managed to survive." Bourdieu thus manages to have his cake and eat it, too, arrogating a place for Paris as the true seat of a modernity in high culture. In his construction of a global cultural dichotomy lurks an established French *parti pris*. More than that, however, his reading of globalization as Americanization by stealth blinds him to the way French intellectuals and artists before him have discovered, adapted, and adopted forms of American commercial culture, such as Hollywood movies.

In his description of the social universe that sustains a cultural international in Paris, he mentions the infrastructure of art-film houses, of a *cinémathèque*, of eager audiences and informed critics, such as those writing for the *Cahiers du cinéma*. He seems oblivious to the fact that in the 1950s precisely this potent ambience for cultural reception led to the French discovery of Hollywood movies as true examples of the *cinéma d'auteur*, of true film art showing the hand of individual makers, now acclaimed masters in the pantheon of film history. Their works are held and regularly shown in Bourdieu's vaunted *cinémathèque* and his art-film houses. They were made to work, like much other despised commercial culture coming from America, within frameworks of cultural appropriation more typically French, or European, than American. They may have been misread in the process as works of individual "auteurs" more than as products of the Hollywood studio system. That they were the products of a cultural infrastructure totally at variance with the one Bourdieu deems essential may have escaped French fans at the time. It certainly escapes Bourdieu now. This should only make us more intellectually cautious before we jump to facile readings of commercial culture as necessarily a threat to things we hold dear.

The Modularizing Mind and the World Wide Web

Among other dreams, the Internet has inspired those of a return to a world of total intertextuality, of the reconstitution of the full body of human thinking and writing. It would be the return to the "City of Words," the labyrinthine library that, like a nostalgic recollection, has haunted the human imagination since the age of the mythical library of Babylon. Tony Tanner used the metaphor of the city of words to describe the central quest inspiring the literary imagination of the twentieth century.[23] One author who, for Tanner, epitomizes this quest is Jorge Luis Borges. It is the constructional power of the human mind that moves and amazes Borges. His stories are full of the strangest architecture, including the endless variety of lexical architecture to which man throughout history has devoted his time—philosophical theories, theological disputes, encyclopaedias, religious beliefs, critical interpretations, novels, and books of all kinds. While having a deep feeling for the shaping and abstracting powers of man's mind, Borges has at the same time a profound sense of how nightmarish the resultant structures might become. In one of his stories, the library of Babel is referred to by the narrator as the "universe," and one can take it as a metaphysical parable of all the difficulties of deciphering man's encounters in existence. On the other hand, Babel remains the most famous example of the madness in man's rage for architecture, and books are only another form of building. In this library every possible combination of letters and words is to be found, with the result that there are fragments of sense separated by "leagues of insensate cacophony, of verbal farragos and incoherencies." Most books are "mere labyrinths of letters." Since everything that language can do and express is somewhere in the library, "the clarification of the basic mysteries of humanity ... was also expected." The "necessary vocabularies and grammars" must be discoverable in the lexical totality. Yet the attempt at discovery and detection is maddening; the story is full of the sadness, sickness, and madness of the pathetic figures who roam around the library as around a vast prison.[24]

What do Borges's fantasies tell us about the Promethean potential of a restored city of words in cyberspace? During an international colloquium in

Paris at the *Bibliothèque nationale de France,* held on June 3rd and 4th, 1998, scholars and library presidents discussed the implications of a virtual memory bank on the Internet, connecting the holdings of all great libraries in the world. Some saw it as a dream come true. In his opening remarks, Jean-Pierre Angremy referred to the library of Babel as imagined by Borges, while ignoring its nightmarish side: "When it was proclaimed that the library would hold all books, the first reaction was one of extravagant mirth. Everyone felt like mastering an intact and secret treasure." The perspective, as Angremy saw it, was extravagant indeed: all the world's knowledge at your command, like an endless scroll across your computer screen. Others, like Jacques Attali, spiritual father of the idea of digitalizing the holdings of the new *Bibliothèque nationale,* took a similarly positive view. Whatever the form of the library, real or virtual, it would always be "a reservoir of books." Others were not so sure. They foresaw a mutation of our traditional relationship toward the written text, where new manipulations and competences would make our reading habits as antiquated as the reading of papyrus scrolls is to us.

Ironically, as others pointed out, texts as they now appear on our screen are like a throwback to the reading of scrolls, and may well affect our sense of the single page. In the printed book, every page comes in its own context of pages preceding and following it, suggesting a discursive continuity. On the screen, however, the same page would be the interchangeable element of a virtual data bank that one penetrates into by the use of a key word that opens many books at the same time. All information is thus put at the same plan, without the logical hierarchy of an unfolding argument. As Michel Melot, longtime member of the *Conseil supérieur des bibliothèques,* pointed out, randomness becomes the rule. The coherence of traditional discursive presentation will tend to give way to what is fragmented, incomplete, disparate, if not incoherent. In his view, the patchwork or cut-and-paste approach will become the dominant mode of composition.[25]

These darker views are suggestive of a possible American imprint of the Internet. They are strangely reminiscent of an earlier cultural critique in Europe of the ways in which American culture would affect European civilization. Particularly the contrast seen between the act of reading traditional books and of texts downloaded from the Internet recalls a contrast between Europe and America that constitutes a staple in the work of many European critics of American culture. Europe, in this view, stands for organic cohesion, for logical and stylistic closure, whereas America tends towards fragmentation and recombination, in a mode of blithe cultural bricolage, exploding every prevailing cultural canon in Europe. Furthermore, we recognize the traditional European fear of American culture as a leveling force, bringing everything down to the surface level of the total interchangeability of cultural items, oblivious of their intrinsic value and of cultural hierarchies of high versus low.[26]

Yet, in the views expressed at the Paris symposium, we find no reference to America. Is this because America is a subtext, a code instantly recognized by French intellectuals? Or is it because the logic of the Internet and of digital intertextuality has a cultural impact in its own right, similar to the impact of American culture, but this time unrelated to any American agency? I would go no further at this point than to suggest a Weberian answer. It seems to be undeniably the case that there is a *Wahlverwandtschaft* —an elective affinity—between the logic of the Internet and the American cast of mind, which makes for an easier, less anguished acceptance and use of the new medium among Americans than among a certain breed of Europeans.

There is, it seems to me, a further way to explore this elective affinity. Most of the discussion at the Paris colloquium focused on the *use* of texts available via the Internet rather than on the *production* of texts, in other words on the act of reading rather than writing. At one point, though, the question came up as to whether the logic of the Internet might not also lead to novel forms of literature. According to the report in *Le Monde*, no one could yet foresee the possible impact on creative writing. Yet one could venture a little farther than this. From a librarian's point of view, the Internet can be seen as having generated a virtual library in cyberspace, linking all available texts ever produced by writers. Through the use of key words and related search techniques, every visitor to this library can determine his or her own particular trajectory through the lexical labyrinth, producing a textual collage to fit the particular needs of individual readers. It is, in this case, individual readers who, on the basis of available texts, generate their own individual recombination and rearrangement of textual fragments. The logical next step, then, would be the production of precisely such a body of textual fragments, as an act of creative writing, where the author would provide the key words, known as hyperlinks, that would allow the reader to cruise through the textual fragments, and to arrange them in any number of combinations. The result would be what we might call a hypertext novel.

As it happens, the challenge has been taken up. Hypertext novels do exist, not on the shelves of real libraries anywhere in the world but, as their logic dictates, in the virtual library in cyberspace. They can be downloaded as so many fragments and then, by clicking on any of the hyperlinks provided by the author, arranged by the individual reader sitting at his or her own computer.[27] This creative leap into cyberspace has something Promethean about it. It invites the reader to become his or her own individual author and to act out the dream that is so central to an age that has proclaimed the death of the author. No longer, it would seem, does the hypertext novel tie the reader down to forms of narrative flow and structure set entirely by the author. The very logic of the hypertext novel demands that readers actively construct their own texts.

Again, I would argue, this daring step was typically one for American writers to make first. It does seem to fit in with a more general American modularizing cast of mind, with a greater willingness to break up coherent wholes and to leave it to individual consumers to recombine the fragments as they please. Yet the idea of the hypertext novel seems more daring than any actual examples I have seen. The idea ties in with the dream of the lost library where an author would do no more than set the reader off on a journey through the labyrinth of the human imagination, out into uncharted territory. The idea is one of a text that is structurally open, fraying at the edges, providing hyperlinks into the unknown. The hypertext in its present form is a far cry from this, however. It is entirely self-enclosed, referring back to its own constituent elements only, allowing of no escape beyond the structural closure set by the author. It is reminiscent of the attempts at building a robot that would not be a simple replica of man but an improvement upon our present stage of evolution. The result has always been of a Prometheus bound and shackled in retribution for his acts of hubris.

Like the robot, the hypertext novel is no more than a clumsy replica of reading as we have always known it and done it. The act of reading texts in their traditional form has always been one of the active construction of hyperlinks. One book always reminds us of other books. Our mind produces its own links and associations. Reading one book, we get up and open other books to verify our associative hunches. We hear voices of other authors reverberating in unison with the voice of any particular author we happen to be reading. Sometimes the reverberation is a matter of authorial intent, sometimes it is a case of the reader's mind wandering. But all reading is intertextual, all fiction a hypertext. Europeans have always produced fiction in a self-conscious awareness of its intertextuality, from Shakespeare and Cervantes to Julian Barnes and Julián Ríos. And so have Americans. In the cultural games that Americans play, they may experiment in ways that strike Europeans as typically American, yet the dream of life in cyberspace is the contemporary version of dreams that we all share.

After reviewing these two exhibits of cultural anti-Americanism as a subtext, taking French attitudes as its typical expression, what conclusions can we draw? One is that fears of an American way with culture, due to either its commercial motives or its modularizing instincts, are too narrow, too hidebound. Discussing Bourdieu's views, I mentioned counterexamples where compatriots of his, in the 1950s, thoroughly reevaluated the body of cinematography produced in Hollywood. They moved it up the French hierarchy of taste and discovered individual auteurs where the logic of established French views of commercial culture would have precluded the very possibility of their existence. This is a story that keeps repeating itself. Time and time again French artists and intellectuals, after initial neglect and rejection, have discovered redeeming cultural value in American jazz, in American hard-boiled detective novels, in rap music, in Disney World, and other forms of American mass culture. What they did—and this may have been typically for French, or more generally European, intellectuals, to achieve—was to develop critical lexicons, constructing canonic readings of American cultural genres. It is a form of cultural appropriation, making forms of American culture part of a European critical discourse, measuring it in terms of European taste hierarchies. It is a process of subtle and nuanced appropriation that takes us far beyond any facile, across-the-board rejection of American culture due to its commercial agency.

How about the second ground for rejection, America's blithe leveling of cultural components to the level of interchangeable bits and pieces? As I argued in my review of the second exhibit, America may have been more daring when it ventures out in this field, yet we can find parallels and affinities with Europe's cultural traditions. A catalytic disenchantment of the world, as part of a larger secularization of Europe's Weltanschauung, had been eating away at traditional views of God-ordained order before Americans joined in.[28] Again, facile rejections of what many mistakenly see as Americanization by stealth, when confronted with more radical manifestations of the modularization of the world, miss the point. I suggested the possibility that what the World Wide Web brings us in terms of endless digital dissection and reassemblage of "texts" may have more to do with the inherent logic of the digital revolution than with any American agency. A more or less open aversion to this happening should be seen, therefore, as antimodernity rather than as anti-Americanism. It reveals a resentment against the relentless modernization of our world that has been a continuing voice of protest in the history of Western civilization.

It is a resentment, though, that should make us think twice. Clearly, we are not all Americans, taking America as a metaphor for the Promethean exploration of the frontier of modernity. This is not the same as saying that those who are not "Americans" are therefore the Bin Ladens in our midst. But their resentment is certainly akin to what, in other parts of the world, has turned into blind hatred of everything Western civilization stands for.

Notes

1. John Kirkpatrick, ed., *Charles E. Ives Memos* (New York, 1972), 120.
2. André Siegfried, *Les Etats-Unies d'aujourdhui* (Paris, 1927), 347.
3. For Huizinga's views on the mechanization of contemporary life, see his *Mensch en menigte in Amerika* (Haarlem, 1918), and his *Amerika denkend en levend: Losse opmerkingen* (Haarlem, 1927), 14ff. Both books have come out in an English translation by Herbert H. Rowen in one volume, entitled *America: A Dutch Historian's Vision—From Afar and Near* (New York, 1972). The first quotation is from *Mensch en menigte*, 61; the second, from ibid., 129; and the third, from *Amerika levend en denkend*, 14, 15.
4. Huizinga, *Amerika levend en denkend*, 21.
5. André Siegfried, preface to André Philip, *Le problème ouvrier aux Etats-Unies* (Paris, 1927), xi.
6. Georges Duhamel, *Scènes de la vie future* (Paris, 1931).
7. Adolf Halfeld, *Amerika und der Amerikanismus: Kritische Betrachtungen eines Deutschen und Europäers* (Jena, 1927).
8. Ibid., 37.
9. Ibid.
10. Richard Müller-Freienfels, "Amerikanismus und Europäische Kultur," *Der deutsche Gedanke*, 4, no. 1 (1927): 30-35; quotations on 34, 35.
11. Hermann Keyserling, *Amerika: Der Aufgang einer neuen Welt* (Stuttgart, 1931), 425.
12. Herbert George Wells, *The Future in America: A Search after Realities* (Leipzig, 1907), 44.
13. Ibid., 47f.
14. Ibid., 63.
15. Ibid., 57.
16. I may refer the reader to my survey of such French views of American modernity. See Rob Kroes, *Them and Us: Questions of Citizenship in a Globalizing World* (Champaign, Ill., 2000), chapter 9.
17. See, e.g., Annick Foucrier, *Le rêve californien: Migrants francais sur la côte Pacifique (XVIIe-XXe siècles)* (Paris, 1999).
18. See my *If You've Seen One, You've Seen the Mall: Europeans and American Mass Culture* (Champaign, Ill., 1996).
19. Quoted in Denis Lacorne, Jacques Rupnik, and Marie-France Toinet, eds., *L'Amérique dans les têtes* (Paris, 1986), 61.
20. Quoted in ibid., 62.
21. Hubert Védrine, *Les cartes de la France à l'heure de la mondialisation* (Paris, 2000).
22. Pierre Bourdieu, "Questions aux vrais maîtres du monde," *Le Monde, sélection hebdomadaire*, 23 October 1999, 1, 7.
23. Tony Tanner, *City of Words: American Fiction 1950-1970* (New York, 1971).
24. For the Borges quotations, see Tanner, *City of Words*, 41.
25. For my summary of the proceedings at the Paris colloquium, I have used a report published in *Le Monde, Sélection Hebdomadaire*, 2589, 20 June 1998, 13.
26. For a fuller analysis of the metaphorical deep structure, underlying the European critique of American culture, I may refer the reader to my *If You've Seen One, You've Seen the Mall*.
27. A site specializing in hypertext novels is <www.eastgate.com>.
28. I argue this more at length in the concluding chapter of my book, *If You've Seen One, You've Seen the Mall*, entitled "Americanization: What are we talking about?"

CALIFORNIA BLUE
Americanization as Self-Americanization

◆ ◆ ◆

Winfried Fluck

The "Toolbox" View of Culture

My first encounter with American popular culture took place in bombed-out Berlin in 1949. I was five years old at the time. Among our neighbors was a woman who managed to support herself by entertaining American GIs on the weekends. On Saturday mornings, she would call my friend and me up to her apartment and ask us to do her grocery shopping for the weekend. Then, upon our return, she would reward us with chewing gum and Superman comics. My friend and I enjoyed the pictures, but we could not yet read, neither German nor English, and thus could not really make sense of the text. The pleasures we derived from those comics came from a more elementary level. I particularly remember the strong presence of an intense blue in Superman's dress as well as in the sky through which he moved, a blue that gained an almost magical quality in our dreary, colorless surroundings. My father had once told me that there was a country called California where the sky was always blue, and so, in an act of arbitrary but creative linkage, the blue of Superman comics became a vision of "California blue" for me.

This transformation of a piece of cheap, cheesy popular culture into an almost magical object illustrates three points I want to make in the following essay on Americanization.[1] To start with, it illustrates a point of agreement the Americanization debate appears to have reached on the key question of effect. In this debate, something like a bottom-line consensus has emerged. Past descriptions of Americanization as a form of cultural imperialism, the argument goes, were based on a surprisingly naive theory of effect and completely disregarded the possibility that different uses could be made of the

---

Notes for this section begin on page 232.

same text or program. In his discussion of theories of cultural imperialism, John Tomlinson summarizes the objections: "The general message of empirical studies—informal ones like Ang's and more large-scale formal projects like Katz's and Liebes's—is that audiences are more active and critical, their responses more complex and reflective, and their cultural values more resistant to manipulation and 'invasion' than many critical media theorists have assumed."[2] In most discussions of Americanization, the cultural imperialism thesis has therefore been replaced by more complex models of reappropriation, negotiation, and creolization.[3] One of the pioneers of the argument that cultural material is never simply absorbed as a model but reappropriated in different contexts for different needs and purposes is the Swedish anthropologist Ulf Hannerz, who, in his essay "Networks of Americanization," applies this "toolbox" view of culture to the question of Americanization: "As an alternative to the phrase 'the American influence on Sweden,' we could speak of 'American culture as a resource for Swedes,' and then find that it consists of a great many parts, of different appeal to different people."[4] My own childhood focus on the magic of color provides an example for such selective, often highly idiosyncratic forms of reappropriation.[5]

My willful transformation of "Superman blue" into "California blue" also foregrounds a second point: the uses recipients will make of popular culture remain unpredictable, because users often attach utopian longings to seemingly banal objects that originate in entirely different historical and personal circumstances. Thus, culture, including popular culture, can represent something that goes far beyond the overt level of meaning and can hardly be understood by others. These hidden sources of aesthetic experience play a crucial role in the gratification cultural objects provide. This, in turn, draws attention to a third point: somatic responses to the "immediate experience" of image, color, and sound can trigger such transfer processes more easily and effectively than moral claims or intellectual arguments. One may argue, as I do in this essay, that the much debated issue of identification with fictional texts is not so much, or at least not primarily, a question of identification with a particular character but with much more elementary dimensions of aesthetic experience.

Why are these important points for a reconsideration of the issue of Americanization? Discussions of Americanization remain incomplete and unconvincing as long as they do not take the phenomenon of selective appropriation, the fact of different contexts of use, and the varying, often unpredictable effects cultural objects can have into consideration. This also means that cultural Americanization cannot be analyzed convincingly by merely identifying economic or political interests. It is certainly important to register and document such interests, which often play an underestimated role, as Volker Berghahn has demonstrated in his recent analysis of the role of American cultural politics in postwar Germany.⁶ However, such economic and political interests can only be realized if the material they offer is effective. Discussions of cultural Americanization therefore have to attempt to account for the worldwide resonance of American popular culture. What my childhood example suggests is a point I have emphasized repeatedly in debates on Americanization: the complicating fact about Americanization is that it often takes the form of self-Americanization. In the final analysis, we are not being Americanized. We Americanize ourselves!

American Popular Culture as Modern Culture

To counter fears of Americanization by pointing out that its impact is weakened and its meaning transformed in the act of reception is still a defensive argument, however. Fortunately, things do not seem to be quite as bad as expected. Nevertheless, the premises on which fears of Americanization were based in the past—the apocalyptic vision of an invasion that destroys authentic cultures—still provide the basis for this argument. Yet, the extent to which the issue of Americanization has changed since the 1950s—which remain the favorite point of reference for discussions of an Americanization of Germany—is illustrated by a recent article in the German news magazine *Der Spiegel*. American television series, the article informs us, are actually in retreat in Germany: either they are dropped altogether or they have been relegated to the late-night hours, way after prime time.⁷ This in itself is surprising enough, but the explanation given is even more amazing. In effect, with a grain of salt, one could almost consider it a candidate for the final word on the Americanization debate; and, as is often the case in history, what began as a grand melodrama of victimization appears to end as provincial farce. The reason given in *Der Spiegel* for the declining role of American television exports is that a new generation of American series are too sophisticated, too irreverent, too self-ironic, too fast-paced for a German audience that has come to prefer a more homely and home-grown product. For someone who has witnessed years of dire predictions that, as a consequence of Americanization, quality programs will be displaced by standardized mass fare, this triumph of provincial German pop culture over a by now more sophisticated American product certainly provides an amusing turn in the debate. In the context of our discussion, it also illustrates a second line of defense in the Americanization debate that may be called the regionalization argument, in contrast to the cultural toolbox argument. As the case of diminished market shares of American television shows reveals, regional tastes can defeat global marketing strategies, thereby confirming the growing importance of national or regional adaptations in a period of globalization.

At first sight, the article in *Der Spiegel* may be seen to provide further, and perhaps final, proof that fears of Americanization are unfounded. However, it can also be read differently, because, depending on one's point of view, one may argue that it confirms the apprehensions of critics of Americanization. German television series may have successfully asserted themselves against American competitors, Turkish-German rap groups may have successfully established their own local version of hip-hop, the German video clip station VIVA may hold its own against MTV, but the format in each case is still American. My examples of national or regional self-assertion therefore do not necessarily confirm that Americanization is in retreat. On the contrary, the point can be made that Americanization has been so successful and all-pervasive in its influence that it has inspired its own regional off-shots. This is, after all, the claim that lies at the center of the critique of American mass culture by Max Horkheimer and Theodor W. Adorno and several generations of critical intellectuals in their wake.

Horkheimer and Adorno's chapter on the American culture industry in their book *Dialectic of Enlightenment* is not a discussion of the Americanization of Germany but of the historical emergence and growing dominance of a new type of culture, described as either American mass culture or as a culture industry, a standardized, completely commercialized product that, in the bleak views of Horkheimer and Adorno, is on the way to become *the* representative modern culture.[8] When we discuss the problem of a possible Americanization of German culture, we are not thinking of Ernest Hemingway or Saul Bellow or Toni Morrison, but of American mass or popular culture. At a closer look, Americanization is thus really another word for the fear that a particular type of American popular culture—symbolized by Hollywood and similarly powerful institutions of the American culture industry—may become the exemplary and dominant form of modern culture. From this point of view, the toolbox argument, which argues that uses of culture are selective and that therefore we cannot simply equate the product with its function and effect, may be valid as far as it goes, but it does not address the more central question. Ultimately, the question of what we think of Americanization depends on what we think of American popular culture as a specifically modern culture.

A Brief History of American Popular Culture

This shift in focus leads us back to what I regard as the major explanatory challenge in the Americanization debate. How can the stunning worldwide resonance of American popular culture be explained?[9] In the cultural imperialism paradigm, this popularity reflects the clever manipulation of audiences and markets; in liberal counterarguments, it is the high professionalism or democratic promise of American popular culture, which, in the toolbox and regionalization versions, is then taken back to the unpredictable use-value of single components. My own answer has been presented in more expansive form in other contexts and publications to which I may refer those looking for more than the following condensed version of a detailed historical account.[10] In view of limited space, I summarize here an extended argument in the shortest possible form.

The significance of the phenomenon of popular culture for cultural history lies in its response to the problems of cultural access and accessibility (in the sense of cultural literacy). Traditionally, access to cultural life in Western societies depended on social standing, economic means, and a high degree of cultural literacy. For example, books before the nineteenth century were expensive and often required an education in classical languages and mythology. The phrase "popular culture" basically refers to cultural forms that undermine or abolish these conditions of access.[11] In this process, American society was especially effective for a number of reasons, among them the lack of strong national cultural centers that would be able to shape cultural expression on the basis of the aesthetic or educational criteria of an elite.[12] Cultural elites in America never had enough authority to establish nationally accepted cultural standards.

Within a socially, regionally, and ethnically diversified context, two factors made American popular culture unique, gave it a head start internationally, and provide an explanation for its amazing worldwide popularity. Both factors are tied to the multiethnic composition of American society. First, American popular culture profited from a variety of multiethnic influences. This is most obvious in the realm of popular music, where the resulting hybrid mixed European and African traditions in a highly original fashion and was clearly something no other country had to offer at the time. Second, because of the multiethnic composition of its audiences, American popular culture faced a market that resembled today's global market in its diversity and multilinguistic nature, so that a need emerged early on to find a common language that would be able to overcome the heterogeneity of audiences.[13] In other words, before the Americanization of other societies could occur, American culture itself had to be "Americanized."

The response of American popular culture to this challenge—and, by implication, to the questions of access and accessibility—was simplification and reduction. The novel, which is the first medium of modern popular culture in the Western world, is already a reduction of the epic; the dime novel, in turn, is a reduction of the novel in terms of narrative complexity and psychological characterization. Each of these reductions increases cultural accessibility, and, because this means increased sales and cheaper production, the possibility of social access also increases. However, in order to read a dime novel, one still has to read English. In terms of accessibility, writing, no matter how reduced it is in its requirements for cultural literacy, has obvious limits. Images and music, on the other hand, have obvious advantages. While even the image still requires a certain cultural literacy in the sense of the ability to master a visual code, music can reduce such potential barriers of accessibility even further. Thus, film and television, but above all popular music, have therefore been the driving forces in the Americanization of modern culture.

Traditionally, it is exactly this phenomenon of reduction that is the target of cultural critics, because it is seen as result of a race for the bottom line in taste. But when silent movies directors like D.W. Griffith tried to develop a filmic language that would be superior to theatrical melodrama in terms of accessibility and effect, they did not do so in search of the lowest common denominator in taste. For his part, Griffith pursued his goals as part of his artistic ambitions, because he realized that the reduction in cultural literacy made possible by filmic images opened up entirely new possibilities of expression. The reduction to which I refer here is, in other words, primarily the result of a transformation of cultural expression by technological developments like printing, film, amplified music, and so on—developments that facilitate accessibility but, at the same time, also create new possibilities of expression and aesthetic experience.

In my view, this development has gone in an unmistakable direction, redefining in the process criteria of cultural literacy. Cultural access and accessibility are constantly widened.[14] At the same time, the individual's wishes for imaginary self-empowerment have been served more and more effectively— up to a point, for example, where the representation of violence has been taken almost completely out of moral or social contexts and is now presented largely for its own sake, that is, for the thrill it gives Hollywood's main target group, young (or not so young) males. This is an important point because it captures the major paradox produced by the development I have sketched. Contrary to the conventional wisdom of standardized mass production, resulting in growing conformity, American popular culture has been driven by a promise of providing ever more effective ways for imaginary self-empowerment and self-fashioning.[15] In this sense, it has contributed to an ever-accelerating process of individualization in society.

By individualization I do not mean a movement toward individual autonomy (that would be individuality),[16] but a growing dissociation from the authority of social claims and hence a pluralization of lifestyles. If popular culture is driven by increasing possibilities for imaginary self-empowerment and cultural self-fashioning, then Americanization, understood as worldwide dissemination of a certain type of culture, means that a process that for a number of reasons is most advanced in the United States is taking hold in other parts of the world as well. This process is usually driven by the demands of a younger generation in flight from traditions it considers restrictive.[17] What many cultural critics, including Americans who are embarrassed to have American society associated primarily with consumer culture and fast food icons, often do not understand is that even the most conventional and maligned symbols of American consumer culture such as Coca-Cola or McDonald's bear a connotation of informality that can still be experienced as liberating by young people in many parts of the world.[18]

Seen this way, Americanization is an effect of modernization—not in the sense of sociological and economic modernization theory with its teleology of progress and liberation, but in the sense of modernity's promise of self-development, which has been put at the center of cultural modernity in Marshall Berman's brilliant book *All That Is Solid Melts into Air*.[19] The problem is, however, that it is an unforeseen, almost embarrassing result of modernity's promise for self-development, for in place of self-cultivation and growing self-awareness, we get unrepentant forms of imaginary self-empowerment and self-fashioning. This, in effect, is the explanation for the strident dismissal of popular culture in the mass culture debates of the 1950s and thereafter, in which mass culture is seen as betrayal of the true task of culture, namely, to function as a counter-realm to the instrumental rationality of modernity.[20] What we have to realize and acknowledge in dealing with American popular culture, however, is that, contrary to its image as a mindless, standardized mass product, it is not the deplorable counterpoint to a modern culture of self-development but an unexpected manifestation and consequence of it.

"Embodiment": Popular Culture and Aesthetic Experience

What do I actually mean by imaginary self-empowerment? To answer this, I want to return to the claim I made at the start of this essay of the existence of a bottom-line consensus in the current Americanization debate: the "culture as toolbox" thesis of selective appropriation and creative adaptation. Scholars have become fond of using this argument, but they do not seem interested in taking it one step further and inquiring about the reasons for the selectivity on the side of the recipient. As a rule, the obviously welcome implication seems to be that, fortunately, even the "masses" are much more resilient and self-determined than cultural critics were willing to assume in the past. For some, such as Dick Hebdige and members of the British Cultural Studies movement, the creative reassembly of elements of the dominant culture demonstrates the potential of youthful subcultures for cultural resistance.

But if such explanations were true, selective appropriation would have to be a restricted phenomenon, since, obviously, not everybody can be equally resilient and creative. However, selective use is an across-the-board phenomenon. There is, by definition, no reception of any text that is not selective. Other reasons must exist, then, for the phenomenon. Again, I have to condense a complex argument developed in other contexts.[21]

The elementary fact about aesthetic objects is that, in order to acquire meaning, they have to be actualized by means of a transfer. This is most obvious in the case of literature. Since we have never met literary characters such as Huck Finn or Madame Bovary and do in fact know that they never existed, we have to bring them to life by investing our own associations, feelings, and even bodily sensations. This means that in the act of reception, the text or object comes to represent two things at the same time: the world of the text and imaginary elements added to it by the reader in the act of actualizing the words on the page. It is exactly this "doubleness" that can be seen as an important source of aesthetic experience, because it allows us to do two things at the same time: to articulate imaginary elements and to look at them from the outside. Aesthetic experience is a state "in-between" in which, as result of the doubling structure of fictionality, we are, in the words of Wolfgang Iser, "both ourselves and someone else at the same time."[22]

This may sound convincing in the case of reading, but it also applies to the case of film or other forms of visual representation. Although, in watching a film, we see Humphrey Bogart or Rita Hayworth in front of us and thus do no longer have to imagine what characters like Rick or Gilda may look like, we still have to invest feelings and bodily sensations of our own in order to understand, to give but one example, what it means to be disappointed in love. In effect, one may argue that the development I have traced, from print to image to sound, also describes a development in which our own involvement as recipients becomes more and more direct, unmediated and therefore body-centered. In this context, it is important to take into account that the transfer I have described does not merely apply to characters. It pertains to every aspect of the text or object.[23] We also have to actualize the villains, the emotional conflicts, even the representation of rain by means of our own imagination, our feelings, and our own bodily sensations.[24] In this way, we spread our own interiority all over the text. This, then, is what I mean by imaginary self-empowerment: not a scenario of imaginary wish fulfillment or self-aggrandizement but an extension of the interiority of the recipient in the act of actualization that provides the basis for aesthetic experience.

The trigger to engage in transfer processes that extend one's own interiority is becoming ever more powerful in the history of modern culture. To be drawn into a novel so that one forgets the outside world is already a form of complete absorption that can involve strong experiences of pain as well as a well-deserved relief from emotional turmoil at the end. The reader feels in the grip of the story and has to "work" for his pleasure. The German term *Lesehunger*, the hunger for reading, draws attention to the addictive dimension such emotional involvement can have. In the next step, the dime novel, where requirements of mental processing are reduced, emotions are triggered in a more superficial, but also a more direct and sensationalist manner. Long-drawn emotional labor is replaced by short, quick "cheap thrills." In the culture of performance around the turn of the century, in which physical attraction and skills are now displayed for their own sake, a heightened awareness of the body is created not only on the level of representation but also on that of reception. Since such cultural forms as the new "animal dances" or the physical pleasures and thrills of the amusement park do not claim to have any deeper meaning, they invite somatic responses in direct, unmediated fashion.

The tremendous impact of film lies in its successful combination of the emotional involvement (and psychological grip) of the novel with the direct physical involvement of the culture of performance. "To go to the movies" is an event because, as a rule, it links cognitive activity, emotional turmoil, and bodily sensations in a tightly knit, skillfully orchestrated package. Experience can thus become more important than content: "Legions of viewers and critics proclaim their abhorrence of the politics of Ford and Capra films, to say nothing of Leni Riefenstahl's *The Triumph of the Will*, yet willingly submit, and repeatedly resubmit, to these films' emotional resonance."[25] Such involvement would not be possible, if it would result merely from an identification with character or plot, as Affron points out by drawing on Claudine Eizykman's "energetics" of response: "Claudine Eizykman provides strong counter-argument to the notion of passive spectatorship at the cinema in her elaboration of an 'energetics' (*énergétique*) of response. She evokes the violent effect made by film on the viewer who, after leaving the movie house, feels 'extremely undone, perforated, shaken by a thousand intensities much stronger than those of television, by a thousand light beams more refractive than those of any pictorial, musical, or theatrical space.' A desire for such violence runs counter to a desire for repose and passivity." (11) The hyperactive quality and sensory overload of recent Hollywood movies—resulting from high-speed cutting, an all-encompassing bombardment of the senses and a preference for directly visceral genres such as the horror or the action movie—presents a new stage in the creation of an immediate somatic experience.

However, in this "embodiment" popular music can go even further, because there is no longer any need to process words on the page or link images in a narrative flow. As the colloquial German term *Ohrwurm* suggests, popular music is highly effective in "worming" its way into the listener's ear almost imperceptibly. No intellectual or cognitive processing of its content is required because it makes no claim to inform, instruct, or represent meaning. Instead, its effect is based on moods and bodily sensations. The characteristic form in which music activates the imagination is by short evocations of decontextualized images, or a sensation of being one with the music, both of which do not have to be integrated into any meaningful narrative. Listeners of popular music need no longer "earn" their aesthetic experience through participation. Contrary to prior visual forms of cultural expression, including the movies, there is no need for continuity in the flow of images; contrary to what happens with a novel, no mental translation is required because the sensuous effect of music creates associations that are shaped not by narrative but by mood. In the video clip, this effect becomes the key principle for textual organization.

The development of popular culture from novel to image to sound has thus created cultural forms of expression that are increasingly effective for the purposes of imaginary self-empowerment and self-extension. In the process, the individual's engagement with the cultural object gets more and more somatic, so that the gratification derived from popular culture becomes increasingly "embodied."[26] The process of individualization I have postulated is thus, upon closer analysis, also a process of increasing embodiment, until "self-empowerment" derives from the unquestioned authority of a directly felt somatic experience in which the body provides both the basis for, and the measure of, the power of an aesthetic experience. The development of American popular culture I have traced is driven by an ongoing search to maximize this effect until, as in techno music, to give but one recent example, it is reduced to bass sounds of such forcefulness that the body is literally penetrated and shaken up. However, such a "pain" appears welcome. Clearly, the individual not only in Western societies is searching for ever more intense experiences of "embodiment."[27] As applied to the history of popular culture, individualization, then, means to search for experiences that support and confirm one's own sense of self as an "embodied" interiority.[28] It is this search that transforms Americanization into self-Americanization.

As Richard Shusterman, in following the late Michel Foucault, has pointed out, such an individual use of culture changes culture's function: from self-development to the "care of one's self": "Life poses an artistic project in calling for creative self-expression and aesthetic self-fashioning."[29] We have moved from a representative aristocratic culture and a bourgeois culture of self-development to an American culture of the self. American popular culture played a crucial role in this process, but the process goes far beyond popular cultural forms and includes contemporary high culture, which also focuses on developing "embodied" forms of aesthetic experience. As Shusterman makes clear, the actual irony in the popular culture debate (and, by implication, the Americanization debate) consists in the fact that this phenomenon does not lead us away from aesthetics but right to what must be seen as a contemporary redefinition of it.[30]

A Guest in the House

If we look at the issue of Americanization from the point of view presented here, today's major challenge consists neither of the question of national ownership (which has become increasingly muddled in an age of economic globalization), nor of content, for, as we have seen, the same cultural object can have different functions in different contexts of use. Globalization has undermined both arguments because it has created a situation in which an American popular culture-type of modern culture is no longer necessarily American. And because of a worldwide process of self-Americanization, the question whether this form of modern culture is desirable or not has become almost obsolete. We have to accept it as a reality of modern life. As a rule, we have learned to integrate it into an ever-diversified cultural menu. High culture and regional culture have not become endangered species; on the contrary, they, too, have prospered in an increasingly differentiated cultural field.

Can the issue of Americanization then be put to rest? Not in one very specific sense; namely, the question of how, on what principles, culture should be organized and financed in the future. For me, the real challenge emerging from Americanization is no longer whether we get the wrong kind of culture but whether we are drifting toward an American model of organizing and financing culture. The problem is not how much American culture we want but how far we want to go in the commercialization of culture. Why not extend the market principles that have driven the worldwide success of American popular culture to culture as a whole? Should European societies continue cultural policies to subsidize local film industries, public radio and television networks, opera houses, theaters, symphony orchestras, that is, all those cultural forms that would have a hard time surviving in the market, even if foundations and philanthropists would try to compensate?

In my view, this kind of state support for culture should be continued. For making this argument, we do not have to go back to the Americanization debate in its original form and claim that the culture deserving subsidization is the artistically or qualitatively superior culture. Anybody who has witnessed the results of several decades of public financial support for the German film industry will not seriously want to make such a claim any more. More to the point, one should argue for a cultural variety that goes beyond regional variants of American popular culture; this involves political decisions about which forms of culture should remain important elements of the public sphere. A second argument is to emphasize national or regional interests in media industries for economic reasons.[31] Just as no pure market policies exist in economic life, not even in the United States, it is counterproductive to expose media industries with a weak capital base to the market without protection or support. If one wants to compete, one has to support capital-intensive media until they can survive in the marketplace. Finally, although the market has always played a role in the arts since patronage went out of fashion, an argument can be made that culture should not rely entirely on the market. In the final analysis, this decision revolves around which values take priority in a society. This issue, in effect, provides the point of departure for the continuation of the Americanization debate. It is one thing to welcome somebody as a guest in the house, but quite another to make sure that he does not take over the whole house.

Notes

1. Throughout the following essay, the use of the word "Americanization" will be restricted to the issue of cultural Americanization.
2. John Tomlinson, *Cultural Imperialism* (Baltimore, 1991), 49-50. For a more recent assessment of the Americanization debate from a similar perspective, see the essay by Ronald Inglehart and Wayne E. Baker, "Modernization's Challenge to Traditional Values: Who's Afraid of Ronald McDonald," *The Futurist* 35 (2001): 16-21. As the authors argue: "The impression that we are moving toward a uniform 'McWorld' is partly an illusion. The seemingly identical McDonald's restaurants that have spread throughout the world actually have different social meanings and fulfill different social functions in different cultural zones." (18) "Economic development tends to push societies in a common direction, but rather than converging they seem to move along paths shaped by their cultural heritages. Therefore we doubt that the forces of modernization will produce a homogenized world culture in the foreseeable future." (20) From a semiotic perspective, this variability of interpretation is opened up by the fact that different codes are applied, as Umberto Eco already pointed out in the 1960s: "The Receiver transforms the Signal into Message, but this message is still the empty form to which the Addressee can attribute various meanings depending on the Code he applies to it." "Towards a Semiological Guerrilla Warfare," *Travels in Hyperreality* (New York, 1986), 139.
3. See, for example, Ulf Hannerz, *Cultural Complexity* (New York, 1992) and Joana Breidenbach and Ina Zukrigl, *Tanz der Kulturen. Kulturelle Identität in einer globalisierten Welt* (Hamburg, 2000).
4. *Networks of Americanization. Aspects of the American Influence in Sweden,* ed. Rolf Lunden (Uppsala, 1992), 15.
5. In his influential book, *Subculture: The Meaning of Style* (London, 1979), Dick Hebdige employs the transformation of a "humble object" into a "magic object" as exemplary case for a description of the process of cultural reappropriation: "The struggle between different discourses, different definitions and meanings within ideology is therefore always, at the same time, a struggle within signification: a struggle for possession of the sign which extends to even the most mundane areas of everyday life. To turn once more to the examples used in the Introduction, to the safety pins and tubes of vaseline, we can see that such commodities are indeed open to a double inflection: to 'illegitimate' as well as 'legit-

imate' uses. These 'humble objects' can be magically appropriated; 'stolen' by subordinate groups and made to carry 'secret' meanings: meanings which express, in code, a form of resistance to the order which guarantees their continued subordination." (17f.) See also Hebdige's book *Hiding in the Light* (London, 1988), in which he applies this argument to American popular culture: "American popular culture (...) offers a rich iconography, a set of symbols, objects and artifacts which can be assembled and re-assembled by different groups in a literally limitless number of combinations. And the meaning of each selection is transformed as individual objects (...) are taken out of their original historical and cultural contexts and juxtaposed against signs from other sources." (74)

6. Volker Berghahn, *America and the Intellectual Cold Wars in Europe. Shepard Stone between Philanthropy, Academy, and Diplomacy* (Princeton, 2001).

7. As a recent article in the *International Herald Tribune* points out, this appears to be a worldwide trend: "'Whereas American TV shows used to occupy prime-time slots, they are now more typically on cable, or airing in late-night or weekend slots,' said Michael Grindon, president of Sony Television International. 'The most valuable slots in the television landscape—network prime time—are now really reserved for locally produced shows.'" The article continues, "Given the choice foreign viewers often prefer homegrown shows that better reflected local tastes, cultures and historical events to American programs, executives said." The article ends with the—in the light of the Americanization debate—stunning conclusion: "'The worldwide television market is growing,' said David Hulbert, president of Walt Disney Television International, 'but America's place in it is declining.'" "American TV losing out in global ratings war," *International Herald Tribune*, 2 January 2003. In the meantime, Neal Gabler has responded by arguing for a somewhat reduced and readjusted version of the Americanization thesis: "Still, one shouldn't mourn the end of American cultural domination quite yet. There will always be the movies. And the truth is, American movies, not TV shows, are the truly potent examples of U.S. cultural imperialism." "U.S. cultural hegemony lives on in movies, not TV," *International Herald Tribune*, 10 January 2003.

8. See Max Horkheimer and Theodor W. Adorno, "The Culture Industry: Enlightenment as Mass Deception," *Dialectic of Enlightenment* [1944] (New York, 2002), 120-67. Horkheimer and Adorno's view of this development is bleak, because for them the new forms of culture erase the true task of culture, namely, to function as a counter-realm to the instrumental rationality of modernity. The only hope for resistance against the growing dominance of this instrumental rationality would be a radical culture of negation. American mass culture is a culture of negation on the level neither of content nor of form. On the contrary, it provides an especially effective, "modern" form of domination, because it has found ways to inscribe itself into the psyche of its consumers: "The analysis Tocqueville offered a century ago has in the meantime proved wholly accurate. Under the private culture monopoly it is a fact that 'tyranny leaves the body free and directs its attacks at the soul' (...) As naturally as the ruled always took the morality imposed upon them more seriously than did the rulers themselves, the deceived masses are today captivated by the myth of success even more than the successful are. Immovably, they insist on the very ideology which enslaves them." (133f.)

9. See the cautious way in which Tomlinson tries to move away from left orthodoxy on this question: "These are difficult generalisations to make with any certainty, but we can safely say that a substantial number of people in developed societies are willing recipients of 'imperialist media texts' such as *Dallas*. This is not to say they are consequently the dupes of their ideological messages and values. There is also *prima facie* evidence that plenty of people in the 'underdeveloped world' are enthusiastic about the cultural products of the

West though, again, the uses and meanings attached to them cannot be easily assumed." *Cultural Imperialism,* 94.

10. See my essays "Emergence or Collapse of Cultural Hierarchy? American Popular Culture Seen from Abroad," *Popular Culture in the United States,* Peter Freese and Michael Porsche, eds. (Essen, 1994), 49-74, "'Amerikanisierung' der Kultur. Zur Geschichte der amerikanischen Populärkultur," *Die Amerikanisierung des Medienalltags,* ed. Harald Wenzel (Frankfurt am Main, 1998), 13-52, and "Amerikanisierung und Modernisierung," *Transit* 17 (1999): 55-71.

11. Of course, religious culture also was a "popular" alternative to aristocratic and bourgeois forms of culture, but still in a very ritualized and hence highly restricted form. As Neal Gabler argues, however, there is a point of convergence of religion and popular culture in American cultural history in evangelical Protestantism, "a form of worship that would have been unrecognizable to most Europeans." *Life: The Movie. How Entertainment Conquered Reality* (New York, 1998), 24. Gabler continues by pointing out "the similarities and affinities between evangelicalism and entertainment." (25)

12. In his study *Highbrow/Lowbrow. The Emergence of Cultural Hierarchy in America* (Cambridge, Mass., 1988), Lawrence Levine traces the emergence of the idea of highbrow culture in America. However, it is significant that his narrative stops before the arrival of American modernism with its dehierarchized, often vernacular, and racially hybrid forms. In the way it is described by Levine, highbrow control over American culture is a phenomenon of the late Victorian period.

13. One of the answers at the time of increased immigration around 1900 was the development of a nonverbal culture of performance, which draws its attraction from the presentation of spectacular skills and physical attractions "for their own sake," that is, without implying any deeper meaning. Important aspects of this development around the turn of the century are described by John Kasson, *Amusing the Million. Coney Island at the Turn of the Century* (New York, 1978); Lewis Erenberg, *Steppin' Out. New York Nightlife and the Transformation of American Culture, 1890-1930* (Chicago, 1981); Robert Snyder, *The Voice of the City. Vaudeville and Popular Culture in New York* (New York, 1989); David Nasaw, *Going Out. The Rise and Fall of Public Amusements* (Cambridge, Mass., 1993); William Leach, *Land of Desire: Merchants, Power, and the Rise of a New American Culture* (New York, 1993); Kathy Peiss, *Cheap Amusements: Working Women and Leisure in Turn-of-the-Century New York* (Philadelphia, 1986); Lauren Rabinowitz, *For the Love of Pleasure. Women, Movies and Culture in Turn-of-the-Century Chicago* (New Brunswick, N.J., 1998); Miriam Hansen, *Babel and Babylon. Spectatorship in American Silent Film* (Cambrige, Mass., 1991), and by various essays in the book *Cinema and the Invention of Modern Life,* Leo Charney and Vanessa Schwartz, eds. (Berkeley, 1995). In order to describe the special contribution of the silent film to this new culture of performance and exhibition, Tom Gunning has introduced the concept of a "cinema of attractions." The concept draws attention to the fact that, in their initial stage, silent movies gave priority to the extraordinary spectacle or the spectacular technological effect over narrative continuity and plausibility.

14. I am using the term "individual" here in the Tocquevillian sense of the smallest social unit, not as a word for a philosophical concept of individuality.

15. The term "self-empowerment" is employed here in a much larger sense than that of an identification with a better version of oneself. Because of the processes of reduction to easily accessible visual and aural forms and because of the growing textual fragmentation of cultural objects into short segments, single images, or musical moods, the individual encounters ever more favorable conditions for satisfying imaginary longings, emotional needs, and bodily sensations.

16. Critical theory, following in the wake of Horkheimer and Adorno, has argued, of course, that the rise of popular culture signals the end of culture's function to nourish a process of self-development in which the individual grows in self-awareness. Instead, the culture industry produces "pseudo-individuality": "In the culture industry the individual is an illusion not merely because of the standardization of the means of production. He is tolerated only so long as his complete identification with the generality is unquestioned. Pseudo individuality is rife: from the standardized jazz improvisation to the exceptional film star whose hair curls over her eye to demonstrate her originality. What is individual is no more than the generality's power to stamp the accidental detail so firmly that it is accepted as such. The defiant reserve or elegant appearance of the individual on show is mass-produced like Yale locks, whose only difference can be measured in fractions of millimeters." *Dialectic of Enlightenment*, 154. Obviously, this description of "mass-produced individuality" depends on a normative concept of individualization as leading up to a unique individuality, as Axel Honneth points out: "*Den normativen Rahmen aber, in dem diese geschichtsphilosophische Argumentation eingebettet ist, stellt eine ästhetische Theorie der gelingenden Ichbildung dar...*" ["The normative frame of reference for this philosophical argument is provided by an aesthetic theory of successful ego-formation..." (author's translation)]. "Foucault und Adorno. Zwei Formen einer Kritik der Moderne," '*Postmoderne' oder Der Kampf um die Zukunft*, ed. Peter Kemper (Hamburg, 1988), 140.
17. The habitual criticism of the destruction of native cultural traditions through American culture never considers the possibility that, as a form of cultural self-definition, these traditions may be very limited and may be experienced even as suffocating by the individual, because, in reflecting a strict social hierarchy, they only provide one possible role and source of self-esteem. Usually, the demise of these pre-individualistic traditions is bemoaned by those Western individuals on the outside who would like to escape the leveling effects of democracy by having a whole array of cultural choices spread out before their eyes. On this point, see the acute observation by John Tomlinson: "The critique of homogenization may turn out to be a peculiarly Western-centered concern if what is argued is that cultures must retain their separate identities simply to make the world a more diverse and interesting place." *Cultural Imperialism*, 135.
18. The crucial role "youth" has played in the worldwide reception of American popular culture is emphasized by David Ellwood in his essay *Anti-Americanism in Western Europe: A Comparative Perspective*, Occasional Paper No. 3, European Studies Seminar Series (Bologna, 1999), 25-33. See also Volker Berghahn in his introduction to the German Historical Institute conference "The American Impact on Western Europe": "On the German side the 'Americanizers,' it seems, were very much young people who responded positively, indeed enthusiastically, to what arrived from across the Atlantic. The resistance to these imports came from an older generation who rejected rock and jazz, James Dean and Coca-Cola as products of an *Unkultur*." "Conceptualizing the American Impact on Germany: West German Society and the Problem of Americanization," available at <www.ghi-dc.org>. In his essay "Über die Europäisierung Amerikas" ("On the Europeanization of America") in the paper *Das Parlament*, Gero Lenhardt gives an example for the easy fit between fast food and youth: "To go to fast food restaurants means to be liberated from the strictures of class etiquette. It is a liberation from the strain of presenting oneself properly in the public sphere. (...) To be sure, everything is standardized but this also has an egalitarian dimension. Questions of social rank become irrelevant. Everybody is taken equally serious as a customer who pays." *Das Parlament. Beilage.* (26 December 1987), 13 (author's translation). Lenhardt goes on to argue that this must be especially attractive for children and young people who are usually treated as inferior.

19. See Marshall Berman, *All That Is Solid Melts into Air. The Experience of Modernism* (London, 1983), who analyzes cultural modernity as a culture of restless individualism, driven by a promise of self-development, and chapter 5 of John Tomlinson's study *Cultural Imperialism*, in which he writes, "Cultures are 'condemned to modernity' not simply by the 'structural' process of economic development, but by the human process of *self-development*." (141)
20. Cf. the anthologies edited by Bernard Rosenberg and David Manning White, *Mass Culture. The Popular Arts in America* (New York, 1957) and *Mass Culture Revisited* (New York, 1971), as well as the volume *Culture for the Millions? Mass Media in Modern Society*, ed. Norman Jacobs (Boston, 1961). The argument that the United States has been an importer as well as an exporter of culture—useful as it is in drawing attention to complex forms of cultural contact and exchange—therefore misses the essential point in the critique of American popular culture—namely, the fact that within the American context a new type of culture has been created that betrays culture's "true" function. It is therefore also besides the point to contrast "American" versus "European" views on the subject, because there are also numerous American critics of American popular culture who question its status as culture, as Paul R. Gorman has pointed out in his book *Left Intellectuals and Popular Culture in Twentieth-Century America* (Chapel Hill, 1996). The issue of Americanization is, in the final analysis, not a debate about the merits of American culture but about the direction modern culture is taking.
21. See the following essays: "Aesthetics and Cultural Studies," *Aesthetics in a Multicultural Age*, Emory Elliott, Lou Carton, and Jeffrey Rhyne, eds. (New York, 2001), 79-103; "Aesthetic Experience of the Image," *Iconographies of Power. The Politics and Poetics of Visual Representation*, Ulla Haselstein, Berndt Ostendorf, and Hans Peter Schneck, eds. (Heidelberg, 2003), 11-41; and "The Role of the Reader and the Changing Functions of Fiction: Reception Aesthetics, Literary Anthropology, Funktionsgeschichte," *European Journal of English Studies* 6 (2003): 253-71.
22. Wolfgang Iser, "Representation: A Performative Act," *Prospecting: From Reader Response to Literary Anthropology* (Baltimore, 1989), 244.
23. This is one of the reasons why I find the concept of transfer more fitting here than the psychoanalytical concept of transference. Transference presupposes a deeply felt psychic drive, but not all aspects of the actualizing of the text will be shaped by the unconscious.
24. As Carol J. Clover puts it, "We are both Red Riding Hood *and* the Wolf; the force of the experience, the horror, comes from 'knowing' both sides of the story." "Her Body, Himself. Gender in the Slasher Film," *Fantasy and Cinema*, ed. James Donald (London, 1989), 95. Arguing against the theory of spectator positioning in apparatus theory, Steve Neale provides a helpful reminder of the continuous mobility of the viewer by drawing on John Ellis's book *Visible Fictions*: "Ellis argues that identification is never simply a matter of men identifying with male figures on the screen and women identifying with female figures. Cinema draws on and involves many desires, many forms of desire. And desire itself is mobile, fluid, constantly transgressing identities, positions, and roles. Identifications are multiple, fluid, at points even contradictory." "Masculinity as Spectacle," *Screening the Male. Exploring Masculinities in Hollywood Cinema*, Steven Cohan and Ina Rae Hark, eds. (London, 1993), 10. This nomadic mobility is even further enhanced, once we go beyond processes of identification and start at a more elementary level, that of actualizing a text or object by means of a transfer.
25. Charles Affron, *Cinema and Sentiment* (Chicago, 1982), 12.
26. My use of the term "embodiment" is thus not restricted to cultural constructions of the male or female body in representation and, hence, to a theory of gender identity as performance. It refers to a more elementary process of aesthetic experience "through" the

body. In several books Richard Shusterman has provided interesting contributions to the conceptualization of a body aesthetic, which he calls "somaesthetics": "Somaesthetics is devoted to the critical, ameliorative study of one's experience and use of one's body as a locus of sensory-aesthetic appreciation (*aesthesis*) and creative self-fashioning." *Performing Live. Aesthetic Alternatives for the Ends of Art* (Ithaca, 2000), 138. See also his *Pragmatist Aesthetics* (Oxford, 1992) and *Practicing Philosophy* (London, 1997).

27. The fact that "our body (…) now gets elevated, as our central medium, to the status of constructor and locus of the real" does not mean, however, that "this lived body is claimed as a 'primordial presence' that we directly grasp and directly move without any representation." Shusterman, *Performing Live*, 144, 149. To start with, our somatic responses rely "on prior constructions, on habits of response formed through the influence of historical and social conditions already in place." (150) Moreover, our responses are reciprocally conditioned by the object they structure. To describe the history of popular culture as a process of individualization that moves increasingly toward experiences of embodiment thus does not aim at the recovery of an elusive authenticity or spontaneity outside of cultural constructions but points out different means through which such constructions take hold. However, I postulate that representation and the individual's interiority that seeks articulation are never entirely identical. Although a cultural history of individualization and a theory of subjection are much closer related than the two terms "individualization" and "subjection" may suggest, a theory of subjection based on the idea of embodiment therefore appears insufficient to me. On the contrary, one may follow Judith Butler here, who has tried to clarify the psychic processes that can explain the possibility of resignification by arguing that discourses of subjection can at the same time function as stimuli for resignification. See her essay "Subjection, Resistance, Resignification: Between Freud and Foucault," *The Identity in Question*, ed. John Rajchman (London, 1995), 229-49.

28. By interiority I mean the full range of inner states, from mental images to moods and bodily sensations, that strive for articulation but can never be fully expressed.

29. Shusterman, *Performing Live*, 10. On page 11, he continues, "Today's aesthetic energies seem powerfully refocused on the art of living." See also his chapter "Postmodern Ethics and the Art of Living," in *Pragmatist Aesthetics*, 236-61.

30. This does not, of course, mean that contemporary aesthetics have become "mindless," as Shusterman points out: "However, the claim that aesthetic experience must involve *more* than phenomenological immediacy and vivid feeling does not preclude that such immediate feeling is crucial to aesthetic experience." *Performing Live*, 21.

31. In his article "U.S. cultural hegemony lives on in movies, not TV," Neal Gabler argues that, in contrast to television, American movies will continue to be universal because they export "the primal aesthetic of excitement and individualism." *International Herald Tribune*, 10 January 2003. But excitement and individualism are no longer exclusively American values. Perhaps one reason for the success of American movies simply lies in the strong capital-base the American movie industry has. That the future area of struggle may no longer be cultural but commercial is indicated by the current clash over expiring copyright laws between the United States and Europe, which, in an obviously protectionist move, have been extended in the United States to 95 years (for works created by groups of people) and 70 years (for individual works), while copyright protection lasts 50 years in Europe—so that, for example, recordings of the early to mid-1950s have begun to enter the public domain in Europe. ("Europe set to sing to expiring copyrights," *International Herald Tribune*, 3 January 2003.

AWKWARD RELATIONS

American Perceptions of Europe, European Perceptions of America

◆ ◆ ◆

Volker R. Berghahn

In this contribution, I would like to raise the question of how far it is possible to "Europeanize" this volume's central themes. The focus here will be on Western Europe, but it should not be forgotten that between 1945 and the 1980s the societies of East Central Europe were also exposed to American cultural influences that pierced the Iron Curtain. To be sure, this occurred in subtler and often subterranean ways in the early postwar decades, until it became more open and direct after the final demise of communism in 1989, if not well before that date.

In this context, I am less concerned with "images" than "perceptions," as indicated by this chapter's title. Image research has no doubt been important as an approach to historical studies, and, indeed, European scholars have examined the "image of America" (singular) many times since the nineteenth century, just as Americans have studied the "image of Europe."[1] However, I wonder if "perceptions" (plural) might not be a more useful term, if only because it can be more easily connected to a shift that our understanding of the concept of Americanization has undergone. There was a time when Americanization, perhaps all too simply, was seen as a process by which the United States, as the hegemonic power of the West, came to Europe, and, like a steamroller, flattened everything in its path to implant its own cultural products and ideas.[2]

But a counter-argument has always existed that gained strength in the 1980s and has since become the dominant view—that is, that American offerings were not swallowed hook, line, and sinker by receiving societies;

Notes for this section begin on page 248.

that there was adaptation, but only after critical scrutiny and negotiation of how far the ideas and products that came from across the Atlantic to Europe could be integrated with indigenous structures and mentalities.[3] The terms "structures and mentalities" were meant to cover not only the social and cultural, but also the political, military, and economic.[4]

This implies that ultimately a blending of the imports with the indigenous has always taken place. The degree of interpenetration depended on the area (politics, economics, culture) and issue (labor relations, marketing, theater, and popular music, federalism, social welfare, etc.); close study of these aspects would reveal whether at the end of the process a lesser or stronger "coloring" of the preexisting structures and mentalities had occurred. In other words, what interpenetration did occur was never uniform and across the board. It was even dependent on the region of a particular European country. Hamburgians dealt with the "American question" differently from Upper Bavarians or Chemnitzeans. Class and generational difference also have to be factored into the equation.

The benefit of this shift in the debate on Americanization was, apart from the fresh research into the subject that it stimulated, that it came to be related to a larger field of scholarship, originally pioneered by anthropologists, interested in the encounter between two or more societies and cultures. The concept of encounter, it is true, has itself come under criticism because of its rather pacific connotations. It is said to veil and hence to downplay in all too many cases the violent ways in which two societies often "encountered" each other in the past. This criticism would seem to be particularly justified when we come to the subject of the encounter between settlers and Native Americans in North America or of European administrators and soldiers during the age of colonialism in Africa, Latin America, and Asia.[5] But it is probably fair to say that the European encounter with America after 1945 has been nonviolent. It was based on negotiation and slow and in many cases still partial blending.

The advantage of this approach to the problem of Americanization is, on the one hand, that it stresses the creative aspects of the transatlantic relationship. The assumption is that we are not dealing with anonymous structures at the European end that somehow change or resist change. Rather we are dealing with groups and individuals who actively respond and concretely shape their socioeconomic, cultural, and political environments. Hence also the usefulness of the concept of negotiation, even where it does not involve negotiation among equals, but a relationship in which one side covertly or overtly gently pressures or occasionally even bullies the other side. But as work on the Nazi occupation has shown, even in the most unequal and repressive conditions, men and women, groups and entire societies, develop ways of not submitting completely to the superior power and force.[6]

The idea the American-European encounter in the twentieth century reflected an interactive process thus allows us not only to differentiate between divergent issues and groups as we study the American impact and responses to it within a particular nation. It also enables us to make intra-European comparisons, that is, to examine how different European societies dealt with imports from across the Atlantic. We can take the United States as the *tertium comparationis* in an initially asymmetrical comparison (U.S. and France; U.S. and Sweden) that can then be expanded to intra-European comparisons in a triangular pattern (France and Britain in relation to the U.S.; Italy and Germany in relation to the U.S.).

The encounter concept also reveals why the notion of perceptions of "the other" may be more helpful than image research. Images, especially if used in the singular, seem to have a static and monolithic quality. Perceptions denote a more active relationship between subject and object. There is, it is true, the point that images often are surprisingly durable. Still, one also finds change over time, and it seems easier to capture it by considering a subject's perceptions in his or her engagement with the environment.

This raises another question that leads beyond the analysis of how the Europeans related to American influences, be they political, military, economic, social, or cultural. As indicated by the title, this contribution is also about American perceptions of Europe and how these in turn influenced Americans' engagement with Europe. Indeed, this is the aspect with which I would like to begin, as I move from conceptual problems to a more empirical analysis. This point of departure will allow me to begin with a few observations on the contemporary situation. I shall then go back in time in order to put the current, seemingly awkward European-American relationship into a deeper historical perspective before returning to the question of Americanism and anti-Americanism in Europe at the beginning of the twenty-first century.

American perceptions of Europe have undergone considerable mood swings during the past five years or so. Supported by the boom of the 1990s and the optimism about the post-Cold War twenty-first century that it generated in connection with revolutionary developments in communications and electronics, Americans regarded Europe in relatively relaxed terms during the presidency of Bill Clinton. There was a strong sense of confident American leadership in economic matters. Europeans were criticized for their inflexible socioeconomic structures and attitudes that, it was said, prevented them from reaping the full benefits of the New Economy.[7] If only, so the argument continued, they adopted the American model of generating jobs and wealth, all would be as well for them as it was for those in the United States. It must be added that disputes existed over trade issues and environmental policies in the Atlantic region. Agricultural protectionism remained the bone of contention it had been for a long time.

However, none of these differences of opinion and controversies ever became so serious as to call into question a basically positive attitude towards the Europeans among the mass of the population in general and in the Clinton administration in particular. As the American political scientist David Calleo has argued, Clinton's basic foreign policy design was more geo-economic than geopolitical. Like the Europeans, Clinton was uneasy about the use of military power. Insofar as an imperial vision did exist, it was conceived more in the Wilsonian tradition.[8]

This approach to international politics and to Europe underwent a first shift when George W. Bush became president in January 2001. He and his advisers not only favored a more Hobbesian view of international relations in general but also were more willing to stress ideological differences. They were also more prepared to use the truly overwhelming military power that the United States had built up during the 1980s. The neoconservatives who now began to dominate the American domestic policy agenda had little sympathy for what they saw as Europe's rather stubborn adherence to the welfare state and their refusal to invest in defense. Indeed, among those in the security field, especially in the Pentagon, a distinct perception existed that the modernization of the armed forces since the Reagan years had given the United States an unprecedented superiority not only in space but also in conventional high-tech weapons. For, while many eyes had remained fixed on Washington's preoccupation with the "Star Wars" strategic defense initiative, all three branches of the armed forces had become equipped with highly sophisticated hardware that enabled them to wage wars in any part of the world, day or night, in all weather conditions.

We have since seen the deployment of this military might in Afghanistan, where air power was brought to bear over long distances and at very high altitudes from only two of the fleet of thirteen aircraft carriers that the United States keeps in permanent service on the oceans around the world. The B-1 bombers started from the American continent to drop their bombs over Afghanistan, while the waves of B-52 bombers flew there from Diego Garcia, an island in the Indian Ocean. According to Yale historian Paul Kennedy, no country has ever before disposed of so much military power as the United States.[9] This is also reflected in military expenditures, which now surpass the defense expenditures of the next nine major powers combined. In the mid-1990s, the United States spent some $260 billion per annum. In 2001, expenditures approached $329 billion. Although Washington has urged the Europeans to increase their defense spending and to create more efficient, rapidly deployable forces, American perceptions of Europe as an inferior partner have only increased, as the Bush administration moved further away from Clinton's geo-economic strategy toward an emphasis on military power and its use. Perceptions of Europe during the early months of the Bush administration and among leaders of the Republican Party also changed in a negative direction, as other ideological differences emerged, for example, over the Kyoto Protocol and environmental policy more generally.

However, all these feelings were swept aside on September 11, 2001, following the Al Qaeda attacks on New York and Washington. The fact that all European governments immediately rallied behind Washington and that millions of Europeans spontaneously expressed genuinely felt sympathies for the victims and a traumatized American population restrengthened transatlantic ties at all levels and in all spheres of life. Once again, American perceptions of the Europeans became more positive even in Washington.

In the meantime, these feelings have changed once again quite dramatically. The proposed invasion of Iraq became the cause of growing tension. The Bush administration in particular, but also wider Republican circles, disliked the European attempt to keep the United States from taking unilateral military action in the Middle East and to engage the superpower in the established system of international law, diplomatic negotiation, and conflict prevention. The war in Iraq has exacerbated perceptions of European disloyalty on this side of the Atlantic. Meanwhile, politicians across the Atlantic have been under strong pressure from their own populations, and even the British Prime Minister Tony Blair continues to feel the heat.[10] If, on the other hand, Bush fails in Iraq, the impression is bound to spread in Washington and among neoconservatives that the defeat was due to the lack of international support. Worse, this lack will be interpreted, as it already has been in recent months, as a growing anti-Americanism. However, this is—it seems to me—a misperception of the situation, which leads me to move to the other side of the Atlantic and to an examination of European perceptions of the United States.

My argument here is a historical one. It does not deny that there is anti-Americanism in Europe, if we define it as a fundamental rejection of the United States as a society and culture. There are men and women, particularly among the intellectual elites, who have a basic aversion to everything that, in their eyes, America represents. But today they represent a small minority, and, in historical perspective, are certainly much weaker than they were fifty years ago, when the balance of forces between those who were open to the American societal model and those who loathed it was quite different from what it is today.

The year 1945 seems to be a good starting point for making this case. It is now widely accepted that the Cold War did not start in earnest the moment the Third Reich was finally defeated in May 1945. At that point, a kind of twilight zone emerged during which even some decision-makers in Washington thought that the wartime alliance with Stalin could be continued and that the "division of the world" might be avoided.[11] During this period, almost all Europeans developed the notion that they could build a "third way" between the American and Soviet models, however large these two powers loomed in Europe because of their military presence right in the heart of the Continent, in defeated and occupied Germany. The visions of Europe that underlay the idea of a "third way" differed from group to group. For some it amounted to a rejection of the liberal-capitalist market economy embodied by the United States, on the one hand, and of a dictatorial Stalinist economy, on the other. It is typical of this vision that it was held not only by socialists in Britain and Continental Europe[12] but also by Christian Democrats who spoke of a "Christian-socialist way."[13] It even existed in countries like Czechoslovakia and East Germany. Those conservatives who saw the world more in terms of political power and empire disapproved of social-democratic reform of the domestic economy, and yet they, too, conceived of a world that would not be dominated by two superpowers, but in which reconstituted British and French empires would exist as equal partners alongside Soviet Russia and the United States.[14]

The beginning of the Cold War stopped the dreams of a "third way." Czechoslovakia, together with the other nations east of the Iron Curtain, was absorbed into the emerging Soviet bloc. Its society, economy, and political system were Stalinized. Meanwhile, the West European, feeling threatened by what they perceived as Soviet aggressiveness, moved under the protective umbrella that the United States held out. West Europeans increasingly came to accept the United States as the power that had emerged as the hegemon in the West in economic, military, and political terms. They saw no alternative, the more so since Washington offered them, through the Marshall Plan, economic support in their effort to rebuild a half-continent devastated by World War II, as well as military protection against the Red Army through the North Atlantic Treaty Organization (NATO).[15]

However, if the Europeans accepted the United States as the hegemonic power of the emerging Atlantic alliance in economic, technological, military, and political terms, this did not mean that they also accepted the country's cultural and social model. On the contrary, in this field we can see the recrudescence of what might be called a European superiority complex that had deep roots in the interwar period. A good deal of research has recently been done on the cultural anti-Americanism of the 1920s and 1930s, although space limitations prevent a detailed description of it here.[16] The more immediately relevant point for this essay is that the rejection of America as a society and culture was once again widespread in Europe by the 1950s on both the ideological Right and Left. For different reasons, and with different arguments, both sides saw the United States as a country that did not really have a culture. As West German intellectuals, and, indeed, many educated people saw it, the United States represented an *Unkultur*. This was not least in reaction to the products of American popular culture that began to arrive again in this period all over Europe.

Many of these products were familiar from the interwar period, above all Hollywood movies that once again began to flood the cinemas of Western Europe. Then came jazz, which many rejected, with blatantly racist overtones, as "nigger music." By the mid-1950s, rock 'n' roll appeared with Elvis Presley and Bill Haley in the lead, giving large concerts, at the end of which the audiences rioted and demolished the concert hall furniture.[17] Many proper middle-class parents were appalled, and criticism of American "trash" and "vulgarity" mounted on both Right and Left of the political spectrum.

It should be added that this kind of criticism also arose at this time in the United States. Here, men like Dwight Macdonald railed at the inferiority of American "masscult" and "midcult" and regarded Hollywood with horror.[18] Others who stressed the perceived conformism and standardization of society supported him. This is also the time when David Riesman published *The Lonely Crowd*, which portrayed Americans as having lost their erstwhile "inner-directedness" and as having become "other-directed," superficial individuals.[19] It did not take long for alternative arguments to be put forward against these pessimistic views of the future of American society. A good digest of them can be found in Daniel Bell's *The End of Ideology*, a book that only in part dealt with the postwar age in which, he asserted, the ideologies that had dominated society before 1945 had disappeared.[20] Large parts of the book are devoted to a vigorous defense of American popular culture, which he views as rich, diverse, colorful, and democratic. In short, the book is in effect a celebration of the achievements of American culture, which Bell saw not only in the field of "high culture" of the arts and sciences but also in popular culture, or what Macdonald and the European critics of American society had termed "low culture."

The optimistic view of American culture and society that Bell projected soon found its supporters in Western Europe. Here it was initially a younger generation that, like Bell, was attracted by the vibrancy of jazz and popular music; that could identify with rebels like James Dean and Marlon Brando; that enjoyed the freewheeling quality of American dance. Not least of all, young women were attracted by what they perceived to be the emancipatory power of American popular culture that encouraged free expression and the blurring of traditional gender boundaries.[21] Indeed, it is often forgotten how formal and conventional postwar European societies were, and not just with respect to sexuality. Here was a younger generation whose members were not anti-American in the sense that they rejected the American model. On the contrary, they accepted the United States as the embodiment of a modernity that they hoped to realize in their own lives.

This Americanism that began in the 1950s among a younger generation of West Europeans, whose arguments, together with Bell's, increasingly gained acceptance among intellectuals and educated people, many of whom had meanwhile visited the United States, continued to proliferate in the 1960s and 1970s. At first glance, this point does not seem to tally with the renewed criticism of the United States voiced in growing volume by the student movements that arose all over Western Europe in the wake of the Vietnam War. With them came the rise of a neo-Marxist critique of Western capitalism and the causes of Third World poverty and deprivation.[22] There were times when it seemed to both opponents of these movements and outside observers as if this was the only agenda of the rebellious students. But with the benefit of hindsight, one sees more clearly that this was too monochromic a perception of the student movements of 1968.

Perhaps less shrill, but certainly no less important to them, was the quest for an acceptance of diversity, for the shedding of laws and conventions that restricted the free development of one's personality and life-style.[23] The idea was to "dare more democracy," as Willy Brandt, the West German social democrat and federal chancellor once put it. If we agree that the initial impetus for all this came from the United States and was partly transmitted through the notions of democracy and civil society that had developed on this side of the Atlantic, but also through American popular culture, we can see how far these ideas and attitudes have taken root in Europe. They are, it is true, also related to the emergence of a consumer society for which the United States served as the model.[24] But they also represent part of a new European acceptance of a much broader definition of culture than existed in the 1950s. At that time, there was only "high culture"; the rest was "primitive" and beyond the pale of an educated person. Today the Europeans have come to support a very broad concept of culture that includes not only the fine arts and the sciences, but also what was once disdained as "low culture"—an import from that country across the ocean that was to be kept out. As the Berlin anthropologist Kaspar Maase put it a few years ago: "Among the upper echelons of business, politics, science and technology, among the academically trained professions, the right to enjoy the bliss of common culture is claimed extensively. Popular art and entertainment have become the culture of all."[25]

This, it seems, also applies to East Central Europe. Long before the 1980s, the Iron Curtain had already become increasingly permeable. In the 1950s, it was still difficult for young people to receive the products of American youth and popular culture. They knew about it and were certainly fascinated by jazz, rock 'n' roll, and American movies. This in turn so worried the Communist authorities that they invented a variety of antidotes to influences they deemed pernicious.[26] With the advent of the transistor radio, it became more and more difficult to uphold this barrier. In countries like Hungary and Poland, where the regimes found it more and more difficult to maintain tight control over the consumption of popular culture, the Iron Curtain had disappeared in cultural terms long before the final collapse of communism. After 1989, the societies of the former Soviet bloc became as fully exposed to American cultural imports as their Western counterparts had been since World War II.

However, in line with the argument put forward at the beginning of this chapter, it should be added that this process of cultural Americanization has not gone so far as to blur all distinctions between the societies of Europe and America. All over Europe, in East and West, we now see complex processes of acculturation, of a blending that deserves much closer study if we want to find out how far Europe finds itself on the "path toward a European society"[27] and how far this path is influenced by what enters Europe every day from across the Atlantic. Traveling in any European country today, it is striking to see how not only the economies have become Americanized, down to the use of the English language in large corporations, but also how many American elements have been absorbed into society and culture. But this does not mean that environment and attitudes have become so similar that one can no longer recognize that a particular place is not Bismarck, North Dakota, but a provincial town in Lower Saxony; that this is not New London, Connecticut, but a port on the Welsh coast of the British Isles. This is where the blending process can be studied comparatively in its variations and permutations, as it can be when we compare, for example, medical systems or primary school education.

The point to be made here is thus twofold. First, fears that the cultures of Europe will be obliterated by the thrust of the American hegemon are greatly exaggerated if we consider the results of the blending that has occurred. At the same time, the processes analyzed in this chapter of cultural change and interaction between Europe and America over the past fifty years or so refute the notion that Europeans have once again become violently anti-American some three years after *Le Monde* proclaimed in the wake of "9/11" that "we are all Americans now."

If relations between the United States and Europe have again become more "awkward," this has little to do with a rejection of American society and culture, but more to do with the policies of the present US administration. At issue then is not anti-Americanism but rather "anti-Bushism." Some of the issues that have contributed to the negative perceptions of the White House were enumerated at this chapter's start. Kyoto, steel tariffs, Vice President Dick Cheney's torpedoing of a deal, supported by 144 countries, to get cheap drugs to countries whose populations have been wiped out by HIV/AIDS and other epidemics—all these issues must be factored into the equation of disillusionment and criticism that Washington misinterprets as anti-Americanism. But what strengthened European anti-Bushism more than anything else was the new strategic doctrine, proclaimed in September 2002. Europeans, as well as the rest of the world, are still grappling with the revolutionary implications of a doctrine that abandoned the notion of deterrence (i.e., a second-strike strategy) and replaced it with a first-strike policy of preemption.

There is now some hope that a reconsideration might occur. Consider the year 1955, for example, when U.S. Secretary of State John Foster Dulles proclaimed the doctrine of "massive retaliation."[28] It amounted to the threat, directed at the Soviet Union, that, if attacked, Washington would use its full arsenal of nuclear weapons to pulverize the Soviets and with them presumably other parts of the world. It did not take long before experts raised their voices questioning this doctrine's wisdom. Soon thereafter, limited war proposals were put forward and advocated in books like Henry Kissinger's *Nuclear Weapons and Foreign Policy*.[29] And a few years later, red telephones were installed in the Kremlin and the White House and the policy of détente, first initiated by President Dwight D. Eisenhower, was stepped up by his successor, John F. Kennedy.[30]

However, as long as this reconsideration of the Bush doctrine has not set in and it is applied not merely to Iraq but also to other members of the "axis of evil" and powers that challenge America's global hegemony, relations with Europe will remain awkward on a political plain. It is at this level that European perceptions of America will be shaped—not at that of culture and society where the process of interaction and interpenetration has markedly increased if seen in historical perspective. Only if transatlantic political relations witness a further steep decline is it conceivable that this latter process may also begin to unravel.

Notes

1. See, e.g., Daniel Boorstin, *America and the Image of Europe* (Gloucester, 1960). See also the contribution by Karsten Voigt in this volume.
2. See, above all, Ralph Willett, *The Americanization of Germany, 1945-1949* (London, 1989); Reinhold Wagnleitner, *Coca-Colonization and Cold War* (Chapel Hill, 1994).
3. For an early expression see Wichard von Moellendorff, *Volkswirtschaftliche Elementarvergleiche zwischen Vereinigten Staaten von Amerika, Deutschland, Grossbritannien, Frankreich, Italien*, vol. I (Berlin, 1930), raising the question of the transferability of experiences. For the more recent arguments see, e.g., Heide Fehrenbach, *Cinema in Democratizing Germany* (Chapel Hill, 1995); Richard Kuisel, *Seducing the French. The Dilemma of Americanization* (Berkeley, 1993); Heide Fehrenbach and Uta Poiger, eds., *Transactions, Transgressions, Transformations. American Culture in Western Europe and Japan* (New York, 2001).
4. On this point, see Volker R. Berghahn, *The Americanisation of West German Industry, 1945-1973* (New York, 1986), 332.
5. See, e.g., Daniel Richter, *Facing East from Indian Country* (Cambridge, Mass., 2001); Richard White, *Roots of Dependency* (Lincoln, 1983); Adam Hochschild, *King Leopold's Ghost* (Boston, 1998).
6. See, e.g., Reuben Ainsztein, *Jewish Resistance in Occupied Eastern Europe* (New York, 1974); Harry Gordon, *The Shadow of Death* (Lexington, Ky., 1992); Israel Gutman, *The Warsaw Ghetto Uprising* (Boston, 1994).
7. See, e.g., Timothy Garton Ash, "Anti-Europeanism in America," *New York Review of Books*, 13 February 2003, 32-34.
8. David Calleo, *Rethinking Europe's Future* (Princeton, 2001).
9. Paul M. Kennedy, "The Eagle Has Landed," *Financial Times*, 2 February 2002.
10. See, e.g., Craig Kennedy and Marshall M. Bouton, "The Real Atlantic Gap," *Foreign Policy*, November/December 2002: 66-74.
11. Wilfried Loth, *The Division of the World* (New York, 1988).
12. See, e.g., Dietrich Orlow, *Common Destiny. A Comparative History of the Dutch, French, and German Social Democratic Parties, 1945-1969* (New York, 2002). On Britain: William I. Hitchcock, *The Struggle for Europe* (New York, 2002), 40ff.
13. See, e.g., Geoffrey Pridham, *Christian Democracy in Western Germany* (London, 1977); Ronald J. Granieri, *The Ambivalent Alliance* (New York, 2002).
14. See, e.g., E. Barker, *Britain between the Superpowers* (London, 1984); Raymond Betts, *France and Decolonization, 1900-1960* (New York, 1991); Miles Kahler, *Decolonization in Britain and France* (Princeton, 1984).
15. See, e.g., Charles S. Maier and Stanley Hoffmann, eds., *The Marshall Plan. A Retrospective* (Boulder, 1984); Gustav Schmidt, ed., *A History of Nato* (New York, 2001).
16. See, e.g., Mary Nolan, *Visions of Modernity* (New York, 1994); Thomas Saunders, *Hollywood in Berlin* (Berkeley, 1994); Philipp Gassert, *Amerika im Dritten Reich* (Stuttgart, 1997).
17. See Uta Poiger, *Jazz, Rock and Rebels* (Berkeley, 2000).
18. See Michael Wreszin, *A Rebel in Defense of Tradition* (New York, 1994).
19. David Riesman et al., *The Lonely Crowd* (New Haven, 1950).
20. Daniel Bell, *The End of Ideology* (Glencoe, Ill., 1960).
21. See Poiger, *Jazz, Rock and Rebels*, 168ff.
22. See, e.g., Carole Fink et al., *1968. The World Transformed* (New York, 1998).
23. Ibid.

24. See, e.g., R.H. Haddow, *Pavilions of Plenty* (Washington, 1997).
25. Kaspar Maase, *Grenzenloses Vergnügen* (Frankfurt, 1997), 274f. See also Herbert J. Gans, *Popular Culture and High Culture* (New York, 1999).
26. Poiger, *Jazz, Rock and Rebels*, 31ff.
27. Hartmut Kaelble, *Auf dem Wege zu einer europäischen Gesellschaft* (Munich, 1987).
28. Richard H. Immerman, ed., *John Foster Dulles and the Diplomacy of the Cold War* (Princeton, 1990).
29. Henry Kissinger, *Nuclear Weapons and Foreign Policy* (New York, 1957).
30. Anne de Tinguy, *US-Soviet Relations During Detente* (Boulder, 1999).

Part 5

OUTLOOK

CRISIS OR COOPERATION?
The Transatlantic Relationship at a Watershed

◆ ◆ ◆

Karsten D. Voigt

Transatlantic relations remain as important now to Germany—indeed, even more so to Europe—as they have ever been in the past. If Europe and the United States were to oppose one other's policies and positions, their shared attempts to address global issues would be jeopardized—in terms of military and economic matters, and also those related to democratic culture and environmental protection. Opportunities for working together for security and democracy in many parts of the world would be lost.

However, I do not foresee an end to the western or transatlantic alliance. Clearly, Germany, the European Union, and the United States find themselves in the midst of a phase of adjustment and reorientation. But, in the past, whenever facts and thinking have changed, partners in this alliance have had to redefine themselves and their relationships to each other time and time again.

In view of the development that has been underway in Europe over the last few years and decades, it is understandable that growing concern exists, particularly in the United States, that the continent wishes to transform itself into a rival to the United States. In the final analysis, I do not believe there is any real danger that Europe will endeavor to define itself in opposition to the United States. Indeed, following the enlargement of the European Union, there will be no majority for a total break from the United States. Specifically defining Europe in opposition to the United States would not be in Germany's interests.

However, I would also like to contradict those in the United States who believe that Europe's increased strength in the sphere of foreign and security policy is a negative development. The opposite is true. Europe's lack of military effectiveness is one of the central problems in transatlantic relations. A

Europe incapable of taking effective action would have little global influence and would not interest the United States as a partner, thus weakening the valuable transatlantic ties developed over decades. A Europe that, as a result of its weakness, sees no hope of exerting influence on the United States could potentially, out of frustration, turn either away from or against the United States. Comments from the United States implying that Germany is irrelevant have diminished rather than increased the readiness of the German public to support American initiatives.

Because I want to strengthen the basis for a joint transatlantic future, I favor making Europe more effective, including militarily. In keeping with the sentiment expressed by Joe Nye of Harvard University in his 2002 book, *The Paradox of American Power: Why the World's Only Superpower Can't Go It Alone*, I would add that the United States is the only true global power in the military sphere. In the economic field, it is one power among many. In economic terms, however, the European Union is almost equal in weight, while in terms of population and its share in world trade, it is more important. At the level of societal and non-state players, the United States used to be more attractive, because of its efforts on behalf of freedom and democracy, than any other country in the world. This attractiveness, rather than military power, was its strongest advantage. After all, "soft power" is also a form of power. In light of current developments in the United States, Nye has warned that America must not lose its social and political appeal by flexing its military muscle too much, thus objectively losing power, which is more than just military might. I share this concern.

There is a long history behind the idea that the world is by nature a place in which states must be rivals, in which a state's security dilemmas can only be lessened by increasing power and not by forming alliances with other states linked by a common legal order or values. I consider this idea, which has many advocates in the United States today, to have been largely proved wrong by Europe's postwar development, even if the traditional idea of the importance of wielding military power still holds sway over many parts of the world. In agreement with many American realists, and in contrast to many Europeans, I am convinced that the deployment of military power is sometimes unavoidable. However, in contrast with American realists, I am also convinced that, with the prospect of a new reality in line with postwar developments, through which Europe was changed from a continent of wars to a continent of peace, we can change our world. Indeed, we should not abandon hope of being able to change the world. Otherwise, politics would be reduced to meaningless action void of goals or values. It will take generations until fundamental changes can be brought about in other parts of the world. However, acceptance of the reality of power and the pursuit of the rule of law, realism, and teleological action do not preclude one another.

The transatlantic relationship is changing. However, changes should not be regarded as negative or as a sign of crisis. For example, the shift in Germany's geostrategic location after 1989 has given rise to unavoidable changes. If we were to retain the modes of conduct and ideas that reflected Germany's geostrategic location during the Cold War, we would undermine rather than strengthen the partnership across the Atlantic. I would therefore like to see a new Atlanticism established by reforming transatlantic policies and transatlantic institutions (in particular, NATO).

November 9, 1989 and September 11, 2001 changed Europe, transatlantic relations, and, ultimately, the world as a whole. The peaceful revolution of 1989 transformed Europe, which had been divided for many decades, and reunited Germany. The second key date was September 11, 2001. The acts of terrorism committed that day accelerated and changed international developments. New threats were recognized. The experience of September 11 led to a new view of the world, first in the United States, then in Europe. The altered awareness in the United States following September 11 was initially underestimated by many Europeans.

What has changed strategically? First, before 1989 Germany had been at the heart of a global conflict for fifty years. It was therefore only logical for John F. Kennedy, as the representative of a global power that was a local protecting power in Berlin, to say that he was proud to be a citizen of Berlin. Now that the Cold War is over, Germany is fortunately no longer at the center of a global conflict. What is more, the centuries-old German question has been resolved by united Germany's membership in the European Union and NATO in a stable, peaceful Europe. Both sides of the Atlantic should rejoice that Germany is no longer a source and cause of crisis. Seen in this context, comments by representatives of the US Administration that Germany has become less relevant lose some of their original polemic harshness.

For the British and French, America's new strategic orientation does not require the same fundamental change in thinking and actions as it does for us. Until 1989, German soldiers were not deployed in military missions outside German territory. I believe that Germany should think increasingly in global terms when it comes to foreign and security policy and that it should also act globally on a selective basis. However, we must decide when we want to act and when not. In view of our limited resources, we will only be able to take military action very selectively. Morality is an important factor influencing policy decisions. Unfortunately, we will also often have to weigh interests against morality whenever our limited resources and influence prevent us from combining them in an ideal fashion. After all, we must also decide whether, like some of our NATO partners, we want to make decisions on military deployment primarily at the national level or whether we always want to make missions dependent on a UN vote, in the context of the European Union, NATO, or a transatlantic consensus. I am certain that, on the basis of its interests as well as commonsense, Germany will continue to decide against giving precedence to decisions at national level.

However, the change in Germany's strategic situation and the reorientation of the United States has presented German policy, as well as the political thinking of most Germans, with new challenges. The military dimension of German foreign policy will have to be further developed. Ultimately, agreement exists on this in the Bundestag and the German government. However, debates about the framework within which Germans want and have to act will continue. Due to Germany's geostrategic location, its integration in NATO and the European Union, as well as its history, multilateralism and international law play a greater role for Germany than for the United States when it comes to weighing interests and objectives rationally. For Germans, multilateralism is a must, while for the United States, it presents one of many options. This difference in perspective is not new, but the conflict over the Iraq war cast it in high relief.

The new security challenges, as well as Germany's new situation, will influence and change our foreign and security policy culture, as well as the decisions our country makes. Through its actions, the United States can have either a positive or a negative influence on this process of creating a new security culture in Germany. It is also crucial now that we ourselves constructively influence the process of adjusting to the new realities by engaging in an even more intensive transatlantic dialogue.

GERMANS AND AMERICANS
Understanding and Managing Change

❖ ❖ ❖

Bowman H. Miller

When I was invited to write this essay in March 2002, it could not have been expected that the task would prove as timely as it has since become. Having been a student of (and, several times, in) Germany for some forty years now, I have spent much of my adult life in thought, conversation, and analysis concerning Germany—a pivotal country, a key ally, and a sometimes troubled regional power.

My background is rather unique for someone in foreign affairs analysis, having done my doctoral work in an analysis of the Baader-Meinhof group's writings espousing terrorism and a master's thesis on the ballads of the nineteenth-century poet Eduard Moerike. However, most of my writing has been devoted to the likes of Helmut Schmidt, Willy Brandt, Helmut Kohl, and now the Schröder-Fischer tandem.

While I fully realize generalizations can be dangerous, and that they provide the raw material for unwanted, often inaccurate stereotypes, nonetheless I am obliged to resort to some sweeping observations in trying to say something useful about nearly sixty years of shared German-American history and cooperation. In my business, we are told to put our key findings up front—lest our busy senior policy-maker clients abandon the read before they see our conclusions, so I offer this chapter's central theses straightaway.

Germans and Americans know and appreciate each other more thoroughly than virtually any other two major partners, and, despite differences of value interpretation and prioritization at times, we have much more in common than that which divides us. But the last fifteen years or so have brought epochal changes in both societies and in our bonds with each other. Our

---

Notes for this section can be found on page 262.

bilateral agenda is more complex, and change in the European Union and NATO adds to the complications of managing bilateral relations.

Following World War II and the institution of the Four-Power occupation in Germany, the United States proved instrumental in helping shape a decentralized, highly federal German democracy. In so doing, the United States presented itself as an antifascist, anticommunist model to the German people, one they generally respected and sought in some ways to emulate. In the succeeding fifty years, federalist practice has deeply embedded itself in Germany, while the luster and unreality of aspects of an overly idealized vision of the United States have been adjusted (some would say have grown tarnished). Nonetheless, Germans are decidedly not anti-American, even if increasingly disappointed and disturbed by certain acts and attitudes they see coming from the United States—often from Washington, but predating the onset of the current administration.

The United States and its European allies, Germany chief among them, have long claimed, as one sees in NATO summit communiqués since 1949, that the Atlantic alliance represents a bond between states with common interests and values. But time and events have shown us where differences between the United States and Germany exist (in attitudes toward the role of the state, the appropriate uses of power, the interpretation and experience of threats, social and criminal justice practices, and international governance and sovereignty, among others). Rather than pretend such differences do not exist, we need to acknowledge them and work together to surmount our differences lest those "toxic" areas of our relationship infect others.

As Germany has moved forthrightly to integrate itself into the European Union and to embrace collaborative multilateralism as its fundamental tenet of foreign and security policy, the United States (over the course of several administrations) has exhibited behavior that is considerably more "sovereignty-insistent," steadfast in proclaiming a basic self-reliance, and is perceived by critics as frequently oblivious to external pressures to conform to international norms and agendas. This disparity in overall approaches, most recently in a broad area of international governance, has led to a new level of acrimony and recriminations in transatlantic and US-German relations. But, one must note, tensions per se are not at all new. Recall, for instance, the Moscow Olympics and intermediate range missile episodes from 1978 to 1987, intermittent misapprehensions concerning EU and NATO competition for stature, and more.

We have not found it all that easy to adjust our relationship to new conditions and expectations, following the joint achievement of Bonn and Washington that forged a rapid, unfettered German unification.

On the German side, unification has brought with it enduring burdens, financial and psychopolitical, but it has also essentially ended a prolonged period of direct security dependence on the United States and the status of a semisovereign nation. German external policy has featured great continuity but also has begun shedding the cliché of being an "economic giant but political dwarf." (Today, Germany's economy itself suffers stagnation and some structural strangulation.) German leaders have cast aside some of the limits on Berlin's freedom of maneuver, as we expected. US leaders also expected, or at least hoped, that Germany would acknowledge and articulate policies in terms of interests (a point to which I will return below). The political change in Germany in 1998 also marked the end of an era—a generational transition, and the advent of a government with some new priorities, different instincts, and special challenges.

On the US side, things have evolved as well. As President George Bush's 2002 National Security Strategy leads off, "Today, the United States enjoys a position of unparalleled military strength and great economic and political influence," and yet we Americans have witnessed the first hostile foreign attack on the US homeland (sic) since 1941—and much closer to home than Pearl Harbor. September 11 left an enormous, indelible imprint on this country, on its sense of security, and its national temperament.

As we focus on vulnerabilities and security, Europeans would be wise not to expect the United States to strengthen national gun control laws or to jettison capital punishment any time soon, regardless of the arguments pro and con. The value Germans and Americans place on freedom, the sanctity of human life, and on open, democratic societies is shared, but how we define the components that shape and encourage those values differs—and will likely continue to do so.

While routinely reminding ourselves of our sole status as superpower, clear majorities of Americans are uncomfortable with the risks, rhetoric, and resource costs of a "go it alone" foreign policy, as many polls, including the German Marshall Fund's *Transatlantic Trends 2003* study, show us.[1] Sustained national sovereignty, clearly an icon or article of faith in the United States, has been relegated in Germany and broadly among Europeans engaged in the European Union integration effort. Pooling sovereignty is the hallmark of postwar intra-European interaction and the presumed way of the future. In the United States, rightly or wrongly, many with influence believe we can only count on ourselves, ultimately, and thus must maintain and use our power to our own advantage and protection. Moreover, many Americans hold fast to a mythology of exceptionalism. Thus, September 11 represented not merely a massive, malicious terrorist assault but an evil attack directed at the "city on the hill." To understand it otherwise is to misconstrue the national reaction and the depth of many Americans' disgust and anger.

Not surprisingly, we, Germans and Americans, are different—but the differences do not present insurmountable challenges. We share those first-order values of democracy, rule of law and equal justice, the individual's importance, basic freedoms, free markets and enterprise, and the unending quest for peace. But, the picture Germans gained of the United States has changed dramatically since 1945. We do not share the same political space or cultures; we differ enormously in terms of power and our understanding of what constitutes power and how it should be used. Many Germans, I fear, believe that the United States is overly militaristic in its predilections and priorities, first and foremost a *Militärmacht.*

Although this is changing, too few Germans consider *Macht*, or power, a legitimate aspiration for and instrument of the state. Indeed, the idea of articulating German interests remains underdeveloped; however, when and if these interests are articulated, other issues will emerge. History explains these differences and sensitivities. The venerable Prof. Fritz Stern has remarked, both in his seminal histories of Germany and to this author, that "when Germans think of their future, others think of their past." One can ask, I think, if Germans looking at today's America lament the abandonment of what they deem our "creative, post-WW II past" (when Bretton Woods, NATO, the United Nations, and such were put in place); they and others question America's commitment to common action and structures for international cooperation, both political and economic.

During the period when I first visited Germany, in 1965, Germans still actively admired, almost worshipped, John F. Kennedy; but his assassination, and later those of his brother and Martin Luther King, jarred them as it did us. During the Vietnam War, Germans worried not only that America had resorted to warfare but, as always, that the war deflected attention from Europe, especially Germany. The special post-World War II German-American relationship, unique in its origins and in the vast numbers of personal contacts that helped sustain it, rested heavily on the concatenation of occupation, then protecting forces, and then presence as NATO allies. The half million US forces several decades ago now number barely 75,000; 53 *Amerikahäuser* have all but disappeared. Germany's elite came to the United States in droves as students, official visitors, and USIA grantees, for example. This is not the case today. Indeed, neither do the Germans qualify for such priority concern as they once did nor are these otherwise valuable programs as well funded or regarded as heretofore. This excludes, of course, the citizens of eastern Germany, who constitute one fourth of the unified population and who, up until 1990, had been reared on a steady diet of anti-US, anti-NATO propaganda. Their quite different, if not ignorant, attitudes toward the United States reflect a work in progress; indeed, the author of the next chapter, Karsten Voigt, has been a leader in exposing emerging leaders in the five new *Länder* to America, its attitudes, and its society.

Defending Germany throughout the Cold War always blended the contradictory perceptions that US forces and nuclear weaponry represented a security blanket and also a policy straitjacket. This contradiction was at its most acute, in my recollection, during the period from 1979 to 1987, when Helmut Kohl encountered a real threat to peace and social stability over US missile deployments—those that Helmut Schmidt had demanded, Francois Mitterrand had seconded, and were deployed only to be negotiated away.

In the Two-plus-Four Process of 1989/90, the United States had perhaps its finest diplomatic hour in helping steward Germany's unification over Soviet objections and clear, even vocal, French and British misgivings. But, as Georgi Arbatov reminded us in an 8 December 1987 *New York Times* article, some would regret the passing of the USSR since it provided the very glue that bound our Allies to us.[2] Some of that glue, however, reflected security dependence and an outdated *Feindbild.*

Neither America nor Germany feels today as bound to each other as before 1989/90. German security dependence is attenuated; German and American threat perceptions have diverged. Germany attends to Washington but tends to give first hearing and attention to Brussels and Paris as it formulates policy together with its EU counterparts. Germany no longer represents a special, primary concentration or concern among US leaders.

I shall close with a question often reserved for trying to explain the seemingly perennial dysfunctionality of the American-French relationship: how does each society and nation understand itself in terms of claimed "exceptionalism?" France and the United States both consider themselves the cradle of Western democracy, societies worthy of foreign emulation, and endowed with special rights and qualities for leadership. Germany, long divided and thus in some ways distorted as a national actor, is also exceptional: defeated in war, it modeled itself in key ways after the United States and put its benefactor on a high moral pedestal, overly idealizing its most powerful, most trusting Western ally and protector. Today, many Germans join a significant number of Americans in their concern over the staying power and legacy of the US commitment to those critical multilateral institutions that Americans such as Dean Acheson, Harry S. Truman, and George C. Marshall were instrumental in founding after 1945. They worried (and we continue to worry) that some of the values and goals the US proclaims and projects, as seen from abroad, may not square with what has made America the envy of—and desired new homeland for—much of the outside world. But Germany, too, is a magnet attracting many outsiders to it as a new home. And we both suffer the social ills of modernizing, postindustrial, pluralistic societies.

Are Germans becoming more anti-American? Is the United States becoming a state or society less worthy of envy and emulation? There are, indeed, troubling signs of both, demanding diligent diplomacy, open dialogue, and new avenues of cooperation in order to bridge a widening transatlantic divide.

Notes

The views expressed in this discussion are solely those of the author and do not claim to represent the views of the Department of State or the US government.

1. *Transatlantic Trends 2003,* the German Marshall Fund of the United States and the Compagnia di San Paolo, Turin, Italy, July 2003.
2. Georgi Arbatov, "It Takes Two to Make a Cold War", *New York Times* (August 12, 1987) A38.

SELECTED BIBLIOGRAPHY FOR THE PERIOD 1945 TO THE PRESENT

Adams, Willi Paul, and Knud Krakau, eds. 1985. *Deutschland und Amerika: Perzeption und historische Realität.* Berlin: Colloquium.
Aguilar, Manuela. 1996. *Cultural Diplomacy and Foreign Policy: German-American Relations, 1955-1968.* New York: Lang.
Alfred Herrhausen Gesellschaft, ed. 1998. *Pax Americana?* Munich: Piper.
"The American Occupation of Germany in Cultural Perspective." 1999. *Diplomatic History* 23, no. 1: 1-77.
Angster, Julia. 2003. *Konsenskapitalismus und Sozialdemokratie: Die Westernisierung von SPD und DGB.* Munich: Oldenbourg.
Barber, Benjamin R. 1995. *Jihad vs. McWorld.* New York: Times Books.
Barclay, David E., and Elisabeth Glaser-Schmidt, eds. 1997. *Transatlantic Images and Perceptions: Germany and America since 1776.* Cambridge: Cambridge University Press.
Bauschinger, Sigrid, Horst Denkler, and Wilfried Malsch, eds. 1975. *Amerika in der deutschen Literatur: Neue Welt – Nordamerika – USA.* Stuttgart: Reclam.
Beck, Earl R. 1968. *Germany Rediscovers Amerika.* Tallahassee: Florida State University Press.
Berghahn, Volker R. 1986. *The Americanisation of West German Industry, 1945-1973.* Cambridge: Cambridge University Press.
———. 2001. *America and the Intellectual Cold Wars in Europe: Shepard Stone between Philanthropy, Academy and Diplomacy.* Princeton: Princeton University Press.
Berghahn, Volker R., Anselm Doering-Manteuffel, and Christof Mauch, eds. 1999. "The American Impact on Western Europe: Americanization and Westernization in Transatlantic Perspective." Available at http://www.ghi-dc.org/conpotweb/westernpapers. Accessed 21 November 2003.

Berman, Russell A. 2003. "Demokratischer Krieg, repressiver Frieden: Über den real existierenden Antiamerikanismus." *Merkur* 57, no. 7: 570-82.

Bigsby, C.W.E., ed. 1975. *Superculture: American Popular Culture and Europe*. Bowling Green: Bowling Green University Popular Press.

Blair, John G., and Reinhold Wagnleitner, eds. 1997. *Empire: American Studies. Selected Papers from the Bi-National Conference of the Swiss and Austrian Associations for American Studies at the Salzburg Seminar, November 1996*. Tuebingen: Narr.

Bohrer, Karl Heinz, and Kurt Scheel, eds. 2000. "Europa oder Amerika? Zur Zukunft des Westens." *Merkur* Sonderheft, 9/10.

Bredella, Lothar, and Dietmar Haack, eds. 1988. *Perceptions and Misperceptions: The United States and Germany. Studies in Cultural Understanding*. Tuebingen: Narr.

Breitenkamp, Edward C. 1953. *The U.S. Information Control Division and Its Effect on German Publishers and Writers, 1945-1949*. Grand Forks: University Station.

Broder, Henryk M. 2002. *Kein Krieg, Nirgends: Die Deutschen und der Terror*. Berlin: Berlin Verlag.

Bude, Heinz, and Bernd Greiner, eds. 1999. *Westbindungen: Amerika in der Bundesrepublik*. Hamburg: Hamburger Edition.

Bundeszentral für politische Bildung. 2001. *Die Zukunft der transatlantischen Beziehungen im Kontext der Globalisierung: Eine deutsch-amerikanische Konferenz*. Bonn: Ost-West-Kolleg der Bundeszentrale für politische Bildung.

Bungenstab, Karl-Ernst. 1970. *Umerziehung zur Demokratie! Re-education-Politik im Bildungswesen der US-Zone 1945-1949*. Duesseldorf: Bertelsmann.

Chargaff, Erwin. 1994. *Armes Amerika- Arme Welt: Ein Essay*. Stuttgart: Klett-Cotta.

Clemens, Gabriele, ed. 1994. *Kulturpolitik im besetzten Deutschland 1945-1949*. Stuttgart: Steiner.

Cohen, Jean-Louis. 1995. *Scenes of the World to Come: European Architecture and the American Challenge, 1893-1960*. Paris: Flammarion.

Coleman, Peter. 1989. *The Liberal Conspiracy. The Congress for Cultural Freedom and the Struggle for the Mind of Postwar Europe*. New York: Free Press.

Corbin, Anne-Marie. 2001. *L'image de l'Europe à l'ombre de la guerre froide: La revue* Forum *de Friedrich Torberg à Vienne (1954-1961)*. Paris: L'Harmattan.

Crockatt, Richard. 2003. *America Embattled: September 11, Anti-Americanism, and the Global Order.* London: Routledge.
"Cultural Transfer or Cultural Imperialism?" 2000. *Diplomatic History* 24, no. 3: 465-528.
Czempiel, Ernst-Otto. 2002. *Weltpolitik im Umbruch: Die Pax Americana, der Terrorismus und die Zukunft der internationalen Beziehungen.* Munich: Beck.
Dean, John, and Jean-Paul Gabilliet, eds. 1996. *European Readings of American Popular Culture.* Westport: Greenwood Press.
Dettke, Dieter, ed. 1985. *America's Image in Germany and Europe. Papers of a Seminar on 'Anti-Americanism in Germany: Slogan or Reality?'* Washington: Friedrich Ebert Stiftung.
Diefendorf, Jeffry M., Axel Frohn, and Hermann-Josef Rupieper, eds. 1993. *American Policy and the Reconstruction of West Germany, 1945-1955.* Cambridge: Cambridge University Press.
Dienstag 11. September 2001. 2001. Hamburg: Rowohlt.
Diner, Dan. 1996. *America in the Eyes of the Germans: An Essay on Anti-Americanism.* Princeton: Markus Wiener.
Dirke, Sabine von. 1997. *"All Power to the Imagination!" The West German Counterculture from the Student Movement to the Greens.* Lincoln: University of Nebraska Press.
Divers, Gregory. 2002. *The Image and Influence of America in German Poetry since 1945.* New York: Camden House.
Doering-Manteuffel, Anselm. 1999. *Wie westlich sind die Deutschen? Amerikanisierung und Westernisierung im 20. Jahrhundert.* Goettingen: Vandenhoeck & Ruprecht.
Dudden, Arthur Power, and Russell R. Dynes, eds. 1987. *The Fulbright Experience, 1946–1986: Encounters and Transformations.* New Brunswick: Transaction Books.
Duignan, Peter, and L. H. Gann. 1992. *The Rebirth of the West: The Americanization of the Democratic World, 1945-1958.* Cambridge: Blackwell.
Durzak, Manfred. 1979. *Das Amerika-Bild in der deutschen Gegenwartsliteratur: Historische Voraussetzungen und aktuelle Beispiele.* Stuttgart: Kohlhammer.
Ellwood, David W., and Rob Kroes, eds. 1994. *Hollywood in Europe: Experiences of a Cultural Hegemony.* Amsterdam: VU University Press.
Engelbrecht, Lloyd C. 1987. "*Bauhäusler*: A Case Study of Two-Way Traffic across the Atlantic." *Yearbook of German-American Studies*, vol. 22: 149-72.

Epitropoulos, Mike-Frank G., and Victor Roudometof, eds. 1998. *American Culture in Europe: Interdisciplinary Perspectives.* Westport: Praeger.

Ermarth, Michael, ed. 1993. *America and the Shaping of German Society, 1945-1955.* Providence/Oxford: Berg.

Fehrenbach, Heide. 1995. *Cinema in Democratizing Germany: Reconstructing National Identity after Hitler.* Chapel Hill: University of North Carolina Press.

Fehrenbach, Heide and Uta G. Poiger. 2000. *Transactions, Transgressions, Transformations: American Culture in Western Europe and Japan.* New York: Berghahn.

Fluck, Winfried. 1992. "The 'Americanization' of History in New Historicism." *Monatshefte* 84, no. 2: 220-28.

Frankel, Charles. 1965. *The Neglected Aspect of Foreign Affairs: American Educational and Cultural Policy Abroad.* Washington: The Brookings Institution.

Frenz, Horst, and Hans-Joachim Lang, ed. 1973. *Nordamerikanische Literatur im deutschen Sprachraum seit 1945. Beiträge zu ihrer Rezeption.* Munich: Winkler.

Gaida, Burton C. 1989. *USA-DDR: Politische, kulturelle und wirtschaftliche Beziehungen seit 1974.* Bochum: Brockmeyer.

Gassert, Philip. 1999. "Amerikanismus, Antiamerikanismus, Amerikanisierung: Neue Literatur zur Sozial-, Wirtschaft- und Kulturgeschichte des amerikanischen Einflusses in Deutschland und Europa." *Archiv für Sozialgeschichte* 39: 531-61.

Gehring, Hansjörg. 1976. *Amerikanische Literaturpolitik in Deutschland 1945-1953: Ein Aspekt des Re-Education-Programms.* Stuttgart: Deutsche Verlags-Anstalt.

Gelfert, Hans-Dieter. 2002. *Typisch amerikanisch: Wie die Amerikaner wurden, was sie sind.* Munich: Beck.

Gemünden, Gerd. 1998. *Framed Visions: Popular Culture, Americanization, and the Contemporary German and Austrian Imagination.* Ann Arbor: University of Michigan Press.

Gerhards, Jürgen, ed. 2000. *Die Vermessung kultureller Unterschiede: USA und Deutschland im Vergleich.* Wiesbaden: Westdeutscher Verlag.

German-American Cultural Relations: A Summary Record of a Conference Held at Harrison House, Glen Cove, L.I., New York. January 16-18, 1975. Washington: Superintendent of Documents.

Gienow-Hecht, Jessica C. E. 1999. *Transmission Impossible: American Journalism as Cultural Diplomacy in Postwar Germany.* Baton Rouge: Louisiana State University Press.

Giovanopoulos, Anna-Christina. 2000. *Die amerikanische Literatur in der DDR: Die Institutionalisierung von Sinn zwischen Affirmation und Subversion.* Essen: Die Blaue Eule.
Goedde, Petra. 2003. *GIs and Germans: Culture, Gender, and Foreign Relations, 1945-1949.* New Haven: Yale University Press.
Good, David F., and Ruth Wodak, ed. 1999. *From World War to Waldheim: Culture and Politics in Austria and the United States.* New York: Berghahn.
Grabbe, Hans-Jürgen. 1986. "Das Amerikabild Konrad Adenauers." *Amerikastudien* 31, no. 3: 315-23.
Große, Jürgen. 1999. *Amerikapolitik und Amerikabild in der DDR 1974-1989.* Bonn: Bouvier.
Haller, Gret. 2002. *Die Grenzen der Solidarität: Europa und die USA im Umgang mit Staat, Nation und Religion.* Berlin: Aufbau.
Hanuschek, Sven, Therese Hörnigk, and Christine Malende. 2000. *Schriftsteller als Intellektuelle: Politik und Literatur im Kalten Krieg.* Tuebingen: Niemeyer.
Hardt, Ursula. 1996. *From Caligari to California: Erich Pommer's Life in the International Film Wars.* Providence: Berghahn.
Harpprecht, Klaus. 1982. *Amerika der fremde Freund.* Stuttgart: Deutsche Verlags-Anstalt.
Haskell, Barbara, and Lisa Phillips. 1999. *The American Century. Art and Culture, 1900-2000.* 2 vols. New York: Whitney Museum of American Art.
Hein-Kremer, Maritta. 1996. *Die amerikanische Kulturoffensive: Gründung und Entwicklung der amerikanischen Information Centers in Westdeutschland und West-Berlin 1945-1955.* Cologne: Böhlau.
Herm, Gerhard. 1964. *Amerika erobert Europa.* Duesseldorf: Econ.
———. 1980. *Amerika ist an allem schuld: Die Amerikanisierung der Alten Welt.* Munich: Heyne.
Hertsgaard, Mark. 2002. *The Eagle's Shadow: Why America Fascinates and Infuriates the World.* New York: Farrar, Straus and Giroux.
Herzinger, Richard, and Hannes Stein. 1995. *Endzeit-Propheten oder Die Offensive der Antiwestler: Fundamentalismus, Antiamerikanismus und Neue Rechte.* Hamburg: Rowohlt.
Hess, Jürgen C., Hartmut Lehmann, and Volker Sellin. 1996. *Heidelberg 1945.* Stuttgart: Steiner.
Hochgeschwender, Michael. 1998. *Freiheit in der Offensive? Der Kongreß für kulturelle Freiheit und die Deutschen.* Munich: Oldenbourg.
Hoenisch, Michael, Klaus Kämpfe, and Karl-Heinz Pütz. 1980. *USA und Deutschland: Amerikanische Kulturpolitik 1942-1949. Bibliographie – Materialien – Dokumente.* Berlin: John F. Kennedy Institut.

Hogan, Michael J. 1987. *The Marshall Plan: America, Britain, and the Reconstruction of Western Europe, 1947-1952.* Cambridge: Cambridge University Press.

Höhn, Maria. 2002. *GIs and Fräuleins: The German-American Encounter in 1950's West Germany.* Chapel Hill: University of North Carolina Press.

Hollander, Paul. 1995. *Anti-Americanism: Irrational and Rational.* New Brunswick: Transaction Publishers.

Holler, Manfred J. 2002. "Artists, Secrets, and CIA's Cultural Policy." In *Finanzpolitik in der Informationsgesellschaft: Festschrift für Gunther Engelhardt,* B. Priddat and H. Hegmann, eds. Marburg: Metropolis.

Horkheimer, Max, and Theodor W. Adorno. [1944.] "Kulturindustrie: Aufklärung als Massenbetrug." Horkheimer, Max, and Theodor W. Adorno. 2000. *Dialektik der Aufklärung: Philosophische Fragmente.* Frankfurt: Fischer. 128-77.

Hörnigk, Therese, and Alexander Stephan, eds. 2002. *Jeans, Rock und Vietnam: Amerikanische Kultur in der DDR.* Berlin: Theater der Zeit.

Horwitz, Richard P., ed. 1993. *Exporting America: Essays on American Studies Abroad.* New York: Garland.

Huntington, Samuel. 1996. *The Clash of Civilizations and the Remaking of World Order.* New York: Simon & Schuster.

Huyssen, Andreas. 1986. *After the Great Divide: Modernism, Mass Culture, Postmodernism.* Bloomington: Indiana University Press.

Huyssen, Andreas, and Klaus R. Scherpe, ed. 1986. *Postmoderne: Zeichen eines kulturellen Wandels.* Hamburg: Rowohlt.

Iriye, Akira. 1997. *Cultural Internationalism and World Order.* Baltimore: Johns Hopkins University Press.

Jarausch, Konrad, and Hannes Siegrist, eds. 1997. *Amerikanisierung und Sowjetisierung in Deutschland 1945–1970.* Frankfurt: Campus.

Johnson, Chalmers. 2000. *Blowback: The Costs and Consequences of American Empire.* New York: Metropolitan.

Junker, Detlef. 2003. *Power and Mission: Was Amerika antreibt.* Breisgau: Herder.

———, ed. 2001. *Die USA und Deutschland im Zeitalter des Kaltes Krieges 1945-1968: Ein Handbuch.* 2 vols. Stuttgart: Deutsche Verlags-Anstalt.

Kagan, Robert. 2003. *Of Paradise and Power. America and Europe in the New World Order.* New York: Knopf Verlag.

Kaiser, Karl, and Hans-Peter Schwarz, eds. 1978. *America and Western Europe. Problems and Prospects.* Lexington: Lexington Books.

Kamalipour, Yahya R. 1999. *Images of the U.S. around the World: A Multicultural Perspective.* New York: State University of New York Press.

Kamps, Klaus, ed. 2000. *Trans-Atlantik-Trans-Portabel? Die Amerikanisierungsthese in der politischen Kommunikation.* Wiesbaden: Westdeutscher Verlag.

Kellermann, Henry J. 1978. *Cultural Relations as an Instrument of U.S. Foreign Policy: The Educational Exchange Program between the United States and Germany, 1945-1954.* Washington: U.S. Department of State.

Kleinschmidt. Johannes. 1997. *'Do not fraternize.' Die schwierigen Anfänge deutsch-amerikanischer Freundschaft 1944-1949.* Trier: Wissenschaftlicher Verlag.

Klepper, Martin, and Joseph C. Schöpp, eds. 2001. *Transatlantic Modernism.* Heidelberg: Winter.

Klöckner, Thomas. 1993. *Public Diplomacy – Auswärtige Informations- und Kulturpolitik der USA: Strukturanalyse der Organisation und Strategien der United States Information Agency und des United States Information Service in Deutschland.* Baden-Baden: Nomos.

Krabbendam, Hans, J. Verheul, and Hans Bak, eds. 1999. *Through the Cultural Looking Glass: American Studies in Transcultural Perspective.* Amsterdam: VU University Press.

Krampikowski, Frank, ed. 1990. *Amerikanisches Deutschlandbild und deutsches Amerikabild in Medien und Erziehung.* Baltmannsweiler: Pädagogischer Verlag Burgbücherei Schneider.

Krätzer, Anita. 1982. *Studien zum Amerikabild in der neueren deutschen Literatur: Max Frisch – Uwe Johnson – Hans Magnus Enzensberger und das 'Kursbuch'.* Bern: Lang.

Krewson, Margrit B. 1995. *German-American Relations: A Selective Bibliography.* Washington: Library of Congress.

Kroes, Rob. 1996. *If You've Seen One, You've Seen the Mall. Europeans and American Mass Culture.* Urbana: University of Illinois Press.

———, ed. 1999. *Predecessors: Intellectual Lineages in American Studies.* Amsterdam: VU University Press.

Kroes, Rob, Maarten van Rossem, and Marcus Cunliffe, eds. 1986. *Anti-Americanism in Europe.* Amsterdam: VU University Press.

Kroes, Rob, Robert W. Rydell, D. F. J. Bosscher, and John F. Sears, eds. 1993. *Cultural Transmissions and Receptions: American Mass Culture in Europe.* Amsterdam: VU University Press.

Krohn, Claus-Dieter, and Patrik von zur Mühlen, eds. 1997. *Rückkehr und Aufbau nach 1945: Deutsche Remigranten im öffentlichen Leben Nachkriegsdeutschlands.* Marburg: Metropolis.

Krohn, Claus-Dieter, Erwin Rotermund, Lutz Winkler, Irmtrud Wojak, and Wulf Koepke, eds. 1991. "Exil und Remigration." *Exilforschung.* Vol. 9. Munich: edition text + kritik.

Kupchan, Charles A. 2002. *The End of the American Era: U.S. Foreign Policy and the Geopolitics of the Twenty-first Century.* New York: Knopf.

Lange, Wigand. 1980. *Theater in Deutschland nach 1945: Zur Theaterpolitik der amerikanischen Besatzungsbehörden.* Frankfurt: Lang.

Larres, Klaus, and Torsten Oppelland, eds. 1997. *Deutschland und die USA im 20. Jahrhundert: Geschichte der politischen Beziehungen.* Darmstadt: Wissenschaftliche Buchgesellschaft.

Leggewie, Claus. 2000. *Amerikas Welt: Die USA in unseren Köpfen.* Hamburg: Hoffmann und Campe.

Lehmann, Hartmut. 1995. *Alte und neue Welt in wechselseitiger Sicht: Studien zu den transatlantischen Beziehungen im 19. und 20. Jahrhundert.* Goettingen: Vandenhook & Ruprecht.

Lenz, Günter H., and Klaus J. Milich, eds. 1995. *American Studies in Germany: European Contexts and Intercultural Relations.* Frankfurt: Campus.

Lindemann, Beate, ed. 1995. *Amerika in uns: Deutsch-amerikanische Erfahrungen und Visionen.* Mainz: Hase & Koehler.

Lorenz, Sebastian, and Marcel Machill, eds. 1999. *Transatlantik: Transfer von Politik, Wirtschaft und Kultur.* Opladen: Westdeutscher Verlag.

Ludes, Peter. 1991. *Kulturtransfer und transkulturelle Prozesse: Amerikanisierung und Europäisierung des Fernsehprogramms in der Bundesrepublik.* Heidelberg: Winter.

Lüdtke, Alf, Inge Marßolek, and Adelheid von Saldern, eds. 1996. *Amerikanisierung: Traum und Alptraum im Deutschland des 20. Jahrhunderts.* Stuttgart: Steiner.

Maase, Kaspar. 1992. *Bravo Amerika: Erkundungen zur Jugendkultur der Bundesrepublik in den fünfziger Jahren.* Hamburg: Junius.

———. 1997. *Grenzenloses Vergnügen: Der Aufstieg der Massenkultur 1850-1970.* Frankfurt: Fischer.

Milich, Klaus J. 1996. *Die frühe Postmoderne. Geschichte eines europäisch-amerikanischen Kulturkonflikts.* Frankfurt: Campus.

Milich, Klaus J., and Jeffrey M. Peck. 1998. *Multiculturalism in Transit: A German-American Exchange.* New York: Berghahn.

Moeller, Robert G., ed. 1997. *West Germany under Construction: Politics, Society, and Culture in the Adenauer Era.* Ann Arbor: University of Michigan Press.

Moltmann, Günter. 1976. "Deutscher Anti-Amerikanismus heute und früher." In *Vom Sinn der Geschichte,* Otmar Franz, ed. Stuttgart: Seewald. 85-105.

Moore, R. Laurence, and Maurizio Vaudagna, eds. 2003. *The American Century in Europe.* Ithaca: Cornell University Press.

Mueller, Agnes C. 1999. *Lyrik 'Made in USA': Vermittlung und Rezeption in der Bundesrepublik.* Amsterdam: Rodopi.
Müller, Emil-Peter. 1986. *Antiamerikanismus in Deutschland: Zwischen Care-Paket und Cruise Missile.* Cologne: Deutscher Instituts-Verlag.
Müller, Winfried. 1995. *Schulpolitik in Bayern im Spannungsfeld von Kultusbürokratie und Besatzungsmacht, 1945-1949.* Munich: Oldenbourg.
Ney, John. 1970. *The European Surrender: A Descriptive Study of the American Social and Economic Conquest.* Boston: Little, Brown.
Ninkovich, Frank A. 1995. *The Diplomacy of Ideas: U.S. Foreign Policy and Cultural Relations, 1938 – 1950.* Chicago: Imprint Publications.
Nowell-Smith, Geoffrey, and Steven Ricci, eds. 1998. *Hollywood and Europe: Economics, Culture, National Identity: 1945-95.* London: British Film Institute.
O'Connell, Mary Ellen. 2003. "Enforcing International Law in National Courts: The German and American Experiences Compared." In *Konflikt der Rechtskulturen? Die USA und Deutschland im Vergleich,* Knud Krakau and Franz Streng, eds. Heidelberg: Winter. 83-91.
Osterle, Heinz D., ed. 1987. *Bilder von Amerika. Gespräche mit deutschen Schriftstellern.* Muenster: Englisch Amerikanische Studien.
———, ed. 1989. *Amerika! New Images in German Literature.* New York: Lang.
Passerini, Luisa, ed. 2000. *Across the Atlantik: Cultural Exchanges between Europe and the United States.* Brussels: Lang.
Paulsen, Wolfgang, ed. 1976. *Die USA und Deutschland: Wechselseitige Spiegelungen in der Literatur der Gegenwart.* Bern: Francke.
Pells, Richard. 1997. *Not Like Us: How Europeans Have Loved, Hated, and Transformed American Culture since World War II.* New York: Basic Books.
Piltz, Thomas, ed. 1975. *1776-1976: Zweihundert Jahre deutsch-amerikanische Beziehungen.* Munich: Moos.
Pilz, Peter. 2003. *Mit Gott gegen alle: Amerikas Kampf um die Weltherrschaft.* Stuttgart: Deutsche Verlags-Anstalt.
Poiger, Uta G. 2000. *Jazz, Rock and Rebels: Cold War Politics and American Culture in a Divided Germany.* Berkeley: University of California Press.
Polster, Bernd, ed. 1995. *Westwind: Die Amerikanisierung Europas.* Cologne: DuMont.
Pommerin, Reiner, ed. 1995. *The American Impact on Postwar Germany.* Providence: Berghahn.
Preuß, Ulrich K. 2003. *Krieg, Verbrechen, Blasphemie: Gedanken aus dem alten Europa.* Berlin: Wagenbach.

Probst, Alfred. 1989. *Amideutsch: Ein kritisch-polemisches Wörterbuch der anglodeutschen Sprache.* Frankfurt: Fischer.

Ramet, Sabrina P., and Gordana P. Crnković, eds. 2003. *Kazaaam! Splat! Ploof! The American Impact on European Popular Culture since 1945.* Lanham: Rowman & Littlefield.

Rauhut, Michael. 1993. *Beat in der Grauzone: DDR-Rock 1964 bis 1972 – Politik und Alltag.* Berlin: BasisDruck.

Rentschler, Eric. 1996. "How American Is It: The U.S. as Image and Imaginary in German Film." In *Perspectives on German Cinema*, Terri Ginsberg and Kirsten Moana Thompson, eds. New York: G.K. Hall. 277-94.

Rittberger, Volker, and Fariborz Zelli. 2003. *Europa in der Weltpolitik: Juniorpartner der USA oder antihegemoniale Alternative?* Tübinger Arbeitspapiere zur internationalen Politik und Friedensforschung. 41. Tuebingen: Institut für Politikwissenschaft.

Ritter, Alexander, ed. 1977. *Deutschlands literarisches Amerikabild: Neuere Forschungen zur Amerikarezeption der deutschen Literatur.* Hildesheim: Olms.

Rollin, Roger, ed. 1989. *The Americanization of the Global Village: Essays in Comparative Popular Culture.* Bowling Green: Bowling Green University Popular Press.

Rosellini, Jay. 2000. *Literary Skinheads? Writing from the Right in Reunified Germany.* West Lafayette: Purdue University Press.

Ryback, Timothy W. 1990. *Rock around the Bloc: A History of Rock Music in Eastern Europe and the Soviet Union.* New York: Oxford University Press.

Sammons, Jeffrey. 1996. "Zu den Grundlagen des Antiamerikanismus in der deutschen Literatur." In *Alte Welten – neue Welten. Akten des IX. Kongresses der Internationalen Vereinigung für Germanische Sprach- und Literaturwissenschaften*, Michael S. Batts, ed. Vol. 1. Tuebingen: Niemeyer. 33-47.

Sardar, Ziauddin, and Merryl Wyn Davies. 2002. *Why Do People Hate America?* New York: Disinformation.

Saunders, Frances Stonor. 2000. *The Cultural Cold War: The CIA and the World of Arts and Letters.* New York: New Press.

Schildt, Axel. 1995. *Moderne Zeiten. Freizeit, Massenmedien und "Zeitgeist" in der Bundesrepublik der 50er Jahre.* Hamburg: Christians.

———. 1999. *Ankunft im Westen: Ein Essay zur Erfolgsgeschichte der Bundesrepublik.* Frankfurt: Fischer.

———. 1999. *Zwischen Abendland und Amerika: Studien zur westdeutschen Ideenlandschaft der 50er Jahre.* Munich: Oldenbourg.

Schildt, Axel, and Arnold Sywottek, eds. 1998. *Modernisierung im Wiederaufbau: Die westdeutsche Gesellschaft der 50er Jahre.* Bonn: Dietz.

Schildt, Axel, Detlef Siegfried, and Karl Christian Lammers, eds. 2000. *Dynamische Zeiten: Die 60er Jahre in den beiden deutschen Gesellschaften.* Hamburg: Christians.

Schissler, Hanna, ed. 2001. *The Miracle Years: A Cultural History of West Germany, 1949-1968.* Princeton: Princeton University Press.

Schivelbusch, Wolfgang. 1998. *In a Cold Crater: Cultural and Intellectual Life in Berlin, 1945-1948.* Berkeley: University of California Press.

Schlanstein, Beate. November 12, 1999. *Eiskalt – Coca-Cola und das Dritte Reich: Eine deutsche Erfrischungsgeschichte.* Television Documentary, WDR, Cologne, Germany.

Schmiese, Wulf. 2000. *Fremde Freunde: Deutschland und die USA zwischen Mauerfall und Golfkrieg.* Paderborn: Ferdinand Schöningh.

Schneider, Irmela, ed. 1992. *Amerikanische Einstellung: Deutsches Fernsehen und US-amerikanische Produktionen.* Heidelberg: Winter.

Schneider, Irmela, Christian Werner Thomsen, and Andreas Nowak, eds. 1991. *Lexikon der britischen und amerikanischen Serien, Fernsehfilme und Mehrteiler in den Fernsehprogrammen der Bundesrepublik Deutschland, 1953-1985.* 3 vols. Berlin: Spiess.

Schnoor, Rainer, ed. 1999. *Amerikanistik in der DDR: Geschichte – Analysen – Zeitzeugenberichte.* Berlin: trafo Verlag.

Schrenck-Notzing, Caspar. 1965. *Charakterwäsche: Die amerikanische Besatzung in Deutschland und ihre Folgen.* Stuttgart: Seewald.

Schumacher, Frank. 2000. *Kalter Krieg und Propaganda: Die USA, der Kampf um die Weltmeinung und die ideelle Westbindung der Bundesrepublik Deutschland, 1945-1955.* Trier: Wissenschaftlicher Verlag.

Schwan, Gesine. 1999. *Antikommunismus und Antiamerikanismus in Deutschland: Kontinuität und Wandel nach 1945.* Baden-Baden: Nomos.

Schwartz, Richard A. 1998. *Cold War Culture: Media and the Arts, 1945-1990.* New York: Checkmark Books.

Scott-Smith, Giles. 2002. *The Politics of Apolitical Culture: The Congress for Cultural Freedom, the CIA and Post-War American Hegemony.* London: Routledge.

Seliger, Helfried W. 1974. *Das Amerikabild Bertolt Brechts.* Bonn: Bouvier.

Sichelschmidt, Gustav. 1990. *Amerikanismus: Der Weltfeind Nr. 1.* Berg: Türmer.

———. 1996. *Deutschland – eine amerikanische Provinz: Der große Seelenmord.* Berg: VGB-Verlagsgesellschaft.

Siebald, Manfred, and Horst Immel. 1985. *Amerikanisierung des Dramas und Dramatisierung Amerikas*. Frankfurt: Lang.

Skard, Sigmund. 1958. *American Studies in Europe. Their History and Present Organization*. Philadelphia: University of Pennsylvania Press.

Stephan, Alexander, ed. Forthcoming. *American Culture in Europe: Americanization and Anti-Americanism after 1945*. New York: Berghahn.

———. Forthcoming. "The End of Anti-Americanism? German Reactions to 9-11 in Their Historical Context." In *America's Image Abroad After September 11*, Vladimir Shlapentokh, ed.

Stich, Sidra. 1987. *Made in U.S.A.: An Americanization in Modern Art, the 50s & 60s*. Berkeley: University of California Press.

Strack, Manfred. "Amerikanische Kulturbeziehungen zu (West-) Deutschland 1945-55. *Zeitschrift für Kulturaustausch* 37 (1987): 283-300.

Tent, James F. 1982. *Mission on the Rhine: Reeducation and Denazification in American-Occupied Germany*. Chicago: University of Chicago Press.

———. 1988. *The Free University of Berlin: A Political History*. Bloomington: Indiana University Press.

———, ed. 1998. *Academic Proconsul: Harvard Sociologist Edward Y. Hartshorne and the Reopening of German Universities 1945-1945: His Personal Account*. Trier: Wissenschaftlicher Verlag.

Thomsen, Christian W., ed. 1989. *Cultural Transfer or Electronic Imperialism? The Impact of American Television Programs on European Television*. Heidelberg: Winter.

Thornton, Thomas Perry, ed. 1988. "Anti-Americanism: Origins and Context." *The Annals of the American Academy of Political and Social Science*. Vol. 497.

Todd, Emmanuel. 2003. *Weltmacht USA. Ein Nachruf*. Munich: Piper.

Tomlinson, John. 1991. *Cultural Imperialism: A Critical Introduction*. Baltimore: Johns Hopkins University Press.

———. 1999. *Globalization and Culture*. Chicago: University of Chicago Press.

Trommler, Frank, and Joseph McVeigh, eds. 1985. *America and the Germans: An Assessment of a Three-Hundred-Year History*. Philadelphia: University of Pennsylvania Press.

Trommler, Frank, and Elliott Shore, eds. 2001. *The German-American Encounter: Conflict and Cooperation between Two Cultures. 1800-2000*. New York: Berghahn.

Trumpbour, John. 2001. *Selling Hollywood to the World: U.S. and European Struggles for Mastery of the Global Film Industry, 1920-1950*. Cambridge: Cambridge University Press.

Tuch, Hans. 1990. *Communicating with the World. U.S. Public Diplomacy Overseas*. New York: St. Martin's Press.
Tüngel, Richard, and Rudolph van Wehrt. 1958. *Auf dem Bauche sollst du kriechen...: Deutschland unter den Besatzungsmächten*. Hamburg: Wegner.
Wagner, Bernd, ed. 2001. *Kulturelle Globalisierung: Zwischen Weltkultur und kultureller Fragmentierung*. Frankfurt: Klartext.
Wagnleitner, Reinhold. 1994. *Coca-Colonization and the Cold War: The Cultural Mission of the United States in Austria after the Second World War*. Chapel Hill: University of North Carolina Press.
———. 2001. "'No Commodity is Quite so Strange as This Thing Called Cultural Exchange': The Foreign Policy of American Pop Culture Hegemony." *Amerikastudien* 3: 443-70.
Wagnleitner, Reinhold, and Elaine Tyler May, eds. 2000. *'Here, There and Everywhere': The Foreign Politics of American Popular Culture*. Hanover: University Press of New England.
Weidenfeld, Werner. 1996. *America and Europe: Is the Break Inevitable?* Guetersloh: Bertelsmann.
Weigelt, Klaus, ed. 1986. *Das Deutschland- und Amerikabild: Beiträge zum gegenseitigen Verständnis beider Völker*. Melle: Knoth.
Weissman, William J. 1990. *Kultur- und Informationsaktivitäten der USA in der Bundesrepublik Deutschland während der Amtszeiten Carter und Reagan: Eine Fallstudie über Alliierten-Öffentlichkeitsarbeit*. Pfaffenweiler: Centaurus.
Weisz, Christoph. 1994. *OMGUS Handbuch: Die amerikanische Militärregierung in Deutschland, 1945-1949*. Munich: Oldenbourg.
Wenzel, Harald, ed. 1998. *Die Amerikanisierung des Medienalltags*. New York: Campus.
Weßel, Daisy. 1989. *Bild und Gegenbild: Die USA in der Belletristik der SBZ und der DDR (bis 1987)*. Opladen: Leske + Budrich.
White, Donald W. 1996. *The American Century: The Rise and Decline of the United States as a World Power*. New Haven: Yale University Press.
Wierlemann, Sabine. 2002. *Political Correctness in den USA und in Deutschland*. Berlin: Schmidt.
Willett, Ralph. 1989. *The Americanization of Germany, 1945-1949*. London: Routledge.
Winter, Rolf. 1995. *Little America: Die Amerikanisierung der Deutschen Republik*. Hamburg: Rasch und Röhring.
Woodward, C. Vann. 1991. *The Old World's New World*. New York: New York Public Library and Oxford University Press.
Zimmer, Dieter E. 1997. *Deutsch und anders die Sprache im Modernisierungsfieber*. Reinbek: Rowohlt.

Contributors

David Bathrick is the Jacob Gould Schurman Professor of Theatre, Film and Dance and German Studies at Cornell University. He did his graduate work at the University of Chicago, where he received a Ph.D. in Germanic languages and literatures in 1970. From 1970 to 1987, he was a professor of German at the University of Wisconsin, when he joined Cornell. He has also been a visiting professor at universities in Germany and the United States. He served as chair of the German Studies Department at Cornell from 1991 to 1994 and the Theatre, Film and Dance Department from 1995 to 2002. His publications include *The Dialectic and the Early Brecht* (1976), *Modernity and the Text* (1989, coedited with Andreas Huyssen), *The Powers of Speech: The Politics of Culture in the GDR* (1995), for which he was awarded the 1996 DAAD/GSA Book of the Year Prize, and numerous articles on the theory and history of twentieth century literature and cultural studies. He is a cofounder and coeditor of *New German Critique*, an interdisciplinary journal of German studies. His areas of specialization include the history and theory of modern drama, the theater of Bertolt Brecht and Heiner Müller, twentieth century German literature, critical theory, Weimar culture, the cultural politics of East Germany, European film, Holocaust studies, and Nazi cinema. He is currently completing a book on the Holocaust and film.

Volker R. Berghahn is the Seth Low Professor of History at Columbia University. His research interests are in modern German and European history. His publications include *Germany and the Approach of War in 1914* (1973), *Modern Germany* (1982), *The Americanisation of West German Industry, 1945-1973* (1986), *Imperial Germany, 1871-1914* (1994), *America and the Intellectual Cold Wars in Europe* (2001), *Europa im Zeitalter der Weltkriege* (2002).

Russell A. Berman is the Walter A. Haas Professor in the Humanities at Stanford University, with appointments in the departments of German Studies and Comparative Literature. He has written widely on topics in German literary and cultural history from the eighteenth to the twentieth century, as well as on problems in cultural theory and contemporary politics, especially relations between the United States and Europe. His publications include *The Rise of the Modern German Novel: Crisis and Charisma* (1986), *Modern Culture and Critical Theory: Art, Politics and the Legacy of the Frankfurt School* (1989), *Cultural Studies of Modern Germany: History, Representation, and Nationhood* (1993), *Enlightenment or Empire: Colonial Discourse in German Culture* (1998).

Thomas Elsaesser is professor in the Department of Media and Culture at the University of Amsterdam and chair of Research in Film and Television Studies. He is an executive board member of the Amsterdam School of Cultural Analysis and general editor of the series *Film Culture in Transition*, published by Amsterdam University Press. His essays on film theory, genre, film history, television, and digital media have appeared in numerous collections and anthologies, including essays translated into French, German, Italian, Spanish, Polish, Portuguese, Danish, Chinese, Korean, Japanese, and Dutch. Among his recent books as author and editor are *Fassbinder's Germany: History, Identity, Subject* (1996), *Cinema Futures: Cain Abel or Cable?* (1998), *The BFI Companion to German Cinema* (with Michael Wedel, 1999), *Weimar Cinema and After* (2000), *Metropolis* (2000), *Studying Contemporary American Film* (with Warren Buckland, 2002) and *Früher Film und Kinogeschichte* (2002).

Michael Ermarth is professor of history at Dartmouth College in Hanover, New Hampshire. His primary research interests have been in German and European intellectual history, the theory of history and the humane studies, hermeneutics, and modern German history. He has published on the thought of Wilhelm Dilthey, Karl Jaspers, Martin Heidegger, Bernard Groethuysen and the Dilthey school, Georg Gervinus, and modern hermeneutics. He has published articles on German and European attitudes toward modernity, modern civilization, and "Americanization." He is currently completing a two-volume study entitled *Germany's Inner America: Americanization, Counter-Americanism and Transmodernity in the Twentieth Century*.

Heide Fehrenbach is associate professor of history at Northern Illinois University and has held previous positions at Emory and Colgate universities. She has written on cultural and gender dimensions of postwar German reconstruction, with particular focus on national identity, film, masculinity, and, most recently, race. She is author of *Cinema in Democratizing Germany: Reconstructing National Identity after Hitler* (1995) and editor, with Uta Poiger, of *Transactions, Transgressions, Transformations: American Culture in Western Europe and Japan* (2000). Recent essays, relevant to her discussion in this volume, include "'Ami-Liebchen' und 'Mischlingskinder,'" in K. Naumann, ed., *Nachkrieg in Deutschland* (2001); "Of German Mothers and '*Negermischlingskinder*': Race, Sex, and the Postwar Nation," in H. Schissler, ed., *The Miracle Years: A Cultural History of West Germany, 1949-1968* (2001); and "Rehabilitating Father*land*: Race and German Remasculinization," Special Forum on German Masculinity in *Signs: Journal of Women in Culture and Society* 24, no. 1 (fall 1998). Currently she is completing a book, to be published by Princeton University Press, on the reformulation of "race" in postfascist Germany that highlights the gendered and transnational character of the process.

Winfried Fluck is professor and chair of American Culture at the John F. Kennedy Institute for North American Studies of the Freie Universität Berlin. He studied in Berlin, Harvard University, and the University of California, Berkeley, and holds a Ph.D. from the Freie Universität. He has been a visiting scholar at Harvard, Yale, and the University of California, Irvine, a guest professor at Princeton, a fellow at the National Humanities Center and the Rockefeller Study Center, and professor at the University of Konstanz before his return to Berlin. He has published widely on American literature and culture in the nineteenth and twentieth centuries and on questions of literary and cultural theory. His books include *Theorien amerikanischer Literatur* (1987), *Inszenierte Wirklichkeit* (1992), and *Das kulturelle Imaginäre: Eine Funktionsgeschichte des amerikanischen Romans 1770-1900* (1997). In the United States, his most recent publications include "Aesthetics and Cultural Studies," in *Aesthetics in a Multicultural Age*, Emory Elliott, Louis Freitas Caton, and Jeffrey Rhyne, eds. (2002), "Fiction and Justice," in *New Literary History* 34, no. 1 (2003), "The Modernity of America and the Practice of Scholarship," in *Rethinking American History in a Global Age*, Thomas Bender, ed. (2002), "The Humanities in the Age of Expressive Individualism and Cultural Radicalism," in *The Future of American Studies*, Donald E. Pease and Robyn Wiegman, eds. (2002).

Bernd Greiner is director of the research unit History and Theory of Violence at the Hamburg Institute for Social Research and adjunct professor of history at the University of Hamburg. He studied at universities in Germany and the United States and holds a Ph.D. in political science. He has published books on the National Security Council under Truman and Eisenhower (1986), the Cuban Missile Crisis (1988), the controversies about the Morgenthau Plan and postwar economic planning for Germany (1995), and the "Americanization" of West-Germany (1999). He is a frequent contributor to such journals as *Mittelweg 26, Geschichte und Gesellschaft, Diplomatic History, Blätter für deutsche und internationale Politik,* as well as to major German daily and weekly newspapers. He is currently finishing a book on American war crimes in Vietnam and the responses in American political and social life. Building on long-term studies about the "societal impact" of war in the twentieth century, he has also convened a series of conferences dealing with a comparative perspective on the Cold War in east and west.

Sabine Hake is professor of German and film studies at the University of Pittsburgh. She is the author of four books—*German National Cinema* (2002), *Popular Cinema of the Third Reich* (2001), *The Cinema's Third Machine: German Writings on Film 1907-1933* (1993), *Passions and Deceptions: The Early Films of Ernst Lubitsch* (1992)—as well as numerous articles on Weimar culture. Her current research project deals with urban architecture and mass utopia in Weimar Berlin.

Jost Hermand has been professor of German at the University of Wisconsin, Madison, since 1958, W.F. Vilas Research Professor since 1968, and Honorary Professor at the Humboldt University in Berlin since 2003. He received his Dr. phil. from the University of Marburg in 1955. Among his most important publications relating to this book's topic are *Kulturgeschichte der Bundesrepublik, 1949-1985* in 2 vols. (1986/88), *Geschichte der Germanistik* (1990), *Zuhause und anderswo. Erfahrungen im Kalten Krieg* (2001), *Nach der Postmodern. Ästhetik heute* (2004).

Rob Kroes is the chair of American Studies at the University of Amsterdam. He is a past president of the European Association for American Studies (1992-1996) and the author, coauthor, or editor of thirty-two books, including *The Persistence of Ethnicity* (1992), *If You've Seen One, You've Seen the Mall: Europeans and American Mass Culture* (1996), and *Them and Us: Questions of Citizenship in a Globalizing World* (2000). He founded the Netherlands American Studies Association in 1977 and is the general editor of two series, published in Amsterdam: European Contributions to American Studies, and Amsterdam Monographs in American Studies.

Kaspar Maase teaches at the Ludwig-Uhland-Institut für Empirische Kulturwissenschaft at the University of Tübingen. He studied German literature, sociology, art history, and cultural theory in Munich and Berlin and earned his Ph.D. from Humboldt University in Berlin. Afterwards he worked as a freelance editor, writer, university lecturer, and as a fellow at institutes for social research in Frankfurt and Hamburg. He earned his *Habilitation* in cultural studies at Bremen University. Since 1995, he has been teaching and conducting research at various universities in Berlin, Zurich, Basel, Marburg, and Tübingen. His current research focuses on the history of popular culture in the nineteenth and twentieth century, on the aestheticization of everyday life, and on cultural Americanization. Among his publications are *BRAVO Amerika. Erkundungen zur Jugendkultur der fünfziger Jahre in der Bundesrepublik* (1992), "A Taste of Honey: Adorno's Reading of American Mass Culture," in *European Readings of American Popular Culture*, John Dean and Jean-Paul Gabilliet, eds. (1996), *Grenzenloses Vergnügen: Der Aufstieg der Massenkultur 1850-1970* (1997), "Establishing Cultural Democracy: Youth, 'Americanization', and the Irresistible Rise of Popular Culture," in *The Miracle Years: A Cultural History of West Germany, 1949 - 1968*, Hanna Schissler, ed. (2001), *Schund und Schönheit. Populäre Kultur um 1900* (coeditor Wolfgang Kaschuba, 2001), *Unterwelten der Kultur. Themen und Theorien der volkskundlichen Kulturwissenschaft* (coeditor Bernd Jürgen Warneken, 2003).

Bowman H. Miller is director of European Analysis in the United States Department of State, a position he has held since May 1987. He previously held US government positions as lead analyst for Germany and as chief of the Threat Analysis Group in the State Department and as a counterintelligence/counter-terrorism analyst in the United States Air Force. He holds a doctorate from Georgetown University, where his dissertation treated "The Language Component of Terrorism Strategy: A Text-Based Linguistic Case Study of Contemporary German Terrorism" (1983). His research interests include transatlantic relations, European integration, and the language factor in ethnic conflict. He is a member of the editorial board of *International Studies Perspectives* and of the Academic Advisory Council to the American Institute of Contemporary German Studies, Johns Hopkins University.

In addition to various published articles and papers dealing with terrorist profiles and tactics, his publications include: "German Unity and the Politics of German History," in *America and Europe: Prospects for the 1990s*, J.J. Lee, ed., "The EU's Common Foreign and Security Policy: An American Perspective," in *The EU on the Path to a Common Foreign and Security Policy* [in German], Oliver Thraenert, ed., Research Institute of the Friedrich Ebert Foundation (1992), and "Responsibility of the EU and the US for Stability, Security, and Peace in the World," in *Renewal of the Transatlantic Partnership* (2001).

Richard Pells is professor of history at the University of Texas, Austin. He is the author of three books: *Radical Visions and American Dreams: Culture and Social Thought in the Depression Years* (1973), *The Liberal Mind in a Conservative Age: American Intellectuals in the 1940s and 1950s* (1985), and *Not Like Us: How Europeans Have Loved, Hated, and Transformed American Culture since World War II* (1997). He is currently at work on *From Modernism to the Movies: The Globalization of American Culture in the Twentieth Cen-

tury, to be published by Yale University Press. He has received fellowships from the Charles Warren Center for Studies in American History at Harvard University, the Rockefeller Foundation, the Woodrow Wilson International Center for Scholars in Washington, D.C., and the Guggenheim Foundation. He has held five Fulbright senior lectureships and chairs, as well as other visiting professorships at universities in The Netherlands, Denmark, Germany, Austria, Finland, Brazil, and Australia. He has lectured extensively throughout Canada, Latin America, Europe, Turkey, Southeast Asia, Australia, and New Zealand.

Alexander Stephan is professor of German, Ohio Eminent Scholar, and Fellow of the Mershon Center for the Study of International Security and Public Policy at Ohio State University. Previously he taught at Princeton University, the University of California, Los Angeles, and in Florida. Major book publications include *Im Visier des FBI. Deutsche Exilschriftsteller in den Akten amerikanischer Geheimdienste* (1995 and 1998; published in 2000 in English as *'Communazis.' FBI Surveillance of German Emigré Writers*), *Christa Wolf* (1991), *Die deutsche Exilliteratur* (1979), *Max Frisch* (1983), *Anna Seghers im Exil* (1993), *Anna Seghers: 'Das siebte Kreuz'. Welt und Wirkung eines Romans* (1997. He is the editor of the book series *Exil-Studien/Exile Studies* and has made numerous contributions to radio and television in Germany and the United States on Bertolt Brecht, Marlene Dietrich, Anna Seghers, Thomas Mann, and other topics. He produced a documentary film for German television titled *Im Visier des FBI. Deutsche Autoren im US-Exil* (1995).

Publications and activities related to the topic of the book include *Jeans, Rock und Vietnam. Amerikanische Kultur in der DDR*, ed. with Therese Hörnigk (2002), proceedings of a conference at the Literaturforum Berlin, January 2002, *American Culture in Europe: Americanization and Anti-Americanism after 1945* (forthcoming 2005), *Das Amerika der Autoren. Beispiele aus der deutschsprachigen Literatur und Publizistik des 20. Jahrhunderts*, International Symposium at the Kulturwissenschaftliche Institut, Essen, Germany, December 2003 (with Jochen Vogt, forthcoming book, 2004), "The End of Anti-Americanism? German Reactions to 9-11 in Their Historical Context," in *America's Image Abroad After September 11*, Vladimir Shlapentokh, ed. (forthcoming 2004).

Karsten D. Voigt has been the coordinator of German-American cooperation at the German Federal Foreign Ministry since February 1999. He has been a member of the German Parliament (1976–1998), a member of the Parliamentary Assembly of NATO (1977–1998), chairman of Defence and Security Committee of the Parliament Assembly of NATO (1989–1993), vice president of the Parliamentary Assembly of NATO (1992–1994), and president of the Parliament Assembly of NATO (1994–1996). Responsible for the strengthening of transatlantic relations, he tracks the wide variety of existing governmental and private programs, and suggests ways to strengthen German-American political and cultural cooperation. In order to intensify transatlantic relations, the coordinator meets with decision makers from all spheres of American and Canadian society, especially members of the administration and Congress, think tanks, universities, and research establishments.

INDEX

A

Abosch, Hans, 35
Acheson, Dean, 261
Achternbusch, Herbert, 172
A-culture, 73
Adams, Henry, 204, 208
Adenauer, Konrad, 35, 44–45, 108
Adenauer Period, 101, 162, 171
Adlon, Percy, 174
Adorno, Theodor, 41, 68, 71, 72, 142, 178, 224
Afghanistan, 4, 28, 241
Afro-American, 117
Age of Innocence, The (1993), 174
Air Force One (1997), 180
Alarm im Zirkus (1954), 159
Allen, Woody, 195, 197
All That Is Solid Melts into Air (Berman), 227
Al Qaeda, 242
Altman, Robert, 195
Amenábar, Alejandro, 176
American Beauty (1999), 195
American Forces Network, 92
Americanism
    counter-Americanism and, 25–27
    as democratic capitalism, 22, 37–38
Americanization
    aesthetic experience of, 222–32
    as concept of the century, 30–35
    definition of, 17
    features of, 32
    feminization associated with, 151
    forms of, 3
    French views of, 29–30
    German critics of, 29–30
    historical approaches to, 120–21
    mass dynamic of, 38, 45, 46, 121
    in modernization of postwar West Germany, 31–47
    polarization around, 25–26, 32, 33
    as self-Americanization, 221–32
    as social transformation, 12–13
"Americanization of the Holocaust, The" (Rosenfeld), 130
Americanization of the World, The (Stead), 189
American popular culture
    history of, 224–27
    international popularity of, 189–201, 223–32
    as modern culture, 223–24
Amerika: Der Aufgang einer neuen Welt (Keyserling), 207
Amerikanismus, 149
Amerika und der Amerikanismus (Halfeld), 205
Amery, Jean, 43–44
Anders, Günther, 35
Andorra, 143
Angremy, Jean-Pierre, 216
Animals, 177, 178
Annaud, Jean Jacques, 181
Annie Hall (1977), 195
anti-Americanism
    careful anti-Americanism, 28, 35
    Communist variant of, 17–18, 19–20
    contemporary European discourse of, 208–12

cultural criticism as, 21–22
defined, 14
European anti-modernism and,
    202–19
forms of, 3
French discourse of, 21–22
German discourse on, 15–17
as global judgment and stereotype,
    22–23
as independent of Americanization,
    15–19
postdemocratic, 18, 20–21
predemocratic type of, 17, 18
as rhetoric of opposition to
    emancipation, 17
settings of, 15
sources of, 12–23
anti-Bushism, 3, 246
anti-modernism, 202–19
Antonioni, Michelangelo, 176, 194
AOL-Time Warner, 98, 190
Appadurai, Arjun, 97
Arbatov, Georgiy, 261
*Arbeitsgemeinschaft der Rundfunkanstalten
    in Deutschland* (ARD), 91, 92, 93
Arendt, Hannah, 59, 132
Armstrong, Louis, 73
art, Western trends in Germany and
    Europe, 71–75
art informel, 72
Attali, Jacques, 216
"*Auferstehung der Kultur in Deutschland*"
    (Adorno), 68
August, Bille, 181
Auschwitz, 56, 132, 135
Australia, multicultural society of, 200

B

Bach, Johann Sebastian, 67
Ballhaus, Michael, 173, 174
Barber, Benjamin, 198
Baring, Arnulf, 32
Barlach, Ernst, 69
Baudelaire, Charles, 210
Baudrillard, Jean, 21
Bauhaus movement, 193
BBC, 89, 96
Beat Club, 92
Beatty, Warren, 196

Beauvoir, Simone de, 212
Becher, Johannes R., 68, 70, 71
Beethoven, Ludwig van, 67
Beirut, 28
Bell, Daniel, 244
Bellow, Saul, 224
Belmondo, Jean-Paul, 196
Benoist, Alain de, 11
Berenbaum, Michael, 130
Bergen-Belsen, 131, 132, 135, 139
Berghahn, Volker, 43, 222
Bergman, Ingmar, 172, 194, 200
Berkely, Busby, 203
Berlin, as center of the Cold War, 152–53
Berlin Ecke Schönhauser (1958), 159, 160,
    161
Berlin Wall, 11
Berlusconi, Silvio, 182–83
Berman, Marshall, 227
Bernhard, Jack, 180
Bernstein, Leonard, 194
Bertelsmann, 183
Besson, Luc, 176
Bibliothèque nationale de France, 216
Blair, Tony, 242
Bloch, Ernst, 98
Bogart, Humphrey, 196, 228
Bonnie and Clyde (1967), 195
boogie-woogie culture, 69
Borges, Jorge Luis, 215–16
Borman, John, 176
Bourdieu, Pierre, 213–15, 218
Brahms, Helma Sanders, 172
Bram Stoker's Dracula (1992), 174
Brando, Marlon, 160, 196, 244
Brandt, Willy, 245, 257
Braque, Georges, 194
Brauner, Atze, 181
Breathless (1959), 194
Brecht, Bertolt, 35, 156, 197
Bredonck, 133
Bredow, Hans, 80
Brehm, Bruno, 35
Bretton Woods, 43, 260
British Forces Network/British Forces
    Broadcasting Service, 92
broadcasting
    American influences in postwar
        Western Germany, 78–98

dual system of, 79
See also radio broadcasting;
television broadcasting
Broccoli, Albert, 181
Buchenwald, 131, 132, 133, 135
Bürger, Peter, 73
Bush, George, foreign policy of, 26
Bush, George W.
on America's enemies, 183–84
European views of, 1
National Security Strategy of, 259
promoting regime change in Iraq by, 27–28, 242
tactics compared with Hitler, 19–20, 26
unilateralist foreign policy of, 26, 189, 241

C

Cabaret (1972), 172
Cage, John, 72
Cahiers du cinéma, 170, 177, 214
Calleo, David, 241
Camus, Albert, 193
Canady, John, 74
Capra, Frank, 229
Carter, Erica, 151
Casablanca (1942), 196
Cassirer, Ernst, 94
Central Intelligence Agency (CIA), 5, 40, 72
Chabrol, Claude, 177
Chaplin, Charlie, 194, 197, 203
Chayesky, Paddy, 130
Cheney, Richard, 246
Chicago Defender, The, 117
Child Welfare League, 117
Christian Democratic Union (CDU), 37, 44, 82, 91
Christiane F.-Wir Kinder vom Bahnhof Zoo (1981), 179
Christian Social Union (CSU), 82, 91
Cinema Paradiso, 200
Citizen Kane, 195
Clausewitz, Carl von, 26
Clay, Lucius, 39, 114
Clincy, Everett, 114
Clinton, William J., 240, 241
Coca-Cola, 73, 198, 227

Cold War
anti-Americanism in Berlin DEFA films, 148–63
beginning of, 242
civil rights movement during, 107–21
end of, 11
European view of Americanism during, 36
power blocs of, 1
propaganda war during, 5
Soviet hegemony in, 52
third way between American and Soviet models, 243
Cold War Civil Rights (Dudziak), 116
Cole, Tim, 138
Colombani, Jean-Marie, 208–9
Commune 1, 55
Compagnie Générale des Eaux, 183
Congress for Cultural Freedom, 5
Connery, Sean, 181
convergence doctrine, 37
Cooper, Gary, 195
Copland, Aaron, 194
Coppola, Francis Ford, 174, 177, 179, 195, 197
counter-Americanism
associated with West German reconstruction, 25–27
as Old Shatterhand, 45–47
as Other concept, 30–35
social liberal and social democratic doctrines of, 35–45
Crèvecoeur, Michel Guillaume Jean de, 209
Cries and Whispers (1972), 200
Crouching Tiger, Hidden Dragon (2000), 200
cultural imperialism, 3, 7
Cultural League for the Democratic Renewal of Germany, 68
culture, American forms of, 67–75
culture industry, 72
Curtius, Ernst Robert, 68
Curtiz, Michael, 172, 196

D

Dachau, 131, 132, 135–36
Dada-Pop, 74

Daily Fascism (Lettau), 53
Daimler-Chrysler, 182
Dalfiume, Richard, 110
Dallas series, 199
Das Arche Noah Prinzip (1984), 179
Das Boot (1981), 179
Das Kunstwerk, 74
Davis, Angela, 52, 54
Davis, Bette, 196
Dean, James, 72, 196, 244
Death Mills (1946), 132, 136
de Bont, Jan, 176, 180
Decline of the West (Spengler), 36
DEFA Berlin Films, 5, 148–63
de Grazia, Victoria, 97
de Laurentiis, Dino, 181
democratic capitalism, 22, 37–38
De Niro, Robert, 196
Deputy, The (1963), 143
Der Deutsche Gedanke, 206
Der Spiegel, 53, 55, 58, 139, 141, 223
Desegregation of the U.S. Armed Forces (Dalfiume), 110
Dialectic of Enlightenment (Horkheimer and Adorno), 224
Diary of Anne Frank (1959), 136–41
Dickens, Charles, 211
Die deutsche Katastrophe (Meinecke), 68
Die Halbstarken (1956), 161
Die Leiden des jungen Werther (Goethe), 59
Die neuen Leiden des jungen W. (Plenzdorf), 59
Die Revolution in der modernen Kunst (Sedlmayr), 69
Dietrich, Marlene, 196
Dietrich, Otto, 37
Die unendliche Geschichte (1984), 179
Die Welt, 55
Die Zeit, 58
Diner, Dan, 58, 60
Disney
    comics, 171
    Disneyland, 190, 191, 198
    Disney World, 219
    movies, 175
Disney, Walt, 191, 197
Doering-Manteuffel, Anselm, 32
Dörrie, Doris, 181

Dos Passos, John, 192, 193
Dreyer, Carl, 194
Dudow, Slatan, 150–51, 156–59, 161
Dudziak, Mary, 116
Duhamel, Georges, 205, 212
Dulles, John Foster, 247
Dürer, Albrecht, 56
Dussel, Konrad, 89
Dutschke, Rudi, 57

E

East Germany
    anti-Americanism of Cold War films by, 5, 148–63
    images of America during Vietnam War, 59
    stance on music and art by, 70, 72
Ebony, 110, 114, 117, 118
ecology, international agenda for, 11–12
economic humanism, 43
E-culture, 73, 75
Edel, Uli, 174, 180
Edison, Thomas, 33
education, American models of, 14
Ehe im Schatten (1945), 153
Eichinger, Bernd, 6, 181–83
Eine Berliner Romanze (1956), 150
Eisenhower, Dwight D., 110, 132, 247
Eisenstein, Sergei, 194
Ellington, Duke, 73
Elsaesser, Thomas, 145
Emerson, Ralph Waldo, 33
Emmerich, Roland, 6, 174, 179–80
End of Ideology, The (Bell), 244
Enzensberger, Hans Magnus, 55, 59–60
Erhard, Ludwig, 43
Eucken, Walter, 35, 41
Euro-bashing in American press, 7
Europe
    anti-modernism and anti-Americanism, 202–19
    common cultural identity of, 6
    encounters with Americanism, 238–47
    transatlantic relationships and alliances of, 253–56
Europeanism, as democratic socialism, 37
European Union (EU), 29, 253, 258
Europe's postmodern paradise, 2

Eurotrash, 2
"Extermination of the Jews as Soap Opera, The" (Lietzmann), 142

F

farbige Besatzungskinder, farbige Mischlingskinder, Negermischlingskinder, 107–21
Fascism, 37, 55
Fassbinder, Rainer Werner, 143, 170, 171, 172, 173, 174, 181
Faulkner, William, 193
Federal Republic of Germany, 5
Fehrenbach, Heide, 151
Fellini, Frederico, 194, 197
Fichte, Johann Gottlieb, 57
Figgis, Mike, 176
film
- Americanization of Holocaust in Germany, 129–45
- anti-Americanism in Berlin DEFA films, 5, 148–63
- Bollywood industry of, 176
- Europe-Hollywood oppositions in, 167–68
- festivals of, 175
- Hollywood hegemony in German film, 166–84
- Hong Kong industry of, 176, 200
- James Bond, 169, 181
- *See also* German film

Filmkritik, 170
Fischer, Joschka, 27, 257
Fluck, Winfried, 79, 97
Forces Programme, 89, 96
Ford, John, 170, 197, 229
foreign policy
- go it alone, 3
- *See also specific country or leader*

Foreman, Milos, 176
Foster, Stephen, 192
Foucault, Michel, 230
France
- anti-Americanism discourse of, 21–22
- cultural exemptions by, 212, 213
- future in American-French relationships, 261–62
- response to September 11 events, 21–22, 209
- views of Americanization, 29–30

Frank, Anne, 136–41
Frank, Otto, 138–39
Frankfurter Allgemeine Zeitung, 58, 142
Frankfurter Rundschau, 55
Frankfurt School, 35
Frauenschicksale (1952), 150, 156–59
Free University of Berlin, 14
Freiburg school, 43
Freie Deutsche Jugend (FDJ), 153, 158
Freud, Sigmund, 199, 211
Freund, Karl, 174
Friedrich, Paul, 43
Frisch, Max, 143
Fuller, Sam, 172
Funk-Verband Ostsachsen, 87

G

gag art, 74
Gäng, Peter, 57
Gangs of New York (2002), 174
Garbo, Greta, 196
Garncarz, Joseph, 169
"Gaskammern à la Hollywood," 141
Gassert, Philipp, 30
Geldzahler, Henry, 74
General Agreement on Tariffs and Trade (GATT), 11, 182
German-American Friendship Day, 28
German broadcasting
- Americanization of, 73, 78–98
- post World War I programs of, 78
- *See also* radio broadcasting; television broadcasting

German Democratic Republic (GDR), 5, 70
German film
- anti-Americanism in Cold War films of, 148–62
- *Autorenfilm*, 167
- Hollywood hegemony in, 166–84
- impact of Nazism on, 178–80
- New German Cinema in, 167–74
- Young German Film in, 167–74

German Marshall Fund, 259
German Socialist Students' Association, 51

Germany
    in future German-American
        relationships, 257–62
    popular culture of, 177
    postwar culture in, 67–75
    Sonderfall of cultural
        Americanization, 4, 5
    transatlantic relationships and
        alliances of, 253–56
    unification of, 261
Germany in Autumn (1977), 170, 172
Gershwin, George, 194
Gesellschaft, 114, 115, 116
Gibson, Mel, 176
Gilbert, Gustav M., 134
globalization
    changes with, 11
    commercialism in, 212–15
    cultural protection from, 212–15
    as form of Americanization,
        29–30, 32, 202
    impact of, 27
glocalism, 27
Godard, Jean-Luc, 177, 180, 194, 195
Godfather, The (1972), 195
Goebbels, Joseph, 88, 89
Goering, Hermann, 134
Goethe, Johann Wolfgang von, 16, 23,
    59, 67
Goethe Institute, 175
Gombrich, Ernest, 214
Goodfellas (1990), 174
Goodrich, Francis, 136
Grafe, Frieda, 170
Grant, Cary, 196
Great Britain
    filmmakers from, 176
    popular music groups from, 13,
        177, 178
    radio broadcasting in, 79, 89
Green, Gerald, 138
Grenada, 60
Griffith, D. W., 226
Guback, Thomas, 168
Guerillas (Hochhuth), 53
Gulf War, 11, 60

H

Habermas, Jürgen, 42–43
Hackett, Albert, 136, 137, 138
Haley, Bill, 244
Halfeld, Adolf, 205–6
Hamburg Declaration, 170
Hannerz, Ulf, 222
Hansen, Miriam, 97, 98
Harlin, Rene, 176
Hausenstein, Wilhelm, 69
Hauser, Kaspar, 173, 174
Hawks, Howard, 170, 197
Hayworth, Rita, 228
Hebdige, Dick, 227
Hegel, Georg Wilhelm Friedrich, 43, 57
Heidegger, Martin, 37
Heimat (1984), 172, 173
Heimatfilm (2002), 72, 177, 178
Hellpach, Willy, 38
Hemingway, Ernest, 192, 193, 224
Hepburn, Katharine, 196
Herf, Jeffrey, 33, 142
Herzinger, Richard, 60
Herzog, Werner, 171, 173, 179
Hilldring, John, 39
Hiroshima, German views of, 28
Hitchcock, Alfred, 170, 180, 197
Hitler, Adolf, 19, 26, 28, 52
HIV/AIDS, 246
Hochhuth, Rolf, 53, 143
Hofmannsthall, Hugo von, 67
Holocaust
    cinematic Americanization of,
        129–45
    images of, 131–36
Holocaust (1978), 130, 138, 141–45, 172
Horkheimer, Max, 41, 178, 224
Horlemann, Jürgen, 57
House of the Spirits, The (1993), 181
Huizinga, Johann, 204, 207, 208, 211
Hyussen, Andreas, 143

I

IG Farben, 154
Il Postino (1994), 200
Im Lauf der Zeit (1976), 171
Incident at Vichy (1973), 138
Independence Day (1996), 180

Information Media Guarantee Program, 169
International Council of Christians and Jews, 114
International Court of Justice, 1
international law, 1
Internet, 199, 212, 213, 216–17
In the Line of Fire (1993), 180
Investigation, The (Weiss), 143
Iran, 28
Iraq
    German-American disagreement on war in, 1, 4, 27, 242, 256
    occupation of Kuwait by, 11
Iron Curtain, 3, 245–46
Irons, Jeremy, 181
Iser, Wolfgang, 228
Israeli-Palestinian conflict, 11
Ives, Charles, 204

J

Jackson, Peter, 176
Jackson, Robert L., 134, 135
James, Henry, 208
Japan, post World War II reconstruction of, 28
Jaspers, Karl, 41, 135
jazz, 13, 72, 73, 74, 244
Jefferson, Thomas, 209
Jenet, Jean Pierre, 176
Jewish populations
    Nazi extermination of, 129–45
    as steering American foreign policy, 21
Jim Crow, 109, 116
Joel Brand (1965), 143
Joey (1985), 179
Joffe, Josef, 28
Johnson, Lyndon B., 52, 57
Jordan, Neil, 176
Joyce, James, 192
Judgment at Nuremberg (1961), 138
Jud Süss (1940), 154
Jules and Jim (1962), 195
Jung, Carl, 207
Junker, Detlef, 96

K

Kanin, Garson, 136, 139
Kassel Documenta, 72
Kellogg, E. R., 133
Kennedy, John F., 11, 19, 209, 247, 255, 260
Kennedy, Paul, 241
Kerouac, Jack, 56
Kettenacker, Lothar, 32
Keyserling, Hermann, 207
King, Martin Luther, Jr., 260
Kipphardt, Heinar, 143
Kirch, Leo, 182, 183
Kirch Media, 182
Kissinger, Henry, 247
Klee, Paul, 74
Klein, Fritz, 59
Klein, Gerhard, 150, 159, 160, 161
Kluge, Alexander, 143, 170, 172
Koeppen, Wolfgang, 35
Kohl, Helmut, 257, 261
Kohlhaase, Wolfgang, 150, 159, 160, 161
Kollwitz, Käthe, 69
Konchalowsky, Andrej, 176
Konsalik, Heinz Günther, 72
Kramer, Stanley, 138
Kraus, Peter, 44
Kuby, Erich, 35
Kuhle Wampe (1932), 156
Ku-Klux-Klan, 114
Kurosawa, Akira, 194
Kyoto Protocol, 12, 242, 246

L

La Dolce Vita (1960), 195
Lafayette, Marquis de, 209
Lang, Fritz, 170, 174, 180, 194
Langer, Lawrence, 138
L'Avventura (1960), 195
Leigh, Vivien, 196
Le Monde, 208, 213, 217, 246
Lenau, Nikolaus, 16
Lerner, Alan Jay, 194
Lessing, Gotthold Ephraim, 67
Lettau, Reinhard, 53
Lichtenstein, Roy, 74
Lidice, 53
Lietzmann, Sabine, 142
Life is Beautiful (1997), 200

Loewe, Frederick, 194
Lonely Crowd, The (Riesman), 244
Lubitsch, Ernst, 170, 174, 180
Lukács, Georg, 70, 71
Lyne, Adrian, 176

M

Maase, Kaspar, 162, 245
Macdonald, Dwight, 244
Maetzig, Kurt, 150–51, 153–54, 159, 161
Mailer, Norman, 196
Majdanek, 132
Malle, Louis, 176
Mann, Heinrich, 70
Mann, Thomas, 70
Marcuse, Herbert, 52
Marshall, George C., 261
Marshall Plan, 5, 148, 154
Marßolek, Inge, 85
Marx, Karl, 18, 55, 206
mass democratization, 96
Mastroianni, Marcello, 196
Matthias, L. L., 53
Mauriac, François, 212
Mauthausen, 131, 133, 135–36
Maxi, unser Negerbub, 115, 116
May, Karl, 46
Mayer, Louis B., 197
McDonald's, 227
McWorld, 198
Meinecke, Friedrich, 68
Melot, Michel, 216
memory culture, 27
Mencken, H. L., 75
Merritt, Richard, 39
Messier, Jean Marie, 183
Meyer, Ernst Hermann, 70
Microsoft, 190
Middenhoff, Thomas, 183
Mitterrand, François, 261
Modern Times (1936), 203
Moerike, Eduard, 257
Morrison, Toni, 224
Moscow Art Theatre, 196
Mosse, George, 33
Motion Picture Export Association, 168
Mozart, Wolfgang Amadeus, 67, 192
Müller, Robert, 33–34

Müller, Rudolf, 45
Müller-Freienfels, Richard, 47, 206–7
Munich-Geiselgasteig Studios, 182
Murdoch, Rupert, 29, 31, 182
Murnau, F. W., 170, 174, 194
music
    British invasion of, 13
    pop music in, 74
    radio programming of, 85–86
    response to jazz and rhythm, 13, 72, 73, 74, 244
Musik im Zeitgeschehen (Meyer), 70–71
My Fair Lady (1964), 194

N

Name of the Rose, The (1986), 181
Nashville (1975), 195
National Association for the Advancement of Colored People (NAACP), 117–19
National Council of Christians and Jews, 114
National Democratic Party of Germany (NPD), 52
National Security Strategy of the United States of America, The, 7
Native American population, 239
Naumann Gruppe, 35
Nazi Concentration Camps (1945), 132–36
Nazi Germany
    modern America as, 53
    moving forward from history of, 36, 39, 41–42, 52, 89, 91
    'racial state' of, 107–8
Nazism, 37, 55–56
Negro jazz, 73, 89, 158, 244
Nell-Breuning, Oskar, 41
Neo-Dada, 74
Networks of Americanization, 222
New Economy, 29
New German Cinema, 6
Newsweek, 114
New Yorker, 138
New York Pop Art, 74
New York Times, 141, 142, 261
nongovernmental organizations (NGOs), 18, 21

North Atlantic Treaty Organization
(NATO), 1, 16, 243, 255–56, 258, 260
North Korea, 247
Novick, Peter, 139
Noyce, Phil, 176
Nuclear Weapons and Foreign Policy (Kissinger), 247
Nuremberg trials, 53, 54, 60, 132, 134
Nye, Joe, 254

O

Oberhausen Manifesto, 170
Office of Strategic Services (OSS), 40
Ohrdruf, 131, 133, 135
Oldenburg, Claes, 74
Ophuls, Max, 170, 180
Oppenheimer, Franz, 43
Oradour, 53
Origins of Totalitarianism, The (Arendt), 132
Ortega y Gasset, José, 36
Ostendorf, Berndt, 97
Ozick, Cynthia, 138

P

Pannwitz, Rudolf, 45–46
Papst, G. W., 194
Paradox of American Power, The: Why the World's Only Superpower Can't Go It Alone (Nye), 254
Parker, Alan, 176
Patalas, Enno, 170
Patriot, The (2000), 180
Pechel, Rudolf, 43
Pentagon, attacks on, 189
Petersen, Wolfgang, 6, 173, 174, 179, 181
Pew Research Center, 29
Peymann, Claus, 22
phlogiston, 31
Picasso, Pablo, 194, 197
Pittsburgh Courier, 117
Plenzdorf, Ulrich, 59
poesie pure, 70
Poiger, Uta, 151
Polanski, Roman, 176
Pollock, Jackson, 74
Pommer, Erich, 182

Ponti, Carlo, 181
Presley, Elvis, 72, 73, 244
Proust, Marcel, 192
Pulp Fiction (1994), 195
Puttnam, David, 176, 181
Pygmalion (Shaw), 194

R

race
    black U.S. soldiers in postwar Germany, 107–21
    Nazi 'racial state' of, 107–8
    postwar changing concept of, 108–21
    Rasse as extinct category, 107, 108, 113
Radio Bremen, 92
radio broadcasting
    advertising on, 80, 81, 93
    American influences in West Germany, 78–98
    centralized state broadcasting system of, 81
    changes in norms and objectives of, 90–93
    competition with television, 81–82
    dual system of, 82
    educational paradigm of, 79, 86–87, 90–93
    history of German programming in, 83–88
    as instrument of propaganda, 88, 89
    listeners' musical preferences in, 84–85
    programming during World War II, 88–89
    public broadcasting stations in, 81
    radio as luxury item, 86
    regulation and control of, 80
    U.S.-American music on, 70
    in World War II Great Britain, 89
Radio Luxembourg, 89, 92
Radkau, Joachim, 46
Rat der Götter (1950), 154
Rauschenberg, Robert, 74
Ray, Nick, 172
Ray, Satyajit, 194
Reagan, Ronald, 11, 175, 241

reflective modernity, 34
Reitz, Edgar, 144–45, 170, 172, 173, 179
Reuther, Thomas, 38
Revel, Jean-François, 12
Revolt of the Masses, The (Ortega y Gasset), 36
Richter, Horst-Eberhard, 58
Riefenstahl, Leni, 203, 229
Riesman, David, 212, 244
Rivette, Jacques, 177
rock 'n' roll music, 73, 74
Rogin, Michael, 180
Rohrbach, Günter, 182
Rolling Stones, 177, 178
Roman einer jungen Ehe (1952), 150, 153–54, 155, 158
Röpke, Wilhelm, 35, 41–42, 43
Rosenfeld, Alvin H., 130
Run Lola Run (1999), 200
Rüstow, Alexander, 35, 41, 42

S

Sartre, Jean-Paul, 193, 212
Scandinavization of Germany, 40
Scheffler, Karl, 69
Schlegel, Friedrich, 69
Schlöndorff, Volker, 172, 174, 181, 183
Schlöndorff, Werner, 143
Schmidt, Helmut, 257
Schmitt, Carl, 25
Schneider, Irmela, 94
Schneider, Lambert, 41
Schnoor, Rainer, 59
Schönberg, Arnold, 71, 72
Schrader, Paul, 177
Schremp, Jürgen, 182
Schröder, Gerhard, 27, 28, 257
Schumpeter, Joseph, 202
Schutz, Anneliese, 138
Scorsese, Martin, 174, 177, 195, 197
Scott, Ridley, 176
Scott, Tony, 176
second-order modernity, 34
Sedlmayr, Hans, 69
self-Americanization, 221–32
Selling of the Holocaust (Cole), 138
Selz, Peter, 74
September 11, 2001, events of
    American responses to, 259
    European responses to, 242, 246, 255
    as extreme anti-Americanism, 12
    French responses to, 21–22, 209
    German responses to, 18–20, 25
    global terrorism of, 2
serum modernism, 34
Seven Samurai (1954), 195
Shaw, George Bernard, 194
Shoah, 130
Shoot the Piano Player (1960), 194–95
Shusterman, Richard, 230
Sieburg, Friedrich, 35
Siegfried, André, 204–5
Siodmak, Robert, 170, 180
Sirk, Douglas, 170, 172
Skouras, Spyros, 168
Sloterdijk, Peter, 19
Sobibor, 132, 142
Social Democrats, 37, 40, 43
Socialist Unity Party, 70
Society for Christian-Jewish Cooperation, 114
"Song of the Managers," 42–43
Sontheimer, Kurt, 36
Sound of Music, The (1965), 177, 178
Sovietism, 37–38
Soviet Occupation Zone, 70
Soviet Union, defeat of, 11
Spacey, Kevin, 195
Spengler, Oswald, 36
Spielberg, Stephen, 177, 195, 197
Stalin, Joseph, 242
Standard Oil, 154
Starship Troopers (1997), 180
Star Wars (1977), 169, 200
Stead, William, 189
Stein, Hannes, 60
Steiner, George, 142
Stern, Fritz, 33, 260
Stevens, George, 132–33, 135, 139, 140
Stravinsky, Igor, 192
Streep, Meryl, 181
Streetcar Named Desire, A (1951), 196
Stroheim, Erich von, 180
Süddeutsche Zeitung, 55
Survey, The, 114
swing, 73
Syberberg, Hans-Jürgen, 11, 143, 172, 173, 179

T

Tamahori, Lee, 176
Tanner, Tony, 215
Tarantino, Quentin, 180
television broadcasting
    advertising on, 81, 93
    as competition with radio, 82
    dual system of, 82
terrorism
    global views of, 2
    See also September 11, 2001, events of
Theweleit, Klaus, 21
Thoma, Helmut, 92
Thome, Rudolf, 170
Thoreau, Henry David, 57
Time Warner, 175, 190
Titanic (1997), 198, 200
Tivoli, 191
Tocqueville, Alexis de, 209, 210
Tolstoy, Leo, 192
Tomlinson, John, 222
Total Recall (1990), 180
transatlantic alliances, 253–56
"Transition from Today to Tomorrow, The" (Pannwitz), 45
transmodernity, 34
Treblinka, 132
Tressler, Georg, 160
Triumph of the Will, The (1934), 203, 229
"Trivialization of the Holocaust," 141
Truffaut, François, 177, 194–95, 197
Truman, Harry S., 261
Turner, Ted, 182

U

U-culture, 73, 75
Ulmer, Edgar, 180
United Nations (UN), 1, 20, 28
United States
    American-French relationships, 261
    European and foreign influences on American culture, 189–201, 238–47
    in future German-American relationships, 257–62
    High Commission for Germany (HICOG) of, 34, 39
    Office of Military Government (OMGUS) of, 34, 39
    transatlantic relationships and alliances of, 253–56
Unser täglich Brot (1949), 156
Urban League, 117
U.S. Displaced Persons Commission, 117
U.S. Holocaust Museum, 130
U.S. News & World Report, 114

V

Valenti, Jack, 168
Védrine, Hubert, 212
Verhoeven, Paul, 176, 180
Verlag, Lambert Schneider, 138
Versailles Treaty, 16
Vershofen, Wilhelm, 43
Vietnam War, 245
    American protesters to, 53–54, 55–56, 57, 58
    German reactions to, 3, 7, 28, 52, 54–55, 56–59, 260
    movies about, 197
    My Lai massacre during, 53, 58
VIVA, 224
Vivendi-Universal, 183
von Trotta, Margarethe, 172

W

Waldleitner, Luggi, 181
Wall, The (1982), 138
Walser, Martin, 18–19
Walsh, Raoul, 172
Warhol, Andy, 56, 74
Washington, George, 209
Wayne, John, 195
Weber, Alfred, 35, 37–38, 40
Weber, Max, 37, 96, 206
Weimar, 133
Weimar Republic, 4, 16, 31, 40, 43, 52, 61, 68, 86, 149, 172, 180
Weir, Peter, 176
Weiss, Peter, 143
Welles, Orson, 197
Wells, H. G., 208
Wenders, Wim, 6, 170-174, 181, 198
Wendlandt, Horst, 181
Westdeutsche Rundfunk (WDR), 92, 141
West Germany

Americanization in postwar
reconstruction of, 31–47
military zones of occupation in,
108–11
postwar black occupation children
in, 107–21
responses to Western art trends in,
71–75
West Side Story (1961), 194
"What the World Thinks in 2002" (Pew
Research Center), 29
White, Walter, 117, 118
Whitman, Walt, 33, 210, 211
Wiebeau, Edgar, 59
Wiesel, Elie, 141, 142–43, 179
Wild Bunch, The (1969), 195
Wilder, Billy, 136, 170, 180
Wilder, Thornton, 56
Wild West Show, 191, 192
Williams, Tennessee, 56
Wilson, Dooley, 196
Wirsing, Giselher, 37
Wirtschaftswunder, 168
Wolff, Karl Dietrich, 51–52

women
fraternization with American
occupation troops, 107–21
role in Cold War films, 151–60,
161
Worker's Radio Club, 84
World Brotherhood, 114, 115
World Trade Center, attacks on, 19, 20,
189
World Wide Web, 212, 215–19
World Youth Festival, 153
Wortmann, Söhnke, 181

Z

Zbinden, Hans, 41
Zehrer, Hans, 35
Zhdanov, Andrei, 70
Zietlow, Carl, 114
Zweites Deutsches Fernsehen (ZDF), 91, 93

www.ingramcontent.com/pod-product-compliance
Lightning Source LLC
Chambersburg PA
CBHW071221080526
44587CB00013BA/1458